Complete
Geography

Simon Chapman

Philip Amor

Chris Drew

Rosemary Hector

Peter Simonds

Michael Yeabsley

OXFORD
UNIVERSITY PRESS

OXFORD
UNIVERSITY PRESS

Great Clarendon Street, Oxford OX2 6DP

Oxford University Press is a department of the University of Oxford.
It furthers the University's objective of excellence in research, scholarship,
and education by publishing worldwide in

Oxford New York

Athens Auckland Bangkok Bogotá Buenos Aires Calcutta
Cape Town Chennai Dar es Salaam Delhi Florence Hong Kong Istanbul
Karachi Kuala Lumpur Madrid Melbourne Mexico City Mumbai
Nairobi Paris São Paulo Shanghai Singapore Taipei Tokyo Toronto Warsaw
with associated companies in Berlin Ibadan

Oxford is a registered trade mark of Oxford University Press
in the UK and in certain other countries

ISBN 0 19 913398 0

First published 1998
Reprinted 1999, 2000

Typeset in ITC Garamond light and ITC Officina Sans

Printed in Spain by Gráficas Estella

Acknowledgements

The publisher and authors would like to thank the following for permission
to reproduce photographs and other copyright material:

CHAPTER 1
Geoscience: pp 9, 22 (all); Landforms: p 18; Popperfoto: p 13;
P. Simonds: p 21; Tony Stone Images: p 17; Trip Photo Library: pp 14,
19 (both);

CHAPTER 2
Aerofilms: pp 32, 33 (both); Ecoscene: p 35 (middle); Leslie Garland:
p 38; Geoscience: p 25; Landforms: pp 28, 31 (top), 34, 35 (top); Skyscan:
p 36; Trip Photo Library: p 289 (both); Tony Waltham: p 31 (bottom), 35
(bottom); Simon Williams/Weymouth Portland Borough Council: p 39 (both);

CHAPTER 3
Geoscience: pp 43 (bottom), 46 (bottom), 49 (bottom), 50, 51 (top);
Landforms: pp 45 (top), 46 (top), 51 (middle & bottom);
John Cleare/Mountain Camer: pp 41, 49 (top); P. Simonds: p 43 (top);
Tony Waltham: pp 45 (bottom), 48; Trip Photo Library: p 47;

CHAPTER 4
Corbis UK Ltd/Papilio/Steve Austin: p 61 (both); Geoscience: pp 55
(bottom), 56, 64 (bottom right & left); Holt Studios: pp 63, 64 (top left);
Landforms: pp 60 (left), 62; Still Pictures: p 60 (right), 64 (top right), 65;
Trip Photo Library: p55 (top);

CHAPTER 5
Geoscience Photo Library: p 74 (bottom); Holt Studios: pp 66 (both),
67 (both), 68 (left & middle), 69 (left & middle); 70, 71 (both), 72 (top),
75, 78 (all), 87 (top left); Landforms: p 84; Panos Pictures: p 82; Skyscan:
p 74 (top); Tony Stone Images: pp 72 (bottom), 86; Trip Photo Library:
pp 69 (right), 81, 83, 87 (top right & bottom); Jacolyn Wakeford/ICCE:
p 68 (right);

CHAPTER 6
Geoscience: pp 91 (top, middle & bottom right), 98; Holt Studios: pp 90,
91 (bottom left), 93; Popperfoto: p 90 (top & middle); Tony Waltham: p 102
(left); Still Pictures: p 102 (right);

CHAPTER 7
Ecoscene: pp 119 (bottom), 125; Geoscience: p 116; Impact: p 105 (top);
Landforms: pp 114, 115; Popperfoto: pp 110, 121; Trip Photo Library:
pp 105 (bottom), 112;

CHAPTER 8
Geoscience: p 126; Landforms: p 130; Popperfoto: p 128; Trip Photo
Library: p 129; Tony Waltham: p 134; Andy Williss: p 134;

CHAPTER 9
Aerofilms: p 139 (top & middle); David Hoffman: p 139 (bottom); Impact:
p 153 (top); Rex Features: p 153 (bottom); Science Photo Library: p 136
(bottom); Tony Stone: pp 136 (top & middle), 148;

CHAPTER 10
Ecoscene: p 162; Impact: p 157 (middle); Melanie McRae: p 159; Popperfoto:
pp 157 (top), 160; P Simonds: p 163; Still Pictures: p 165 (right); Trip Photo
Library: p 157 (bottom); Tony Waltham: p 165 (right);

CHAPTER 11
Mark Azavedo: pp 174 (bottom right), 179; Ivan J Beltcher: p 190; Heather
Angel/Biofotos: p 184 (top); Corbis UK Ltd: /Jeremy Horner p 166 /Robert Holmes
p 191; Image Bank: p 189 (top right, bottom left & middle bottom); Impact: p 174
(top right); Photofile: p 188; Science Photo Library: p 169; David Simson: p 174
(middle right); Still Pictures: p 174 (top left); Still Moving Pictures: p 174 (bottom
left); Telegraph Colour Library: p 189 (top); Trip Photo Library: p 177;
John Walmsley: p 176 (both); Janine Wiedel: pp 174 (middle left), 184 (bottom);

CHAPTER 12
Hutchison Photo Library: p 203; Panos Pictures: p 193 (both), 196 (top),
197 (both); Still Pictures: pp 196 (bottom right), 200; Tony Stone: pp 195 (both),
196 (bottom left), 198;

CHAPTER 13
Aerofilms: p 210 (middle right); Ecoscence: p 212; Geoscience: p 210 (middle
right); David Hoffman: p 210 (bottom); Panos Pictures: p 213 (top); Tony Stone:
p 210 (top & middle left); Trip Photo Library: pp 206, 213 (middle & bottom);

CHAPTER 14
Aztec: p 222; IBM: p 223; Skyscan: p 227; Tony Stone: p 231; Toyota: p 217;
Tony Waltham: pp 219, 225;

CHAPTER 15
Heather Angel/Biofotos: p 244 (middle); Phil Chapman/ICCE: p 245; Ecoscene:
p 247; David Hoffman: p 246 (top); P Simonds: pp 239 (right), 241 (left), 242
(middle), 244 (top); Skyscan: p 239 (left); Tony Stone Images: pp 234, 240
(bottom), 242 (middle); Trip Photo Library: pp 240 (middle), 244 (bottom);
Tony Waltham: p 236; Andy Williss: p 246 (bottom); Windrush: p 241 (right).

Cover image by Lonny Kalfus/Tony Stone Images.

The Ordnance Survey map extract on p 238 is reproduced with the permission of
the Controller of Her Majesty's Stationery Office © Crown Copyright.

Illustrations by Michael Eaton, Gary Hincks, Julie Tolliday, and Michael Aston.
Computer-generated artwork by Oxford Illustrators and Hardlines.

The authors would like to thank Ray Alexander at Glasgow City Council for his help
in obtaining statistics.

Every effort has been made to trace and contact copyright holders of material
reproduced in this book. Any omissions will be rectified in subsequent printings if
notice is given to the publisher.

Introduction

Complete Geography has been written to meet the needs of students sitting GCSE and Standard Grade examinations.

The themes, topics, and case studies are drawn from current examination syllabuses, giving a book that is rich in content and innovative in the variety and diversity of activities set. The carefully-written text is organised into double-page spreads, while activities are clearly identified and structured, including two examination-style decision making exercises. Written by six experienced and practising teachers, this is a 'complete' geography course in one book.

Simon Chapman – Head of Geography, Warwick School

Contents

The surface of the earth is shaped by many processes. These processes include earthquakes and volcanoes. To understand why volcanoes and earthquakes happen, it is necessary to understand what goes on beneath the surface of the earth.

Figure 1 is a cross-section through the earth. It shows that the planet is made up of a series of layers. The outer layer is a thin, rigid crust, only a few tens of kilometres thick. The crust can be divided into two main types: **continental crust** and **oceanic crust**. The continental crust covers the land surfaces. It is both thicker and lighter than the oceanic crust, which covers the floor of the world's oceans (Figure 2). Both types of crust float on a layer of semi-molten rocks, called the **mantle**. Molten rock in the mantle is called **magma**.

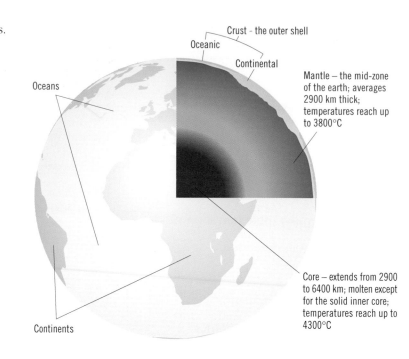

Crust - the outer shell
Oceanic
Continental
Oceans
Continents

Mantle – the mid-zone of the earth; averages 2900 km thick; temperatures reach up to 3800°C

Core – extends from 2900 to 6400 km; molten except for the solid inner core; temperatures reach up to 4300°C

▶ Figure 1 **A cross-section through the earth**

▼ Figure 2 **Composition of the crust**

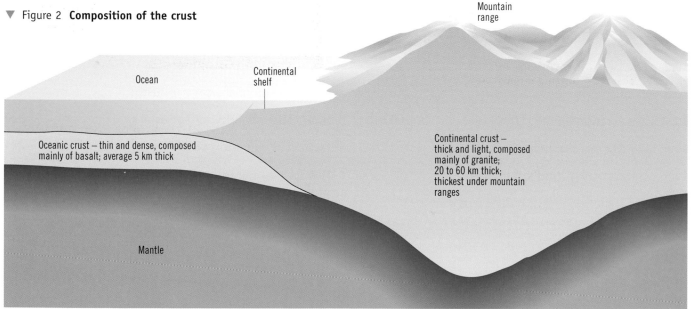

Mountain range

Ocean

Continental shelf

Oceanic crust – thin and dense, composed mainly of basalt; average 5 km thick

Continental crust – thick and light, composed mainly of granite; 20 to 60 km thick; thickest under mountain ranges

Mantle

Radioactive decay in the core creates heat. As this heat escapes towards the surface, it generates convection currents in the molten rocks of the mantle (Figure 3). In some places, these currents are tearing the crust apart, dividing it into huge fragments. These fragments are called **tectonic plates**. Where this occurs, plates are moving away from each other (**diverging**) in a process called spreading. Elsewhere, plates are being pushed together (**converging**). The convergence and divergence causes the crust to fold and fracture.

Individual crustal plates are pushed across the earth's surface at about 50 mm per year like floating pieces of a jigsaw puzzle. This movement has constantly changed the position and size of the continents over millions of years, in a process called **continental drift**.

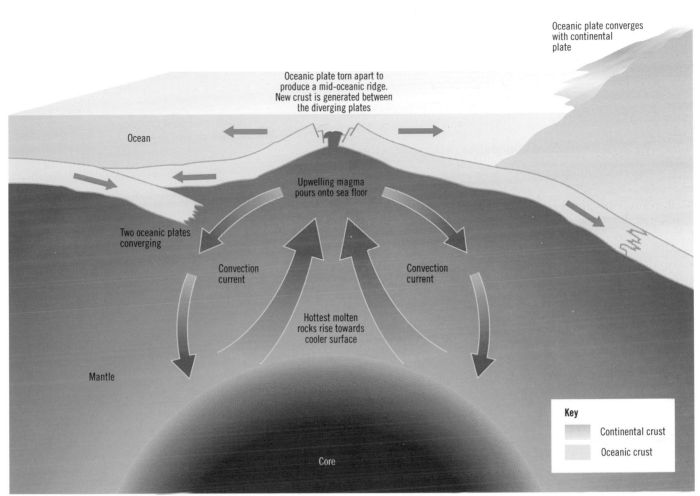

Oceanic plate converges with continental plate

Oceanic plate torn apart to produce a mid-oceanic ridge. New crust is generated between the diverging plates

Ocean

Upwelling magma pours onto sea floor

Two oceanic plates converging

Convection current

Convection current

Hottest molten rocks rise towards cooler surface

Mantle

Core

Key

| | Continental crust |
| | Oceanic crust |

Figure 3 **Convection currents in the mantle**

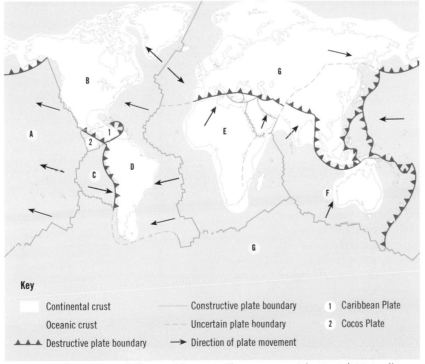

Key

	Continental crust		Constructive plate boundary	1	Caribbean Plate
	Oceanic crust	---	Uncertain plate boundary	2	Cocos Plate
▲▲▲	Destructive plate boundary	→	Direction of plate movement		

Figure 4 **Major plates of the earth's crust** There are seven large and 12 small plates altogether, although some boundaries are difficult to identify.

1 Using a copy of the plate boundary map (Figure 4; also on page 248) and an atlas, label the plates A – G using the list of names given below.

Eurasian; Nazca; North American; African; Pacific; South American; Indo-Australian; Cocos; Antarctic; Philippine.

2 What type of movement (diverging or converging) is taking place between the following plates:
 a Pacific and Nazca?
 b Pacific and Philippine?
 c Eurasian and North American?
 d Cocos and North American?
 e African and Eurasian?

3 What differences are there between continental crust and oceanic crust?

4 What drives the movement of plates across the earth's surface?

5 What evidence could you look for to prove that continents have drifted across the earth?

Plate boundaries

The boundaries between crustal plates can be classified into three main types according to the direction of movement of the plates on either side of the boundary.

- diverging or **constructive boundaries**, where the plates are forced apart and new crust is created in between

- converging or **destructive boundaries**, where one plate collides with another. One plate may slide under the other or both may crumple together, depending on what type of plates are colliding.

- **slipping boundaries**, where two plates move horizontally past one another.

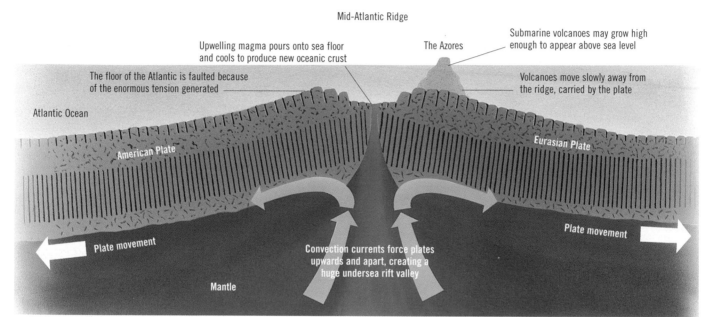

Mid-Atlantic Ridge

Upwelling magma pours onto sea floor and cools to produce new oceanic crust

The Azores

Submarine volcanoes may grow high enough to appear above sea level

The floor of the Atlantic is faulted because of the enormous tension generated

Volcanoes move slowly away from the ridge, carried by the plate

Atlantic Ocean

American Plate

Eurasian Plate

Plate movement

Plate movement

Convection currents force plates upwards and apart, creating a huge undersea rift valley

Mantle

Figure 1 **A constructive boundary** Two plates are forced apart. This usually occurs under the ocean but may also take place on the land.

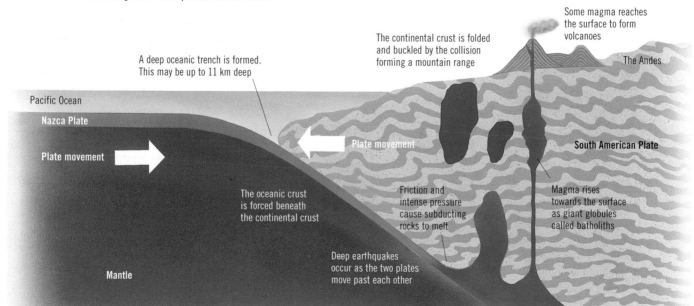

Some magma reaches the surface to form volcanoes

The continental crust is folded and buckled by the collision forming a mountain range

The Andes

A deep oceanic trench is formed. This may be up to 11 km deep

Pacific Ocean

Nazca Plate

Plate movement

Plate movement

South American Plate

The oceanic crust is forced beneath the continental crust

Friction and intense pressure cause subducting rocks to melt

Magma rises towards the surface as giant globules called batholiths

Deep earthquakes occur as the two plates move past each other

Mantle

Figure 2 **A destructive boundary** Where two plates collide, the heavier oceanic plate slides below the lighter continental plate. This process, called **subduction**, occurs along most of the west coast of North and South America.

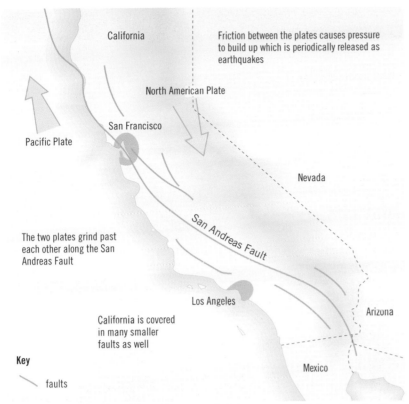

Figure 3 **A slipping boundary** Two crustal plates move or 'slip' past each other.

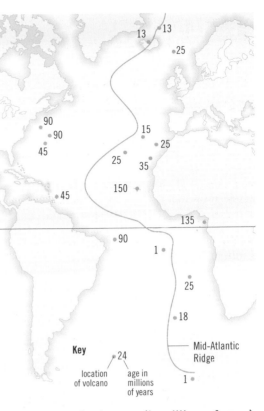

Figure 4 **Ages of volcanoes (in millions of years) in the Atlantic Ocean**

Figure 5 **The Himalayas** Young fold mountains form where two continental plates converge. The mountains are still growing.

Figure 6 **Creating mountains**

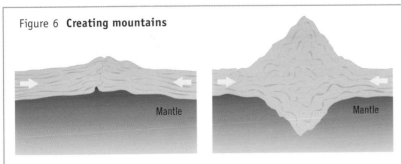

Wherever two plates collide, crustal rocks are crumpled and folded upwards to form **fold mountains** in a process called **mountain building**. This usually occurs along **subduction zones** where different types of crust converge but some of the world's highest mountains have been formed where two continental plates meet.

1 What is meant by each of the following terms:
  a subduction?
  b a constructive plate boundary?
  c a destructive plate boundary?

2 Why do earthquakes occur along:
  a subduction zones?
  b slipping boundaries?

3 **a** Using your copy of the plate boundary map from page 248, mark on it the following fold mountains: Himalayas; Alps; Atlas; Pyrenees; Andes; Rockies.

  b Between which plates does each chain of fold mountains lie?

4 Study Figure 4.
  a What happens to the age of volcanoes as you move away from the Mid-Atlantic Ridge?

  b Explain why this pattern develops.

5 **a** Which large island is found directly in the middle of the Mid-Atlantic Ridge?

  b Explain why it is volcanically active.

6 Using an atlas, find the names of volcanic islands that lie along the mid-ocean ridges in the Pacific and Indian Oceans.

1.3 Earthquakes

Earthquakes are tremors or ground movements caused by shock waves. They have long been a source of both fascination and terror for humans. Pliny the Elder, in AD 200, wrote that earthquakes were Mother Earth's way of protesting against those people who mined for gold, silver and iron.

We now understand that major earthquakes normally occur at boundaries. Plate movement causes stress to build up within the crustal rocks until the rocks break along the line of a **fault** or cracks in the earth's crust. The actual movement of the material may be only a few centimetres but the sudden release of seismic (earthquake) energy can be enormous.

The point at which the rocks break within the crust is the **focus** of the earthquake. This may be some distance below the surface and the seismic energy emitted from the focus travels in all directions as **seismic waves**. The point on the earth's surface above the focus is the **epicentre** (Figure 1). An earthquake is likely to be more powerful the longer the time that stress has had to build up and the closer the location of the focus of the seismic energy to the surface.

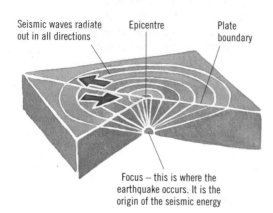

Figure 1 **Focus of an earthquake**

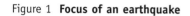

Figure 2 **Recording earthquakes**

Earthquakes are recorded using a seismograph. It has a base that shakes with the earthquake while a pen attached to a weight records ground movements. This produces a seismogram. Earthquakes are measured on the Richter scale.

What makes an earthquake hazardous?

Many thousands of earthquakes occur each year but only a few are centred near populated areas and are strong enough to cause loss of life. There are a number of immediate or **primary effects** from the violent shaking of the ground during an earthquake. Buildings may collapse killing people inside them, shattered window glass may shower on to streets below and huge cracks may open in the ground. Roads and railways may be damaged. Services such as mains water and electricity may be cut off.

The primary effects of earthquakes can also generate other problems or **secondary effects**. A large number of deaths occur after an earthquake when food and water are in short supply. The ability of a country to cope with secondary effects will often determine the final death toll. Secondary effects include:

- fires, set off as gas or oil leak from fractured pipes
- disease, brought about by lack of medical care and clean drinking water
- tsunamis, which are huge waves caused when earthquakes occur under the sea. The waves can travel at 1000 km per hour in open water; they slow to about 65 km per hour close to land when they reach up to 15 metres in height.

The Richter scale		
Richter scale	*Effects*	*Average annual occurence worldwide*
Under 3.5	Detected only by seismographs	300 000
3.5 – 5	Felt by all hanging objects; trees sway	55 000
5 – 6	Walls crack; becomes hard to stand	800
6 – 7	Chimneys and tree branches fall; houses collapse	120
7 – 8	Many houses and bridges collapse; ground opens wide	18
8+	Total destruction	1

In parts of the world where earthquakes are common, governments can take measures to reduce the effects of tremors. Buildings that will not collapse as the earth shakes can be designed and citizens can be properly prepared for earthquakes. Figures 3 and 4 show some of the steps that can be taken. One of the best ways to reduce the impact of an earthquake is to identify areas of high risk and to limit development in these areas. In California, for example, no new building may be built within 40 metres of a known fault line.

Panels of marble and glass flexibly anchored to steel superstructure

Rolling weights on roof to counteract shock waves

Reinforced lift shafts with tensioned cables

'Birdcage' interlocking steel frame

Reinforced latticework foundations deep in bedrock

Rubber shock absorbers between foundations and superstructure

Figure 3 **Earthquake-proofing in a modern building**

Earthquake preparation

1 Have flashlights and portable radio with extra batteries ready.

2 Have first aid kit and fire extinguisher ready.

3 Store a few gallons of water per family member.

4 Store one week's food outside the house.

5 Strap down boiler.

6 Place beds away from windows and mirrors.

7 Agree on a plan to reunite the family by day or night.

Figure 4 **Preparing Californians for an earthquake**

Case study | Khilari, India 1993

Date:	30 September 1993
Time:	4 a.m. (local time)
Location:	Maharashtra State, central India
Strength:	6.2 on the Richter scale
Damage:	9 800 dead
	7 000 homes destroyed
	10 000 left homeless

The epicentre of the tremors occurred in an area where Indian seismologists categorised the earthquake risk as very low. The town of Khilari is more than 1000 km from the Himalayas, India's major seismic zone, where rocks from the Indian and Eurasian plates are being forced together. Occasionally though, areas far from the collision zone feel the effects of stresses within the two plates.

The Khilari earthquake had a magnitude of 6.2, which is quite often exceeded elsewhere in the world. The earthquake was so damaging because of the poor quality of the buildings in the area and the slow response to the disaster. There are no regulations in Maharashtra State to ensure that buildings are earthquake-resistant. Many people lived in two-storeyed stone houses which quickly collapsed. Tonnes of rocks crashed down on victims as they slept. In the worst affected surrounding villages, army rescue teams did not arrive until at least 36 hours after the first tremor. The area is remote and inaccessible, and lacked the equipment to dig out buried survivors in the first crucial hours after the quake. Fierce rain also hampered operations and rotting corpses sparked fears of disease.

Figure 5 **Location of Khilari**

Case study | Kobe, Japan 1995

Date: 17 January 1995

Time: 5.46 a.m. (local time)

Location: Kobe, Japan

Strength: 7.2 on the Richter scale

Damage: 5 500 people dead
7 500 houses destroyed by fire
171 000 houses collapsed
70 000 people made homeless
Total cost of damage estimated
at £64 billion.

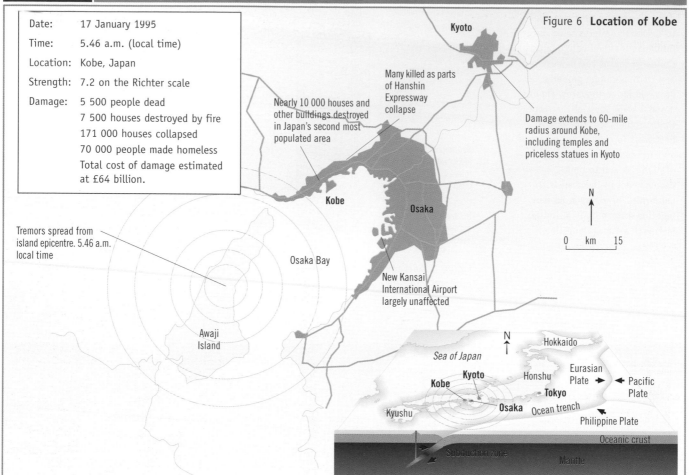

Figure 6 **Location of Kobe**

Many killed as parts of Hanshin Expressway collapse

Nearly 10 000 houses and other buildings destroyed in Japan's second most populated area

Damage extends to 60-mile radius around Kobe, including temples and priceless statues in Kyoto

Tremors spread from island epicentre. 5.46 a.m. local time

New Kansai International Airport largely unaffected

Osaka Bay

Awaji Island

Kobe

Osaka

Kyoto

N

0 km 15

Sea of Japan

Hokkaido

Honshu

Eurasian Plate

Pacific Plate

Kobe

Kyoto

Tokyo

Osaka

Ocean trench

Philippine Plate

Kyushu

Oceanic crust

Subduction zone

Mantle

Figure 7 **Personal accounts of several people who experienced the Kobe earthquake**

"I quickly got into my car after the tremor and went out to assess the extent of the damage. As I approached the poorer industrial area of the city I could see fires blazing on every corner. Entire rows of wooden houses had been razed to the ground – presumably with everyone inside. I came across one distraught man amid the ruins and managed, with the help of some other people, to pull the body of his son-in-law from the rubble."

Kobe policeman

"My wife and I quickly collected a few belongings before we had to flee from our house which was on fire. We didn't even have time to change out of our pyjamas. Our car was in flames so we had to leave it behind. There seemed to be nowhere to go so we ended up in this children's playground with dozens of other people from our district. We have kept warm around a large fire we built using furniture we found nearby. I have seen no sniffer dogs and almost no cranes or diggers. The odd helicopter flies over but these are mainly from television stations."

Elderly inhabitant of Kobe, two days after the earthquake

"We saw on TV that the train station and supermarket next to her house had completely burnt down but we haven't been able to contact her. The trains aren't running because of derailments and the roads are jammed. People are being warned not to travel because some of the highways have collapsed and many buildings are about to fall down. We are just sitting and waiting."

Mother awaiting news of her daughter who lives in central Kobe.

"There would have been much greater loss of life if our tough regulations did not insist that every new building must incorporate devices to counteract the effects of earthquakes. Our modern skyscrapers withstood the quake well and this helped. Unfortunately, many smaller buildings collapsed because they were too low to sway and damage was severe among houses built before regulations came in during the 1960s. Our traditional buildings in Kobe are mainly made of wood and many of these became deadly fire traps after the earthquake. A key question that remains is: why did so many highways and railways collapse?"

Civil engineer working for Kobe District Authority, speaking two weeks after the earthquake

"Walking through the damage, there is a chill silence broken only by the sirens of the rescue vehicles. The only lights are the headlights of vehicles caught in bumper-to-bumper traffic jams both ways as people try to leave the city or get into it to see if their homes still stand. Emergency aid convoys carry medical supplies. One convoy is led by a dozen Japanese army trucks, each towing a water tank but they are unable to move because of the congestion. The surface of the road is cracked every 10 metres and all the traffic lights are out of order."

Journalist writing in Osaka newspaper a day after the earthquake

Month / year	Location	Richter scale reading	Fatalities
June 1995	Greece	6.2	17
May 1995	Russia	7.5	2 000
January 1995	Kobe, Japan	7.2	5 500
October 1994	off Hokkaido, Japan	8.2	16
August 1994	Algeria	5.6	150
February 1994	Indonesia	6.5	37
January 1994	Indonesia	6.8	7
January 1994	Los Angeles, USA	6.6	57
September 1993	India	6.4	9 800
July 1993	Okushiri, Japan	7.8	158
December 1992	Indonesia	6.8	1 912
June 1992	California, USA	7.3	1
April 1992	California, USA	6.9	0
March 1992	Turkey	6.8	1 000
February 1991	Pakistan	6.8	1 200
July 1990	Philippines	7.7	1 621
June 1990	Iran	7.7	50 000
December 1988	Armenia	6.9	25 000
September 1985	Mexico	8.1	9 500

Figure 8 **Some recent major earthquakes**

Figure 9 **In the days following the earthquake, traffic struggles past the collapsed section of the Hanshin Expressway**

1 Copy out and complete the following paragraph using the words supplied in the list below.

Earthquakes occur when two _____ try to move past each other in different directions. This normally occurs at a _____ or a _____ plate boundary. The rocks are put under a great deal of _____ and start to _____. Eventually, when the stress is too great, the rocks suddenly break along a _____. Energy in the form of _____ _____ radiates out in all directions, causing the ground to _____.

bend; shake; seismic waves; line; slipping; fault; plates; stress; destructive

2 Study the information about the Khilari earthquake on page 11. List the different factors that produced the high death toll.

3 Along what type of plate boundary did the Kobe earthquake occur?

4 Read the personal extracts in Figure 7 about the Kobe earthquake. Describe the impact of the earthquake under the following headings:

Transport; Buildings; Industry; People

5 a What is the difference between the primary and the secondary effects of an earthquake?

b List the primary and secondary effects of the Kobe earthquake.

6 In what ways do you think the Kobe earthquake would have been more or less destructive if it had occurred three hours later?

7 Compare what happened at Khilari and Kobe. Why are earthquakes likely to be more dangerous in less developed countries (LDCs) like India than in developed countries like Japan?

8 Why do you think so many people choose to live in areas that suffer from earthquakes?

9 Working in pairs, either design your own earthquake-proof house or design a poster containing some of your own ideas about how people should prepare for and act during an earthquake.

Geothermal heat is released from the earth's core at the surface mainly through volcanoes. Magma is forced up through cracks in the crustal rocks and pours onto the surface as **lava**. Not all volcanoes are alike. Their shape and explosiveness depend on the type of lava emitted. Some lava is viscous like treacle and is called **acid lava**. Lava that is thinner and more runny is called **basic lava**. Figures 2 and 3 show how acid and basic lava volcanoes are formed.

▶ Figure 1 **Mount Ngauruhoe, New Zealand – a steep-sided acid lava volcano. It last erupted in 1975.**

Figure 2 **An acid lava volcano**
This type of volcano is most common along destructive plate boundaries. Here the magma is derived from the melting of basaltic oceanic crust and marine sediments as they slide beneath continental crust. Example: Mount Mayon, the Philippines.

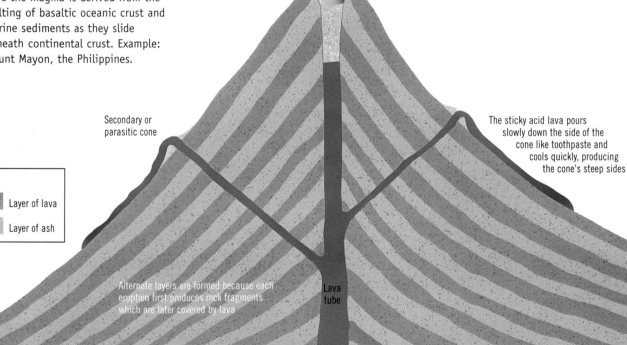

A rock plug may be left from a previous eruption. This will be blown off violently in a future eruption, creating a hail of ash and rock. The top of the cone may collapse

Crater

Secondary or parasitic cone

The sticky acid lava pours slowly down the side of the cone like toothpaste and cools quickly, producing the cone's steep sides

Key
Layer of lava
Layer of ash

Alternate layers are formed because each eruption first produces rock fragments which are later covered by lava

Lava tube

The viscous magma traps hot gases within it, releasing them suddenly during an eruption. As it was originally oceanic crust, the magma also contains large volumes of water which, as steam, increases the pressure within the lava tube. This makes a violent eruption more likely.

Magma chamber

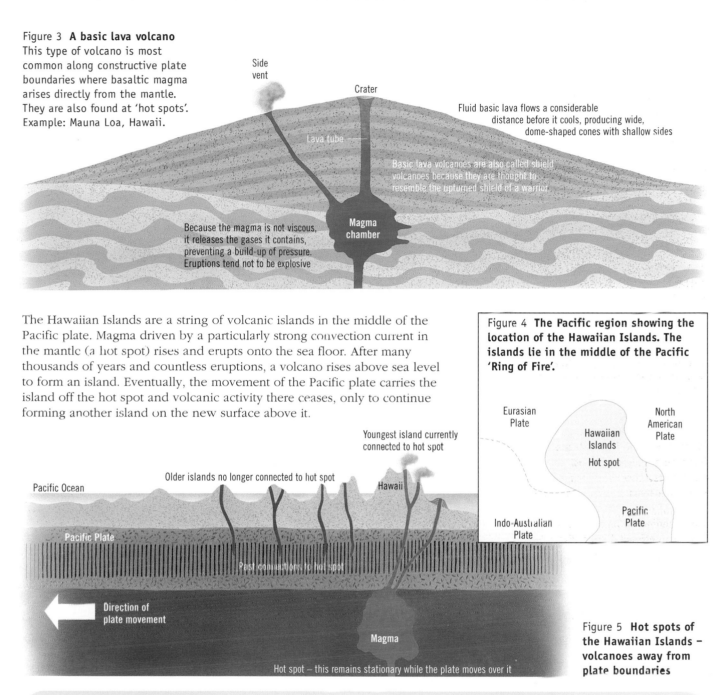

Figure 3 **A basic lava volcano**
This type of volcano is most common along constructive plate boundaries where basaltic magma arises directly from the mantle. They are also found at 'hot spots'. Example: Mauna Loa, Hawaii.

Side vent

Crater

Fluid basic lava flows a considerable distance before it cools, producing wide, dome-shaped cones with shallow sides

Lava tube

Basic lava volcanoes are also called shield volcanoes because they are thought to resemble the upturned shield of a warrior

Because the magma is not viscous, it releases the gases it contains, preventing a build-up of pressure. Eruptions tend not to be explosive

Magma chamber

The Hawaiian Islands are a string of volcanic islands in the middle of the Pacific plate. Magma driven by a particularly strong convection current in the mantle (a hot spot) rises and erupts onto the sea floor. After many thousands of years and countless eruptions, a volcano rises above sea level to form an island. Eventually, the movement of the Pacific plate carries the island off the hot spot and volcanic activity there ceases, only to continue forming another island on the new surface above it.

Figure 4 **The Pacific region showing the location of the Hawaiian Islands. The islands lie in the middle of the Pacific 'Ring of Fire'.**

Eurasian Plate

North American Plate

Hawaiian Islands

Hot spot

Indo-Australian Plate

Pacific Plate

Youngest island currently connected to hot spot

Older islands no longer connected to hot spot

Hawaii

Pacific Ocean

Pacific Plate

Past connections to hot spot

Direction of plate movement

Magma

Hot spot – this remains stationary while the plate moves over it

Figure 5 **Hot spots of the Hawaiian Islands – volcanoes away from plate boundaries**

1 Read pages 14 and 15 carefully and copy the table below into your exercise book. Complete the table by writing in the correct descriptions from the list given:

Differences between an acid lava volcano and a basic lava volcano

Characteristic	Acid lava volcano	Basic lava volcano
Cone shape		
Type of plate boundary		
Where it occurs		
Origin of magma		
Characteristics of lava		
Violence of eruption		
Example		

Shallow-sided shield shape
Often erupt violently

Steep-sided cone shape
Along destructive plate boundaries
Directly from mantle as upwelling molten rock
Mainly runny lava which flows rapidly and cools slowly
Along constructive plate boundaries and at hot spots
Ash, hot gases, lava bombs and viscous lava that cools rapidly
Eruptions usually quite gentle
From the melting of wet oceanic crust and marine sediments

2 Study Figure 4 and your map of plate boundaries. Suggest why the Pacific 'Ring of Fire' is so called.

3 Using an atlas and your map of plate boundaries (page 248), name the type of volcano (acid or basic) you would expect to find in each of the following places:
a Iceland **b** Chile **c** Alaska **d** Hawaii **e** Japan.

Case study | Mount St Helens, Washington State, USA 1980

Mount St Helens, in the Cascade Range of Washington State, USA, erupted violently on 18 May 1980. The eruption had many of the characteristics of an explosive acid volcano that lay over a subduction zone (Figure 6). It caused considerable damage to the surrounding landscape but its effects were also felt much further away.

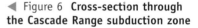

◀ Figure 6 **Cross-section through the Cascade Range subduction zone**

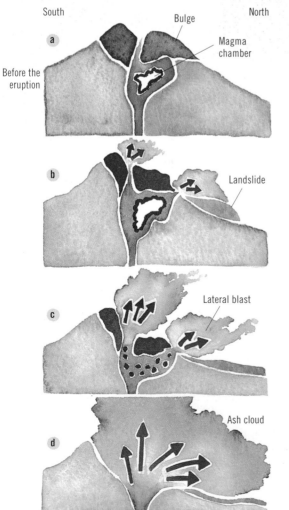

The volcano finally erupted following an earthquake of magnitude 5.0. The tremor caused a massive landslide, removing the bulge on the north flank (a).

The sudden release of pressure produced by the landslide caused a simultaneous lateral blast of steam, hot gases, pumice and ash (called a **pyroclastic flow**) towards the north (b). This hot blast moved at up to 300 km per hour, devastating more than 360 sq. km of land, flattening and incinerating surrounding fir and pine trees. The landslide reduced the mountain's height by 365 m.

Mudflows caused by hot magma melting the mountain's snow cap were channelled down surrounding rivers at up to 35 m per second, sweeping away bridges (Figure 8). A giant mushroom-shaped cloud rose 24 km into the sky and up to 15 cm of ash fell on the surrounding area, blocking out the sun and causing traffic chaos (c and d). Airline flights were cancelled and damage to crops and farm machinery from the ash was estimated at $175 million. Ash blown high into the atmosphere was swept eastwards by wind, causing particularly colourful sunsets across Europe for several months after the eruption. The landscape surrounding Mount St Helens was changed almost beyond recognition.

Only 61 people lost their lives in the eruption, not only because the area had been sparsely populated but also because of the numerous warnings and forced evacuation. Most of those who died were photographers and geologists trying to study the eruption.

◀ Figure 7 **Stages in the eruption of Mt St Helens**

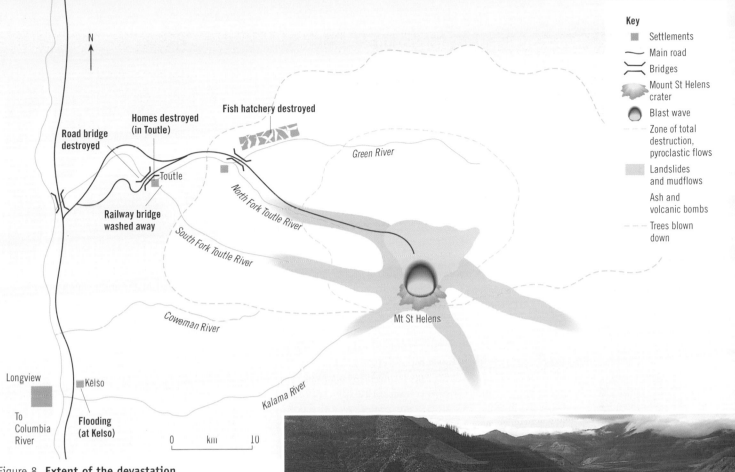

Figure 8 **Extent of the devastation**

Key

- ■ Settlements
- ⌇ Main road
- ⟩⟨ Bridges
- 🌋 Mount St Helens crater
- ⬤ Blast wave
- Zone of total destruction, pyroclastic flows
- Landslides and mudflows
- Ash and volcanic bombs
- Trees blown down

Road bridge destroyed
Homes destroyed (in Toutle)
Fish hatchery destroyed
Green River
Toutle
North Fork Toutle River
Railway bridge washed away
South Fork Toutle River
Coweman River
Mt St Helens
Kalama River
Longview
Kelso
To Columbia River
Flooding (at Kelso)

0   km   10

Figure 9 **Fully grown pine and fir trees were flattened by the blast a few miles north of the crater**

Figure 10 **Countdown to the eruption**	
1980	
20 March	Earthquake measured at 4.0 on the Richter scale, ending a 123 year dormant period for the volcano
25 March	47 earthquakes of at least 3.0 on the Richter scale
26 March	'Hazard alerts' issued to the local population
27 March	First emissions of steam and a new 70-m crater appears in the snow on the summit
28 March	A plume of steam and ash rises 3 km from the crater. Water levels in the Swift Reservoir, south of the mountain, are intentionally lowered by 8 m as a precaution against floodwaters from snowmelt if an eruption occurs
29 March	Second crater appears
30 March	Many small eruptions of steam and ash
3 April	A bulge begins to grow on the north flank of the volcano, protruding 100 m by 12 April
29 April	The new summit craters have joined up to become one large crater, 500 m across
30 April	A 30-km radius danger zone is put around the mountain to keep sightseers away
10 May	Several earthquakes of at least 4.0 on the Richter scale occur; the bulge on the northern flank grows by 1.5 m a day now
18 May	The volcano erupts

1 Why have volcanoes formed in the Cascade Range?

2 What warning signs were there that Mount St Helens might erupt?

3 How did an earthquake play a part in the eruption?

4 List the different substances that were emitted during the eruption.

5 Describe the effects of the eruption on each of the following:
a rivers and lakes
b vegetation
c communications and services
d other human activity.

6 Why do you think the eruption did not claim more lives?

7 Design and write the front page of a Washington State newspaper for the day after the eruption, describing the course of the eruption and its effects.

Case study | Nevada del Ruiz, Colombia, 1985

Nevada del Ruiz – the name means *The Sleeping Lion* – is the northernmost active volcano in the Andes. It is situated 128 km west of the Colombian capital, Bogota. On 13 November 1985, a cloud of hot ash erupted from the volcano and melted the surrounding snow cap and glaciers, producing millions of tonnes of meltwater. The ash and meltwater, combined with rock debris from the eruption, formed a 40-metre high mudflow or **lahar** which rushed down the valley of the Lagunillas River at up to 50 kph.

The town of Armero (population 22 000), 45 km from the summit, was buried by up to eight metres of mud. As the catastrophe occurred between 10 and 11 p.m., many residents were already asleep. Over 20 000 people died, buried by mud. Relief efforts by the International Red Cross and United Nations Disaster Relief Organisation were hampered by the thin mountain air and thick dust which made it difficult for helicopters to operate. There was also a shortage of two-way radios for communication.

There had been earlier warnings of possible volcanic activity. Earthquakes had been recorded in late 1984 and there were small emissions of gas and ash periodically throughout 1985. On 8 November an official warning of a threat from lahars was issued to the inhabitants of Armero and, on 13 November, the evacuation of the town was recommended as Nevada del Ruiz emitted a strong sulphur smell. The population did not respond. The fertile volcanic soils on the mountain's slopes supported wealthy coffee farms which local people were reluctant to leave and many inhabitants feared that, if they left Armero, their homes would be ransacked.

Figure 11 **Within minutes buildings were buried in the mud which later solidified**

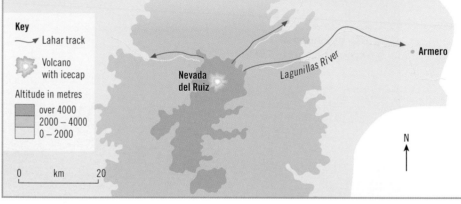

Key
- → Lahar track
- Volcano with icecap
- Altitude in metres
  - over 4000
  - 2000 – 4000
  - 0 – 2000

Nevada del Ruiz

Lagunillas River

Armero

0   km   20

N

Caribbean Sea

Venezuela

Pacific Ocean

Armero

Colombia

Key
- Mountains
- ▲ Active volcanoes
- National boundary

Ecuador

Peru

0   km   200

Figure 12 **Location of Nevada del Ruiz**

Figure 13 **The hazards of a volcano**

Ash cloud – often blown high into the atmosphere and carried a considerable distance; can cause death by asphyxiation

A hot avalanche (nuée ardente) or pyroclastic flow – a glowing cloud of hot ash, rocks, steam and gases; may move at over 300 kph; very dangerous

Lava is usually the last element to be erupted and rarely flows very far; of little danger

A mudflow or lahar – composed of melted snow or water from a crater lake, mixed with volcanic ash; follows river valleys for some distance at high speed; very dangerous

Village

Volcanic rock weathers to produce fertile soil ideal for agriculture. This encourages people to live ever-closer to volcanoes, putting themselves at more risk

Geothermal activity

In areas with geothermal activity, the crust is thin and magma is present at quite a shallow depth. The magma heats the rocks above it and temperatures may exceed 350°C at a depth of less than 5 km. Groundwater, percolating down from above, is heated and then driven upwards by convection through cracks in the crust. Closer to the surface this **superheated** water begins to boil and is then emitted onto the surface as shown in Figure 14.

Fumerole (1)
The superheated water may turn to steam instantly as it reaches the surface because of the sudden drop in pressure.

Mudpool (2)
Where steam condenses near the surface, soil is liquified to produce a bubbling pool of mud.

Hot spring (3)
Superheated water mixes with cold groundwater to form a hot spring at the surface.

Geyser (4)
A regular eruption of hot water and steam is fed from a chamber beneath. Superheated water flows into the chamber and begins to boil until the steam forces it quickly to the surface. The water ejected from the chamber is then replaced by surrounding groundwater and the cycle begins again. The size of the chamber and the temperature below the ground determine how frequently a geyser erupts.

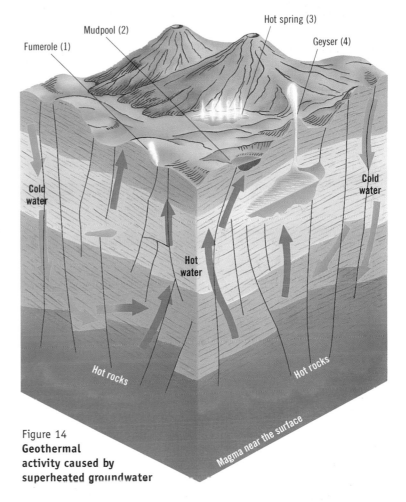

Figure 14
Geothermal activity caused by superheated groundwater

Figure 16 **Geysers like these in New Zealand are valuable tourist attractions**

Figure 15 **The Wairakei Geothermal Power Station providing energy for New Zealand's North Island. Steam from below the ground drives its turbines**

1 What is a lahar?

2 Why were so many people killed at Armero?

3 Why is rescue work generally so difficult following a volcanic eruption?

4 What are the advantages of volcanic activity for humans?

1.5 Igneous intrusions

Volcanoes are part of what is called **extrusive igneous activity**. This means that magma is poured out onto the earth's surface, then cools and solidifies. However, magma may also well up from the mantle and not reach the surface. Instead it is **intruded** (injected) into cracks in the rocks below the surface and cools there. Granite is a common intrusive rock and Figure 2 shows the different types of intrusion.

The largest igneous intrusion is the **batholith**, a huge dome-shaped mass of granite that may extend up to 1000 km across. If the rocks above the batholith are eroded away over millions of years, it may eventually become exposed at the surface. This can happen to all igneous intrusions. Much of Devon and Cornwall lie on top of a large batholith which appears above ground at Dartmoor, Bodmin Moor and Land's End (Figure 1).

Where magma is injected into sedimentary rocks, it may force its way along bedding planes where it cools and solidifies to form a horizontal sheet called a **sill**. Some sills form at an angle. An example is the Great Whin Sill in Northumberland.

Vertical sheets of igneous rock are called **dykes**. These form when magma is forced up through a vertical fault or is left behind in the magma tube of a volcano. A dyke exposed at the surface will form a **ridge** if it is more resistant than the surrounding rock. If the dyke is less resistant than the surrounding rock, it will be eroded more quickly to form a **trench**. An example is the Cleveland Dyke in the North York Moors.

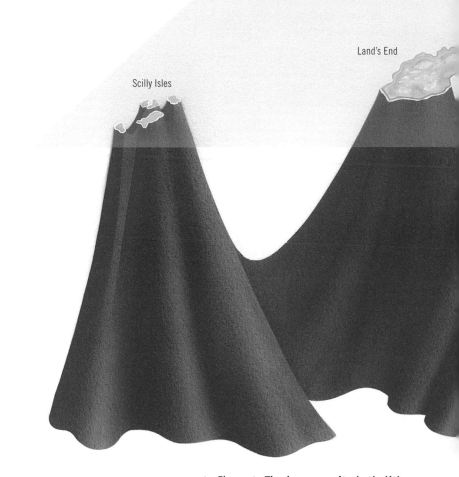

▲ Figure 1 **The huge granite batholith beneath the south-west of England showing areas where it has been exposed by erosion of the surface**

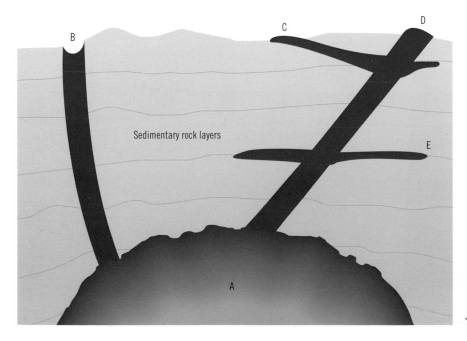

◀ Figure 2 **Igneous intrusions**

Bodmin Moor

Dartmoor

Figure 3 **A tor on Dartmoor** Here a granite batholith has become exposed at the surface. Joints in the rock have been attacked by the elements to produce the tor's 'block-like' appearance.

1 On a copy of the igneous intrusions diagram (Figure 2; also on page 249), label the features marked A – E with the following captions, using the text as a guide.

- dyke forming a ridge at the surface

- part of an underlying batholith

- sill

- dyke forming a trench at the surface

- sill forming an escarpment at the surface.

Rocks are continually being created and destroyed. The processes by which this happen are shown in Figure 1.

New rock is formed when molten lava cools and solidifies, either on the surface as **extrusive igneous rock**, or below the earth's surface as **intrusive igneous rock**.

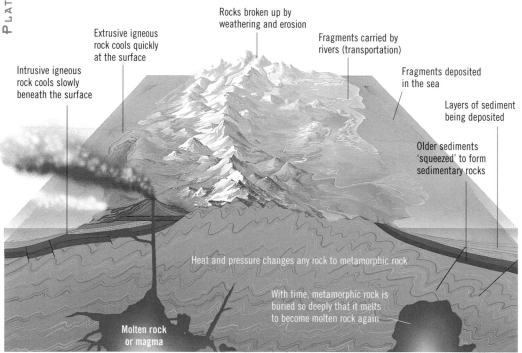

Intrusive igneous rock cools slowly beneath the surface

Extrusive igneous rock cools quickly at the surface

Rocks broken up by weathering and erosion

Fragments carried by rivers (transportation)

Fragments deposited in the sea

Layers of sediment being deposited

Older sediments 'squeezed' to form sedimentary rocks

Heat and pressure changes any rock to metamorphic rock

With time, metamorphic rock is buried so deeply that it melts to become molten rock again

Molten rock or magma

Figure 1 **The rock cycle in action**

Over time, these rocks are worn down by weathering and erosion. The broken down rock particles are transported to the sea where they are deposited. These deposits become compressed as more and more particles are added, which eventually results in new sedimentary rock being formed. As the rocks are buried deeper and deeper they are put under great pressure and experience more heat from the earth's interior. This can result in such rocks being metamorphosed (changed) to form new **metamorphic rock**. These rocks may in turn be subjected to such great heat and pressure that they melt to form molten rock or **lava**, which then rises towards the earth's surface and the whole process starts all over again.

Rock types

There are three main types of rock:

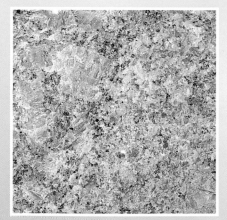

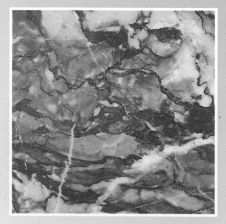

Igneous rock is formed by the cooling of molten rock or magma. If magma cools before it reaches the surface of the earth it is called **intrusive**. Granite is an example of such rock. If it reaches the surface before cooling then it is called **extrusive**. Basalt is an example of this type of rock.

Sedimentary rock is formed by the laying down or deposition of rock particles that have been weathered and eroded. Deposition can take place in the sea, in rivers, underneath glaciers and ice sheets or by the wind. Sandstone is an example of a sedimentary rock.

Metamorphic rock is formed by pressure and extreme heat applied to existing rocks within the earth's crust causing them to change their mineral structure and texture. Marble, which is formed from the sedimentary rock limestone, is one example of a metamorphic rock.

Weathering

Weathering is the break down of rocks at or near the earth's surface. There are two main types of weathering – **physical weathering** which happens when rocks break up due to stress and **chemical weathering** which is where rocks are broken down by chemical reactions.

Chemical weathering

Carbonation – Rainwater absorbs carbon dioxide as it falls through the air and soaks through the soil. This makes it quite acidic. It will attack rocks composed of calcium carbonate, such as limestone, producing some very dramatic features.

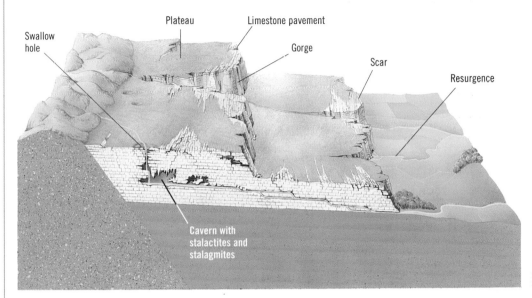

Oxidation – Metals and metallic minerals in rocks combine with oxygen from the air to form another substance. Rocks containing iron are especially weathered by this process.

Hydrolysis – Some rock minerals combine with rainwater and break down into other chemical forms. This process of hydrolysis is important in producing sand and clay when water combines with granite.

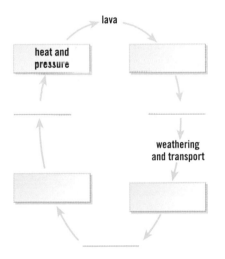

1 Complete the simplified diagram (above) to show the processes operating in the rock cycle. Use the following labels: cooling; compression, sedimentary rock; igneous rock; pressure; metamorphic rock.

2 **a** Look at the pictures of the various rock types. Describe their appearance (texture, colour, etc.).

b Try and find at least another two examples of each rock type.

Physical weathering

Freeze-thaw or frost shattering – Water expands by about one tenth when it freezes. When the temperature falls below 0°C, ice crystals grow and exert pressure on the joint. The rock may split as a result of the pressure.

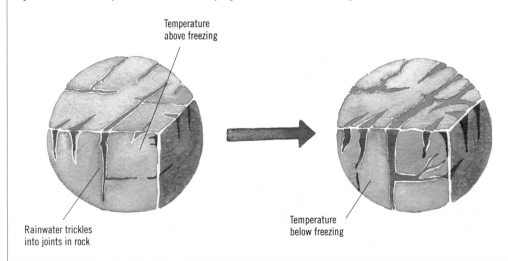

The coast can be defined as the point where land and sea meet. It includes cliffs, sand dunes and the shore.

Coasts are the most varied and rapidly changing of all the natural environments. **Wave erosion** causes some coasts to retreat while **wave deposition** causes others to advance. Many processes occur along coastlines, either on the land or in the sea and some unnatural features are constructed to cope with the effects of these processes, such as groynes or sea walls.

Waves

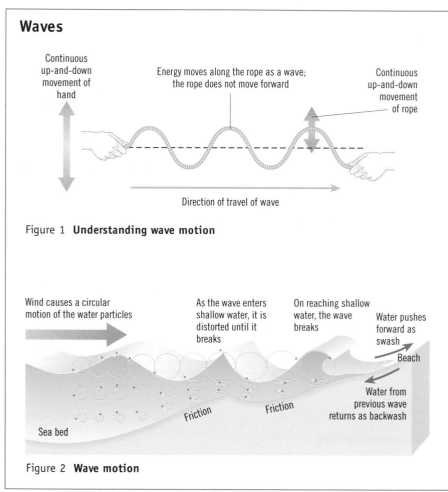

Figure 1 **Understanding wave motion**

Figure 2 **Wave motion**

Waves are caused by the wind. The friction of the wind on the water tugs at the surface of the oceans causing the wave shape to move. Within a wave each water particle moves in a circular motion and returns to its starting point.

It is the surge of energy that actually moves forward and not the water particles. This can perhaps be best demonstrated by shaking a piece of rope. The wave shape travels down the piece of rope but the rope itself remains in the same place. Only the wave travels forward; neither the rope, nor the sea.

When a wave moves into shallow water near the coast, it is slowed down by the frictional drag between the sea and the sea-bed, and eventually it will break. From this moment onwards it is not only the energy of the wave that is moving forward but also the water itself. Water moves up the beach as **swash** and drains back down the beach again as **backwash**.

Different types of waves

Constructive waves cause sediment to build up on the beach. They are most common when the fetch is large and the beach angle is gradual. The waves are flat and low, and have a much stronger swash than backwash. Sediment builds up slowly onshore (between six to eight waves break per minute).

Destructive waves help remove sediment from the beach. They are more common when the fetch is short and the beach angle steep. The waves are steep and high, with a stronger backwash than swash. This allows sediment to be dragged off shore (between ten and 14 waves break per minute).

Figure 3 **Constructive waves**

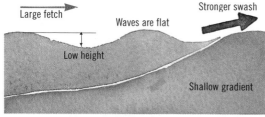

Figure 4 **Destructive waves**

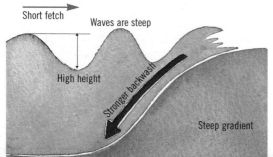

Wave refraction

When a wave approaches the shore it is affected by the sea floor and behaves in a different manner. In shallow areas due to friction, the wave moves more slowly than it does in deep water. The wave is bent; it changes shape so that eventually it is parallel to the coastline.

This is best illustrated where a headland separates two bays. As each wave crest nears the coast it tends to drag in the shallow water near to the headland so that the part of the wave in deeper water moves forward faster. This has the effect of 'bending' the waves and concentrating their energy on the headland, causing greater erosion.

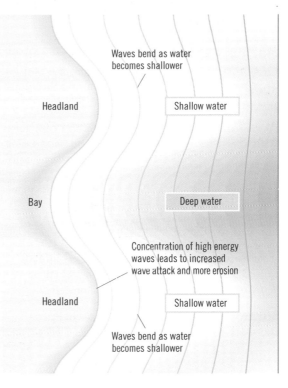

Waves bend as water becomes shallower

Headland

Shallow water

Deep water

Bay

Concentration of high energy waves leads to increased wave attack and more erosion

Headland

Shallow water

Waves bend as water becomes shallower

Figure 5 **Wave refraction**

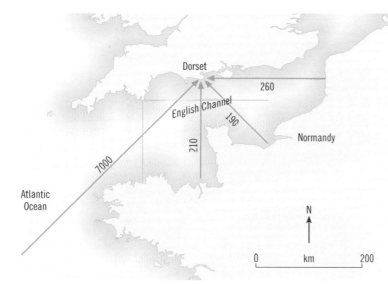

Dorset

260

English Channel

190

210

Normandy

7000

Atlantic Ocean

N

0   km   200

Fetch

The height and strength of the wave depends on the speed of the wind, how long it has been blowing and the distance over which it has travelled. This distance is known as the **fetch**. Figure 6 shows the different fetches affecting the Dorset coastline. A south-easterly wind from the Normandy area of France will not produce large, powerful waves because the fetch is less than 200 km while a south-westerly wind will produce very large waves because its fetch, from the Atlantic Ocean, may be as great as 7000 km.

Figure 6 **Fetch of the waves on the Dorset coast**

1 Define the following terms: swash, backwash, fetch, wave refraction.

2 On a copy of Figure 7 use the data below to draw a scattergraph showing how the fetch influences the size of a certain wave.

Fetch (km)	Wave height (metres)
50	2.4
100	3.5
150	4.2
200	4.6
250	4.9
300	5.1

These figures assume that the wind is blowing at 10 km an hour and that the wind has been blowing for at least 20 hours.

3 What trend does your graph show?

4 Why might this be the case?

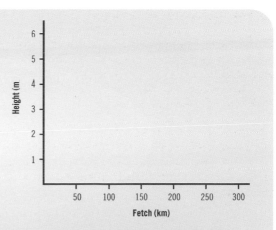

Figure 7 **Scattergraph: how the fetch influences the size of a wave**

Marine erosion

Erosion by the sea takes place where the cliff meets the water.
The relentless wave attack both during the night and day will erode the cliff in four main ways.

Abrasion is the most effective method of coastal erosion with cliffs being worn away by boulders, pebbles and sand being hurled against them.
It is particularly effective during storm conditions.

Hydraulic action occurs when a parcel of air is trapped and compressed in cracks and crevices in the rocks by the encroaching water. As the wave retreats the air may expand explosively, weakening the joints and cracks and causing the rock to shatter.

Attrition is where rocks and boulders already eroded from the cliffs are hurled against the shore and against each other by the breaking waves.
They are gradually broken down into smaller and more rounded pieces.

Solution occurs on limestone and chalk coasts. The sea water dissolves the calcium carbonate in these rocks and weakens them.

These processes of erosion can produce a variety of landforms.

Cliff

Generally any steep rock face adjoining the coast forms a cliff.
The type of cliff depends on the nature of the rock, its resistance to erosion and the angle of dip of the layers of rock – called the **rock strata**. Horizontal and vertical strata are more likely to produce vertical cliffs such as the White Cliffs of Dover. Strata which dip inland may produce an overhang and those dipping seawards may cause a gently sloping cliff.

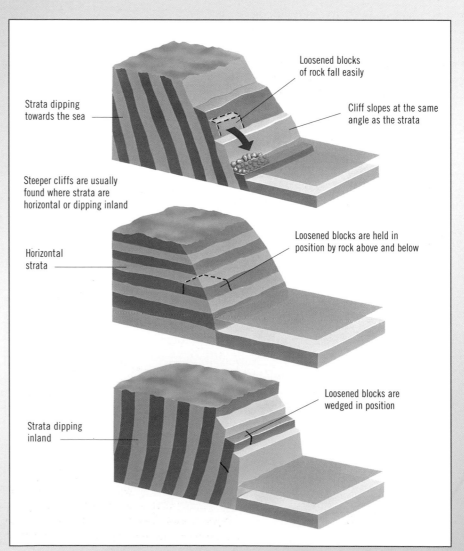

Strata dipping towards the sea

Loosened blocks of rock fall easily

Cliff slopes at the same angle as the strata

Steeper cliffs are usually found where strata are horizontal or dipping inland

Horizontal strata

Loosened blocks are held in position by rock above and below

Strata dipping inland

Loosened blocks are wedged in position

▶ Figure 1 **How the angle of dip of rocks influences the steepness of cliffs**

Figure 2 **Wave erosion has caused these boulder clay cliffs to slump at Holderness**

Where weaker rock is present often the cliffs are not as dramatic. The sands and clays which were deposited by ice sheets cannot support high cliffs and they are easily worn away by sea erosion. One of the best examples of this in the UK can be seen along the 60-kilometre Holderness Coast, north of the Humber estuary in Yorkshire, between Flamborough Head and Spurn Head. The coastline is receding by an average of two metres per year under the relentless attack of waves from the north and north-east. Dozens of towns and villages have been lost during this process and it is thought that up to 4 km of coastline has been removed since Roman times.

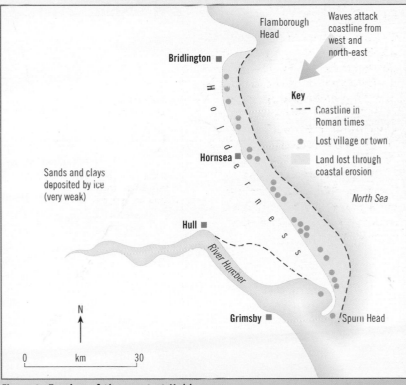

Figure 3 **Erosion of the coast at Holderness**

1 Describe four different processes of erosion.

2 Describe and explain the major controls on cliff formation.

3 Look at the photograph of erosion at Holderness (Figure 2).
   a What evidence is there that the cliff is actively eroding and retreating inland?
   b Describe the type of material of which the cliff is composed.
   c How might this explain the rapid rate of erosion on this section of coastline?

Wave-cut platform

Continual wave attack at the foot of a cliff results in gradual undercutting to create a **wave-cut notch**.

As this notch is under constant attack, slowly the cliff will be eroded away at its lower layers and will collapse. The process of marine erosion at the rock base, followed by cliff collapse will be repeated and as the cliff retreats, a gently sloping **wave-cut platform** will be formed.

Figure 4 **Waves have cut a notch in the rocks near high tide level**

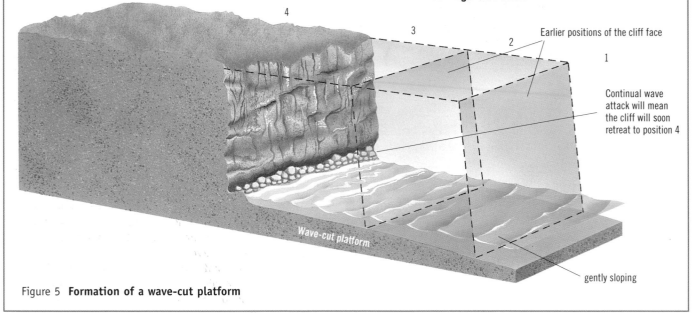

Earlier positions of the cliff face

Continual wave attack will mean the cliff will soon retreat to position 4

Wave-cut platform

gently sloping

Figure 5 **Formation of a wave-cut platform**

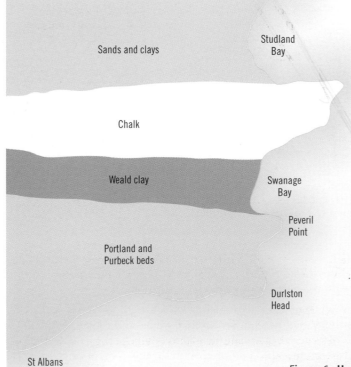

Sands and clays

Studland Bay

Chalk

Weald clay

Swanage Bay

Peveril Point

Portland and Purbeck beds

Durlston Head

St Albans Head

Figure 6 **Headlands and bays along the Dorset coastline**

Headlands and bays

The shape of the coastline results from erosion of the various types of rock. **Bays** have been formed where weaker, exposed rocks have been eroded at the coast; **headlands**, where the more resistant rocks remain as outcrops.

Figure 6 of the south Dorset coast, shows that several headlands extend out into the sea between which the bays made up of softer rock have been eroded. This uneven, or indented, coastline (with the rocks structure running at right angles to the coast) is called a **discordant** coastline. Where the rocks outcrop parallel to the coast, often the coast will be much straighter; it is called a **concordant** coastline.

Figure 7 **The Foreland, Dorset**

Cave, arch, blow-hole, stack and stump

Prolonged wave attack on cliffs of resistant rock will attack areas of local weaknesses, such as a joint or a fault. The waves will excavate holes in the cliff called **caves** (A). Backward or **horizontal erosion** of this cave will lead to a hole eventually being created right through the headland, forming an **arch** (B). Less commonly, a **blow-hole** may be created where air trapped inside the cave will be compressed and, through **vertical erosion**, force its way up the cracks to the cliff top. A spray of sea-water and a blast of air rushes through the blow-hole each time a wave crashes into the cave below.

Continual marine erosion of an arch will lead to roof collapse and the formation of a **stack** (C). The wearing away of a stack will create a **stump** that, with time, will simply be reduced to a **wave-cut platform** (D).

◀ Figure 8 **Blow-hole on the Hawaiian island of Maui**

1 Using the photograph of the Foreland in Figure 7 to help you, draw four labelled diagrams to explain the formation of a cave, an arch, a stack and a stump.

2 Study the map in Figure 6.
   a Which stretch of coast is concordant and which is discordant?
   b Look at the patterns of bays and headlands. Which rocks do you think are hard and which are soft.

Transport and deposition

Once waves have eroded material, they also transport and deposit it through a number of processes.

Processes of transport

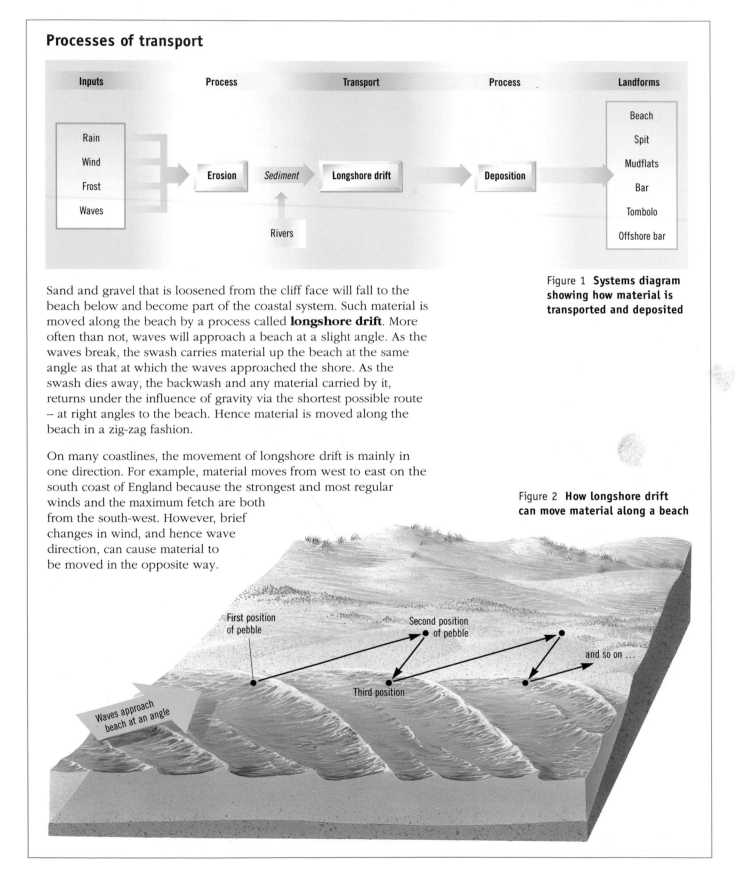

Figure 1 **Systems diagram showing how material is transported and deposited**

Sand and gravel that is loosened from the cliff face will fall to the beach below and become part of the coastal system. Such material is moved along the beach by a process called **longshore drift**. More often than not, waves will approach a beach at a slight angle. As the waves break, the swash carries material up the beach at the same angle as that at which the waves approached the shore. As the swash dies away, the backwash and any material carried by it, returns under the influence of gravity via the shortest possible route – at right angles to the beach. Hence material is moved along the beach in a zig-zag fashion.

On many coastlines, the movement of longshore drift is mainly in one direction. For example, material moves from west to east on the south coast of England because the strongest and most regular winds and the maximum fetch are both from the south-west. However, brief changes in wind, and hence wave direction, can cause material to be moved in the opposite way.

Figure 2 **How longshore drift can move material along a beach**

Figure 3 **Groynes are designed to reduce coastal erosion**

Deposition – a vital form of coastal protection

Longshore drift is a continual process and occurs every time a wave breaks at a slight angle to the shore. Entire holiday beaches can be washed away, sometimes in a single year. To prevent this from happening, large sums of money are spent on sea defences. One common method of protecting the coastline is by using wooden breakwaters or **groynes**. These are fences that run down a beach into the sea and prevent the beach material from being transported away (Figure 3).

One problem with groynes is that they result in less material being transported further down the coast hence those places may well suffer from increased erosion.

The photograph (Figure 4) shows derelict fishing cottages at Hallsands, in Devon. During the 1800s the villagers' fishing boats were kept on the beach which lay between the houses and the sea. However, in 1897, in order to extend the naval dockyard at Davenport, 650 000 tonnes of shingle were removed from the sea bed. This meant that waves could now attack the beach at Hallsands more vigorously and after a few years, the beach which protected the cliff from erosion had disappeared. The waves then proceeded to erode the rocks on which the houses were built and within 20 years, the fishing village had begun to fall into the sea.

▶ Figure 4 **Derelict cottages at Hallsands, Devon**

1 Look at Figure 3. How can you tell longshore drift has occurred?

2 What are the advantages and disadvantages of using groynes to trap sediment?

3 Why did the village of Hallsands fall into the sea?

Landforms produced by wave deposition

Longshore drift provides the link between erosion and deposition along the coast. Material eroded from the cliff in one area will be moved and deposited further along the coast. Several landforms result from this deposition.

Spits

Spits are long, narrow sections of land made up of sand or shingle. One end of the spit is joined to the mainland while the other extends out into the sea or across a river estuary. The spit grows as it is supplied by material from longshore drift. Many spits develop a hooked or **recurved** end. This is probably due to the fact that as the spit grows away from the coastline into deeper water, the sand or shingle is more easily forced towards the land by the stronger waves or occasional changes in wind and wave direction.

◄ Figure 1 **Dawlish Warren, a spit at the mouth of the River Exe, Devon**

Dawlish Warren is a 2 km long spit at the mouth of the River Exe in Devon. One can clearly see the recurved end at the base of the image in Figure 1. Behind Dawlish Warren is a region of fine river deposits that make up an area of **mudflats** and **salt marshes**. Mudflats are covered by every high tide hence they are relatively infertile; salt marshes are covered only by occasional high tides or large floods, which allows them to be used as pasture land.

Since the sea is such a powerful erosive force, spits often change shape over very short periods of time. Possibly the best example this is the Spurn Head Spit growing across the Humber Estuary. Studies of old maps and charts show that the spit has been destroyed and rebuilt three times in the last six centuries. The three breaches took place during heavy storms in 1360, 1608, and 1849. Each time, the spit re-formed through the process of longshore drift from the north. During the winter of 1996, Spurn Head was destroyed for a fourth time and has now started the slow natural process of re-building once again.

Sand dunes

Sand dunes are formed by the presence of strong winds and not through the effects of marine erosion or deposition. The sand blown up from the beach will develop as small hills held together by resistant, long-rooted grasses such as **marram grass**. Where no such vegetation is present, sand dunes that have developed will be easily eroded away thus marram grass is usually planted in an attempt to protect and stabilise the dunes (Chapter 4).

Beaches

Beaches are usually found in sheltered bays where two headlands can protect the area from erosion, for example Lulworth Cove in Dorset. Sandy beaches are usually more gently sloping than shingle (pebble) beaches. The larger the material making up the beach, the steeper the beach. Often at the top of the beach there may be a steep ridge where larger material has been thrown during heavy storms; lower down, gently sloping sand is found as the tide goes out. The beach is an extremely important part of the coastal system as it protects the cliffs behind it from the force of the waves. The energy of the waves is spent on moving beach material instead of attacking the cliff.

◀ Figure 2 **Lulworth Cove**

Bar

A spit rarely extends across the width of a bay since the erosive force of a river flowing into the estuary combined with the waves in deeper water will transport large amount of material out to sea. However, if a spit develops in a bay where no major river flows, it may be able to completely cross the bay from one side to the other to form a **bar**. Bars help to straighten coastlines as they remove indentations from the coast as at Slapton Sands in Devon, for example.

The stretch of water dammed up behind the bar is called a **lagoon**. The lagoon is only a temporary feature as it is soon filled in by material deposited there by waves breaking over the bar or by small streams flowing into the lagoon.

Off-shore bars or **barrier islands** are detached beaches found between eight and 40 km off-shore. The bars form off-shore where waves break in shallow water. If they form near an estuary they are extremely hazardous to ships entering the harbour. One example of this is the Teign estuary in Devon, just south of Dawlish Warren.

▶ Figure 3 **Slapton Sands** The lagoon was formed (to the left) after the bar cut off the water from the sea.

Tombolo

A tombolo is a beach or spit that extends outwards to join with an off-shore island. A known example is the 30 km long Chesil Beach in Dorset, which links the Isle of Portland to the mainland.

Smaller tombolos, around 100 metres in length, are more common and often the island can only be reached at low tide when the tombolo is showing. An example is Burgh Island in Devon.

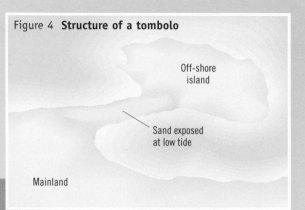

Figure 4 **Structure of a tombolo**

Off-shore island

Sand exposed at low tide

Mainland

Figure 5 **Ard Neackie tombolo, Sutherland**

Cuspate foreland

These are triangular outgrowths of shingle ridges formed by longshore drift from two opposite directions. They can be extremely large in size such as the huge foreland on the Kent coast at Dungeness.

1 Draw your own labelled diagrams to explain how the following landforms have been formed:
   a spit
   b bar
   c tombolo.

2 **a** What is the difference between a mudflat and a saltmarsh?
   b Which is more beneficial to humans? Why?

3 Using an atlas, look up the triangular cuspate foreland at Dungeness, Kent. Draw a sketch diagram of the area and label your diagram to show how this feature has been formed.

4 Using the resources in your school library, produce a short report on *The creation and destruction of Spurn Head Spit*. Find out as much information about its formation, features and recent breaching.

Changes in sea level will have large-scale consequences on the landforms at the coast. During the maximum extent of the last glacial period, approximately 18 000 years ago, there were huge ice masses on the land and thus sea level was at a minimum. The British Isles was connected by land to mainland Europe. As the global temperature warmed up, ice began to melt and for the last 6000 years the average position of sea level has remained relatively constant.

Changes in sea level may therefore lead to areas around the coast either being submerged by melting of the ice or emerging from the sea as the water begins to freeze at the start of an ice age.

Figure 6 **Raised beaches in Sutherland**

Raised beaches

During a glacial period, land is under tremendous pressure from the weight of the overlying ice. It is forced downwards. When the ice melts a huge weight is released allowing the land to 'rebound' and rise up once again. This process is called **isostatic readjustment** and takes thousands of years to completely settle in. The British Isles is still at present adjusting to the release of pressure from the ice that covered Northern Britain 18 000 years ago. In response to the ice melting, isostatic readjustment leads to the formation of **raised beaches** where former wave-cut platforms and their beaches are left as relict features high above the level of the sea. Many of these landforms can be seen on the west coast of Scotland where it is thought land is rising by 4 mm per year.

Figure 7 **A fjord on the Norwegian coast**

Fjords

Perhaps the most known landform resulting from a rise in sea level is the fjord. They are drowned **glaciated valleys**. During the ice age glaciers were able to erode the land down to sea level. When the ice melted, the glacial valleys were flooded to form long, deep, narrow inlets. A good example is Hardanger Fjord, Norway.

Figure 8 **A ria: Salcombe, Devon**

Rias

These are similar features to fjords but are actually drowned **river valleys**. During times of low sea level, flowing rivers were able to erode deep V-shaped valleys. Once the temperature began to increase, sea levels started to rise and the lower part of the river valley was drowned to produce sheltered, winding inlets. Good examples in the UK are Salcombe, Devon (pictured), and Milford Haven, South Wales. Humans are able to utilise rias as they provide deepwater ports. Heavy tankers can be used to transport goods for export and import.

2.6 Managing coastal flooding

Case study | Chesil Beach

Chiswell settlement is located immediately behind the Chesil Beach shingle ridge, on the north-east side of the Isle of Portland. It has been flooded many times. The first major recorded event occurred in November 1824, when 26 people and approximately 80 houses were destroyed or damaged in a devastating storm. Since 1824, 22 storm events have occcured at Chiswell that have endangered lives and put property at risk.

Coastal protection and sea defence works were first undertaken during 1969 – 75. This has formed the basis of the long-term protection of Chiswell. Since then, a number of new protection schemes have been built, at the same time providing an important local amenity: the promenade at the south end of Chiswell.

Chesil Beach is a natural barrier, 27 km long and 200 m wide. It is a coastal feature of international significance, being one of the three major shingle beaches in Britain. Until 1972, beach material was excavated for commercial activities

Figure 1 **Chesil Beach looking north from Portland**

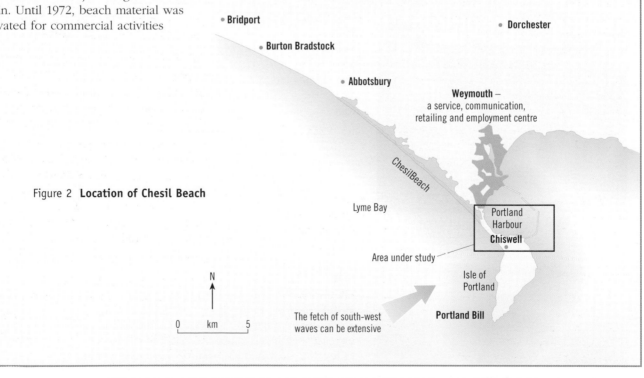

Figure 2 **Location of Chesil Beach**

---

1 Look at Figure 1. What physical features shown on the photograph indicate that Chiswell is at risk from flooding?

2 Portland Harbour is a naval dockyard. What other activities are shown in the photograph?

3 Using the map in Figure 2, describe the main reasons why Chiswell is so prone to flooding from the sea.

4 How might the extraction of beach material increase the chance of flooding at Chiswell?

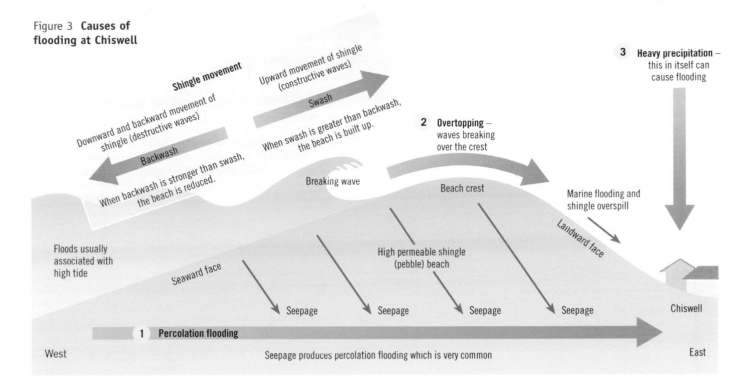

Figure 3 **Causes of flooding at Chiswell**

Shingle movement

Downward and backward movement of shingle (destructive waves)

Upward movement of shingle (constructive waves)

Backwash

Swash

When backwash is stronger than swash, the beach is reduced.

When swash is greater than backwash, the beach is built up.

3 Heavy precipitation – this in itself can cause flooding

2 Overtopping – waves breaking over the crest

Breaking wave

Beach crest

Marine flooding and shingle overspill

Landward face

Floods usually associated with high tide

Seaward face

High permeable shingle (pebble) beach

Chiswell

Seepage   Seepage   Seepage   Seepage

1 Percolation flooding

West

Seepage produces percolation flooding which is very common

East

Flooding at Chiswell

13 December 1978

A deep depression swept in from the Atlantic Ocean and created storm conditions. A combination of heavy rains and strong winds meant that waves of over 4.5 m attacked the shore at regular 12-second intervals. These steep destructive waves with their strong backwash carried away beach material. As the storm continued, Chesil Beach was progressively reduced in height and became even more unstable. Water broke over the highest part of the beach and ran down the other side, eroding the landward slope.

Meanwhile, huge quantities of sea water percolated through the pebbles of Chesil Beach and seeped out through its landward face. Thus, overtopping and percolation led to Chiswell being flooded to a depth of 1.2 m.

Over 30 commercial and residential properties were flooded and families were evacuated to emergency rest centres. Gas, water and electricity lines were cut for 24 hours and emergency services were needed for five days.

13 February 1979

On the morning of 13 February 1979, Chesil Beach was overwhelmed by constructive waves attacking the shore at 18-second intervals. The waves pushed shingle beach forward and tonnes of shingle overspilled the top of Chesil, flattening it out. This allowed water to break over the top of the beach and on to Chiswell below.

Portland was temporarily cut off from the mainland because of the overtopping waves. Over 30 Chiswell properties were flooded and the relevant families evacuated. Again, water, gas and electricity supplies were cut and emergency services were needed for ten days.

After the 1979 flood, everyone has agreed that something had to be done to prevent future flooding.

5 Using the following headings, construct a table to compare the two floods: Wave type; Wave interval; Damage; Time that emergency serves were needed for.

6 Explain the cause of flooding at Chiswell.

7 Imagine you are a member of one of the families in Chiswell at the time of the floods. Describe the events from the onset of the storm to the point of evacuation.

8 The County Council have to decide whether or not to build a flood defence scheme to protect the residents of Chiswell. Write a report either for or against such a scheme, clearly stating your reasons for your decision. You may like to include some of the following points:

● the cost of rehousing residents

● the cost of a defence scheme

● the importance of local industries

● the importance of community spirit

● the problem of providing services when it floods.

9 In February 1979, the Council decided to go ahead with a flood defence scheme. You have been given the task of designing a flood defence scheme for Chiswell. Produce a poster explaining what you would do and how it would work.

The Chesil Beach Sea Defence Scheme

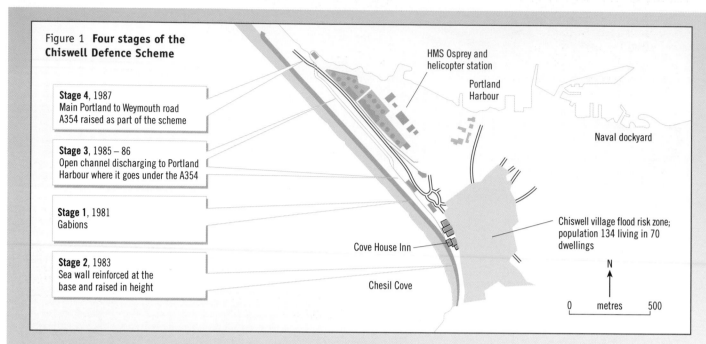

Figure 1 **Four stages of the Chiswell Defence Scheme**

Stage 4, 1987
Main Portland to Weymouth road A354 raised as part of the scheme

Stage 3, 1985 – 86
Open channel discharging to Portland Harbour where it goes under the A354

Stage 1, 1981
Gabions

Stage 2, 1983
Sea wall reinforced at the base and raised in height

HMS Osprey and helicopter station

Portland Harbour

Naval dockyard

Chiswell village flood risk zone; population 134 living in 70 dwellings

Cove House Inn

Chesil Cove

N

0   metres   500

On 14 February 1979, a firm of consultant engineers were contracted to identify and find ways of reducing the flood hazard at Chesil Beach. Funded mainly by the government, the engineers produced an updated flood control system. The systems cost approximately £3 million and was built in four main stages.

Stage 1: 1981

A trial length (150 m) of **gabion mattresses** raised the beach level to 14.5 m. A gabion is a reinforcing cylinder, used in building construction.

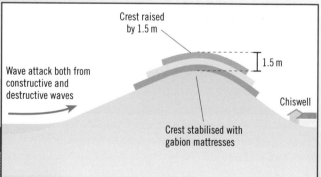

Crest raised by 1.5 m

Wave attack both from constructive and destructive waves

1.5 m

Chiswell

Crest stabilised with gabion mattresses

▲ Figure 2 **Gabion protection of the crest of Chesil Beach**

Figure 3 **Gabion mattresses at Chiswell**

The mattresses strengthened the crest of the beach, reducing the effects of erosion from the constructive and destructive waves. They cost £150 000 and are expected to last approximately 20 years.

Stage 2: 1983

The 300-m sea wall which was constructed 30 years earlier was modified. Easy access was provided for pedestrians and disabled persons by ramps and sea gates along the length of the wall. Access also took into account the needs of the local fishermen. The cost was £350 000.

Figure 4 **Sea wall at Chiswell**

Stage 3: 1985 – 86

This was the most expensive part of construction at £2.5 million. It was to reduce the amount of storm water percolating into Chiswell. A large culvert (drain) with openings in the seaward side and the top has been constructed along the southern end of Chiswell.

At times of flooding, water emerges from the drains and flows northwards along an open ditch towards Portland Harbour.

Stage 4: June 1987

The A354 was raised above the level of the December 1978 flood.

Figure 5 **Drain openings on the seaward side**

Success of the scheme

With the exception of the recommended 1500-metre length of gabion crest protection, the scheme was completed in 1988. A severe storm attacked Portland on 16 December 1989 and proved the efficiency of the sea defence scheme. Flooding was minimal and the interceptor drain flowed at its maximum.

1 For each stage of the flood defence scheme, explain how it works to prevent flooding.

2 In 1990 the government requested an investigation into the effectiveness of the Chiswell Scheme. How would the investigation be carried out?

3 What evidence is there to suggest the scheme is a great success?

4 Apart from improving the beach, what other ways could the flood hazard be reduced at Chiswell?

GLACIATION

About 170 000 years ago, 30% of the surface of the earth was covered by ice. Much of Britain was under ice and many of its present landforms are a direct result of ice erosion and deposition.

Ice began to spread over Britain about 2 million years ago and only disappeared about 10 000 years ago, a time known to geographers as the **Pleistocene** or Ice Age. The Pleistocene period has left a great impact on the landscape. There were many periods of glaciation before the Pleistocene but effects of these earlier ice ages have been overcome by succeeding ice advances.

Clearly, the climate was colder during the Ice Age than it is now, but the Ice Age itself was not one single, simple event. During the last two million years there have been fluctuations in global temperatures of between 5°C and 6°C which have led to cold phases (**glacials**), where ice advanced southwards over Britain, and warm periods (**interglacials**), where ice retreated northwards. Figure 1 shows how the temperature of Britain has changed over the last two hundred thousand years. It shows that the average July temperatures reached as high as 20°C, 200 000 years ago and as low as 5°C, 180 000 years ago.

Britain experienced three major glacial periods during the Ice Age. These are shown on Figure 2.

Figure 1 **Temperature changes in Britain through the last 200 000 years**

G Glacial periods when ice covered much of Britain

I Interglacial periods much like the present day

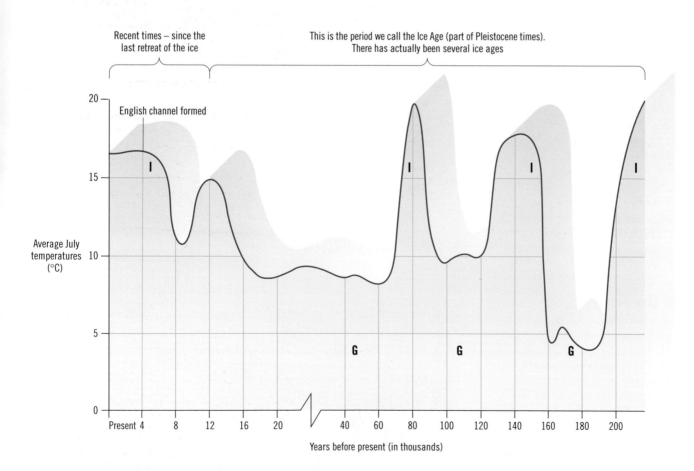

Years before present (in thousands)

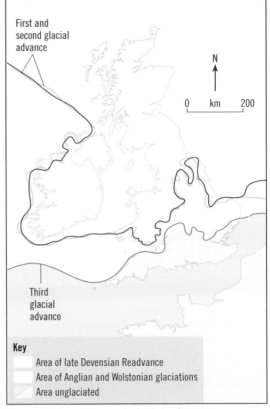

First and second glacial advance

N

0   km   200

Third glacial advance

Key

Area of late Devensian Readvance

Area of Anglian and Wolstonian glaciations

Area unglaciated

Figure 2 **The pattern of glacial advances**

The accumulation of ice

The present climate of the British Isles is no longer cold enough to allow snow to accumulate for long periods of time. If snow falls in winter, then it will melt in the spring. In the uplands, where temperatures are cooler and precipitation greater, snow will remain on the land for longer periods. If the climate was colder, then the winter snow would not melt in spring and it would be added to the following year. Slowly, over a large time period, snow would accumulate on the land.

When snow first falls it appears to accumulate quickly, but much of the thickness (up to 90%) is usually due to the pockets of air trapped between the snowflakes rather than the snow itself. If temperatures remain cold enough, more snow will cause lower layers to be compressed and much of the air will be removed. After one winter the snow will have formed a more compacted structure called **firn** or **névé**. More snowfall weighs the névé down, squeezing yet more air out. This process, over 20 to 30 years, will form glacier ice which is almost impermeable (will not allow water to pass through it).

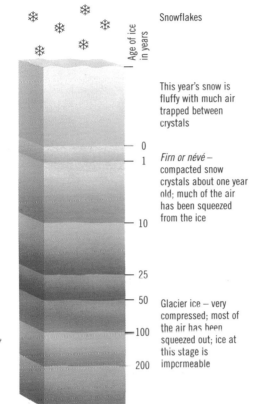

Snowflakes

Age of ice in years

This year's snow is fluffy with much air trapped between crystals

0
1

Firn or névé – compacted snow crystals about one year old; much of the air has been squeezed from the ice

10

25

50

Glacier ice – very compressed; most of the air has been squeezed out; ice at this stage is impermeable

100

200

Figure 3 **The accumulation of ice**

When a mass of ice has formed in a valley it is called a **glacier**. It may, like a river, flow slowly downhill under the influence of gravity as a 'tongue' of ice (Figure 4). At present the largest glaciers are in high mountain ranges such as the Himalayas, Andes, Rockies and Alps. When a continuous mass of ice covers a large land surface, it is called an **ice sheet**. A good example of an ice sheet is at the Antarctic; it covers the south pole.

1 Look at Figure 1.
   a How many times did the ice advance over Britain during the Ice Age?
   b When did the last major glacial period start? How long did it last?
   c What is the difference in the July average temperatures between the glacial period 40 000 years ago and the interglacial period 80 000 years ago?
   d What is the average July temperature for Britain at the present time?
   e What do you think the future pattern of temperature changes might be?

2 Explain how ice is formed.

3 What is the difference between a valley glacier and an ice sheet?

▶ Figure 4 **Yerupaja Glacier, Peru**

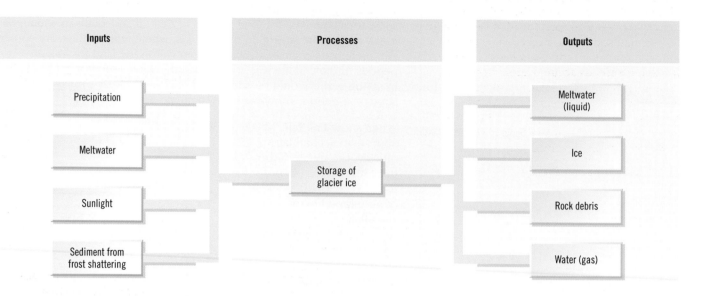

Figure 1 **The glacier as a system**

The glacier operates as a system with inputs, stores, transfers and outputs. The main inputs are snowfall and sediment falling from the valley sides due to frost shattering and other forms of weathering. The principle outputs are evaporation and water from melted snow. Glacier ice is stored within the valley as well as transferred down the valley.

A glacier does not grow indefinitely. It will eventually move into warmer areas where the ice will melt. Its length may be divided into two parts. The upper part of the glacier, where inputs exceed outputs and the glacier is growing or advancing, is known as the **zone of accumulation**; the lower part where outputs exceed inputs, where the glacier is shrinking or retreating, is called the **zone of ablation**. Between the two zones is a line where the rate of accumulation is balanced by the rate of melting. The balance between accumulation and ablation is known as the glacier's **budget** (Figure 2).

Figure 2 **The glacial budget**

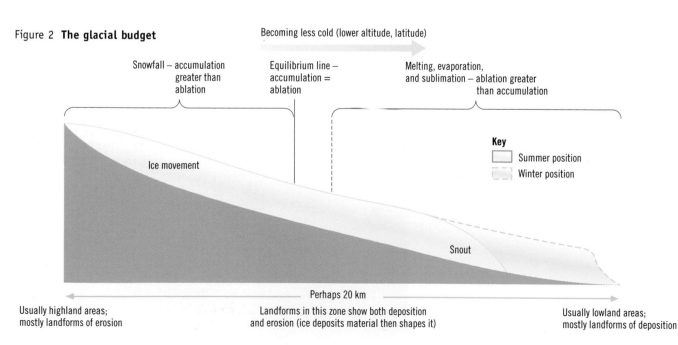

Using the systems approach we can tell if a glacier will advance down the valley or retreat up it. If, over a year, precipitation of snow in the accumulation zone exceeds melting in the ablation zone, then the glacier will advance. If melting exceeds accumulation, however, then the glacier will retreat. Seasonal variations can also be explained using this approach. In summer, a glacier is likely to retreat as melting is greater than accumulation; during winter, precipitation is greater, causing the glacier to advance.

▲ Figure 3 **Snout of Fox Glacier, New Zealand, showing moraine deposits**

◀ Figure 4 **The large valley glacier is joined by several tributary glaciers**

1 Using Figure 1, list the main inputs and outputs from the glacier system.

2 What is the difference between accumulation and ablation?

3 For each of the following, state whether the glacier will advance, retreat or remain stationary.
   a accumulation equals ablation
   b ablation is greater than accumulation
   c accumulation is greater than ablation.

The speed at which glacier ice moves varies greatly, both from glacier to glacier and within each individual glacier. **Cold, polar glaciers** (where temperatures are permanently below 0°C) move extremely slowly because there is little meltwater present. Meltwater in **warmer, temperate glaciers** helps reduce the frictional force, hence allowing them to move at far greater speeds. Speeds vary from about 100 m to 7 km per year.

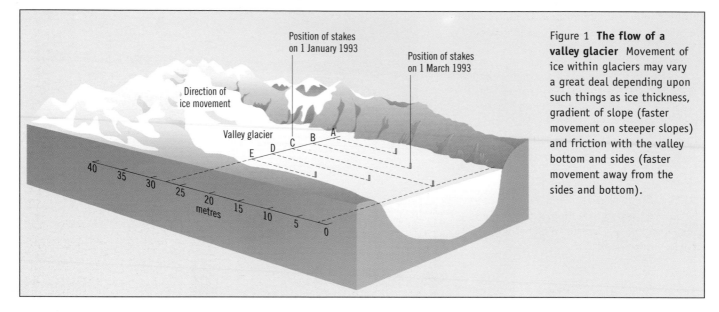

Position of stakes on 1 January 1993

Position of stakes on 1 March 1993

Direction of ice movement

Valley glacier

B A
E D C

40 35 30 25 20 metres 15 10 5 0

Figure 1 **The flow of a valley glacier** Movement of ice within glaciers may vary a great deal depending upon such things as ice thickness, gradient of slope (faster movement on steeper slopes) and friction with the valley bottom and sides (faster movement away from the sides and bottom).

Figure 2 **Glacial erosion and transport of moraine**

Transportation by ice

Figure 4 on page 43 shows that glaciers have the ability to transport large amounts of rock debris. This debris, called **moraine**, may be transported in one of three ways:

■ on the surface of the glacier

■ within the glacier. This material was most likely to have been on the surface of the ice only to be covered and buried by more recent snowfalls.

■ along the floor of the glacier either by the ice or the meltwater streams that are present there.

Cirque

Valley glacier

Lateral moraine

Medial moraine

Movement of ice

Striations

Crevasses

Refreezing and plucking

Partial melting

Roche moutonnée

Ground moraine

Bedrock

Processes of glacial erosion

Abrasion

Rocks carried along at the bottom of a glacier wear away the bedrock like sandpaper smoothing a piece of wood. Abrasion requires a large supply of rocky material to be effective. Often these rocks will scratch the surface they pass over. These scratches, if they are fine and shallow, are called **striations**, or if they are larger and deeper, are **grooves**.

Plucking

As ice flows over obstacles on the valley floor, such as large boulders, increased pressure on the upstream side of the obstacle causes the ice to melt which then refreezes on the downstream side as the pressure decreases. As it refreezes it plucks off loose or weak rocks. It is particularly effective on well-jointed rocks and on rocks previously weakened by freeze-thaw weathering. Plucking is responsible for a landform called a **roche moutonnée**.

Freeze-thaw

The continual melting and re-freezing (on a daily basis) of the bare rock slopes above the valley glaciers provides rock debris which falls on to the ice below.

Meltwater

Water from melted ice plays a vital part in helping glaciers move and, therefore, erode. It can also occur in large enough volumes and travel so quickly as to cause erosion by itself.

Figure 3 **Striations caused by abrasion**

Figure 4 **Roche moutonnée, Yosemite National Park, California**

1 Look at Figure 1. An experiment conducted in the winter of 1993 aimed to calculate the speed of a glacier by inserting stakes across its width.
   a Using Figure 1, calculate:
      (i) the distance in metres moved by each stake, A – E
      (ii) the average speed of the glacier over the two-month period.
   b Why have some stakes moved faster than others?

2 Describe the main processes of glacial erosion.

3 Draw your own labelled diagram to explain how a roche moutonnée is formed.

3.4 Landforms produced by glacial erosion

▲ Figure 1 **A glaciated upland valley – Lauterbrunnen Valley, Switzerland** Many dramatic landforms are created as a result of ice erosion.

◄ Figure 2 **Corrie below the summit of Helvellyn, Cumbria**

Corrie, cwm or cirque

A **corrie** or cirque is a semi-circular, steep-sided basin cut into the side of a mountain, or at the head of a valley. The shape of a corrie is often compared to an armchair because of its steep back wall and side walls, and open front.

Corries start as sheltered, gently sloping hollows on the shady side of a mountain where snow accumulates. Once the snow has filled the hollow, processes of erosion take place and the ice starts to enlarge the hollow to form the characteristic 'armchair' (Figure 2). This process of enlarging the hollow is known as **nivation.**

Two distinct features of the corrie remain once the ice has melted away. **A very steep back wall** is cut progressively steeper by a combination of the processes of freeze-thaw and plucking. **The 'lip' of the corrie** is left as the glacier erodes less powerfully at the edge of the landform than at the base of the hollow. The 'lip' is made up of resistant rock

When the snow melts, it often leaves a small lake or **tarn** in the corrie.

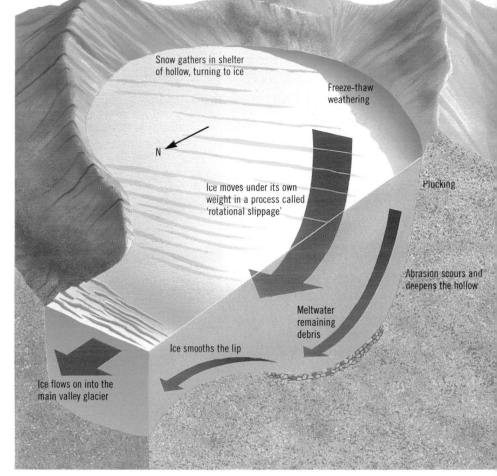

Snow gathers in shelter of hollow, turning to ice

Freeze-thaw weathering

N

Ice moves under its own weight in a process called 'rotational slippage'

Plucking

Abrasion scours and deepens the hollow

Meltwater remaining debris

Ice smooths the lip

Ice flows on into the main valley glacier

Figure 3 **Section through a corrie**

Figure 4 **The Matterhorn, Switzerland, a pyramidal peak**

Arêtes

These are steep sided, knife-edged ridges separating two corries. **Arêtes** are formed when the backs of the back walls of corries are cut.

Pyramidal peak or horn

Figure 4 shows the Matterhorn in Switzerland which is perhaps the most famous **pyramidal peak** in the world. It is created by three or four corries cutting back on each other to form a horn or pyramidal peak at the centre.

1 Based on Figure 2, draw a sketch diagram of the glaciated features around Helvellyn. Label the following features: Helvellyn Summit; steep back wall; steep side walls; corrie lip.

2 Using all the information on this page and with the help of diagrams, explain how the glaciated features you have labelled were formed.

U-shaped glacial trough

Ice from corrie glaciers moves down valley and eventually feeds the main valley glacier. This is much larger in size than the individual corrie glaciers because it is fed by a number of corrie glaciers. The main glacier produces perhaps the most characteristic feature of a glaciated landscape – the broad, flat-bottomed U-shaped valley or **glacial trough** (Figure 5). A previous V-shaped river valley has been both deepened and widened by the powerful erosive action of the glacier ice.

Figure 5 **A gentle U-shaped glacial trough in Wharfedale, Yorkshire Dales** Contrast this with Figure 1 on page 46.

Features of the glacial trough

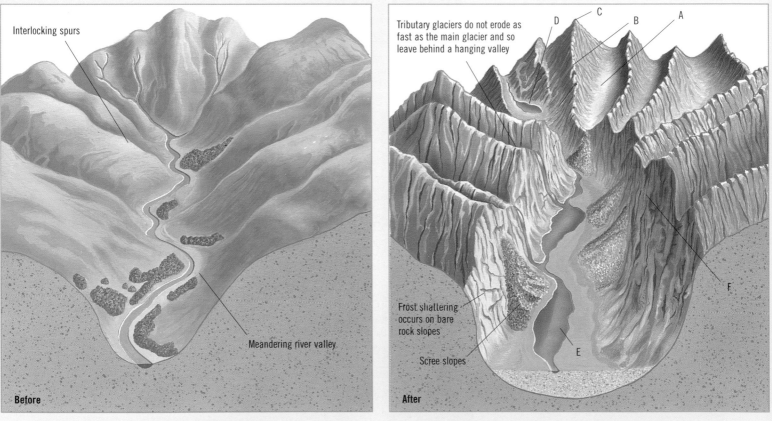

Interlocking spurs

Meandering river valley.

Before

Tributary glaciers do not erode as fast as the main glacier and so leave behind a hanging valley

D   C   B   A

Frost shattering occurs on bare rock slopes

Scree slopes

E   F

After

Figure 6 **The effects of valley glacier erosion**

Truncated spurs

Before glaciation the river valley may have shown evidence of interlocking spurs. However, ice being much less flexible than water, simply flows straight down the valley and will truncate or 'behead' the spurs, leaving a line of steep cliffs along the sides of the glacial trough.

Hanging valleys

The larger, main glacier obviously had much more ice flowing in it than did the smaller tributary glaciers, causing the U-shaped trough to be cut much deeper into the landscape than the feeder glaciers. After melting, these feeder glaciers leave tributary valleys hanging above the main overdeepened trough, often with a stream cascading as a waterfall over the edge.

▶ Figure 7 **Bridal Vale Falls, California, a hanging valley**

Ribbon lake

In some glacial troughs, the power of the ice is so great that it 'overdeepens' the valley floor, creating a large, linear depression. This often becomes filled with water after the ice has melted, to form a ribbon lake.

Misfit streams

These are rivers that flow in the U-shaped glacial trough and often seem far too small when compared to the huge glacial feature. The streams do not 'fit' the width of the glacial trough.

3 **a** On a copy of Figure 6 (see page 250), label the features A – F.
b Explain how each was formed.

Figure 8 **A ribbon lake below the Gerlos Pass, Austria**

As temperatures rise towards the end of a glacial period, the ice will melt and any material being carried will be deposited either on the floor of the glacial trough in highland areas or at the snout of the glacier in lowland areas. Figure 1 shows many of the landforms created by deposition of material from both ice and water.

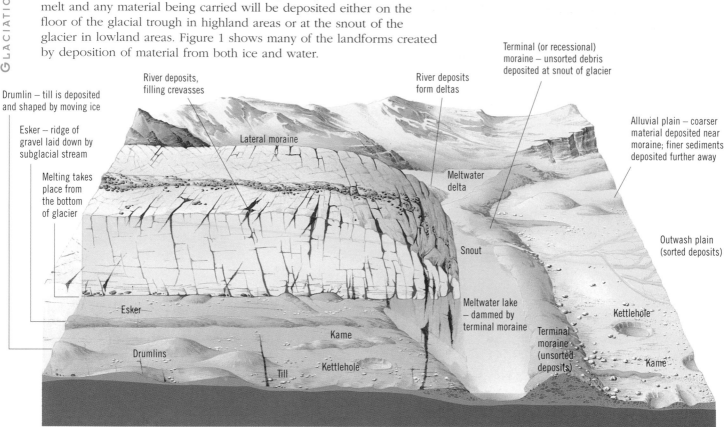

Drumlin – till is deposited and shaped by moving ice

Esker – ridge of gravel laid down by subglacial stream

Melting takes place from the bottom of glacier

River deposits, filling crevasses

Lateral moraine

River deposits form deltas

Terminal (or recessional) moraine – unsorted debris deposited at snout of glacier

Alluvial plain – coarser material deposited near moraine; finer sediments deposited further away

Meltwater delta

Snout

Meltwater lake – dammed by terminal moraine

Outwash plain (sorted deposits)

Kettlehole

Kame

Terminal moraine (unsorted deposits)

Esker

Kame

Drumlins

Till

Kettlehole

Figure 1 **Glacial deposition and its resulting landforms**

Erratics

These are large boulders transported over great distances and deposited by glaciers. Often, they are composed of totally different material to the bedrock they are deposited upon.

Figure 2 **Glacial erratic in northern Canada**

Moraine

Moraine is the erosive material which is transported and later deposited by a glacier. The different types of moraine are named according to the location of its deposition.

Terminal or end moraine

The terminal moraine represents the end of the ice advance and is characterised by a ridge of material across the valley floor. It is composed mainly of **boulder clay** (a mixture of clay and rocks) that was either under, inside or on the valley glacier. It may measure from 20 to 50 m high, up to 100 m wide and can extend several kilometres across the valley. If the terminal moraine is extremely well developed, this may suggest that the glacier was stationary for a long period of time before it melted. Part of the city of York is built on an end moraine.

Lateral moraine

Lateral moraine is carried along at the side of the glacier. The debris is mainly from weathering of the valley sides. On melting, it forms a ridge or bank of material along the valley edges.

Medial moraine

Medial moraine results from the merging together of two lateral moraines from different glaciers joining together. It will be found in the centre of the valley.

Drumlins

Drumlins are smooth, egg-shaped hills that vary in length from 100 to 800 m, and between 25 to 100 m high. The side facing the direction from which the ice came is steeper than the downside of the glacier. Drumlins rarely occur by themselves; often they will be found in **swarms** called **drumlin fields**. They are formed under the glacier by ice which had moulded boulder clay into their distinctive shape. The ice was still moving but was not powerful enough to erode the boulder clay.

▶ Figure 3 **Drumlins in Cumbria**

Figure 4 **Eskers in Glen Shee, Tayside**

Meltwater landforms

As the ice was melting, vast quantities of water flowed over the land. It is estimated that rivers would have flowed 80 times faster during this period compared to today. Such meltwater streams created a number of distinctive features.

Meltwater lakes

Terminal moraine could often dam up a huge lake. The Vale of York, for example, was once formed by such a lake.

Eskers

Eskers are long ridges of deposited material. They usually run parallel to the direction of ice flow and are formed by deposition from meltwater streams which flow under the ice.

Kames

Kames are small mounds of debris which have been washed into crevasses in the ice. This material is dropped on to the ground as the ice melts.

Kettle holes

As the glacier retreats, it leaves behind detached blocks of ice which, on melting, create small kettle holes. The water remains in the hollow and will eventually be lost through evaporation or infiltration.

Outwash plains

As meltwater streams flow away from the glacier, they begin to sort out material and deposit their load. The largest, heaviest particles are dropped first and so create **alluvial fans** and **outwash plains**.

Figure 5 **Kames in Glen Shee, Tayside**

What is soil?

Soil: a definition

Soil makes up the top layer of the earth's crust. Rocks on the earth's surface are ground down over time into many smaller fragments by the erosive forces of rain, wind and the sun, and combine with the rotten remains of plants and animals. Living things and rock type each play a vital role in the formation of soil.

There are many different types of soil. Each individual soil can be identified and described by looking at its **soil profile** (Figure 1), a vertical column of the soil that may be exposed at a pit, or may be extracted from the ground. The soil profile consists of different layers of material called **horizons**. Each horizon has a different colour and texture. The different horizons are parallel to the ground surface and lie above the bedrock.

Properties of soil

All soils are composed of the same basic materials, although the proportions of each vary greatly from one soil type to another. Individual soils are made up of four main components: mineral particles, organic matter, air and water. Figure 2 shows the average proportions of each component in a typical agricultural soil in the UK. Half of the volume of the soil is not solid at all, being made up of air and water.

The four main soil components shown in Figure 2 are intermixed with one another to give three important soil properties:

● **soil texture,** which is the amount of sand, silt and clay in the soil. Texture influences the soil's capacity to retain moisture, air and nutrients.

● **soil structure,** which is the size and shape of individual particles (or peds) within the soil.

● **soil fertility,** which is how suitable the soil is for crop growth.

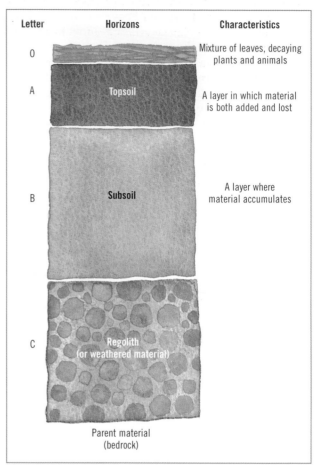

Figure 1 **Soil profile**

Figure 2 **Soil components**

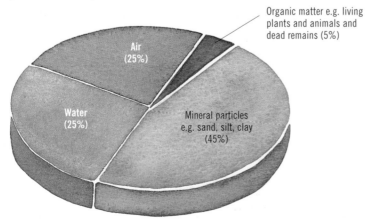

1 What is soil made of?

2 What is a soil horizon?

3 Compare a podzol soil with a chernozem soil under the following headings: Formation; Location: Characteristics.

Classification of soil types

There are numerous ways of classifying the many soil types of the world. Figure 3 shows a classification that links soil types with the global climate and vegetation belts. Some soils develop from the effects of climate where there are no extremes of weathering, relief or drainage (**zonal**). Others result from local factors (**intrazonal**) such as a limestone parent rock, a continuous presence of water, or high altitude. Some soil types are mature having had a long time to develop, whereas others are still young (**azonal**) and soil forming processes have not had time to operate fully.

Each soil type has its own unique characteristics, determined by its location in relation to climate, rock type, drainage, relief, vegetation cover and presence of animals.

Figure 3 **Soil type classification**

Soil type	Example
Zonal (climate and good drainage)	Tundra; Podsol; Chernozems; Desert soils
Intrazonal (parent rock, extremes of drainage, relief)	Rendzina, Terra Rossa; Gleyed; Peat (or bog); Saline (salty)
Azonal (immature)	Alluvium (fluvial); Scree (weathering); Till (glacial); Sand dunes (aeolian and marine); Salt marsh (marine); Volcanic (tectonic)

Case study | Podsols

Podsols are the common soil type in colder and wetter parts of the UK. They are also common in the Boreal Forest region of northern Russia (the word podsol is Russian for 'ash coloured'). Podsols are often associated with coniferous evergreen trees, particularly pines.

The formation of podsols, a process known as **podsolisation**, requires a general movement of water down through the soil. This can occur because precipitation (which is not particularly high) exceeds evapotranspiration due to the generally low temperatures throughout the year. An evergreen forest also casts heavy shade over the ground surface and shelters it from the wind, thus reducing evaporation further.

Figure 4 **The process of podsolisation**

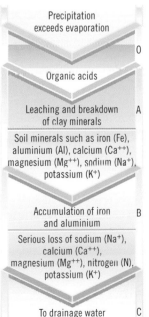

Water flowing down through the soil encourages intense **leaching** (the washing down of soil minerals that are soluble, from the profile). This increases the acidity of the soil. High acidity and increased wetness of the soil encourage the build-up of a thick peat layer at the surface.

Podsols are not good agricultural soils because they are acidic and generally infertile. They are found in many of the wild and semi-wild landscapes of the UK (forest, heather moorland and mountain grassland).

Case study | Chernozems

The **chernozem** soil is found with temperate grassland vegetation such as that of the Prairies in North America and the Steppes in Russia. The climate is generally warmer and drier than in forest areas, though winters may still be very cold. In these grasslands, moisture from the soil evaporates quickly from the ground surface. Much soil moisture can also be lost through transpiration by grasses. Winter frost and summer drought combine to limit the rate of decomposition so that over many years, a very rich and deep A-horizon builds up.

Figure 5 **The process of calcification**

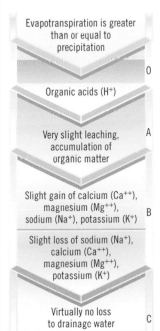

The process of **calcification** occurs in areas with chernozem soils. Unlike podsols, soluble minerals and nutrients are not washed down through the soil profile. These soils are only wetted to a depth of between 1 m and 1.5 m when the moisture begins to evaporate. A layer of calcium carbonate accumulates in the B- or upper C-horizon where little downward moving water reaches.

World biomes

Across the globe are an amazing variety of large-scale natural vegetation types or **biomes**. The location and characteristics of each biome is principally determined by climate: the amount and distribution of precipitation, temperature patterns, number of sunshine hours, length of growing season, rates of evaporation, transpiration and humidity. In addition, factors such as rock type, soils, relief and drainage are important. Figure 1 is a generalised map of global vegetation showing the distribution of the eight principal biomes.

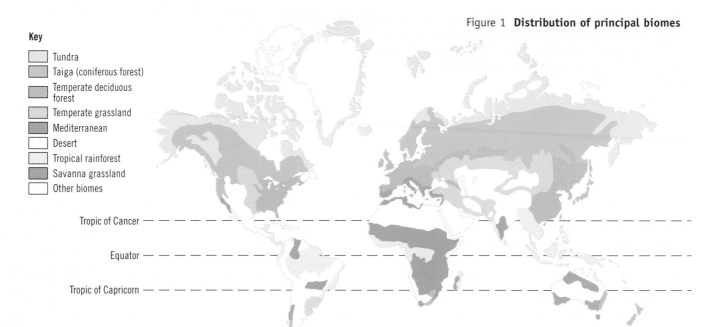

Figure 1 **Distribution of principal biomes**

Key
- Tundra
- Taiga (coniferous forest)
- Temperate deciduous forest
- Temperate grassland
- Mediterranean
- Desert
- Tropical rainforest
- Savanna grassland
- Other biomes

Tropic of Cancer

Equator

Tropic of Capricorn

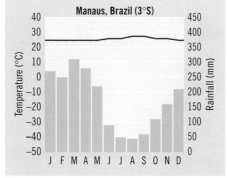

Figure 2

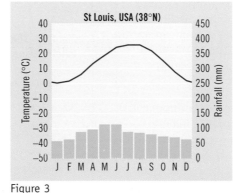

Figure 3

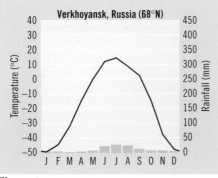

Figure 4

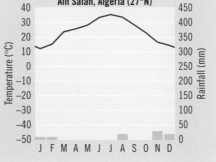

Figure 5

1 Refer to the four climate graphs in Figures 2 to 5. Each graph shows typical climatic characteristics for one of the world biomes. Using Figure 1 and an atlas, match each graph with the appropriate biome.

2 Using an atlas and your graphs, describe the main climatic characteristics for each of these four biomes.

3 Using an atlas, describe the climatic characteristics of each of the remaining biomes in Figure 1.

Savanna grasslands

Distribution

Savanna grasslands are found in central parts of continents away from the coast, approximately between latitudes 5° and 15° north and south of the equator (Figure 1). Parts of Brazil and Venezuela in South America sustain savanna, as does northern Australia and a large belt around the Zaire basin in Africa.

Climate

The savanna climate has a distinctive wet season from May to October with rainfall equalling that of the Equatorial rainforest, and a dry season from November to April when conditions can resemble those of a desert climate. The occurrence of these two climatic extremes is determined by the location of the prevailing winds, the Trade winds, at different times of the year.

Vegetation

A cross-section or transect across the savanna grasslands shows how the natural vegetation changes in response to different climatic conditions (Figure 8). Where the savanna merges with the equatorial rainforest, the vegetation is dense woodland with patches of tall grass. Where it meets the desert, it is reduced to drought-resistant bushes and occasional clumps of grass.

In the wet season, grass seeds germinate and trees produce new leaves. Trees grow quickly in the hot humid conditions, to a height of three to four metres. The landscape becomes awash with greenery and is dominated by Acacia trees with their flattened crowns (Figure 6).

With the onset of the dry season, the grass turns yellow before it dies, trees lose their leaves and the ground becomes a red-brown dust. Some trees produce thorny leaves to keep transpiration to a minimum. Plants like the baobab tree (Figure 7) make use of their xerophytic (drought-resistant) features such as very long roots to tap water supplies deep underground, and thick bark to store water in the trunk.

Figure 6 **Acacia trees are common on the savanna plains**

Figure 7 **The baobab tree is particularly well adapted to the savanna climate**

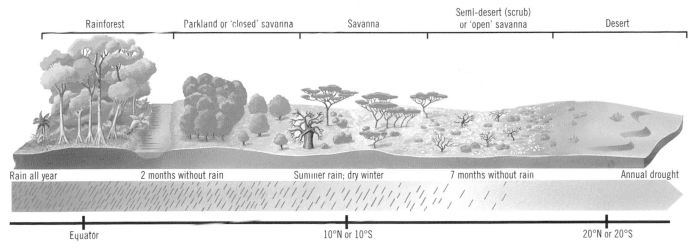

Rainforest	Parkland or 'closed' savanna	Savanna	Semi-desert (scrub) or 'open' savanna	Desert
Rain all year	2 months without rain	Summer rain; dry winter	7 months without rain	Annual drought

Equator   10°N or 10°S   20°N or 20°S

Figure 8 **Changes in vegetation across the savanna grassland**

Loss of the grasslands

Little of natural savanna grassland remains today. It has been modified over the centuries by nature and humans. Fires, whether started intentionally or by electrical storm, have altered the grasslands forever. Areas bordering deserts have experienced extensive desertification (p84) from overgrazing, tree felling for firewood and resultant soil erosion.

4 Using an atlas and Figure 1, describe the distribution of savanna grassland.

5 Describe ways in which the savanna vegetation adapt to their climatic conditions.

Taiga

Distribution

Taiga or coniferous forest covers vast expanses of the North American and Eurasian land masses between approximately 50° and 70° in latitude.

Climate

Long, cold winters last from October to April and temperatures can fall to −30°C or less (Figure 9). Summers are short and cool, with a brief growing season. Annual precipitation, usually in the form of snow, is low. Soils are podsolic.

Vegetation

Coniferous forests dominate. Dominant species are softwood evergreens such as spruce, fir and pine. They attain a height of 40 m or more and are well adapted to living in a harsh environment (Figure 10).

As trees are evergreen, they can photosynthesise (convert sunlight into energy for growth) as soon as conditions allow, without having to wait for new growth. In spring, incoming radiation increases and water becomes available through snowmelt. The needle-like leaves are small and the thick **cuticles** (protective layering) help reduce transpiration in strong winds. Cones protect the seeds and thick bark protects the trunk from extreme winter cold. The cone shape of the trees with their downward sloping branches allows snow to slide off without breaking the branches.

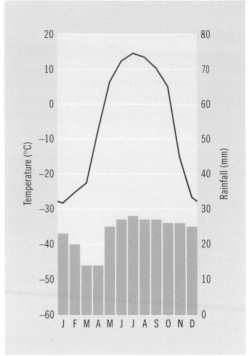

Figure 9 **Climate graph for Dawson, Canada**

In North America and Eurasia, the taiga merges with the tundra to the north, and with the temperate deciduous forests and grasslands to the south (Figure 11). The **tree line** (the altitude above which trees can no longer grow) and the height of the trees themselves is determined by mean monthly temperatures and the length of growing season.

◀ Figure 10 **The structure of coniferous vegetation is suited to the taiga climate**

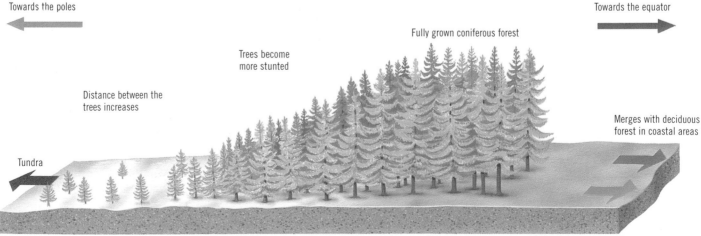

Towards the poles

Towards the equator

Fully grown coniferous forest

Trees become more stunted

Distance between the trees increases

Tundra

Merges with deciduous forest in coastal areas

Figure 11 **Influence of climate on taiga vegetation**

Merges with temperate grasslands in continental interiors

Tropical rainforest

Distribution

Tropical rainforests are found in areas with an equatorial climate and lie within 5° either side of the equator. The Amazon basin in South America and the Zaire basin in Central Africa are the two most extensive areas of tropical rainforest in the world, although in Amazonia the forest is being removed at an alarming rate by human activities.

Climate

An equatorial climate has constantly high temperatures throughout the year with little seasonal variation. It has an annual temperature range of only 2°C as the sun is high in the sky at all times of the year. Annual rainfall is high. It regularly exceeds 2 500 mm p.a. largely due to heavy convectional thunderstorms which occur most afternoons. Figure 12 shows the daily weather pattern which is remarkably uniform throughout the year.

Figure 12 **The daily rhythm of weather in tropical rainforests**

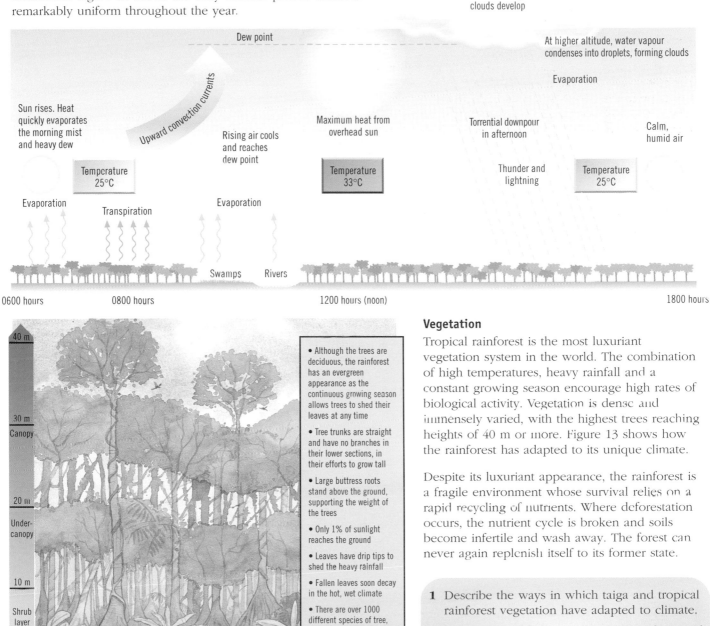

Figure 13 **How rainforest vegetation has adapted to the equatorial climate**

- Although the trees are deciduous, the rainforest has an evergreen appearance as the continuous growing season allows trees to shed their leaves at any time
- Tree trunks are straight and have no branches in their lower sections, in their efforts to grow tall
- Large buttress roots stand above the ground, supporting the weight of the trees
- Only 1% of sunlight reaches the ground
- Leaves have drip tips to shed the heavy rainfall
- Fallen leaves soon decay in the hot, wet climate
- There are over 1000 different species of tree, including mahogany and rosewood

Vegetation

Tropical rainforest is the most luxuriant vegetation system in the world. The combination of high temperatures, heavy rainfall and a constant growing season encourage high rates of biological activity. Vegetation is dense and immensely varied, with the highest trees reaching heights of 40 m or more. Figure 13 shows how the rainforest has adapted to its unique climate.

Despite its luxuriant appearance, the rainforest is a fragile environment whose survival relies on a rapid recycling of nutrients. Where deforestation occurs, the nutrient cycle is broken and soils become infertile and wash away. The forest can never again replenish itself to its former state.

1 Describe the ways in which taiga and tropical rainforest vegetation have adapted to climate.

2 Construct a table contrasting taiga and tropical rainforest under the following headings: precipitation, temperature, vegetation.

The word **ecosystems** refers to the total environment, including soils, vegetation, animals, humans and climate, together with their interactions. Ecosystems consist of living organisms (the organic community) and their physical and chemical environment (the inorganic community), and can be identified using the dominant vegetation e.g. savanna grassland or tropical rainforest. An ecosystem can vary significantly in scale from a world biome, such as the taiga coniferous forest, to a small-scale example, such as a sand dune.

All ecosystems have two major processes: **energy flow** and **nutrient cycling**. These two processes, which are driven by the sun's energy, help to link the component parts of the ecosystem.

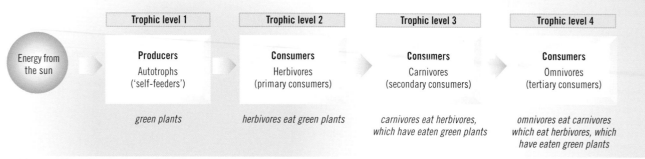

Figure 1 **Energy flows in the food chain**

Energy flow involves the fixing of light energy by green plants (**photosynthesis**) and the passing of this energy through the ecosystem as food along a **food chain** (Figure 1). Each link in the food chain feeds on and obtains energy from the one before it and, in turn, is consumed by and provides energy for the link after it. Eventually this energy is lost from the ecosystem as heat. There are usually four links in the food chain, each link known as a **trophic** or **energy level**. In reality, however, a much more complex **food web** is likely to exist (Figure 2).

Nutrient cycling refers to the circulation of chemical elements from the environment to organisms and back again to the environment. Two of these cycles, the carbon cycle and the nitrogen cycle, are shown in their simplest form in Figure 3.

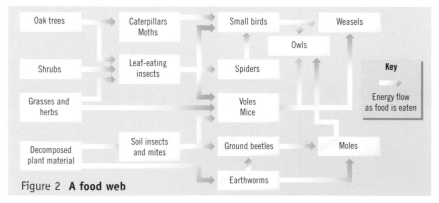

Figure 2 **A food web**

1 Define the following terms: ecosystem, energy flow, nutrient cycle, food chain, food web.

2 Refer to Figure 2. Give examples of the following: Producers, Primary Consumers, Secondary Consumers and Tertiary Consumers.

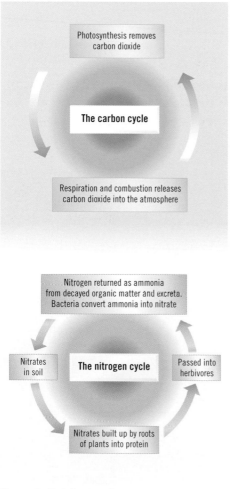

Figure 3 **Nutrient cycles**

A **sere** is a stage in a sequence of events where the vegetation of an area develops over time. A chain of seres begins with a **pioneer community** (the first plants to colonise an area) and ends with a **climatic climax vegetation** (the ultimate vegetation the climate and environment of the area can sustain). **Plant succession** occurs where one plant species replaces another.

Climatic climax vegetation is rarely found in present environments. Human activity has brought about deforestation, desertification, overcultivation and acid rain, each removing the possibility of climatic climax vegetation surviving. Such modified vegetation is called **plagioclimax**.

Figure 4 **Plant succession**

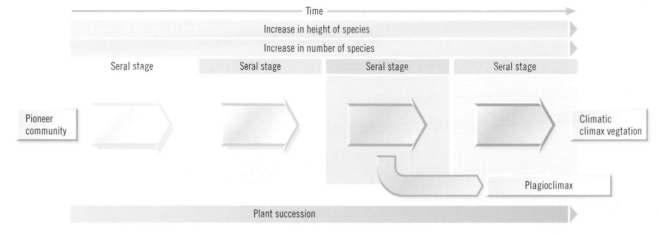

The four basic seres where plant succession takes place are:
- a **lithosere** (rock) e.g. on a new volcanic island
- a **halosere** (salt water) e.g. in a salt marsh
- a **psammosere** (sand) e.g. on sand dunes
- a **hydrosere** (fresh water).e.g. in a lake or pond.

Figure 5 **Plant succession on an emerging rocky coastline**

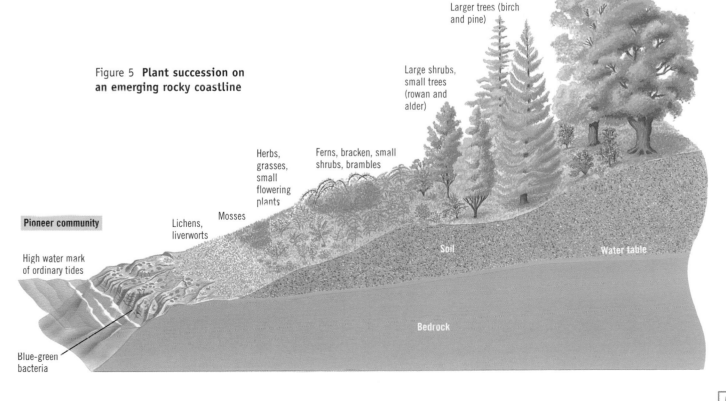

Psammosere

A **psammosere** is a plant succession that takes place on sand. A place where a psammosere might develop is on sand dunes. If conditions allow, plants will colonise and stabilise the dunes with time, progressing through a number of distinct stages. Each stage can be identified by the dominant or most common species (Figure 6).

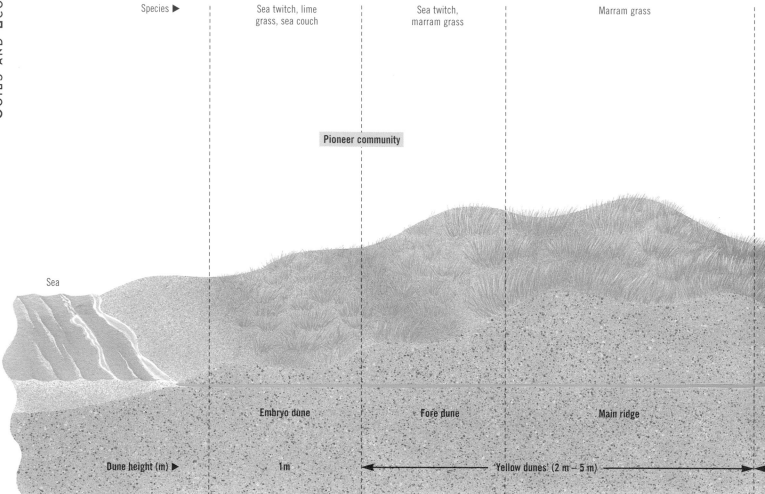

| Species ▶ | Sea twitch, lime grass, sea couch | Sea twitch, marram grass | Marram grass |

Pioneer community

Sea

| Dune height (m) ▶ | Embryo dune | Fore dune | Main ridge |
| | 1m | 'Yellow dunes' (2 m – 5 m) | |

Figure 7 **Sea twitch**

Figure 8 **Marram grass**

Figure 6 **Psammosere succession**

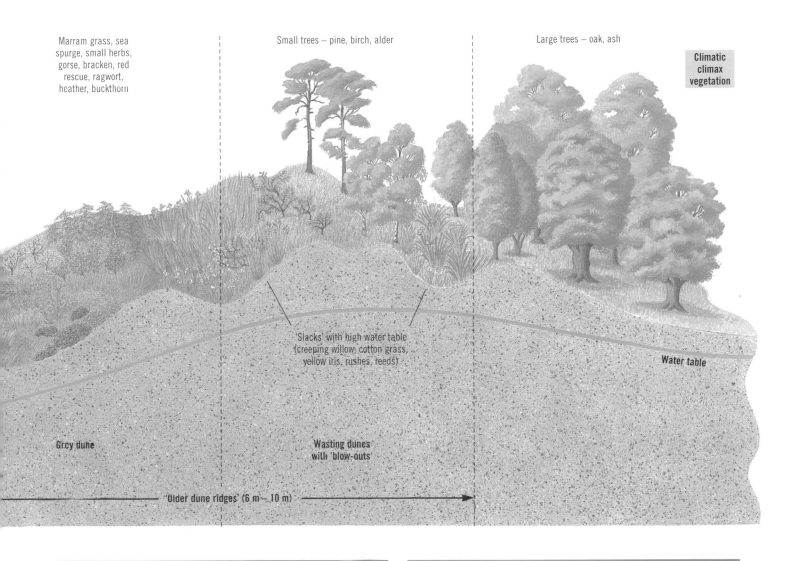

Marram grass, sea spurge, small herbs, gorse, bracken, red rescue, ragwort, heather, buckthorn

Small trees – pine, birch, alder

Large trees – oak, ash

Climatic climax vegetation

'Slacks' with high water table (creeping willow, cotton grass, yellow iris, rushes, reeds)

Water table

Grey dune

Wasting dunes with 'blow-outs'

'Older dune ridges' (6 m – 10 m)

Figure 9 **Birch trees**

Figure 10 **An Ash tree**

SOILS AND ECOSYSTEMS

Soil is the thin store of plant foods (nutrients) and water upon which all vegetation and agriculture depends. **Soil erosion** is the removal of some of this precious store. It is a major environmental problem all over the world. Soil can be removed by wind or water when it is left exposed to erosion by human activities or nature.

Up to 37% of arable land in England and Wales is at risk from soil erosion (Figure 2). Areas that are particularly vulnerable are associated with intensive arable agriculture, sandy or sandy-loam soils and a slope angle of more than 3°. Soil losses can be very high: 250 tonnes per hectare (t/ha) in the South Downs, 160 t/ha in East Anglia and 150 t/ha in West Sussex.

The potential for soil erosion has increased dramatically in recent decades for a number of reasons:

● the spread of arable agriculture into pasture areas

● hedgerow removal

● ploughing and draining of peat soils

● increased recreational pressures on the countryside.

Case study | Water erosion on the South Downs

The South Downs in England is an example of an area badly affected by water erosion. Rates of up to 250 t/ha have been recorded and gullies several metres deep have been created in severe storms (Figure 1).

Principal causes of water erosion

● traditional sheep pastures have been replaced by arable fields on slopes as steep as 20°

● the use of heavier, more powerful machinery not only compacts the soil but creates gullies for water run-off to follow

● EU policy has made it more profitable for farmers to grow winter barley rather than spring-sown crops. These autumn-sown crops leave bare surfaces through the winter.

● many field boundaries have been removed, leaving long open slopes and areas for water to collect

● land is often ploughed directly downslope, even when the slopes are steep

● convex slopes collect water on their flatter, upper sections so the water gains speed as it runs to the steeper, lower sections.

Figure 1 **Water erosion on a ploughed field, following torrential rain**

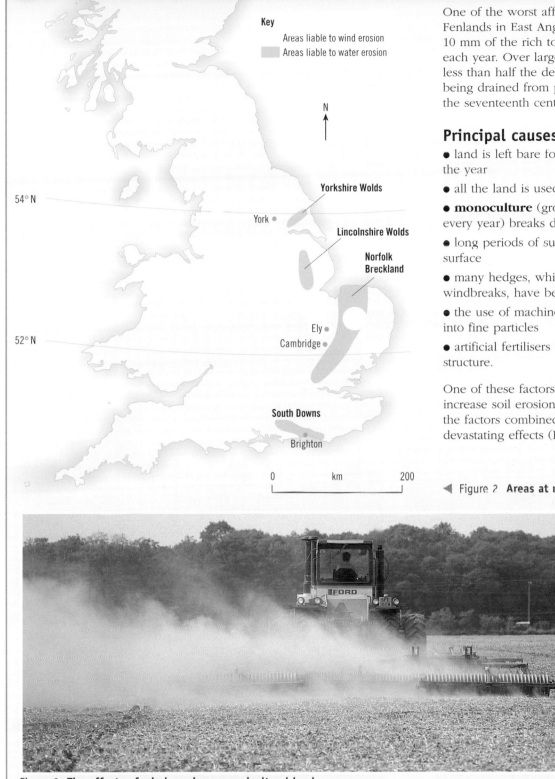

Key

Areas liable to wind erosion
Areas liable to water erosion

N

Yorkshire Wolds

York

Lincolnshire Wolds

Norfolk
Breckland

54° N

Ely
Cambridge

52° N

South Downs

Brighton

0   km   200

One of the worst affected areas is the Fenlands in East Anglia where at least 10 mm of the rich topsoil is blown away each year. Over large areas, the soil is less than half the depth it was after being drained from peaty wetlands in the seventeenth century.

Principal causes of soil erosion

- land is left bare for several months of the year
- all the land is used for arable crops
- **monoculture** (growing the same crop every year) breaks down soil structure
- long periods of sunshine dry out the surface
- many hedges, which act as windbreaks, have been removed
- the use of machinery breaks the soil into fine particles
- artificial fertilisers break down the soil structure.

One of these factors will not greatly increase soil erosion, but some or all of the factors combined can have devastating effects (Figure 3).

◀ Figure 2 **Areas at risk from soil erosion**

Figure 3 **The effects of wind erosion on agricultural land**

1 Referring to the case studies, describe the damage that can be done to agricultural land from soil erosion.

2 What steps do you think British farmers could take to reduce the potential for wind and water erosion?

3 Compare the problem of soil erosion in the UK with that of desertification in the Sahel (p84). How are the activities of farmers (i) similar? (ii) different?

4 It is not only the UK that has a problem with soil erosion. Find out about another country that suffers from it and examine the main causes.

4.5 Soil conservation

Soil erosion is a very real problem in developed countries, such as the UK, but more so in developing countries (Figure 1). Many countries suffering from its effects are seeking effective ways to conserve what soil they have left and to try and prevent further soil erosion in the future. Possible solutions can be classified into mechanical (Figures 2–5), crop, soil and political.

Key

1 **USA**: pressure on soils in the grain areas
2 **Mexico**: erosion and droughts
3 **North-east Brazil**: over 40 million population demanding food
4 **North Africa**: tree belts not very successful
5 **Sahel**: probably worst wind erosion area in the world
6 **Botswana–Namibia**: livestock accelerate erosion
7 **Middle East**: erosion spreading at an increasing rate
8 **Central Asia**: too many livestock, too little careful management
9 **Mongolia**: increasing numbers of herds and people
10 **Yangtze**: China loses over 5 billion tonnes of 'loess' annually
11 **Himalayan foothills**: more than quarter of a million tonnes of topsoil are lost from deforested slopes in Nepal
12 **Baluchistan**: traditional stock-raising and large herds do the damage
13 **Rajasthan**: droughts are becoming a permanent phenomenon
14 **Australia**: long droughts are aggravated by excessive stock

Figure 1 **Areas of severe soil erosion**

Figure 2 **Contour ploughing, where the farmer ploughs across slopes rather than along them**

Figure 3 **Bund-like embankments help retain soil wash**

Figure 4 **A shelter belt, such as a line of trees, slows down wind speed and helps protect the land from wind erosion**

Figure 5 **The building of terraces across slopes help to hold the soil on the land** Eventually the terrace becomes level as the soil is caught when it washes down. The major disadvantage of this solution is that it can take up to 10% of the farmland out of production.

Crop solutions

● take care to maintain a crop cover for as long as possible to protect soil from erosion

● re-introduce crop rotation using grass leys in the cycle, as rates of erosion are very low when the soil is covered by grass (Figure 7)

● introduce intercropping. Rather than leaving land bare between rows of crops, grow other crops in the open spaces e.g. in the tropics rows of coffee are inter-planted with maize (Figure 6).

Figure 7 **A system of crop rotation in operation**				
Field number	Year 1	Year 2	Year 3	Year 4
1	Wheat	Rape	Sown grass	Sown grass
2	Sown grass	Sown grass	Wheat	Rape
3	Rape	Wheat	Sown grass	Sown grass
4	Sown grass	Sown grass	Rape	Wheat
5	Wheat	Rape	Sown grass	Sown grass
6	Sown grass	Sown grass	Wheat	Rape
7	Rape	Wheat	Sown grass	Sown grass
8	Sown grass	Sown grass	Rape	Wheat

▼ Figure 6 **Intercropping of cabbages and bananas in Cuba**

Soil solutions

● add organic matter to the soil e.g. mix animal manure with crop-stubble and straw then plough it back into the soil. This increases the ability of the soil to hold water and restores soil fertility by improving soil structure and, as it decays, by returning nutrients to the soil.

● re-introduce crop rotation (Figure 7), ensuring that nutrient-demanding grain crops such as wheat and barley are alternated each year with soil-restoring crops, such as grass leys and peas

● grow a grass crop to increase the humus content of the soil

● choose the right kind of ploughing which will not grind down and deform soil structures

● install pipe drains into heavy clay and waterlogged soils which can be easily damaged during ploughing

● prevent the break-up of compacted soil by subsoiling (deep ploughing that mixes the surface and subsoil horizons).

Political solutions in the developed world e.g. Britain

Farmers need to be encouraged to produce less from their land rather than more, while keeping up their standard of living. It could be argued that it is the intensive nature of farming in the developed world, the constant drive for greater efficiency and profit maximisation from the land that has caused many of the problems of soil erosion in the first place.

Political solutions in the developing world e.g. Nepal

More investment is needed for research into how to improve the yield of local crops which would allow farmers to produce more in one year and so leave the land fallow to recover the next year. Trained experts to advise farmers on improving farming techniques are also needed. Greater investment in existing projects, such as roads, transport, guaranteed market prices and security in land-holdings to encourage poor farmers in soil conservation, is needed.

A farm can be described as a **system**, with **inputs** into the system, **processes** which take place in it and **outputs** from the system. A farmer may also **feed back** some of the outputs, such as profits, into the system. Figure 1 shows a system in its simplest form. Figure 2 applies these ideas to farming.

Inputs	Processes	Outputs
Physical environment e.g. natural inputs, human economic inputs	Patterns and methods of farming e.g. cultivating, rearing and storage	Products e.g. crops, animals
Expenditure		Profits

Figure 1 **The farming system**

Figure 2 **Factors that affect the farming system**

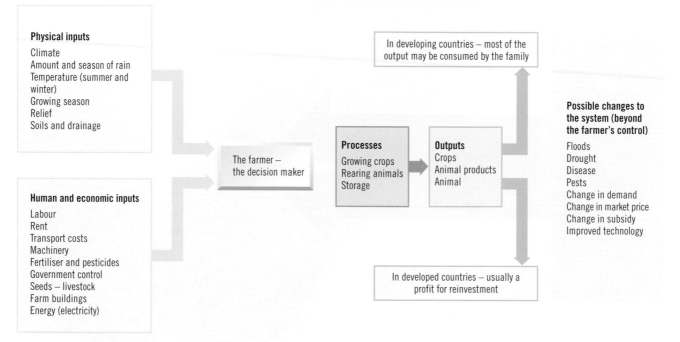

Physical inputs
Climate
Amount and season of rain
Temperature (summer and winter)
Growing season
Relief
Soils and drainage

Human and economic inputs
Labour
Rent
Transport costs
Machinery
Fertiliser and pesticides
Government control
Seeds – livestock
Farm buildings
Energy (electricity)

The farmer – the decision maker

Processes
Growing crops
Rearing animals
Storage

Outputs
Crops
Animal products
Animal

In developing countries – most of the output may be consumed by the family

In developed countries – usually a profit for reinvestment

Possible changes to the system (beyond the farmer's control)
Floods
Drought
Disease
Pests
Change in demand
Change in market price
Change in subsidy
Improved technology

Farming systems vary within and between countries because the inputs, whether physical, human or economic, will be different. The processes and the outputs will therefore be affected. For example, rice farming in India (Figure 3) is quite different from the system of mixed farming in the English Midlands (Figure 4).

Inputs	Processes	Outputs
Plenty of rain Growing season – all year Flat land Rich soils Much labour Hand tools Rice seed	Rice cultivation Land	Rice

= no profit

Figure 3 **System of rice farming in India**

Inputs		Processes	Outputs
Skilled labour	Machines	Land	Pigs
Electricity	Fertiliser	Animals	Cattle
Seeds	Cattle feed	Crops – grass	Barley
Rain all year		barley	Hay
Barns for storage		potatoes	Manure
Low relief and deep soils			Potatoes
Growing season – 8 months			

= profit

Figure 4 **System of mixed farming in the English Midlands**

The farmer as decision maker

Each farmer has to decide which crops to grow or which animals to rear. This decision is based on **physical**, **human** and **economic** factors. The farmer will choose the type of farming that is most suitable to the conditions, using the most efficient method to gain maximum profit.

Types of farming

Each farming type is best suited to the area it occupies. **Arable** farming is the ploughing of the land and the growing of crops. **Pastoral** farmers leave the land under grass and rear animals, usually cattle or sheep, or both. In **mixed** farming, crops are grown and animals are reared.

Key

- Horticulture
- Arable
- Mixed
- Livestock

Only predominant types shown; urban areas not taken into account

Figure 5 **Types of farming in the UK**

Figure 6 **How physical and human inputs in the North-West differ from those in the South-East**

Hill sheep farming in north-west UK

The North-West	The South-East
Cool summers, mild winters, cold on mountains	Warm, sunny summers, cold winters
Heavy rainfall, snow in winter, strong winds	Less rainfall, falls during the growing season
Much highland with steep slopes	Much low-lying, flat land
Poor, thin soils	Rich, deep soils
Small fields (sheep on open moors)	Large farms and fields
Less machinery	More machinery
Less capital	More capital
Further from markets	Near to markets
Limited transport	Good transport
Lower wages	Higher wages

Arable farming in south-east UK

---

1 How can we describe the farm as a system?

2 List the major differences between the two farming systems in Figures 3 and 4.

3 Why would farming systems in the North-West and the South-East of the UK be different?

4 Where would be the most suitable locations for (a) a mixed farming system and (b) a cattle farming system in the UK? Give reasons for your answers.

Types of farming

Case study | **Dairy farming at Panmore Farm, near Southam, Warwickshire**

Panmore is a dairy farm located in an area of the UK dominated by dairy and mixed farming. The farm is 140 hectares (346 acres) in size. It has a herd of 240 pedigree Friesian dairy cows. Each cow produces an average of 4700 litres per year (4500 litres is the national average). The farmer, Mr. Boville, has three full time employees and gets a regular income from two nearby dairies.

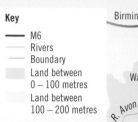

Key
— M6
— Rivers
— Boundary
▨ Land between 0 – 100 metres
▨ Land between 100 – 200 metres

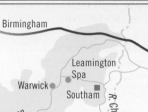

Figure 1 **Southam, east Warwickshire**

Figure 2 **Friesian cows grazing (inputs)**

Figure 3 **Cows in the milking unit (process)**

Figure 4 **Milk ready for delivery (output)**

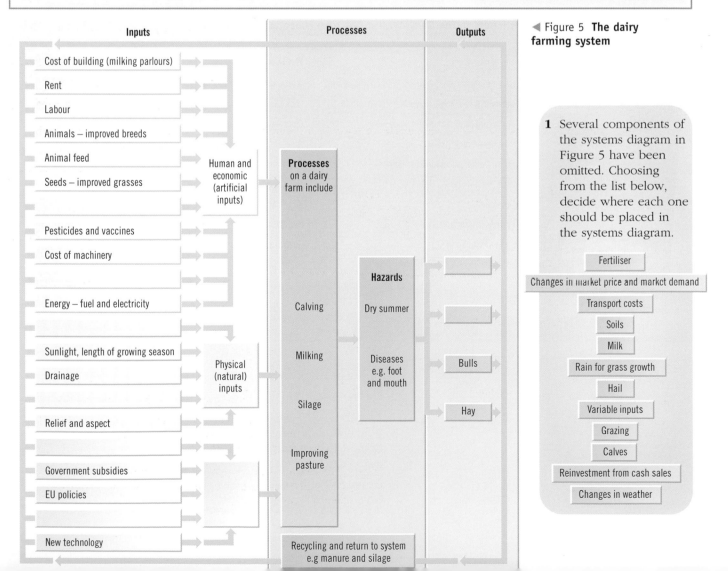

◄ Figure 5 **The dairy farming system**

Inputs

- Cost of building (milking parlours)
- Rent
- Labour
- Animals – improved breeds
- Animal feed
- Seeds – improved grasses

Human and economic (artificial inputs)

- Pesticides and vaccines
- Cost of machinery
- Energy – fuel and electricity
- Sunlight, length of growing season
- Drainage

Physical (natural) inputs

- Relief and aspect
- Government subsidies
- EU policies
- New technology

Processes

Processes on a dairy farm include

- Calving
- Milking
- Silage
- Improving pasture

Hazards
- Dry summer
- Diseases e.g. foot and mouth

Outputs

- Bulls
- Hay

Recycling and return to system e.g manure and silage

1 Several components of the systems diagram in Figure 5 have been omitted. Choosing from the list below, decide where each one should be placed in the systems diagram.

- Fertiliser
- Changes in market price and market demand
- Transport costs
- Soils
- Milk
- Rain for grass growth
- Hail
- Variable inputs
- Grazing
- Calves
- Reinvestment from cash sales
- Changes in weather

Greenwood Farm is a classic example of a hill farm. Hill farming of sheep and cattle in the UK is most common in the western part of Britain due to its relief and high levels of precipitation. Hill farming can be extremely difficult given the physical constraints of the land, climate and poor, thin soils. For the farmer and his family, making a living can be equally demanding. **Farm diversification** is often practised in an attempt to improve on the small profits.

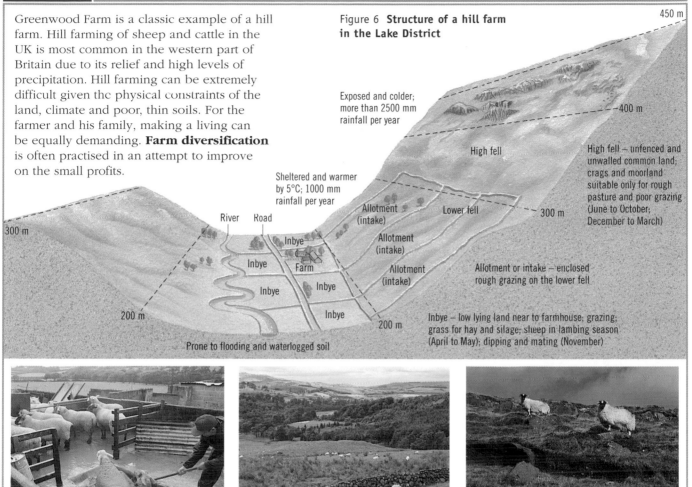

Figure 6 **Structure of a hill farm in the Lake District**

450 m

Exposed and colder; more than 2500 mm rainfall per year

High fell

400 m

High fell – unfenced and unwalled common land; crags and moorland suitable only for rough pasture and poor grazing (June to October; December to March)

Sheltered and warmer by 5°C; 1000 mm rainfall per year

Allotment (intake)

Lower fell

300 m

Allotment (intake)

River   Road

300 m

Inbye

Inbye   Farm

Inbye   Inbye

Allotment (intake)

Allotment or intake – enclosed rough grazing on the lower fell

200 m

Inbye

Inbye

200 m

Inbye – low lying land near to farmhouse; grazing; grass for hay and silage; sheep in lambing season (April to May); dipping and mating (November)

Prone to flooding and waterlogged soil

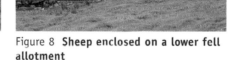

Figure 7 **Sheep dipping on an inbye**

Figure 8 **Sheep enclosed on a lower fell allotment**

Figure 9 **Grazing on unenclosed rough pasture on the high fell**

Farm diversification

As a result of falling sheep prices and higher running costs on the farm, many hill farmers have had to diversify or vary the uses of their land to try and make more money. The most common methods of diversification include:

- caravan and camping sites, activity holidays, bed and breakfast

- pony trekking, horse riding, fishing, farm zoo, farm tours

- farm shop, tea rooms, ice cream shop, cheese making

- golf courses, game/clay pigeon shooting

- logging and timber.

Cloud

Rain shadow

Air expands and cools; the water vapour condenses at dew point

Cooler, dry air descends along the leeward slope and warms

Clouds clear

Rain falls

Onshore wind

Warm, moist air moves towards mountain barrier and is forced to rise

Ocean

Lake District

Figure 10 **Relief rainfall in the western UK**

2 Why is hill farming of sheep and cattle the only type of farming possible in the Lake District?

3 Draw up a calendar for the hill farmer's year. You should include farming tasks, movement of animals, and use of different fields and buildings.

4 What do you think might be the (a) advantages and (b) disadvantages of the methods of farm diversification listed in the text box?

Case study | Arable farming at Trenholm Farm, East Anglia

Figure 11 Location map

Figure 12 **Harvest time on an arable farm**

Destinations of Trenholm Farm produce

- Wheat and barley sent to a processing factory in Manchester as they will keep over the long distance and the demand is in urban markets.
- Peas to local frozen food factory as they need to arrive fresh
- Sugar beet refined locally as it is bulky
- Potatoes sold locally as they are bulky
- Carrots and celery sold locally at market

Arable farming is most common in the east and south of the UK, especially in East Anglia and Lincolnshire. Here the physical conditions are just right.

The flat land and large fields are suitable for labour-saving machinery such as combine harvesters. Although the land was once marshy and badly-drained, extensive river dyking and soil drainage have enabled the natural fertility to be exploited.

Deep and rich soils give good anchorage for roots of cereal crops (such as wheat, oats, maize, corn and barley) and producing high yields.

This region has some of the lowest rainfall in Britain (often under 650 mm per year), ideal for cereal growth. The most rain falls in the summer during the growing season, when it is most needed.

Cold winters (average January temperature is 3°C) with hard frosts break up the soil for ploughing and kill diseases, whereas warm, sunny summers (average July temperature of 17°C) ripen the crops quickly.

Trenholm Farm near King's Lynn in Norfolk is a large arable farm. It is 280 hectares (692 acres) in size. Mr. Geldart, the owner, has contracts with *Sainsbury's* to grow wheat and barley and *Bird's Eye* to grow peas. Sugar beet, potatoes, carrots and celery are also grown.

Figure 13 Land use on Trenholm Farm

	% of land used	Hectares
Wheat	25%	
Barley	22%	
Peas	20%	
Sugar beet	12%	
Potatoes	10%	
Carrots	8%	
Celery	3%	

5 What are the major differences between Trenholm Farm and Greenwood Farm (pages 69 and 70)?

6 Copy and complete Figure 13. Draw a pie chart using the data from your completed table.

7 Read the text box on Destinations of Trenholm Farm produce. What are the complications for the farmer with having his produce going to different destinations?

8 From Figure 14, construct a climate graph to show the climate of King's Lynn, Norfolk.

9 How does the climate graph help explain the type of farming in the area?

Figure 14 Climate data for King's Lynn, Norfolk

	J	F	M	A	M	J	J	A	S	O	N	D
mm	55	48	43	40	42	42	60	62	50	53	55	55
°C	3	4	5	7	11	15	18	19	18	15	11	5

Mechanisation and loss of labour

Machinery has taken on an important role on farms in recent years. Although costly to buy, machines such as tractors, combine harvesters and seed drills save time and money in the long run. The number of workers employed and the costs of employing workers have also fallen. Although farm output in the UK may be high, the number of people involved in agriculture continues to decline (Figure 2). Faced

with increasing rural unemployment, many workers have had to leave the countryside to find alternative jobs in the towns and cities, bringing about **rural depopulation**.

Figure 1 **Advanced agricultural machinery in use**

Figure 2 **Number of people engaged in UK agriculture ('000s) and the number of tractors and combine harvesters on UK farms ('000s)**

Type of work	1975	1985	1995
Full-time regular workers	222	157	104
Regular part-time workers	80	61	46
Seasonal or casual	73	96	112
Salaried managers	7	8	10
Farmers, partners, directors	280	291	303
Total persons employed	662	623	575

Type of machinery	1975	1985	1995
Tractors	500	580	640
Combine harvesters	50	70	85

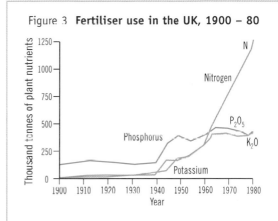

Figure 3 **Fertiliser use in the UK, 1900 – 80**

Increased use of chemicals

Farmers have become increasingly reliant on the use of chemical fertilisers, pesticides and insecticides to improve the quality and quantity of their farm produce (UK farmers currently spend over £400 million per year). For centuries, farmers have been trying to improve the quality of soils by ploughing, draining and adding manures, and to improve the quality of their animals by controlling their grazing and breeding. These traditional practices are continued with a more carefully researched and scientific approach. The chemicals have two main uses: to improve the plant food in the soil, increasing yields, and to kill unwanted weeds, pests and diseases (e.g. parasitic worm killers, slug and snail killers, insecticides and fungicides). Application has been made easier by the use of modern machinery, including aircraft.

Nitrate pollution

The major increase in fertiliser use since 1950 has been in the form of nitrogen (in which soils are most deficient), rather than phosphorous and potassium. This has occurred especially in the east of the UK where most arable farming is located. It has led to excessive nitrate seepage into rivers and public water supplies, polluting water and killing wildlife.

Figure 4 **Spraying a large wheat field**

Greater accessibility

The extensive road building programme of the 1980s and early 1990s has greatly helped farming. The UK now has a comprehensive integrated motorway and A-road network, allowing farmers to get their products to a wider area and to more distant major urban markets in less time. Increased use of refrigerated lorries has allowed milk and many other farm products to travel further yet remain fresh.

1 What do you consider to be the (a) advantages and (b) disadvantages of using machinery instead of workers on farms?

2 What evidence is there of the trend of machines replacing workers in industries as they have in agriculture?

3 **a** Construct graphs to show all the information in Figure 2.
b What trends does your graph is show?

5.4 Agribusiness

Figure 1 **Large-scale activity on an agribusiness farm**

Agribusiness is capital-intensive farming on a large scale which produces food for processing factories and supermarkets. It is popular in the east of the UK where much arable farmland is located.

In **capital-intensive** farming, a great deal of money is invested in the farm. The latest, most efficient machinery and biotechnology (such as fertilisers and pesticides) will be invested to get the highest output from the land.

Agribusiness farms have become popular due to two major changes in the demand for food: an increasing proportion of food is consumed in restaurants and cafes rather than at home, and foods are increasingly frozen and processed before they are bought (e.g. tinned, packeted, dehydrated, ready-made-meals, etc.). Because such an increasing proportion of food is processed after leaving the farm gate, there has been a tendency for food processors to buy land in order to control the quality and quantity of their raw materials. Most food processing companies, frozen food companies and supermarket chains now own and run agribusiness farms in this way.

▶ Figure 2 **Making potato crisps**
This factory would probably be supplied by its own potato farms.

Agribusiness farms have particular characteristics:

- very large in size, often the result of several privately-owned small farms being bought by a factory or supermarket and merged into one large farm

- large fields to allow machinery to operate efficiently

- many hedgerows removed to allow several small fields to be merged into large ones

- the farm will specialise in growing only one or two types of crop, or in rearing only one or two types of animal.

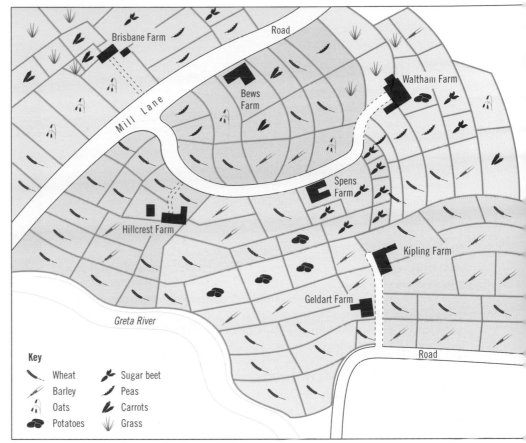

Figure 3 **Farmland before agribusiness set in, 1965**

1 **a** What is an agribusiness farm?
b In what ways do you think an agribusiness farm is different from a family-run farm?
c Why have agribusiness farms become so popular in recent years?

2 What do you consider to be the
(a) advantages and
(b) disadvantages of the agribusiness method of farming?

3 Look at Figures 3 and 4.
a Calculate the percentage of each crop type for the farms.
b Explain what your figures show.

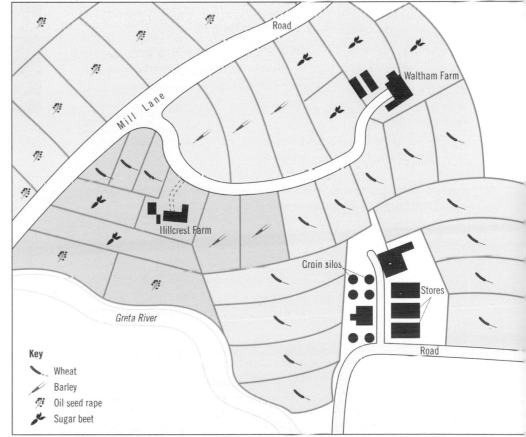

Figure 4 **Farmland after agribusiness, 1995**

Removal of hedgerows

Between 1945 and 1990, 380 000 km of hedgerows (nearly half the UK total) disappeared. Farmers removed hedgerows and trees to create larger fields. Hedgerows had taken up space that could be used to grow crops, they limited the size of machinery that could be used in fields, and were home to many harmful insects and pests. Removal of hedgerows and trees, however, has had a major environmental impact. Soil erosion from wind and running water increased, as the hedges no longer acted as wind-breaks, and the natural habitat of birds, animals and insects was destroyed. In recent years some farmers have reversed their actions by replacing and trimming hedges, encouraging wildlife to flourish once again.

Drainage of wetland

Wetlands are transition zones between land and sea where the soil is frequently waterlogged and the water table is at or near the surface. Draining wetlands to create new farmland has had a disasterous effect upon local wildlife, particularly where tidal sand flats have been destroyed. They would formerly have been the breeding and feeding grounds for many species of birds, animals and insects. Wetland drainage has been halted by law in areas such as East Anglia, and wetland conservation sites are being established in an attempt to redress the harm done.

Soil erosion

Soil erosion is a process that can damage farmland beyond repair and is very difficult to reverse. Certain farming practices encourage it. Harmful activities include:

● Overcultivation of land and monoculture (growing only one type of crop) can impoverish the soil.

● Ploughing up and down hillsides increases surface run-off.

● Overgrazing exposes land to erosion by wind and water.

● Heavy machinery can compact the ground.

● Irrigation without adequate drainage can cause salinity (salt water) and waterlogging.

● Removal of hedgerows and woodland leaves soil exposed to wind and increases water erosion which forms gulleys.

Figure 1 **The fields of this flower-producing farm have been merged after the removal of hedgerows**

Figure 2 **Wetlands have been drained for agriculture**

Figure 3 **Attempts to reduce and prevent soil erosion** Soil erosion can be reduced and productivity sustained with effective practices.

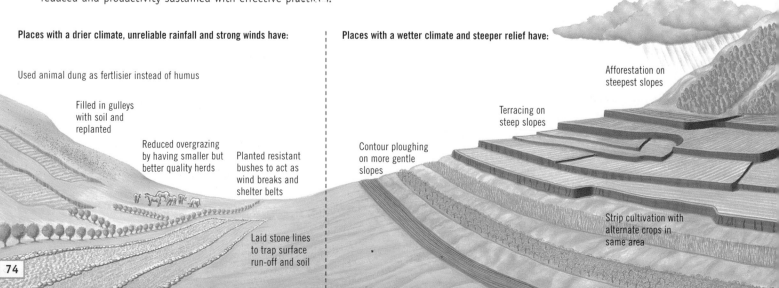

Places with a drier climate, unreliable rainfall and strong winds have:

Used animal dung as fertlisier instead of humus

Filled in gulleys with soil and replanted

Reduced overgrazing by having smaller but better quality herds

Planted resistant bushes to act as wind breaks and shelter belts

Laid stone lines to trap surface run-off and soil

Places with a wetter climate and steeper relief have:

Afforestation on steepest slopes

Terracing on steep slopes

Contour ploughing on more gentle slopes

Strip cultivation with alternate crops in same area

Chemical pollution

The problem of agricultural pollution, where chemical fertilisers, slurry (animal waste) and pesticides find their way into rivers and public water supplies, is now a major concern. More than 200 000 people a year die from pesticide poisoning and a further three million suffer acute symptoms (World Health Organisation estimates). In 1995, 1.5 million people in the UK were drinking water contaminated by nitrate fertilisers. Excess nitrate in drinking water is linked to blood poisoning in babies, gastric cancer and birth defects. Nitrates are highly soluble, so those not taken up by crops percolate slowly into underground aquifers. Seepage can take up to 40 years, making nitrate contamination a long-term problem. Denitrification of water is very expensive. A change in farming practices is needed if the problem is to be brought under control.

Figure 4 **Algal growth caused by excess nitrate in water**

Figure 5 **The techniques of organic farming**

On-farm waste recycling of manure and crop residues is seen to be more in harmony with natural ecosystems than the use of chemical fertilisers and the burning of straw.

Non-manufactured, natural mineral fertilisers (e.g. limestone) are allowed, but only where nutrients are released through weathering or the activity of soil organisms.

Weeds are controlled by:
- mulching (when a layer of organic material e.g. straw, is applied to the soil surface to reduce evaporation and stop weed growth)
- crop rotation
- cultivation rather than spraying
- timed planting to allow the weed seeds to germinate first and emerge before the crop.

Pests and diseases are prevented by:
- using less nitrogen, thus allowing plants to become sturdier and less succulent to pests
- rotating crops to reduce the chance of a pest surviving from one year to the next
- encouraging predators e.g. spiders, birds
- using natural biocides, like pyrethrum and derris
- using resistant crop varieties.

Animal welfare is given a high priority.

Use green manuring and under-sown legumes which fix nitrogen in the soil. Some farmers aim for green cover all year round.

Crop rotations are encouraged, such as:
- a four-year grass/clover ley, then barley, oats, beans, oats
- a four-year ley, then wheat, barley and under-sown clover, ley, wheat, oats
- a two-year ley, then wheat, barley, potatoes, wheat, oats
- beans/peas, then wheat, oats, beans, wheat, rye.

Intercropping, or the mixing or rows of different crops in the same field reduces the risk of pests spreading from one plant to another in the same crop, and makes better use of sunlight.

Organic farming

Organic farming is practised without factory-made chemicals, such as fertilisers, pesticides, herbicides or yield-enhancing drugs for animals. Much less damage is done to the environment because fewer toxic chemicals are released into the soil or find their way into rivers. There are only 1000 organic farmers in the UK, as the demand for organic products is very small. Higher prices have to be charged for their products as organic farming is more costly than modern agriculture and yields are 10 to 20% lower due to greater losses to pests and diseases and lower soil fertility. However, it is an alternative to modern methods and a change in consumer preference could have a fundamental impact on the way food of the future is produced.

1 **a** List the many ways in which farming has damaged the environment.

   b For each type of damage, suggest measures which could be taken to reduce the damage to the environment.

2 Organic farming is better for the environment but food produced organically costs more in the shops. Do you feel it is worth paying more for organic produce? Give reasons for your answer.

European agriculture

Agriculture represents a source of wealth and a guarantee of security in the European Union (EU). Member countries are proud that they produce enough of the major food types to feed themselves (400 million people in 1997). The quantities of cereals, meat, milk, wine and butter produced in the EU account for a significant percentage of the total world production (Figure 1).

In order to achieve these high levels of production and efficiency, member states of the EU have undergone tremendous change in their farming practices. These dramatic changes have been called **the Second Agricultural Revolution**.

Figure 1 **European agriculture's share of world production (%)**

Country	Cereals	Wine	Meat	Milk	Butter
EUR 12	11.8	60.0	18.6	23.3	22.4
USA	26.3	6.0	17.0	13.8	7.3
CIS	14.5	6.3	12.0	22.4	13.9
Japan	0.1	0.2	2.2	1.5	1.1
Canada	2.5	0.2	1.7	1.7	3.8
Rest of world	43.8	27.3	48.5	37.3	51.5

Figure 2 **Types of farming in Europe**

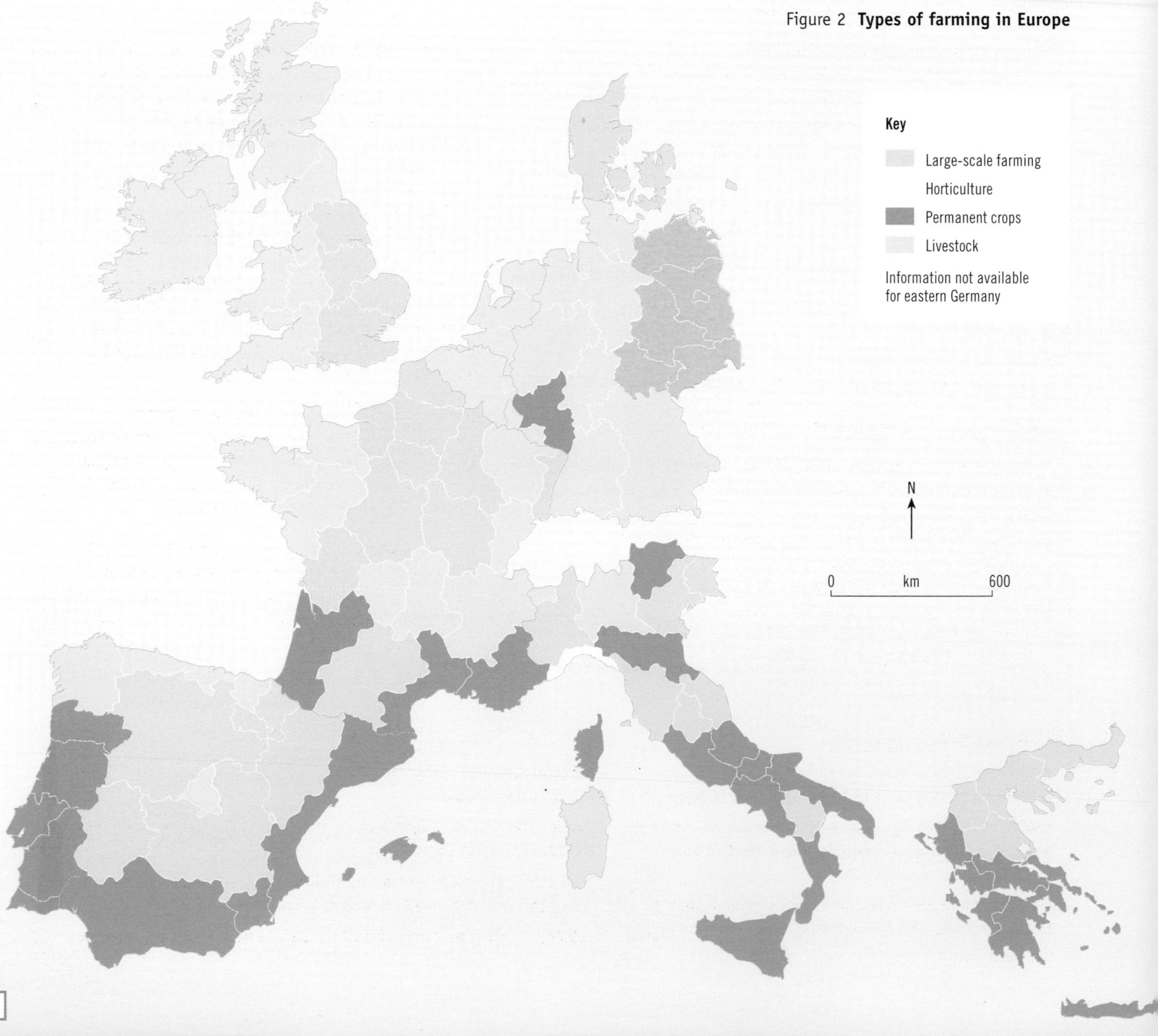

Key

- Large-scale farming
- Horticulture
- Permanent crops
- Livestock

Information not available for eastern Germany

N

0 km 600

The Second Agricultural Revolution

In the 1950s a global population explosion brought about a huge increase in demand for food. Advances in science and technology enabled a growth in the supply of food to match this demand. Investment (machinery, irrigation), chemical inputs (fertilisers, pesticides, etc.) and biotechnology (use of genetically improved seeds and animals) helped to raise the output per unit of land. The outcome has been continuous growth in agricultural production for the last 45 years.

In developed countries, such as those in the EU, production of food has increased greatly (often resulting in surpluses), yet the amount of land farmed has been shrinking and the number of people employed in agriculture has been falling drastically. A study of the EU's **Common Agricultural Policy (CAP)** explains how this has come about.

Figure 3 **Flag of the European Union**

The Common Agricultural Policy (CAP)

The positive

In an attempt to create a single market in agriculture and a secure food supply for its members, the EU implemented the CAP in 1958. It aimed:
- to increase agricultural productivity
- to ensure a fair standard of living for the agricultural community
- to have fair market prices
- to ensure supplies to the consumer at reasonable prices.

Preference would be shown to agricultural products grown in the member states and member states of the EU would finance the CAP, with the wealthier nations contributing more.

The CAP operates in a variety of ways, including managing food prices, controlling food supplies, offering grants and subsidies to farmers and protecting the environment.

Since 1958, the changes brought about by CAP have been remarkable. The EU has become self-sufficient in most major foods including wheat, sugar, barley, butter, beef, cheese, fresh vegetables, chicken, pork, eggs, wine, margerine, milk and potatoes. The EU's ten million farmers are among the most productive in the world. The CAP has also helped reduce mass rural depopulation, and support for those in marginal farming has helped maintain many mountain farming communities

The negative

A number of difficulties have also been created by the CAP. The cost of running the CAP has become increasingly expensive, taking 70% of the EU budget. This figure is too high considering agriculture only contributes to 3% of the EU's wealth.

Throughout the 1980s, farmers were given guaranteed prices for their produce and therefore produced as much as possible. Vast surpluses of food and drink (known as the 'food mountains' and the 'wine lakes') resulted from more being produced than could be sold. The surplus had to be stored at a huge cost (£5.5 billion).

Obsession with increased productivity has resulted in serious environmental problems, such as pollution from nitrates, pesticides and animal waste, and increased soil erosion as a result of removing hedgerows and woodland.

Many landscapes are now threatened. Wetlands (lowland bog, marsh and saltmarsh), meadow, heath, moorland and woodland have all suffered as farmers have tried to increase the area under their cultivation.

Farming terms

Diversification – a farmer decides to develop land uses in addition to farming to make a profit and stay in business

ESA – Environmentally Sensitive Area – land that is farmed in a traditional way to reduce the risk to wildlife and to maintain the attractive landscape

Intervention price – a guaranteed price given by the EU to the farmer for a farm product e.g. wheat

Marginal farming – where the physical conditions only just make farming economically possible

Quota – the amount of farm product that an individual farmer is allowed to produce e.g. on milk production

Set-Aside – where a farmer is paid compensation by the government for not using some of his land for agricultural purposes

Subsidy – money given to farmers by the EU to help them stay in business

Recent EU policies

Production controls (1984 – 92)

In 1984 the EU announced a series of measures aimed at increasing demand and restricting agricultural production. This included guaranteed thresholds on cereals where farmers receive guaranteed prices only up to a specified quantity grown and milk quotas aimed to limit output to 1981 levels. Where farmers exceeded their quotas, they had to pay a super-levy of 75% of the value of the surplus.

Import tariffs

The EU aims to promote trade within Europe and minimise imports from outside. There is a tax on imported foods, although preferential treatment is given to some former colonies.

Set-Aside

Farmers must withdraw 15% of their land from agricultural production if they are to receive EU funding. Set-Aside land must be left fallow, planted with trees or used for non-agricultural purposes (diversification). It is a controversial policy as too few environmental benefits are brought to the countryside and it seems as if farmers are getting paid for growing nothing. By 1997, 8000 UK farmers were involved in the Set-Aside scheme, although the amount of land that had to be withdrawn had reduced to 7%.

Cereal and beef cuts

Between 1993 and 1996, there had been a progressive reduction by 29% in the support price for cereals and an 18% reduction in the support price for beef. This reduction attempted to bring EU cereal and beef prices closer to world prices. Cereal producers get compensation through the Set-Aside scheme.

Tackling food shortages – Rape seed

One of the few agricultural products the EU is lacking is vegetable oil. Growing oil-seed rape was a solution. Rape seed has a 40% oil content (used for cooking oil, margarine and salad dressing) and what is left is high in protein, which is valuable for livestock feed. Oilseed also improves the structure and fertility of the soil.

Figure 5 **Lowland heath, an Environmentally Sensitive Area**

Figure 4 **Farmland under the Set-Aside scheme**

Figure 6 **Oil seed rape**

Recent UK government policies

The Countryside Stewardship Scheme

Farmers are eligible for payments of up to £300 per hectare for conserving and restoring five types of vulnerable landscape: chalk grasslands, lowland heath, coastal vegetation, river meadows and marshes, and heather moorland and hill landscapes.

Environmentally Sensitive Areas

This scheme encourages farmers to safeguard areas of the countryside where the landscape, wildlife habitat or historic interest is of national importance. Its purpose is to support the conservation of traditional farming practices and to encourage measures that will enhance the environment. ESAs in England include The Lake District, Exmoor, the Norfolk Broads and Test Valley. A farmer may join the scheme for a 10-year period, in return, receiving an annual payment per hectare. The highest amount received is when arable land is returned to native grassland.

Nitrate Sensitive Areas

These are ten areas within the UK that suffer from a high nitrate content (from fertilisers) in water supplies. Farmers within such areas are compensated for not applying large quantities of nitrogen fertilisers.

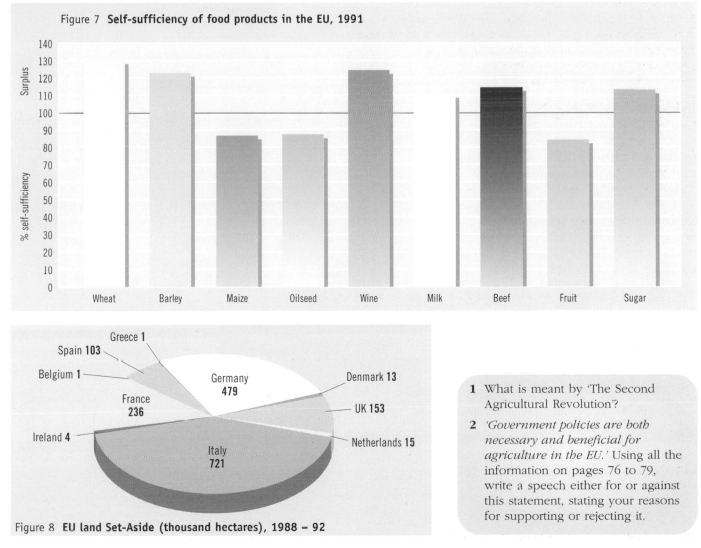

Figure 7 **Self-sufficiency of food products in the EU, 1991**

Figure 8 **EU land Set-Aside (thousand hectares), 1988 – 92**

1 What is meant by 'The Second Agricultural Revolution'?

2 *'Government policies are both necessary and beneficial for agriculture in the EU.'* Using all the information on pages 76 to 79, write a speech either for or against this statement, stating your reasons for supporting or rejecting it.

5.7 Rice farming in India

Figure 1 **World distribution of farming types**

Type of farming	Example
Nomadic hunting and collecting	Australian aborigines
Nomadic herding	Maasai in Kenya
Shifting cultivation	Amerindians of Amazon Basin
Intensive subsistence agriculture	rice in the Ganges Valley
Plantation agriculture	coffee in Brazil
Livestock ranching (commercial pastoral)	beef on the Pampas
Cereal cultivation (commercial grain)	Canadian Prairies and Russian Steppes
Mixed farming	Netherlands
'Mediterranean' agriculture	southern Italy
Irrigation	Nile Valley
Unsuitable for agriculture	Sahara desert

Tropic of Capricorn

Tropic of Capricorn

Tropic of Capricorn

World distribution of rice farming

Specific growing requirements make rice cultivation possible only in a few areas of the world. Rice farming is a type of **labour intensive subsistence farming.** This means that the input of labour is high, the input of capital is low, and only enough rice is produced for the farmers and their families. Figure 1 shows that South East Asia is the main area in which rice farming occurs.

Farming in India

India has many natural resources including fertile soil, abundant water, dense forests and rich mineral deposits. The large areas of fertile arable land, the variety of climates and long growing season have made it possible to grow a variety of crops like cereals, pulses, oil seeds, cotton, sugar cane, jute, tea and coffee (Figure 2). India is the world's second largest producer of rice (growing 20% of the world's total). Rice forms 90% of its total diet and has a high nutritional value.

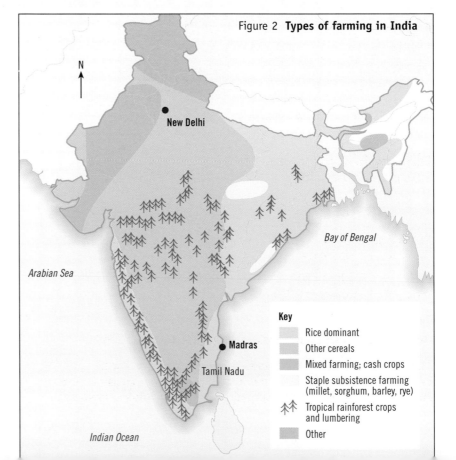

Figure 2 **Types of farming in India**

N

New Delhi

Arabian Sea

Bay of Bengal

Madras

Tamil Nadu

Indian Ocean

Key
- Rice dominant
- Other cereals
- Mixed farming; cash crops
- Staple subsistence farming (millet, sorghum, barley, rye)
- 🌲🌲 Tropical rainforest crops and lumbering
- Other

Features of rice cultivation in India

Rice cultivation involves the maximum use of land with neither fallow or wasted space. Rice is usually grown on river flood plains (e.g. the Ganges), in river deltas and on terraces on steep hillsides. Yields are high enough to support a high population density (up to 2000 per km^2).

The farming is labour intensive with much manual effort needed to construct *bunds* or terraces, to build irrigation channels, to prepare the fields and plant, weed and harvest the crop. Rice has a growing season of only 100 days, so the constantly high temperatures of SE Asia enable two or three harvests of rice in a year.

Figure 3 **Paddy farming in India**

Farming in Tamil Nadu, India

The climate of Tamil Nadu favours agriculture. Rainfall averages 700 mm per year and comes from two **monsoons**: the north-east monsoon (October to December) and the south-west monsoon (June to September). Irrigated rice (**paddy**) is the main crop. Water for **irrigation** is taken from rivers or small reservoirs called tanks. Farmers recognise three rice-growing seasons:

- *kuruvai*: late June – late September
- *thaladi*: late October – February
- *samba*: August – January

Famers also cultivate sugar cane, groundnuts, beans and fruit.

The area does experience devastating famines at times, with cyclones and droughts a constant threat. Population density is high and poverty is widespread, especially among the landless labourers.

1 Where in the world is rice cultivated?

2 Why is India so well suited to the cultivation of rice?

3 What are the disadvantages of rice farming in Tamil Nadu?

5.8 The Green Revolution

The Green Revolution refers to the application of modern, western-type farming techniques to developing countries such as India. In the 1960s, rapid world population growth and a belief that the world's farmers would be unable to feed the increase in numbers led to a search for new ways to increase productivity from the land. Four of the main features of the Green Revolution are outlined below.

High yield varieties

Developed Countries such as the UK, USA, Germany and Australia, provided research and money to develop high yield varieties (**HYVs**) of food grains such as maize, wheat and rice. In 1965 an improved strain of rice called **IR-8** (known as 'miracle rice') allowed yields in India to increase by 300% in areas of good soil and water conditions. IR-8 was followed by wheat and maize HYVs.

Farm output increased dramatically and food prices lowered. The farmland for cereals was used more intensively, allowing **cash crops** to be grown and rural unemployment to fall.

However, HYVs need large amounts of fertilisers and insecticides as they are prone to insect attack. They also require the best conditions of soil and water. As a result, only the more wealthy farmers have benefited from the new strains, increasing inequality in living standards in rural areas.

HYVs are used in the drier (hill rice) regions of India as they are less effective in the main wet paddy regions of the Ganges valley and delta, along the east coast (such as Tamil Nadu) where fields are deep flooded and soils are subject to waterlogging. This is because HYVs are easily submerged. They are also used, as they are short-stemmed and develop heavy heads of grain.

Irrigation

Many developing countries rely heavily on irrigation to increase output from the land. About 45 million hectares of land has been irrigated in India.

Tube wells have been sunk and reservoirs built all over the country. Water projects, however, such as the **Narmada River Project** between Gujarat and Madhya Pradesh, have both benefits and disadvantages. The project plans to build 30 large dams along the river and its tributaries, to irrigate two million hectares of land and provide 400 megawatts of hydro-electric power for rural communities. However, more than 100 000 hectares of forest and good agricultural land will be drowned, one million people will have to abandon their homes and the weight of the water trapped in reservoirs could trigger earthquakes.

Irrigation can bring problems of **waterlogging** to soils and **salinisation** through the upward movement of soil salts. Over six million hectares of irrigated land in India has been impaired in this way.

Figure 2 **The Vijdyawada Dam, Andhra Pradesh, India**

Appropriate Technology (AT)

Most people in developing countries live in rural areas and use low or basic technology. When Western countries try to impose their own high or advanced technology on these countries, it is often with disasterous results. **Appropriate Technology** (sometimes called **Intermediate Technology**) is technology suitable to the state of development of the country in question. AT has five main aims:

● to provide jobs
● to produce goods for local markets
● to replace imported goods with local goods which are of the same quality but the same price or cheaper
● to use local resources, labour, materials and finance
● to provide communities with services like health, water, housing, roads and education.

Figure 1 **Appropriate Technology in use**

Appropriate Technology should help people from developing countries solve their own problems and gain satisfaction from doing so. Appropriate Technology should be designed so as not to harm the environment and to contribute to a sustainable lifestyle.

Examples of Appropriate Technology include low-cost roofing tiles for schools, clinics and houses made from local cement and sand, training in the preserving and marketing of foods, improved techniques for storing rainwater, and training courses for making carpentry and farming tools.

In India, recent Appropriate Technology initiatives have included training courses for animal first-aid workers, design of fuel-efficient stoves and training courses for stove makers, design and manufacture of improved fishing boats, and the design and manufacture of bicycle trailers, wheelbarrows and animal carts.

A great deal of appropriate technology is the introduction of basic, simple techniques, but they can make an enormous difference to the lives of people throughout the developing world.

Land reform

Land reform tries to resolve long-held difficulties with the ownership of land that exists in many developing countries. Land holdings (the size of farms) are small in comparison with those of the developed world. In India for example, 75% of farmers own less than three hectares and 25% own less than 0.5 hectares.

A farmer's land can often be fragmented or broken-up into many small plots spread over a wide area, making it impossible to farm efficiently. The majority of farmland is owned by a few wealthy landowners. Many of the poorer farm labourers own no land at all and suffer great poverty.

Since 1947, land reform in India has aimed to increase average farm size for the small land owners, set an upper limit on the amount of land held by the wealthiest landowners, and has reallocated 2 million hectares of surplus land to the landless. Such reforms have increased the productivity of farms and increased the incomes of farmers.

1 How has the Green Revolution transformed farming in India?

2 What are the negative aspects of the Green Revolution?

3 What other problems need to be overcome before Indian farmers can gain the most from the land?

4 Why is Appropriate Technology more beneficial to many farmers in India than more modern farming methods?

Desertification in the Sahel

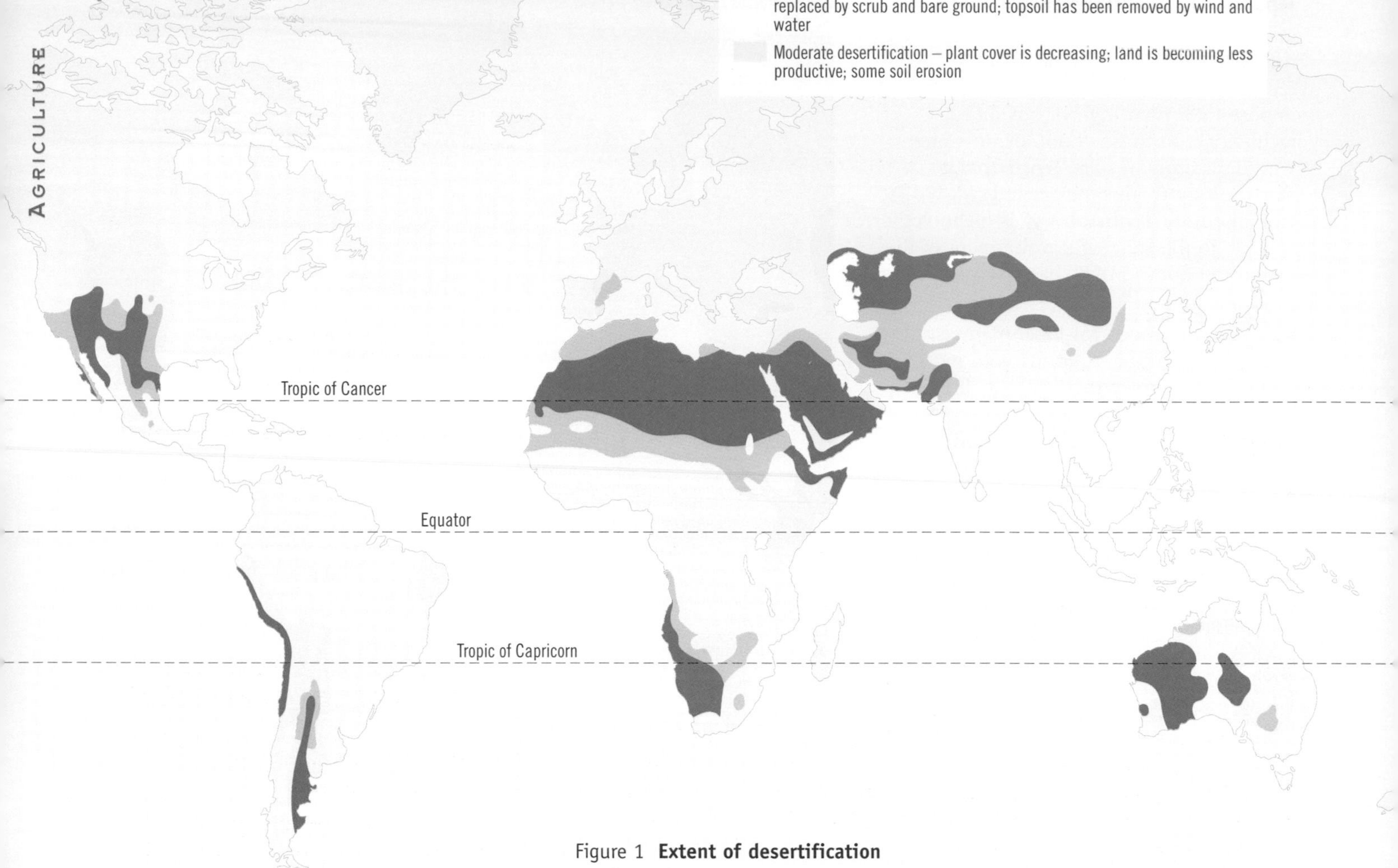

Key

- Land that is naturally desert
- Severe desertification – much less vegetation; stable grasses have been replaced by scrub and bare ground; topsoil has been removed by wind and water
- Moderate desertification – plant cover is decreasing; land is becoming less productive; some soil erosion

Tropic of Cancer

Equator

Tropic of Capricorn

Figure 1 **Extent of desertification**

Desertification is when human and climatic processes reduce biological activity, changing once-fertile farming land to desert-like conditions. Desertification is a global problem (Figure 1), particularly in the susceptible dry lands. Found in developing and developed countries alike, it currently affects the lives of one billion people. Every year another six million hectares of farmland becomes unproductive as a result.

An area of the world seriously affected by desertification is the **Sahel**. This is a belt running west-east across Africa to the south of the Sahara Desert. The countries of the Sahel are Somalia, Ethiopia, Sudan, Chad, Niger, Mali, Burkina Faso, Mauritania and Senegal. The natural vegetation of the Sahel, **savanna** (a mixture of tall grasses, bushes and scattered trees), has been all but destroyed.

Figure 2 **Overgrazing contributes towards desertification**

Causes of desertification

Watering holes

At a local scale, desertification is common around watering holes in desert fringe areas. Large numbers of livestock gather here, leading to overgrazing and degradation of the vegetation. This is a particular problem in years of drought, when **nomadic pastoralists** may take up semi-permanent residence around the watering holes.

Firewood

In developing countries the demand for firewood for cooking and lighting is high. In the countries of the Sahel, over 80% of domestic energy comes from firewood. In rural areas where population density is high, trees and shrubs around villages are cleared. Soils become vulnerable to erosion by wind and water as a result of the loss of the binding effect of the vegetation.

Over-cultivation

When rapid population growth occurs, so too does pressure on farmland (e.g. population of Sudan was nine million in 1950 and will have grown to 34 million by the year 2000). Some farmers are forced to cultivate marginal areas which are more vulnerable to erosion. Some have to grow the same crop year after year on the same piece of land without any rest or **fallow** years. Soils which have limited fertility and fragile structures become exhausted, cannot grow vegetation and become susceptible to wind and water erosion (Figure 2).

Climatic change

Years of drought, which are common in areas such as the Sahel, can cause widespread desertification (Figure 4). The decrease in rainfall means less grazing land and fewer crops. The Sahel ecosystems have adapted to one or two drought years in ten, but with three or four successive drought years, the water stores in the system (in the plants, the soil and the rocks beneath) empty and the whole system begins to break down through lack of water.

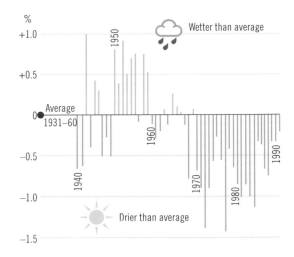

Figure 3 **Annual rainfall in the Sahel since 1931**

1 Study Figure 1. To what extent can desertification be described as a global problem?

2 What are the main causes of desertification in the Sahel?

3 What could be done to stop the spiral into desertification shown in Figure 4?

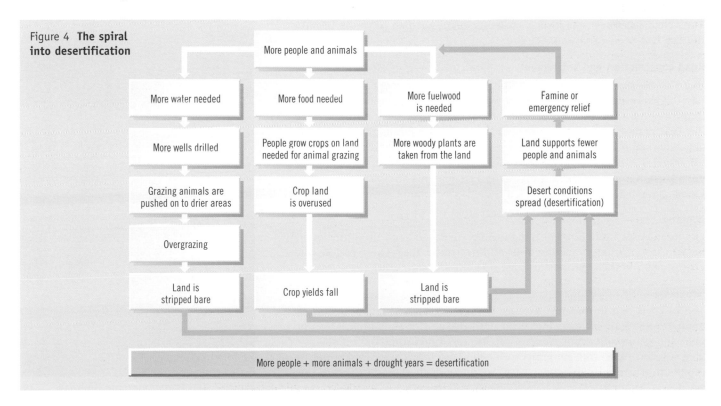

Figure 4 **The spiral into desertification**

More people and animals

More water needed | More food needed | More fuelwood is needed | Famine or emergency relief

More wells drilled | People grow crops on land needed for animal grazing | More woody plants are taken from the land | Land supports fewer people and animals

Grazing animals are pushed on to drier areas | Crop land is overused | | Desert conditions spread (desertification)

Overgrazing

Land is stripped bare | Crop yields fall | Land is stripped bare

More people + more animals + drought years = desertification

AGRICULTURE

Deforestation is the felling and clearance of forest land. Although it has been carried out for centuries, today it is mainly taking place in developing countries which have tropical rainforests as their natural vegetation (Figure 1). The rapid clearances in recent years has made deforestation a key global environmental issue.

The fastest clearances are taking place in **Amazonia**, an area of South America, which is mainly in Brazil but also covers parts of its neighbouring countries.

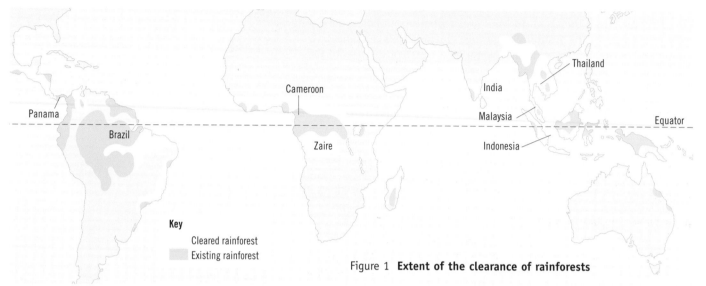

Key

Cleared rainforest
Existing rainforest

Figure 1 **Extent of the clearance of rainforests**

Causes of deforestation in Amazonia

Shifting cultivation

Large areas of land are being cleared and burnt by a growing number of migrants from other parts of Brazil in a process called **'slash and burn'**. They clear the forest, plant their crops for one year then move on because the soil has been exhausted (Figure 3).

Road construction and settlement

In an effort to open up the forest, the Brazilian government has built many new highways (Figure 2). The roads were built to encourage settlement and to aid the transport of minerals and timber out of the forest. Settlers along the new highways have brought with them modern farming methods. Conventional harvesting of land after rainforest removal quickly damages the fragile natural ecosystem. Soils soon become exhausted, the environment degraded, and the land and settlements are often abandoned. Forest clearance is so thorough that there is no hope of regeneration.

Logging

Hardwoods such as ebony and mahogany are logged and used for building construction, furniture making and pulp to make paper. The Japanese and Europeans buy these woods in huge quantities.

Minerals

The forest is rich in minerals that are in high demand. There are extensive mining operations of manganese, tin ore, bauxite (for aluminium), iron ore, gold and diamonds. Many mineral prospectors (**garimpeiros**) operate illegally, and mine with no concern for the land they exploit. Tree loss, pollution of rivers by mercury, waste sediment from mining processes and sewage is common.

Figure 2 **The Trans-Amazonia Highway**

Figure 3 **Evidence of 'slash and burn' in Amazonia**

Figure 4 **The Itaipu Dam, Brazil**

Ranching

Much land has been cleared for pasture for beef cattle. The global demand for beef has increased dramatically, particularly in the beefburger market.

Hydro-Electric Power (HEP)

Large areas of land have been cleared and flooded to construct reservoirs, dams and HEP power stations (Figure 4). The Altamira Complex on the River Xingu has flooded over 10 310 sq. km, creating the world's largest artificial lake.

Effects of deforestation in Amazonia

Loss of forest plants and animals

Many species of birds, insects and animals are lost as their habitats are destroyed.

Loss of medicines

More than 50% of Western medicines come from the rainforests, including remedies for serious diseases such as malaria. If these plants are destroyed then we may be losing possible cures for other diseases.

Figure 5 **Members of the Xikvin tribe**

Loss of Indian groups

Over 90 indigenous Indian groups have been driven from their homes and land by road construction, mining and ranching (Figure 5). These groups and their way of life will soon be lost forever.

Soil erosion

With trees removed, there is increased surface run-off which causes soil erosion and more severe and frequent flooding.

Soil fertility decline

Nutrients are not returned quickly enough to the soil and are washed away (**leached**) by heavy soil because trees have been removed. Within three or four years the soil becomes infertile, unable to support even crops or grass.

Increased carbon dioxide

Forest burning and clearance has increased carbon dioxide emissions into the atmosphere. With trees removed, conversion of carbon dioxide into oxygen is also stopped.

1 Why is the Amazonian rainforest being removed?

2 What are the effects of removing the Amazonian rainforest?

3 *This house believes deforestation in the Amazon rainforest should be stopped.*

For each of the following groups of people, prepare a short speech arguing for or against this motion:

a a native Indian

b a logger

c a mineral prospector

d a rancher

e a Brazilian government official

f a United Nations environmental advisor.

AGRICULTURE

Italy: two nations?

Italy is a wealthy nation, but its wealth is not spread evenly across the country. The north is rich and the south is poor. The north has a high standard of living, is home to most of the country's industry and has good transport links. The south suffers from high unemployment and poor living conditions. Agricultural output is high in the north but low in the south.

The Italian government has worked hard at closing the gap between the rich north and poor south.

The **Cassa per il Mezzogiorno** ('Fund for the South') operated from 1950 to 1984. Most of its funds went on improving and diversifying farming, improving roads and water supplies and draining malarial marshes. Figures 3 and 4 show the changes the Cassa brought about in farming during its years of operation. The Cassa also worked at improving transport links with the north and at attracting large companies to build factories in the south. Fiat, Alfa-Romeo, Olivetti and Pirelli all located near Naples. Steelworks, oil refineries, chemical and cement factories were all attracted by cheap land and government grants and subsidies. However, many of these projects employed few local people, the profits made were sent back to the north and when recession came, these were the first industries to close down.

The **Comunita Montana**, set up in 1984 and still running today, is a rural planning agency aimed at encouraging farmers in the more remote mountainous areas to diversify and to remain on the land. It provides grants for new farm buildings, improved livestock and small irrigation schemes, and has planted trees to reduce soil erosion.

Since 1984, the **Agency for the Promotion of the Development of the Mezzogiorno** has been encouraging small-scale industry to locate in the south and has concentrated on developing the region's tourist potential – the hot sunny climate, warm seas, pleasant beaches and unique sites such as Mount Vesuvius and Pompeii.

Within 50 years the government has succeeded in eliminating the south's widespread poverty and has halted mass south-to-north migration. Although still below those of the north, living standards and prospects have been raised significantly. The south currently receives heavy funding and investment from the EU's fund for disadvantaged areas.

	The north	The south
Climate	a European climate of warm summers and plenty of rain all year round, ideal for high farming yields	a **Mediterranean climate** of hot summers (over 30°C) and long summer droughts, making farming very difficult; known as the **Mezzogiorno**, meaning 'the land of the midday sun'
Relief	plenty of lowland on which to farm e.g. the Lombardy Plain	mostly steep rugged mountains
Soils	rich, deep fertile soils on which to farm	thin and of poor quality; after centuries of forest clearance, suffers from extensive soil erosion and flooding
Land ownership	farmers have their own land	vast private estates called **latifundia** owned by absentee landlords cover much of the area and are farmed by peasant tenant farmers and casual labourers (**braccianti**)
Farming methods	the latest technology is used in farming, with mechanisation and the use of chemicals to maximise yields	modern methods follow on some years later
Location of industry	most industry wants to locate in the north because of its large urban markets such as Milan, Genoa and Turin, its good road and rail networks and its proximity to the rest of Europe	the south is distant from markets and with poor transport links, is an unattractive location for industry.

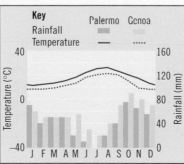

Figure 1 **Climate graph for Palermo and Genoa**

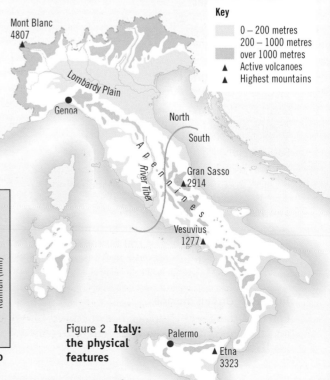

Figure 2 **Italy: the physical features**

Figure 3 **Before Cassa per il Mezzogiorno**

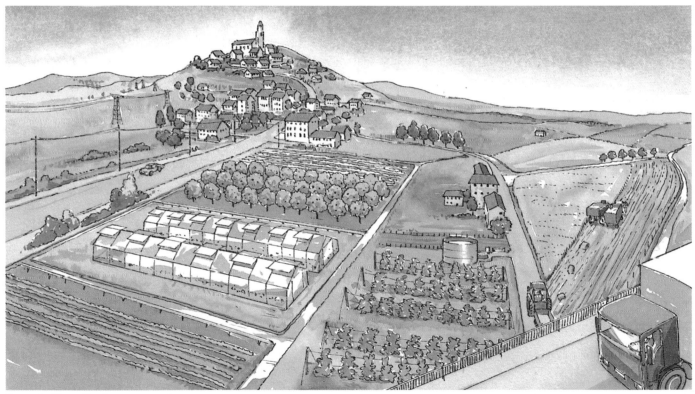

Figure 4 **Since the improvements**

1 What makes the Mezzogiorno a difficult region to farm?

2 **a** What efforts have the government made to improve farming conditions in the south?

b What efforts have been made to close the gap in wealth between the north and south?

3 Study Figures 3 and 4. Describe the changes that have taken place in farming in the Mezzogiorno over the last 50 years.

4 What do you think are the disadvantages of the changes that have been made?

WEATHER AND CLIMATE

Weather affects all our lives on a daily basis. Winter weather has us wearing thicker clothing and will certainly increase heating bills while the summer brings outings to the beach and barbeques in the garden. Bad weather can cause chaos to the transport systems with trees being blown onto roads or snow making railway tracks unsafe. Droughts can lead to water shortages which may have an effect on crop prices if harvests are bad.

The term **weather** is used to describe changes over a short period of time, from hour to hour or day to day. It includes temperature, sunshine, precipitation and wind. Weather is never static and is constantly changing which is why **meteorologists** (scientists who study the weather) find it so difficult to forecast the weather accurately. In the same country weather conditions can vary enormously; it may be raining in Leeds, for example, while London might be experiencing bright sunshine.

Climate is the average condition of the atmosphere over a much longer time period. It is the **expected conditions** for a place rather than the actual conditions. For example, the climate of Malaysia can be described as a hot, wet equatorial climate. This sums up the average conditions of the country throughout the year. In order to obtain accurate climatic conditions of a place meteorologists must record elements of the weather such as rainfall, temperature, humidity, air pressure, winds, clouds and sunshine, every day for a minimum period of 35 years.

Recording the elements of weather and climate

A basic understanding of weather recording can be obtained by looking at a simple weather station. Most school weather stations will contain instruments that can measure temperature, humidity, rainfall and wind speed and direction.

Figure 1 **Cricket at Lord's and Headingley**
Weather conditions can vary enormously at two different places during the same day.

Temperature

As temperatures can vary over different types of surfaces and can change with height above the ground, meteorologists have agreed to use a standard measure of temperature. This is the **shade temperature** or the temperature of the air. The temperature is recorded by **thermometers** in a **Stevenson Screen**. The Stevenson Screen is simply a box painted white to reflect sunlight. It has louvred sides to allow a free flow of air and should stand on stilts one metre above the level of the ground surface, well away from trees and buildings that may affect the temperatures recorded. The screen will usually contain maximum and minimum thermometers as well as wet and dry bulb thermometers.

Maximum and minimum temperatures are measured by two slightly different thermometers. The maximum thermometer, filled with mercury, records the highest temperature reached during the day. It has a constriction in the thread so that once mercury has been forced through, it cannot return to the bulb.

The minimum thermometer, filled with alcohol and a metal indicator, measures the lowest temperature reached during the day. This will most probably occur during the middle of the night or early in the morning. When the temperature drops the alcohol will contract, pulling the indicator towards the bulb.

Figure 2 **A Stevenson Screen**

Humidity

Humidity is measured using a **hygrometer**. A hygrometer consists of two thermometers; one is a **dry bulb thermometer**, the other is a **wet bulb thermometer**. These are both stored within the Stevenson screen. As the air temperature increases, evaporation from the wet thermometer will cause the temperature within it to decrease and hence record a difference between the two readings. Tables can be used to work out the relative humidity of the air. The greater the difference in the readings, the less water there is in the atmosphere and therefore, the lower the humidity. Measurements of equal value suggests that no evaporation has taken place and that the air is saturated. This type of reading is common in areas of high humidity, for example in the tropical rainforests of Brazil.

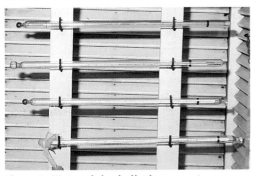

Figure 3 **Wet and dry bulb thermometers inside a Stevenson Screen**

Rainfall

Rainfall is measured using a **rain gauge**. The rain gauge is located in an open area so that it is not sheltered by trees. It is a metal container which houses a conical flask for collecting the rainwater. The container is partly sunk into the ground in order to prevent evaporation and for stability in the wind. It has a rim which stands 30 mm above the ground surface. The rim protects the flask from rain splash. Each day the rainfall can be transferred from the flask to a measuring cylinder and thus total rainfall can be recorded in **millimetres**.

Figure 4 **Rain gauge**

Wind speed and direction

Figure 5 **An anemometer**

Wind speed is measured by an **anemometer**. This may be a hand-held machine or it can be attached to the roof of a building. It consists of three cups mounted on a spindle, which in turn is connected to a rev-counter. The wind blows against the cups causing the spindle to rotate, and the number of revolutions in a specific time gives the wind speed. Wind speed is measured in **knots**.

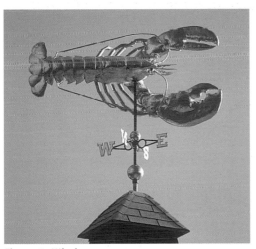

Figure 6 **Wind vane**

Wind direction is shown by a **wind vane**. The arrow points to the direction from which the wind blows.

Pressure

Pressure may be recorded using a **barometer**. Air pressure is usually measured in **millibars**.

---

1 What is the difference between weather and climate?

2 Draw and label the most important features of a rain gauge.

3 Will a rain gauge located in Oxford give a useful measurement when studying rainfall in the UK? Explain your answer.

4 A weather vane was recorded as pointing in the following directions at various times throughout the day. Which way was the wind blowing?
   a north
   b south-east
   c north-east
   d south-west.

Through the studies carried out by meteorologists we now know many of the reasons for differences in climate. We have established why it is that countries located on the equator, such as Brazil, have very hot and wet conditions all year round while countries at higher latitudes, such as the UK, experience a number of different climatic conditions throughout the year.

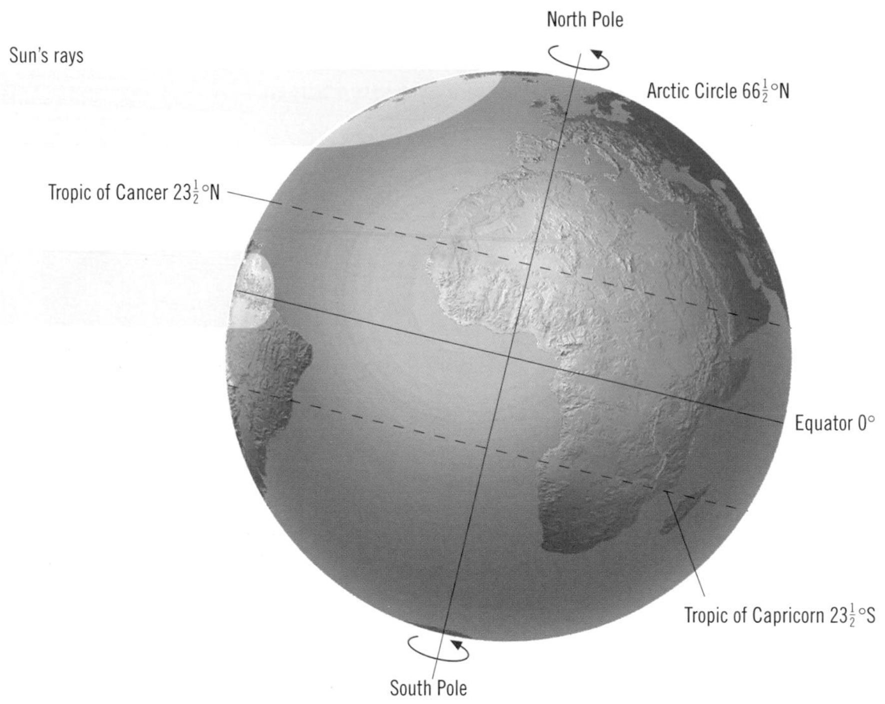

Sun's rays

North Pole

Arctic Circle $66\frac{1}{2}°N$

Tropic of Cancer $23\frac{1}{2}°N$

Equator 0°

Tropic of Capricorn $23\frac{1}{2}°S$

South Pole

Figure 1 **How latitude affects the temperature at the earth's surface**

Latitude

Places nearer to the equator are much warmer than places which are nearer to the poles. This is due to a combination of factors such as the angle of the sun in the sky, the curvature of the earth, and the layer of atmosphere which surrounds the earth.

At the equator the land heats up rapidly because the sun's energy is far more concentrated than at higher latitudes. Further away from the equator the ground will take much longer to warm up as the heat is no longer concentrated within a small area.

Land and sea influences

In summer the land will warm up extremely quickly, while in winter it will not take long to cool down. The sea on the other hand takes long periods of time to both heat up and cool down. This is because land cannot retain heat and cannot disperse it easily. The sea meanwhile, mixes hot and cold easily, so avoiding extremes of temperature. This helps to explain why **continental climates,** areas located in the middle of large land masses, such as Siberia in Russia, experience such extremes in temperature. The summer maximum may reach 22°C while the winter minimum may be as cold as –35°C, a temperature range of 57°C. The climate of areas located near to major oceans is modified by the sea and large extremes in temperature are not found. Britain has a **maritime climate** where the climate is directly affected by the Atlantic Ocean to the west. The British climate has on average a temperature range of between 10° and 15°C, much less than continental areas.

Winds

The temperature of the wind is directly affected by the type of surface which it passes over. If the most frequent or **prevailing** winds blow from the oceans, then the areas over which they blow will be warmer in winter and cooler in summer. If they blow from a large land mass, the temperature will be warmer in summer and colder in winter.

Ocean currents

Ocean currents flow both from the equator to the poles and vice-versa. Like prevailing winds, they can have a great influence on the temperature of a coastal town or city. Warm currents, such as the North Atlantic Drift which flows off the west coast of Britain, raise the air temperature in maritime environments. Cold currents, such as the Labrador, flowing off the north-east coast of North America, carry water to the equator and may decrease the temperature of coastal areas.

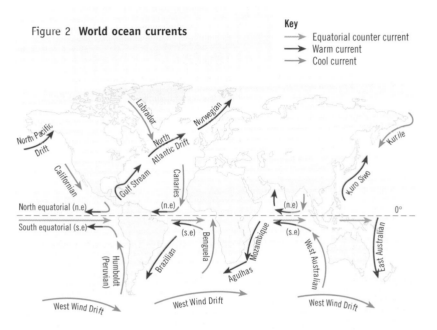

Figure 2 **World ocean currents**

Key
→ Equatorial counter current
→ Warm current
→ Cool current

Figure 3 **In the northern hemisphere, north facing slopes receive less heat than those facing south**

Altitude

As one walks up a mountain such as Snowdon in North Wales, the temperature becomes markedly cooler. This is because heat cannot be retained as easily in the upper atmosphere. Temperature drops by about 1°C for every 100 metres above sea level.

Aspect

Aspect is the direction in which the land faces. Slopes which face **south** in the northern hemisphere will receive much more heat than those in the shade facing north.

---

1 a How does latitude affect temperature in different parts of the world?
b Although being on a lower latitude and by the sea, cities on the north-east coast of the USA often have more severe winters than the UK. Why is this the case?

2 Look at Figure 4.
a Which place has the highest temperature in summer? Is it on the coast or inland?
b Which place has the lowest temperature in summer? Is it on the coast or inland?
c Can you explain your findings?

3 a Draw a scattergraph to show how annual range of temperature varies with distance from the sea. Add a line of best fit.
b Describe and explain what your graph shows.

4 Why is there a difference between the temperature on the valley floor and the temperature on top of mountains in highland areas of Britain?

Figure 4 Climate variations for a continental land mass

Location	Latitude (approx)	Distance from open sea (approx) km	Average summer maximum temperature °C	Average winter minimum temperature °C	Range of temperature
Bergen, Norway	60.5°N	20	15	1	14
Oslo, Norway	60°N	330	17	− 5	22
Stockholm, Sweden	59.5°N	780	16	− 3	19
St. Petersburg, Russia	60°N	1440	17	− 8	25
Hamburg, Germany	53.5°N	110	17	1	16
Berlin, Germany	52.5°N	380	16	− 1	17
Warsaw, Poland	52°N	1120	19	− 3	22
Moscow, Russia	56°N	3300	19	− 10	29
Tomsk, Russia	56°N	3300	18	− 20	38
Irkutsk, Russia	52.5°N	2700	18	− 21	39
Blagoveshchensk, Russia	50°N	1200	21	− 23	44
Okhotsk, Russia	39°N	0	13	− 25	38
Petropsvisvsk, Russia	53°N	0	13	− 8	21

Climatic data for selected places between 50°N and 60°N latitude, Eurasia

Climate differences across the world

Temperature across the world will vary for a large number of reasons. This variation gives rise to a number of different climate types.

Temperate landscape – Oxfordshire, England

Figure 1 **World climate zones**

Verkhoyansk, Russia

Reykjavik, Iceland

London, UK

Palermo, Sicily

Tropic of Cancer   23½°N

Khartoum, Sudan

Equator   0°

Manaus, Brazil

Nzega, Tanzania

Tropic of Capricorn   23½°S

Key

Polar

Desert

Savanna

Temperate

Mediterranean

Equatorial

Other climates

Desert landscape – Simpson Desert, Australia

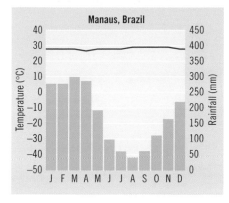

Equatorial

Places with an equatorial climate lie in a narrow band that extends roughly 5° either side of the equator. A typical equatorial climate is hot, wet and humid all year round. This area of the world is unlike any other in that it has no seasons and the weather on a daily basis is repeated virtually every day of the year.

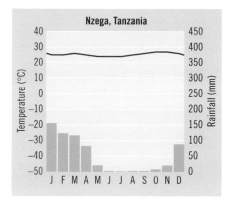

Savanna

Areas with this type of climate are located in the centre of continents approximately between 5° and 15° either side of the equator. This climate has two distinct seasons: a very warm, dry season where temperatures are similar to those found in desert regions and a hot, wet season where temperatures are similar to the equatorial areas.

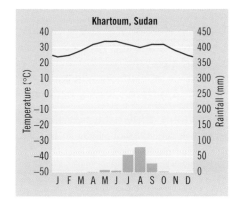

Desert

These areas remain hot and dry for most of the year. They are located between 15° and 30° either side of the equator. Many people think there is no rain in deserts. Rain does occur, however, but not very frequently. When it does rain, it is usually very heavy and for only a short period of time.

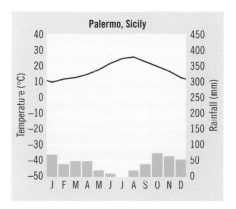

Mediterranean

These areas are mainly located between 30° and 40° either side of the equator and, like savanna areas, they have two distinct seasons. Hot, dry summers are experienced, where the weather is rather like that of deserts, and warm, wet winters when conditions are similar to those in the UK.

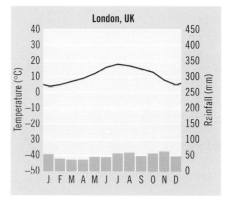

Temperate

Temperate mid-latitude areas lie between 40° and 60° either side of the equator. Most of these areas have cool summers, mild winters and an approximately even distribution of rainfall throughout the year.

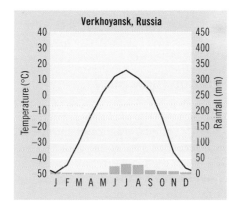

Polar

Polar climates are found above 60° in both the northern and southern hemisphere. Rainfall in these areas is usually low because the air is so cold. Temperatures reach a summer maximum which allows some of the frozen land to thaw.

1 a Using an atlas, write down the latitude of both Verkhoyansk in Russia and Reykjavik in Iceland.

b Plot a climate graph on graph paper using the climate statistics for Reykjavik.

Month	J	F	M	A	M	J	J	A	S	O	N	D
Average temperate (°C)	0	0	2	4	7	10	12	11	9	5	3	1
Average rainfall (mm)	89	64	62	56	42	42	50	56	67	94	78	79

2 Compare the climate graph for Reykjavik with the one for Verkhoyansk.

a What is the temperature range for each area?

b Suggest a reason as to why the temperature falls to such a low figure in Verkhoyansk but not in Reykjavik.

c Suggest one reason why the rainfall is greater in Reykjavik.

Air pressure on the earth's surface can be either high or low. When air is heated up at the earth's surface it is forced to rise, resulting in low pressure at the surface. When air cools, it sinks and pushes down on the earth's surface, creating high pressure.

The patterns of pressure over the earth's surface are very complex and it is easiest to explain these in terms of three distinct latitude bands.

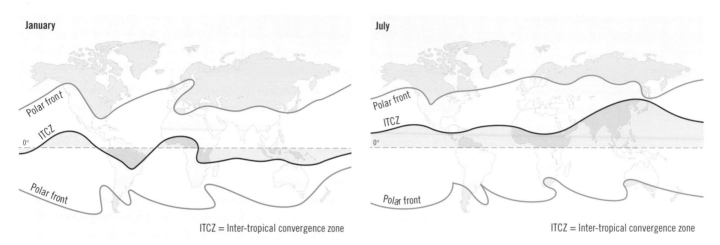

Figure 1 **Pressure systems during January and July**

Equator (0°– 30°)

Strong heating at the equator causes warm air to rise and then cool to form clouds. These clouds regularly release large amounts of rainfall, which is characteristic of equatorial regions. Warm air is also encouraged to rise at the equator by the meeting of warm trade winds from both the northern and southern hemisphere (a process called **convergence**). This area is called the **Inter-Tropical Convergence Zone** (**ITZC**).

As the air rises, it leaves behind an area of low pressure. This area is characterised by light winds as air flows in from the north and south to fill the area of low pressure. Thus, between the tropics, there is a distinct convection cycle. Having been heated and forced upwards, air travels north and south from the equator before cooling and sinking back to earth. It forms two high pressure zones around latitude 30°N and 30°S. The air then returns to the equator as **trade winds** and the process starts all over again.

These movements of air help to create a pattern of vegetation on the earth's surface. Tropical rainforests are found at the low pressure zone of the equator where there are high temperatures and ample regular rainfall. Desert areas occur at 30° north and south, where descending air is warming up, thus giving virtually no rain. In between is the savanna region.

The zones of high and low pressure shift northwards in July. This occurs when the area of maximum solar heating migrates northwards from the equator, taking the area of low pressure with it. In January, the area of maximum solar heating has moved back to the southern hemisphere and so the low pressure zone returns to around the equator. Such movements are responsible for the savanna's wet and dry seasons.

Mid-latitudes (30° – 65°)

Not all the warm air from the equator returns to the earth's surface at 30°. Some air continues into the mid-latitudes. Here, it mixes with colder air travelling down from the polar regions. Where this mixing of warm and cold air occurs, it is called the **polar front**. As the warm air is forced to rise over the dense colder air, low pressure results.

Polar regions (65° – 90°)

Just as at the equator, there is a small cycle of air in this region. Warm air from the mid-latitudes travels into polar regions and descends at the poles. This results in high pressure and the cold air travels back to the mid-latitudes.

Case study │ The Indian monsoon

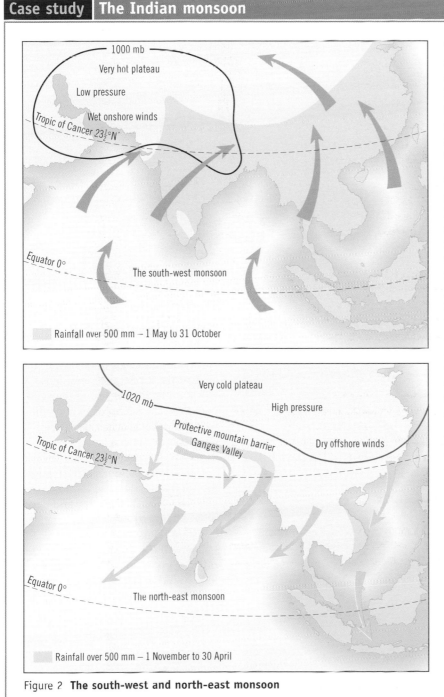

Figure 2 **The south-west and north-east monsoon**

The word monsoon means 'wind reversal' and this is a distinctive feature of the Indian monsoon. The dry season begins in November with moderate temperatures. The wind blows (from the north) from the cool land to the warm sea. Cloudless skies are characteristic of this time of year.

Towards the end of the winter, in March and April, the area of maximum solar heating shifts northwards from the southern hemisphere. This results in an increase in solar energy. The land begins to heat up, creating a low pressure. Air moves from the high pressure to the low pressure as wind. The winds now blow from the south bringing moisture from the Indian Ocean to the land; they have reversed. As they reach the coast (which is hot, due to the increased solar energy), the water condenses and forms clouds. The clouds thicken with the result that violent storms occur. It rains continually from June for three months.

The monsoon rains are concentrated on the coastal mountain ranges of India, on the edges of the Himalayas, and in the north-east of the Indian sub-continent, including Bangladesh.

During September and October, the low pressure weakens. The monsoon dies and the winds return from the north. Eventually, high pressure is restored and the winds from the north prevail once more; another wind reversal.

WEATHER AND CLIMATE

All rain is caused by rising air. As air is heated at the earth's surface, it becomes less dense and it will begin to rise. Warm air at the ground surface can hold much more water than cold air higher up in the atmosphere. Hence, as the light, less dense warm air rises it begins to cool down. When the temperature falls to a critical level known as the **dew point temperature**, the water vapour condenses and clouds are formed. If enough water vapour condenses then rain will occur. The base of the clouds show the height where dew-point temperature is reached (the **condensation level**).

▶ Figure 1 **Cumulus clouds over the Cotswolds** The base of the clouds show the condensation level.

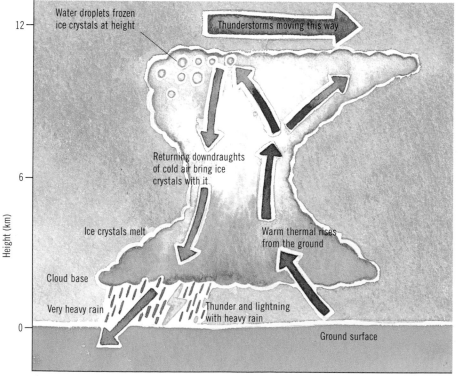

Figure 2 **Convectional rain**

Convectional rainfall

Convectional rainfall is caused by the sun heating the ground. As the moist air warms, it becomes less dense and is forced to rise as strong convectional currents. The warm air will continue to rise until it reaches dew point temperature where it will condense its water droplets and form towering cumulonimbus clouds. These large thunderclouds are seen most afternoons at the equator and explain why equatorial rainforests have a constant daily source of rainfall. In the UK where the ground is not heated as rapidly, convectional rainstorms are less common. However, the South East, and particularly the low-lying flat areas of East Anglia, often experience heavy convectional rainstorms during the summer months. It is for this reason that Cambridge regularly has its wettest month in June, July or August.

Relief or orographic rainfall

Where air blows from the sea across a land surface and towards a mountain range it will be forced to rise. In Britain this occurs where the prevailing south-westerly winds bring moist air from the Atlantic Ocean. On reaching the mountains it is forced to rise up over them. The rising air cools with height until it can no longer hold all the water vapour and condensation occurs, leading to an increase in cloud cover. Eventually rain will fall. Once the air has passed over the mountain it will begin to sink downwards and be slowly warmed by the land. The eastern side of the mountains will have little rain as the air is relatively dry. This area is known as the **rain shadow**.

The western side of Britain receives more rain than the eastern side.

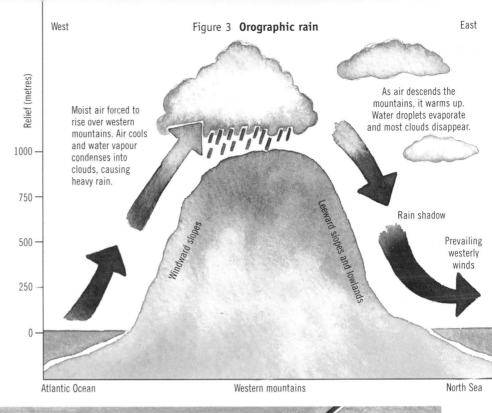

Figure 3 **Orographic rain**

West

East

Moist air forced to rise over western mountains. Air cools and water vapour condenses into clouds, causing heavy rain.

As air descends the mountains, it warms up. Water droplets evaporate and most clouds disappear.

Rain shadow

Prevailing westerly winds

Windward slopes

Leeward slopes and lowlands

Relief (metres)

1000 —
750 —
500 —
250 —
0 —

Atlantic Ocean — Western mountains — North Sea

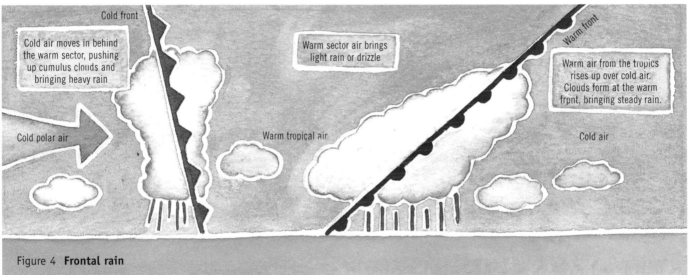

Cold front

Cold air moves in behind the warm sector, pushing up cumulus clouds and bringing heavy rain

Warm sector air brings light rain or drizzle

Warm front

Warm air from the tropics rises up over cold air. Clouds form at the warm frpnt, bringing steady rain.

Cold polar air

Warm tropical air

Cold air

Figure 4 **Frontal rain**

Frontal rainfall

Frontal rain is the result of a warm air mass meeting a cold air mass. As the two air masses are of different temperature, little mixing takes place and the less dense warm air mass is forced to rise over the heavier, colder air. Since the warm, moist air is forced to rise it will soon reach dew point temperature, which leads to condensation, cloud formation and rainfall. Frontal rainfall occurs in depressions and is particularly common in Britain's winter. The warm, tropical air meets the cold polar air over the Atlantic Ocean and is forced to rise, creating a depression. Prevailing winds from the south-west blow the depression over Britain and heavy frontal rain results.

1 Look at Figure 5.
   a Describe the pattern shown by the map.
   b Try to explain this pattern. (To help answer this question, use an atlas to look at a map of the relief of the British Isles.)

Figure 5 **Mean annual precipitation in the British Isles**

Key
mm
2500
1500
1000
750
0

Shetland islands

Falkirk

Armagh

Pembroke

London

In order to forecast the weather in Britain, meteorologists need to know the weather conditions over the Atlantic Ocean and Europe. This is because most of the UK's rainfall and the majority of its dramatic storms are the result of **depressions**.

Depressions are areas of low atmospheric pressure, formed over the Atlantic Ocean when warm air from the tropics meets cold air from the polar regions. Figure 1 shows the life cycle of a depression. Figure 2 explains the typical weather sequence a depression brings as it passes over. It is easy to recognise a depression on a weather chart such as that seen at the beginning of a television forecast or in a national newspaper. A typical chart is shown in Figure 3.

The **warm front** and **cold front** are clearly marked by symbols. The **isobars** join up lines of equal air pressure (although not usually shown, the wind direction has also been marked on Figure 3). The closer together the isobars are, the greater the pressure difference and the stronger the wind.

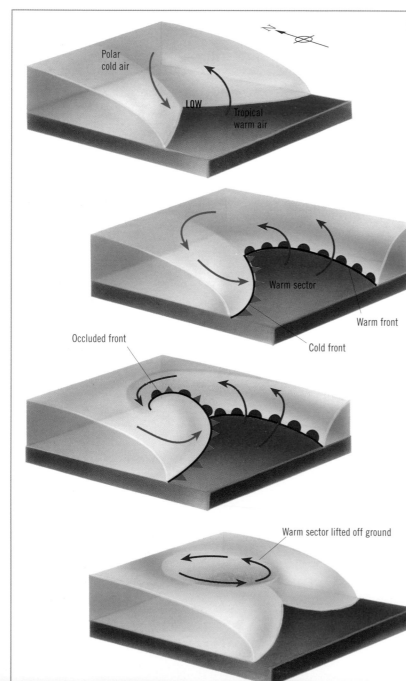

Figure 1 **Stages in the development of a depression**

Stage 1 – Birth

Cold air slowly travelling down from the polar regions meets warm air travelling up from the tropics.
A low pressure is created on the ground where the two air masses meet.
The warm air starts to rise over the denser cold air.

Stage 2 – Youth

The warm air is 'sucked' into the low pressure area, to create a warm sector.
The cold air is 'sucked' in behind the warm air.
This causes the entire air mass to start swirling in an anticlockwise direction.
Where the warm air starts to rise over the cold air, is called the **warm front**.
Where the cold air pushes in behind the warm air, is called the **cold front**.

Stage 3 – Maturity

The warm sector starts to 'climb' above the cold air because it is buoyant.
Underneath the rising air, the cold front catches up with the warm front. It lifts the warm sector off the ground.
Where the warm sector is lifted, is called an **occluded front**.

Stage 4 – Old age and death

Cold air has replaced the warm sector on the ground.
Temperatures even out.
The fronts disappear and the depression dies.

Figure 2   **The passage of a depression over Birmingham**

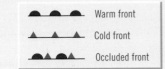

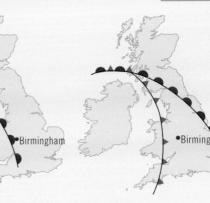

1 A warm front approaches. Skies change from clear, to having high wispy clouds, to developing thicker, lower clouds. Eventually it starts to drizzle.

2 The warm front passes over. Drizzle is replaced by steady rain.

3 The temperature rises in the warm sector. The sky remains grey and overcast. Rain or drizzle continues. The wind blows from the south-west.

4 The cold front approaches, resulting in heavy rain and gusty conditions. Temperatures drop as the front passes over. The wind swings around to the north-west. Behind the cold front, the sky clears. The weather now brings sunny intervals with heavy showers.

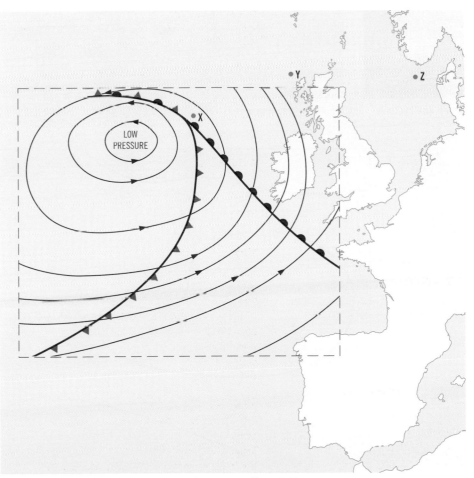

Figure 3   **Weather conditions on Tuesday, 21 April at 6.00 a.m.**

Study all the information on this page.

1 Make a tracing paper copy of the area shown inside the dashed lines on Figure 3. Mark in the fronts, the isobars and the point marked X.

2 You are going to chart the movement of a fast-moving depression. Move the point marked X first to Y and then to Z. Each movement takes six hours, so at Y it is 12 noon, and at Z it is 6.00 p.m. Do this now to see how the depression moves.

3 Write a weather forecast at 6.00 a.m. on 21 April for the next 12 hours, for each of the following:
a ferries in the Irish Sea
b climbers in Scotland
c holiday makers in the Lake District
d farmers in East Anglia
e an air-sea rescue helicopter flying due west from the south-west coast of Ireland.

WEATHER AND CLIMATE

As well as wet weather brought by depressions, the British Isles also experiences periods of dry weather. This is usually caused by the formation of areas of high pressure, called **anticyclones**.

Winter anticyclones

In winter, the cloudless skies often associated with an anticyclone allow heat to escape, cooling the ground rapidly at night and leading to the formation of frost. Fog can also be a problem as the cold air makes water vapour condense into droplets. The fog can linger long into the day until the heat of the sun is sufficient to evaporate it away.

Figure 1 **Weather conditions during a winter anticyclone**

Summer anticyclones

In summer, an anticyclone can bring very different weather. Whereas in a depression air is being lifted up, in an anticyclone air is descending. As the air descends, it warms up, causing any water in the air to evaporate. This prevents clouds from forming. With clear skies, all the sun's energy can reach the earth's surface, raising temperatures dramatically. If the anticyclone remains over the British Isles for several weeks, it produces a **heat wave**. One of the most notable heat waves in Britain occurred in 1976.

Figure 2 **Weather conditions during a summer anticyclone**

Figure 3 shows a summer anticyclone over the British Isles.

1 Compared to the weather map of a depression (page 101), what differences do you notice about:
   a the spacing of the isobars
   b the wind direction?

2 How strong do you think the winds are in an anticyclone? Why?

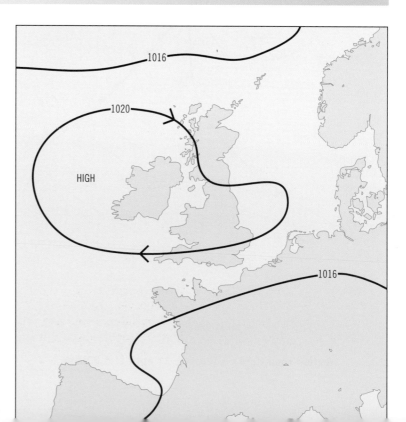

▶ Figure 3 **A summer anticyclone over the British Isles**

Understanding synoptic charts and weather symbols

Using the instruments described in unit 6.1 we can record the elements of the weather from day to day. Weather forecasters use synoptic charts, or weather maps, to plot the conditions of certain areas of the world at any one time. Figure 3 on page 101 and Figure 3 (page 102) are two examples of such charts.

From these charts and Figure 4 below, someone with little knowledge of weather symbols can easily understand six different elements of the weather: pressure, from the isobars, as well as temperature, cloud cover, type of precipitation, wind direction and wind speed from the actual symbol itself.

Figure 4 **Official weather symbols**

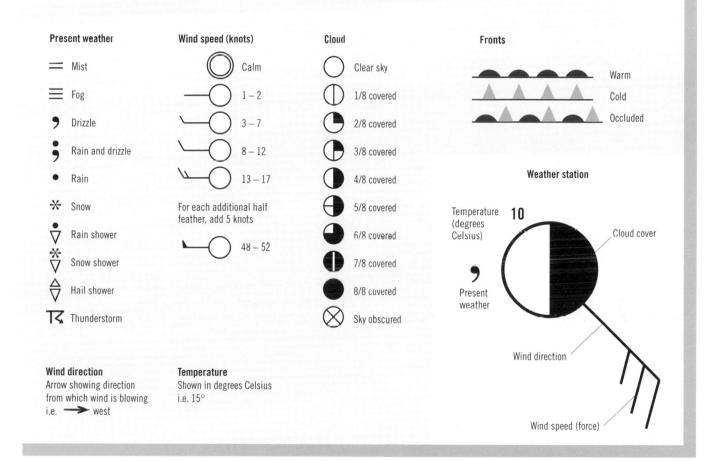

3 The weather conditions in a depression and anticyclone are very different. Make an enlarged copy and complete Figure 5 to show the main differences.

4 Using the weather symbols on Figure 4, describe the six weather conditions.

5 Draw two weather symbols and add the following weather information:
   a Place Y: temperature: – 30°C; present weather: fog; wind direction: NE; wind speed: calm; cloud cover: 3/8 covered.
   b Place Z: temperature: – 6°C; present weather: rain; wind direction: SW; wind speed: 48 – 52 knots; cloud cover: 7/8 covered.

Figure 5 **Comparing depressions and anticyclones**

	Depression	Anticyclone	
Pressure			
Cloud cover			
Wind direction			
Wind speed			
Precipitation			
Temperature		*Summer*	*Winter*

The global hydrological cycle

Hydrology is the study of water. The **hydrological cycle** (or water cycle) is the continuous transfer of water from the oceans into the atmosphere, onto land, then back into the oceans. This cycle is vital in ensuring the earth has a continuous supply of fresh water.

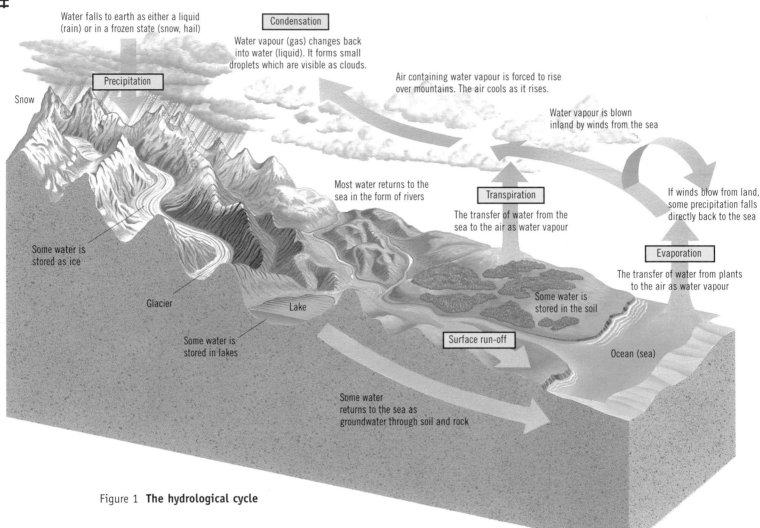

Water falls to earth as either a liquid (rain) or in a frozen state (snow, hail)

Condensation

Water vapour (gas) changes back into water (liquid). It forms small droplets which are visible as clouds.

Air containing water vapour is forced to rise over mountains. The air cools as it rises.

Precipitation

Snow

Water vapour is blown inland by winds from the sea

Most water returns to the sea in the form of rivers

Transpiration

The transfer of water from the sea to the air as water vapour

If winds blow from land, some precipitation falls directly back to the sea

Evaporation

The transfer of water from plants to the air as water vapour

Some water is stored as ice

Glacier

Lake

Some water is stored in lakes

Some water is stored in the soil

Surface run-off

Some water is stored in the soil

Ocean (sea)

Some water returns to the sea as groundwater through soil and rock

Figure 1 **The hydrological cycle**

The recycling of water in the hydrological cycle should mean that water is a sustainable resource, one that does not run out. However, sometimes there are interruptions to the cycle. These can either create a surplus of water on the land, causing **flooding**, or a shortage of water, causing **drought**. Interruptions can be natural or brought about by human activity.

Figure 2 **Hydrology terms**

Precipitation deposition of water from the atmosphere in solid (snow, hail) or liquid form (rain, dew)

Condensation formation of liquid water droplets from water vapour around particles of dust, soot, etc.

Surface run-off the portion of the hydrological cycle connecting precipitation with channel flow. It occurs when ground becomes saturated and can no longer absorb water

Transpiration plant 'perspiration', or the loss of water vapour mainly from the cells of leaves

Evaporation take up of water vapour into the atmosphere from exposed water surfaces, including water loss from lakes, rivers, clouds, saturated soil and plant surfaces. It does not include transpiration loss from plants.

On a global scale, there is enough water to supply each human being. Yet, so often extreme shortages or extreme surpluses of water can have disasterous effects on many lives. These situations are due to imbalances in the hydrological cycle on a more localised scale.

When the rate of precipitation exceeds the rate of run-off, flooding can occur. Bangladesh is a country that suffers from excessive flooding.

When the rate of evaporation exceeds the rate of precipitation, drought can occur. Sudan is a country that suffers from excessive drought.

Figure 3 **Flooding in Bangladesh after the cyclone**

1 Study Figure 5. Using an atlas, locate the areas of the globe most at risk from flooding and those most at risk from drought.

2 Find out about a major flood event. Consider the pattern of precipitation before and during the flood, its intensity, its duration and the effect it had on people and their livelihoods. Could anything have been done to prevent the flood?

Figure 4 **Drought in the Sudan** All the water had evaporated from the dried up river bed

▼ Figure 5 **Areas most at risk from flooding and drought**

Lena

Yenisey

Rhine

Brahmaputra

Mississippi

Ganges   Yangtze

Nile   Indus

Tropic of Cancer

Irrawaddy

Orinoco

Mekong

Amazon

Equator

Tropic of Capricorn

Parana

Colorado

Negro

Key

▢ Areas where severe drought may occur

▢ Major river flood plains

The river valley system

The **river valley system** is the part of the global hydrological cycle that operates on land. It operates as a **system** because it consists of **inputs** (entering the system), **flows** or **transfers** (moving through the system), **stores** (held within the system) and **outputs** (leaving the system).

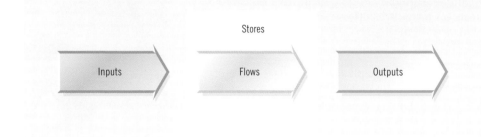

Stores

Inputs → Flows → Outputs

Figure 1 **A simple system**

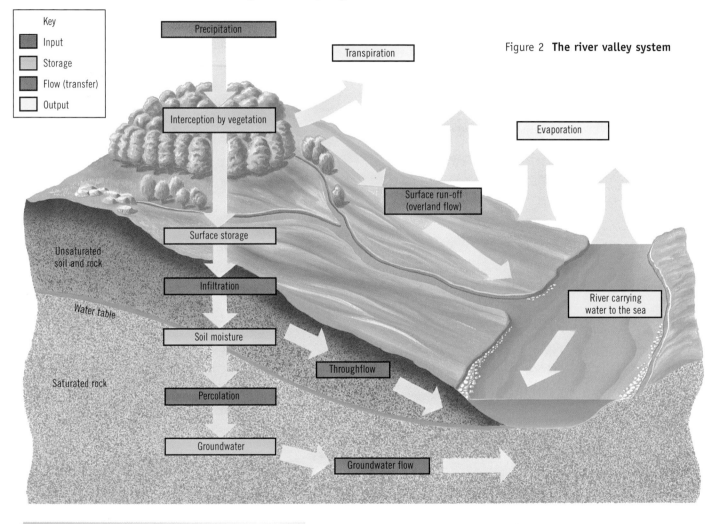

Figure 2 **The river valley system**

Key
- Input
- Storage
- Flow (transfer)
- Output

Precipitation

Transpiration

Interception by vegetation

Evaporation

Surface run-off (overland flow)

Surface storage

Unsaturated soil and rock

Infiltration

Water table

Soil moisture

River carrying water to the sea

Saturated rock

Throughflow

Percolation

Groundwater

Groundwater flow

Figure 3 River valley system terms

Percolation movement of water downwards through soil or rock in the unsaturated zone

Groundwater water stored in rocks following percolation

Infiltration movement of water into soil surface and underlying rocks

Saturation when the soil or rock is full of moisture and can store no more

Water table the level at which saturation occurs in the soil or rock

1 Copy Figure 4 to show the river valley system. Place the words on the right into the correct blank boxes.

2 How will the river valley system be affected by the following conditions:
   a a very hot, dry summer?
   b a long, cold winter with sub-zero temperatures for several weeks?
   c the removal of all trees and plants?
   d a reservoir or dam near to the source of the river?

3 How might a town, with lots of concrete and tarmac surfaces, affect the natural flows of the river valley system?

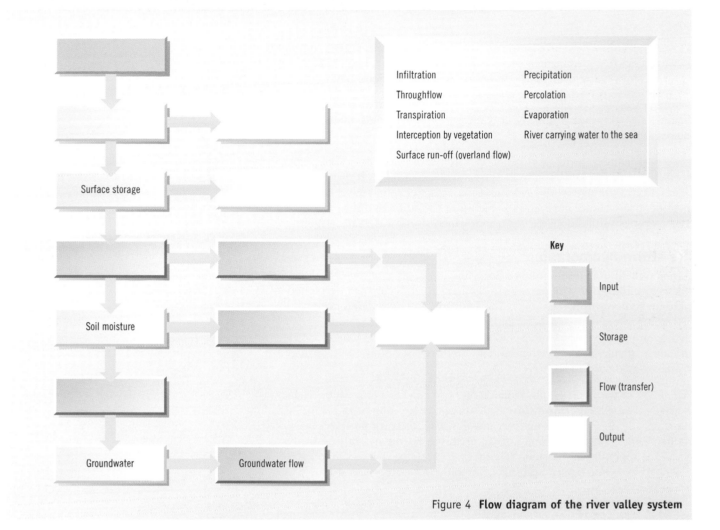

Infiltration   Precipitation

Throughflow   Percolation

Transpiration   Evaporation

Interception by vegetation   River carrying water to the sea

Surface run-off (overland flow)

Surface storage

Soil moisture

Groundwater   Groundwater flow

Key

Input

Storage

Flow (transfer)

Output

Figure 4 **Flow diagram of the river valley system**

Figure 5 **Profiles for different types of rivers**

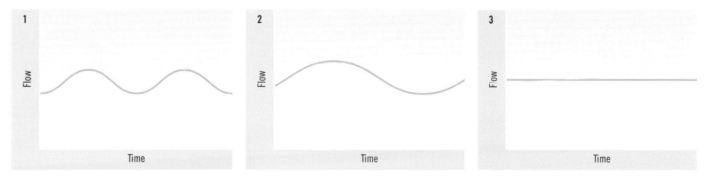

4 Match rivers A, B and C described in Figure 5 with the three graphs above it. Give reasons for the match you have chosen.

5 What other information might be useful in determining which graph belongs to which river?

6 For each river, describe how its inputs, flows and outputs have been affected.

Types of rivers

River A – usually high flow, but has recently experienced a long summer drought

River B – experiences very high flows during storms and snow melt

River C – flow is regulated by a reservoir and dam along its course

Floods

A river will flood when its **discharge** (the volume of water passing through it each second) is greater than the capacity of the river channel. Excess water flows over the river banks and onto the adjacent flood plain.

Discharge can be calculated by finding the cross-sectional area of a river channel and the water's velocity. It is measured at gauging stations, in cubic metres per second or **cumecs**.

A storm is likely to produce flooding if storm water runs off quickly into rivers and streams. This rapidly increases discharge to a level that the river channel can no longer carry. A number of factors encourage this rapid increase in discharge, including the nature of the storm and the characteristics of the drainage basin into which storm water falls (Figure 4).

The storm hydrograph

During and after a storm, a river's discharge increases as it receives extra water from the storm. The change in discharge that occurs can be plotted as a **storm hydrograph** (Figure 1). The **lag time**, the time difference between peak rainfall and peak discharge, can then be calculated. Hydrographs are vital in understanding how and why river floods happen and are particularly useful when normal discharge is disturbed by a sudden storm or rapid snowmelt.

The shape of the hydrograph depends on how quickly storm water reaches the river channel. **Overland flow** is the fastest route. If most of the rainwater travels into rivers and streams this way, then lag time will be short and discharge will rise and fall rapidly. Both the **rising** and **falling limbs** of the hydrograph will be steep (Figure 2). This shape of hydrograph is described as being 'peaky' and it is commonly associated with storms which produce floods.

Where little overland flow occurs and more water reaches the river channel through the soil (**throughflow**) or from groundwater stores (**baseflow**), discharge will rise more slowly. This is because it takes longer for storm water to percolate through the soil and into the bedrock before it reaches rivers and streams. Lag time will be longer and there will be a lower maximum discharge with little risk of flooding. The hydrograph will be flatter and less 'peaky' (Figure 2). Eventually, if there is not another storm soon after, discharge returns to the same level as before the storm, supplied only by baseflow.

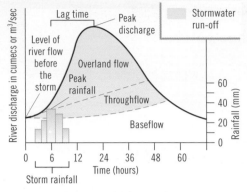

Figure 1 **The storm hydrograph**

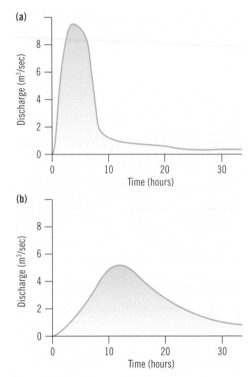

Figure 2 **The shape of the hydrograph**

Figure 3 **The River Severn and the River Wye**

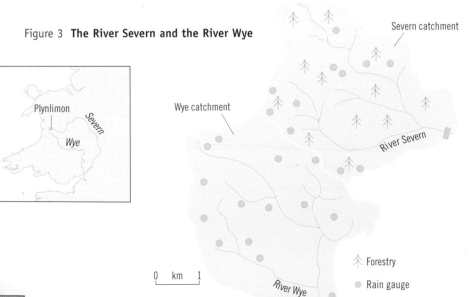

Forestry

Rain gauge

River gauging station

River discharge (cumecs)		Hours after start of rainstorm
River Severn	River Wye	
1.0	1.1	2
1.1	1.3	4
1.2	2.1	6
1.3	2.9	8
1.5	2.5	10
1.55	2.2	12
1.6	1.9	14
1.6	1.7	16
1.5	1.5	18
1.4	1.3	20
1.35	1.2	22
1.3	1.1	24

Figure 4 Factors that affect a river's discharge

Factor	Effect on river discharge
Precipitation	
Type	If precipitation falls as snow, it may be several days or weeks before it melts and runs off into streams. If melting is rapid and the ground beneath is frozen, large amounts of overland flow by meltwater can cause flooding.
Intensity	Intense rain in a thunderstorm may fall too rapidly for the ground to absorb it all. Excess water will run quickly overland into streams, rapidly increasing discharge.
Drainage basin characteristics	
Rock type	Permeable rocks such as limestones (including chalk) and sandstone readily absorb water and reduce levels of overland flow. Instead, storm water reaches the river channel more slowly by flowing through the rocks as baseflow. Flooding is more likely in catchments where the underlying rock is impermeable, such as granite. Impermeable rocks do not absorb water nor allow it to pass through them.
Soil	Sandy soils contain large air spaces which encourage water to infiltrate into the surface and so discourage overland flow. Rapid run-off is more likely in an area where the soil has a high clay content. Clay particles are very small and fit together tightly so rainwater takes much longer to infiltrate the surface. Peat soils have a high water content and so become saturated quickly during a storm, producing overland flow.
Slope gradient	On horizontal or gently sloping ground, rainwater has time to infiltrate the surface and little overland flow occurs. Steep slopes encourage water to run quickly downhill towards the nearest stream, particularly when the underlying rock or soil is impermeable. However, gradient may be relatively unimportant where the rock or soil is very permeable.
Previous weather conditions	Whether a storm produces flooding or not may depend on how much rain there had been in the days before. It takes time for previous storm water to drain away and, if the soil is still wet from earlier rain, it will quickly become saturated when new rain falls and so act as an impermeable surface. Soil that has dried out after weeks without rain will quickly absorb new rainfall and so prevent overland flow.
Land use	**Vegetation** tends to slow down the passage of storm water into streams by intercepting it as it falls. Tree roots obstruct the movement of water over the surface and encourage infiltration. This lowers the risk of flooding, although the effect is reduced in winter if trees have no leaves, or in a wheatfield after the crop has been harvested. The concrete and tarmac surfaces of **urban areas** are very impermeable and encourage rainwater to flow rapidly along the ground into drains. This water is transferred into the nearest river, quickly raising it to flood height. **Agriculture** can also affect the likelihood of flooding. If the plough lines in a field run downhill, they act like a draining board, quickly channelling rainwater downslope into a river. Heavy farm machinery such as tractors can compact the soil in a field making the surface impermeable and encouraging overland flow.

1 State the meanings of the following terms:
 a river discharge
 b storm hydrograph
 c lag time.

2 Figure 2 shows two contrasting hydrograph shapes, A and B. Identify which of the two hydrographs is most likely to correspond to each of the following situations. Give reasons for your answers.
 a an area of sandy soil
 b a steep upland area with outcrops of granite
 c an area that receives a storm after a dry summer
 d a sudden period of warm weather after heavy snow
 e an area of arable farming after the harvest.

3 **a** Using graph paper, draw hydrographs for the rivers Severn and Wye using the data given in Figure 3.
 b Describe and explain the differences in the shapes of your hydrographs.

Case study | Bangladesh

Bangladesh is one of the world's poorest countries. Nearly all of its 120 million people live in the countryside and rely on intensive rice farming for their livelihood. The country lies at the northern end of the Bay of Bengal and at the mouth of several large rivers. About 80% of Bangladesh consists of the flat, low-lying floodplain and deltas of the rivers Ganges, Jamuna (called the Brahmaputra in India) and Meghna (Figure 3). These rivers play a major role in life in Bangladesh and bring severe flooding every year, although they are not the only source of flooding.

River floods

The rivers that flow into Bangladesh deposit silt at their mouths. This has produced a huge delta that extends out into the Bay of Bengal. The delta is made up of many flat islands, most no more than one metre above sea level, divided by river channels. The fertile alluvial soil found on these islands is ideal for growing rice and attracts many farmers to cultivate it. The heavy monsoon rain that falls from June to September across the Himalayas runs off into streams and then into the large rivers that enter Bangladesh. Snowmelt in the Himalayas can add additional water, and flooding is most likely to occur at this time as river channels cannot cope with the dramatic increase in water volume. Silt deposited in the river channels raises the river bed and worsens the problem. This flooding is beneficial if it occurs at a time when farmers are ready to sow their rice but it can be harmful to agriculture if it occurs late in August, when it will damage crops at a critical stage of growth.

Coastal floods

Tropical cyclones (hurricanes) over the Bay of Bengal in late summer bring strong winds gusting up to 180 kph. They whip up large waves which are then funnelled northwards by the shape of the coastline up the Bay of Bengal. Nearer Bangladesh, the sea becomes shallower due to the large amount of silt deposited there by rivers like the Ganges. This causes the waves to grow in height, creating a **storm surge**. The surge may be 4 m high, topped by waves of another 4 m. The wall of water then sweeps inland across the low-lying islands of the delta, causing enormous damage to a poor and defenceless population.

10th September 1988

Bangladesh counts cost of floods

Faisal Ibrahim in Dhaka

Over 2000 people have lost their lives in Bangladesh following some of the worst floods in living memory. About 60% of this low-lying country has been submerged, including two-thirds of the capital, Dhaka, and up to 7 million homes are thought to have been damaged or destroyed. In total, 45 million people could have been affected. The floods followed exceptionally heavy monsoon rain over northern India and Nepal, causing the Ganges, Jamuna and Meghna Rivers all to rise simultaneously and burst their embankments. The country's road and rail network have been severely damaged, with hundreds of bridges washed away, cutting off parts of the country. Farmers have lost their livestock and estimates suggest that this year's rice harvest could be two million tonnes lower than last year. Many farmers cultivate the temporary islands of sediment that build up each year in the River Jamuna but these islands are now several feet under water. Rescue services have been slow to respond because of the destruction to roads and hospitals. There are now fears of an outbreak of cholera as many rural areas have found their wells polluted with river water.

▲ Figure 1 **The 1988 floods**

▼ Figure 2 **Frequent flood damage destroys homes**

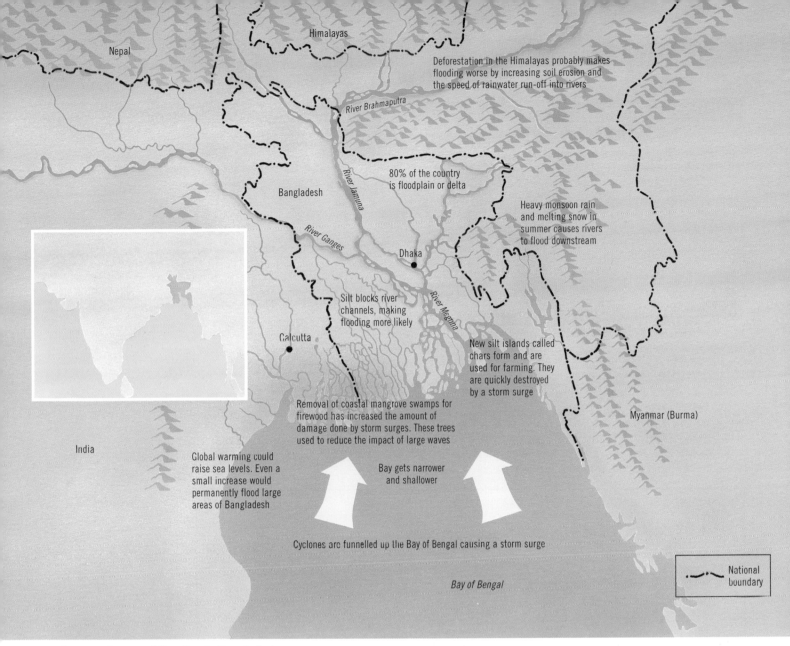

Deforestation in the Himalayas probably makes flooding worse by increasing soil erosion and the speed of rainwater run-off into rivers

80% of the country is floodplain or delta

Heavy monsoon rain and melting snow in summer causes rivers to flood downstream

Silt blocks river channels, making flooding more likely

New silt islands called chars form and are used for farming. They are quickly destroyed by a storm surge

Removal of coastal mangrove swamps for firewood has increased the amount of damage done by storm surges. These trees used to reduce the impact of large waves

Global warming could raise sea levels. Even a small increase would permanently flood large areas of Bangladesh

Bay gets narrower and shallower

Cyclones are funnelled up the Bay of Bengal causing a storm surge

Bay of Bengal

National boundary

Figure 3 **Causes of flooding in Bangladesh**

The Flood Action Plan

A number of flood control measures have been carried out since the 1960s. A Flood Action Plan (FAP) was started in 1990, funded by the World Bank and developed countries. It involves:

● raising and strengthening 260 km of embankments along the Jamuna

● allowing controlled flooding. Land is divided into compartments surrounded by embankments. These can be flooded using sluice gates, thereby taking pressure off areas downstream.

● improved flood forecasting using an increased network of radar stations across the country to monitor the weather and transmit warnings

● coastal embankments and replanting of mangrove swamps

● disaster preparation – building escape centres on high ground, specially designed school buildings and elevated roads.

Other schemes include expensive dam construction upstream and dredging channels to remove silt. However, this is also expensive and channels would soon become choked once again.

1 Name the three largest rivers in Bangladesh.

2 How do each of the following help produce flooding in Bangladesh:
  a climate?
  b relief?
  c silt?

3 What human activity may make flooding more likely?

4 What started the 1988 floods (Figure 3)?

5 What effect did the 1988 floods have on:
  a settlement?
  b transport?
  c agriculture?

6 What problems do you think are encountered when trying to reduce flooding in Bangladesh?

The cost of dams

Case study | The Three Gorges Dam, China

The Yangtze River is the third longest river in the world and one of the two great rivers of China. It rises high on the Tibetan plateau of the Himalayas and flows into the East China Sea at Shanghai. Throughout China's history, the Yangtze has been a source of both life and death; it has provided water and fertile silt for rice cultivation along its banks but it has also flooded large areas annually (Figure 1).

Plans have now been approved to build the world's largest hydro-electric dam on the Yangtze in an area called the Three Gorges, north of Yichang (Figure 2). The dam's 26 turbines will provide 14% of China's electricity demand. It will be the largest HEP project in the world and will stand 185 m high. The scheme will create a reservoir 600 km long (roughly the same as from London to Glasgow), storing 39 billion cubic metres of water.

At a time when China is striving to develop economically, many people see the Three Gorges scheme as vital. Apart from the large quantities of hydro-electric power it will generate, the dam should also prevent the flooding from which so many inhabitants of the Yangtze's floodplain have suffered. However, opinions about the dam are heavily divided.

Key
Severe flooding
Occasional flooding

Figure 1 **Areas subject to severe flooding in China**

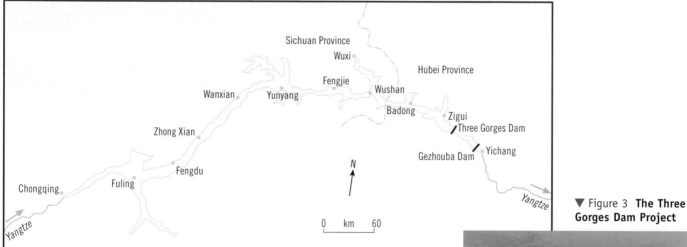

Figure 2 **Location of the Three Gorges Dam**

▼ Figure 3 **The Three Gorges Dam Project**

The River Yangtze and its floodplain

● The Yangtze floodplain provides 66% of China's rice and supports 400 million people.

● The river drains an area of 1.9 million sq.km and discharges 700 cubic km annually.

● Most floods in recent years have come from rivers which join the Yangtze below the site of the Three Gorges dam.

● The region is vulnerable to earthquakes and landslides are common.

● Up to 530 million tonnes of silt are carried through the gorge annually. The first dam to be built on the river lost its capacity due to silting up within seven years.

The Three Gorges Dam Project

- The project will take up to 20 years to build and could cost US $70 billion, possibly diverting funds from other developments.

- Several large towns, including Wanxian (population 140 000) and Fuling (population 80 000) will be flooded.

- It will provide electricity for Shanghai, one of the world's largest cities with a population of over 13 million, and Chongqing, population 3 million, an area earmarked for economic development.

- The dam could protect up to 10 million people from flooding.

- More than 1.2 million people will have to be resettled to make way for the dam and lake. Much of the land used for resettlement is over 800 m above sea level, where the climate is colder, the slopes steeper and the soil barely able to support farming.

- The 90-metre rise in water level created by the dam will allow shipping above the Three Gorges and turn the rapids in the gorge into a lake.

- The dam is likely to trap sediment behind it, eventually causing the reservoir to silt up. Areas downstream would be deprived of sediment.

- The 18 000 megawatts of energy generated will enable China to reduce its dependency on coal and contribute to a reduction in the emission of greenhouse gases.

- Landslides on the steep gorge sides could generate surge waves which would overtop the dam.

- The dam will quickly pay for itself from the electricity generated.

- There are concerns that the dam will interfere with aquatic life, including the already endangered Siberian crane.

Figure 4 **The environmental impact of large dams**

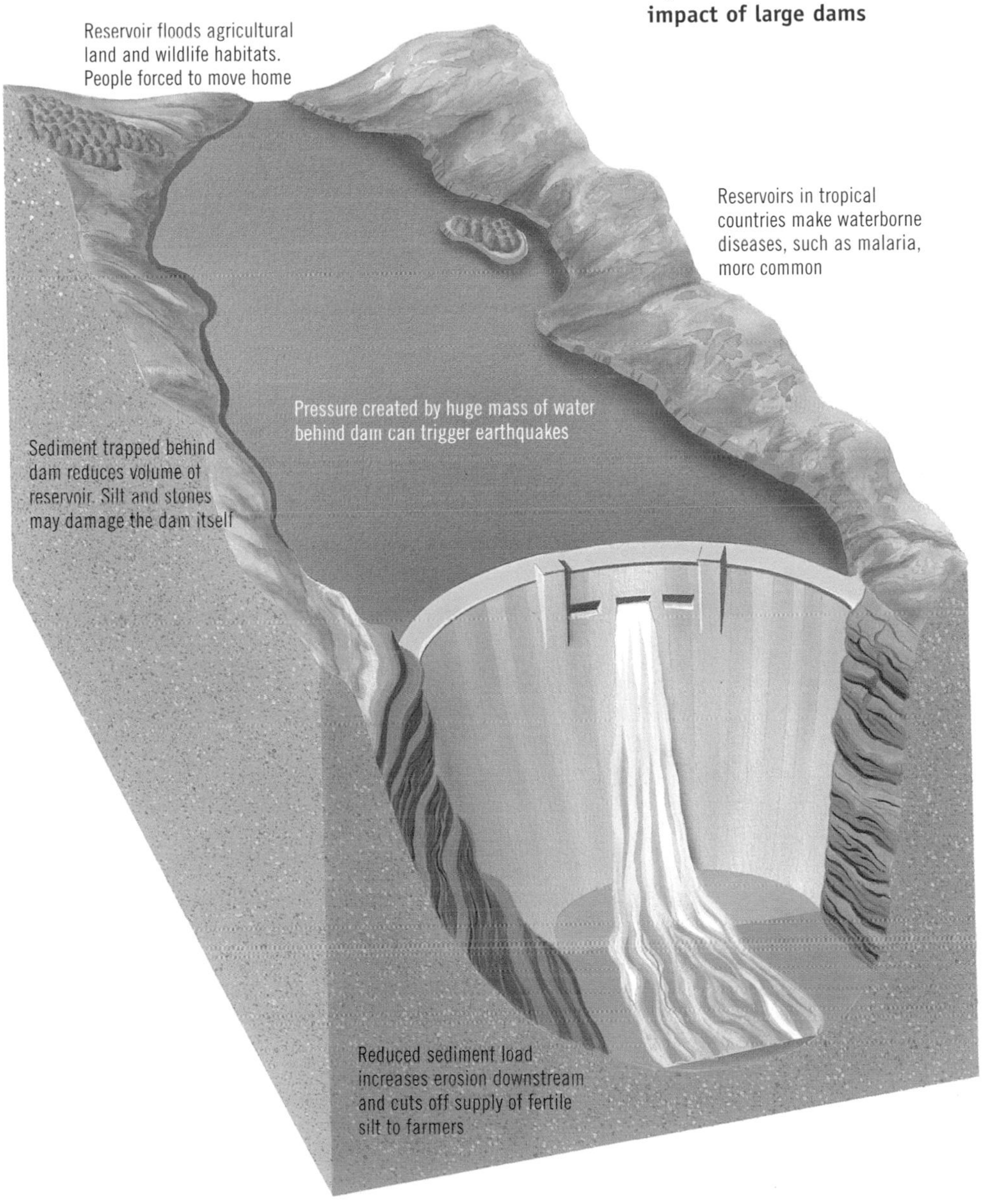

Reservoir floods agricultural land and wildlife habitats. People forced to move home

Reservoirs in tropical countries make waterborne diseases, such as malaria, more common

Pressure created by huge mass of water behind dam can trigger earthquakes

Sediment trapped behind dam reduces volume of reservoir. Silt and stones may damage the dam itself

Reduced sediment load increases erosion downstream and cuts off supply of fertile silt to farmers

1 Construct a two-column table like the one shown. Complete it by identifying the possible advantages and disadvantages of the Three Gorges Dam Scheme.

The Yangtze River Three Gorges Dam Project

Advantages	Disadvantages

2 Imagine you are one of the following people: a Chinese government official, an environmentalist, a peasant farmer or a resident of Wanxian. Write a speech stating whether you are for or against the Three Gorges scheme, and your reasons for your choice.

3 What could China do about flood management if the Three Gorges scheme did not go ahead?

7.6 River processes

Approximately 95% of a river's energy is used to keep the river flowing. As water moves over the bed and banks of a river, friction slows the river down; most of the river's energy is used in overcoming this friction. You might expect a river in its upper course, where the slope of the river bed is steep, to flow faster than a river further downstream. However, the upland river has a small rough channel and uses up more of its energy in overcoming friction, whereas less of the water in a lowland river is being slowed down by the bed and the banks. The result is that the average speed of a mountain stream is very similar to that of a larger river flowing over lowland.

The 5% of energy remaining after a river has overcome friction is used to wear away or erode material from the bed and banks. This material is then transported downstream. If there is a decrease in a river's energy (for example, entering a lake or flowing out onto a wide floodplain), then material may be dropped on to the river bed – a process called **deposition**.

River erosion

A river can erode material from its bed and banks in three main ways:

- **Abrasion** – Moving water throws particles it is carrying against the bed and banks of the river which dislodges more material.

- **Hydraulic action** – The sheer force of water pounding into the bed and banks can dislodge material.

- **Attrition** – Particles being carried downstream knock against each other, wearing each other down. This results in smaller, rounder particles as you move downstream.

Figure 1 **Potholes created through the swirling action of the water and abrasion**

River transportation

Rivers transport material in four main ways:

- **Solution** – Some minerals (particularly in limestone areas) dissolve easily in water and are not visible to the naked eye.

- **Suspension** – As the speed or velocity of a river increases, it is able to pick up and carry larger and larger particles in its flow. Where particles are carried along in the flow and are not in contact with the river bed, they are said to be travelling in suspension.

- **Saltation** – Heavier particles may not be held in the flow all the time but may be bounced along the bed.

- **Traction** – The heaviest particles are rolled along the bed. Such particles may only be moved when the river has a large volume of water in it.

River landforms

The processes of erosion, transportation and deposition are capable of creating a number of distinct landforms. Figure 2 shows one such landform – a waterfall.

▲ Figure 2 **The Huangguoshu Falls, south-west China**

◀ Figure 3 **Formation of a waterfall**

Hard rock

Softer rock undercut by the power of the water

As softer rock is undercut, the harder rock above eventually collapses. The waterfall retreats leaving the river to flow in a sleep-sided gorge

Water reaches the bottom of the waterfall with such force that a plunge pool is carved out

Figure 4 **River Cuckmere meanders over the flood plain near its mouth**

Meandering rivers

In lowland areas, a river often flows across a wide floodplain (Figure 4). In order to balance its energy, a river frequently swings from side to side in a process called meandering. The curved bends of the river are called **meanders**. Meanders are not static, but are constantly changing and shifting position as the processes of erosion, transportation and deposition work.

The formation of a meander

A meander is a bend in a river's course. As the river flows around the bend, the fastest water tends to flow on the outside. This water erodes the outside of the river bank to form a **river cliff**. Deposition takes place in the shallower water of the inside of the river bend, forming a **point bar** which, with time, builds up to create a gentle **slip-off slope**.

It is not fully understood how a meander is formed. During the early stages of formation, the erosion at the outside of the bend causes it to grow in size. This makes the river bed less steep and so slows the speed of the river down. Eventually, the river is travelling slowly enough for erosion to stop. The meander is now said to be 'in balance' with the amount of water flowing down the river.

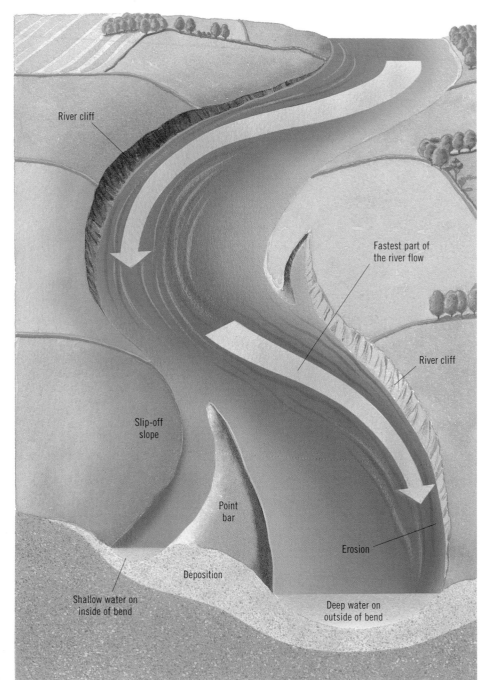

River cliff

Fastest part of the river flow

River cliff

Slip-off slope

Point bar

Erosion

Deposition

Shallow water on inside of bend

Deep water on outside of bend

▶ Figure 5 **Formation of a meander**

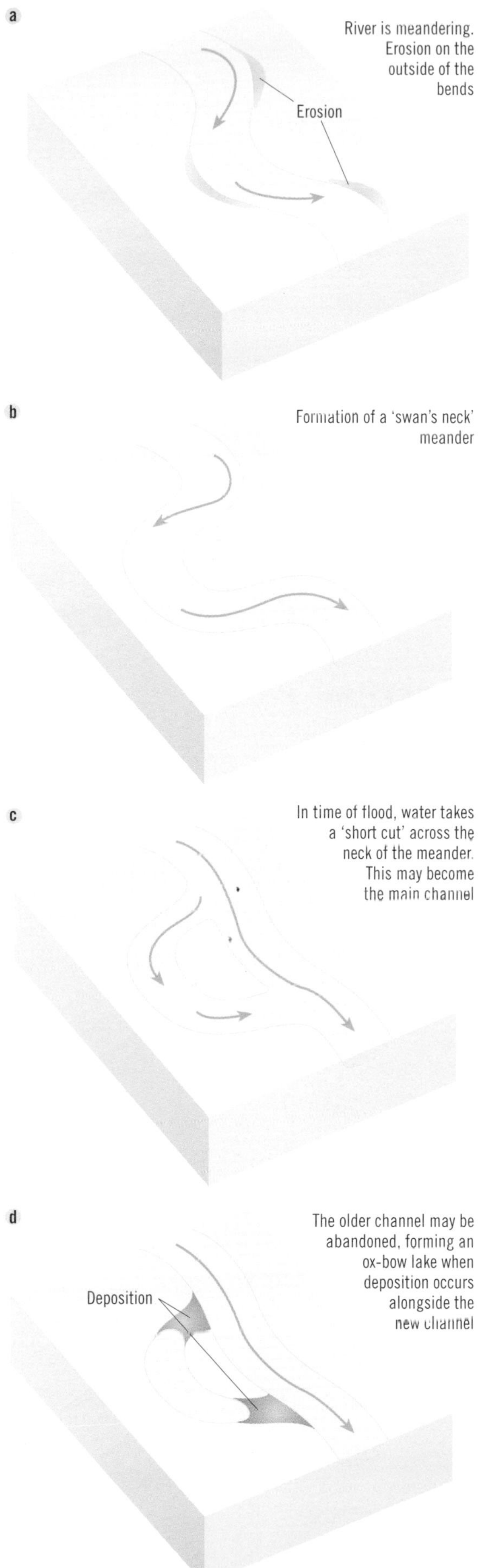

a
River is meandering. Erosion on the outside of the bends
Erosion
b
Formation of a 'swan's neck' meander
c
In time of flood, water takes a 'short cut' across the neck of the meander. This may become the main channel
d
The older channel may be abandoned, forming an ox-bow lake when deposition occurs alongside the new channel
Deposition

Figure 7 **Formation of an ox-bow lake**

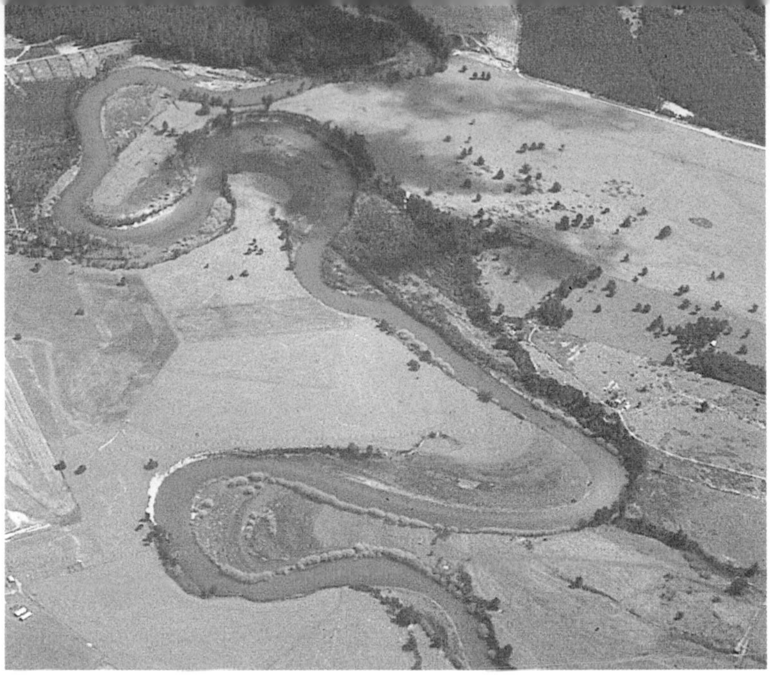

Figure 6 **A 'swan's neck' meander**

1 Look at the data in the table.

Measurements of river particles collected from source to mouth of a river

Particle size (mm)	Distance from source (km)	Particle size (mm)	Distance from source (km)
155	1	77	9
147	2	64	10
139	3	69	11
121	4	61	12
136	5	53	13
97	6	56	14
86	7	41	15
91	8		

a On a copy of the graph below, produce a scattergraph to show how particle size varies with distance downstream.

180
160
140
120
100
80
60
40
20
0
Particle size (mm)
0 1 2 3 4 5 6 7 8 9 10 11
Distance from source (km)

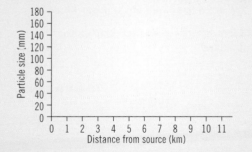

b Draw in a line of best-fit.

c Explain what your graph shows and say why this is the case.

2 Copy the diagram shown below. Mark on it where you would expect to find erosion and deposition taking place.

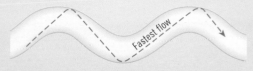

Fastest flow

3 Figure 6 shows a photograph of a meander. Make a sketch of the photograph and mark in the main features. What evidence is there that erosion is taking place?

Water management on the River Rhine

The Rhine is one of the world's greatest commercial rivers, with 10 000 ships carrying some 250 million tonnes of cargo. The Rhine is a navigable river (can be safely travelled by ships) for over 900 km of its 1320 km length. It is the most important link in Europe's inland waterway system, and its importance should increase even more with the completion of the Main-Danube canal and the opening up of Eastern European countries.

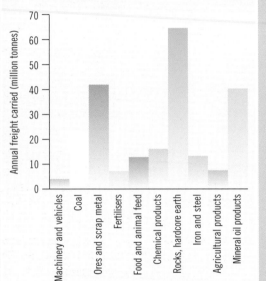

▲ Figure 1 **Trade on the River Rhine**

▶ Figure 2 **The catchment area of the River Rhine**

▼ Figure 3 **Hydro-electric power stations on the Rhine in Switzerland**

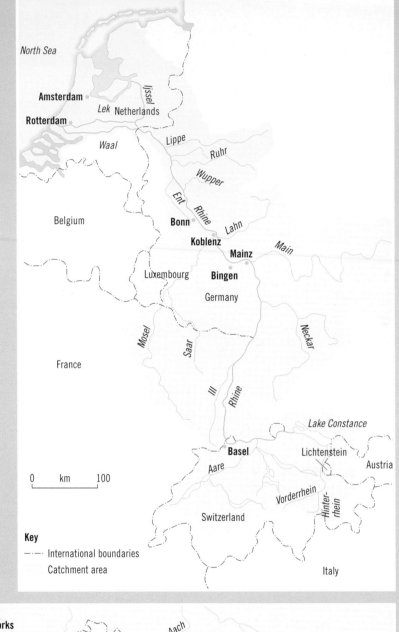

Key

– · – · – International boundaries

Catchment area

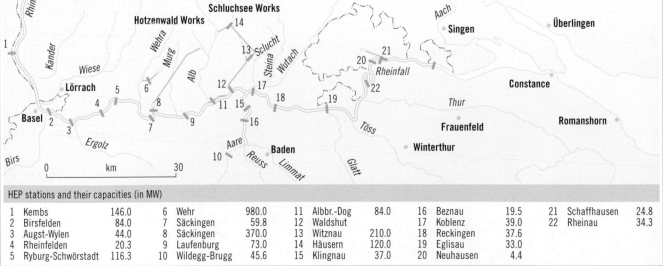

	HEP stations and their capacities (in MW)										
1	Kembs	146.0	6	Wehr	980.0	11	Albbr.-Dog	84.0	16	Beznau	19.5
2	Birsfelden	84.0	7	Säckingen	59.8	12	Waldshut		17	Koblenz	39.0
3	Augst-Wylen	44.0	8	Säckingen	370.0	13	Witznau	210.0	18	Reckingen	37.6
4	Rheinfelden	20.3	9	Laufenburg	73.0	14	Häusern	120.0	19	Eglisau	33.0
5	Ryburg-Schwörstadt	116.3	10	Wildegg-Brugg	45.6	15	Klingnau	37.0	20	Neuhausen	4.4

21	Schaffhausen	24.8
22	Rheinau	34.3

Figure 4 **Tourism on the Rhine**

Figure 5 **Industrialisation on the Rhine**

ACTIVITIES 1

1 Write a short paragraph to explain why the River Rhine is considered to be such an important river for European trade.

2 **a** Using Figure 2 and an atlas, describe the physical characteristics of the area in which the sources of most of the Rhine's tributaries are found?
b What problems may this cause at certain times of the year?

3 **a** Using Figure 1, list the main types of cargo, in order of importance from greatest to least, that are carried along the Rhine.
b Despite being a relatively slow form of transport, why do you think water transport is favoured for such cargoes?
c It takes seven days to travel from Rotterdam to Basel, but only three days from Basel to Rotterdam. Why is this the case?
d Basel is the head of navigation – the furthestmost point upstream that a ship can safely travel. Using an atlas, why do you think that it is impossible for ships to travel further upstream?

4 Using Figure 3 and an atlas, describe the conditions that allow so many hydro-electric power stations to be built on the section of the Rhine between Basel and Lake Constance.

Controlling Rhine water

The Rhine is a river that is difficult to control. In the mountains it is fast-flowing, with large variations in its seasonal flow. After Basel, it travels more slowly, carrying with it large amounts of silt which build up and force it to change course. Historically, the river overtopped its banks following autumn rains and spring snow thaws. However, much of the river bank meadows and marshes soaked up the floodwater.

In the last 150 years or so, this river bank scenery has been changed dramatically (Figure 1). Many other attempts have been made to control the floodwater (Figures 2 and 3).

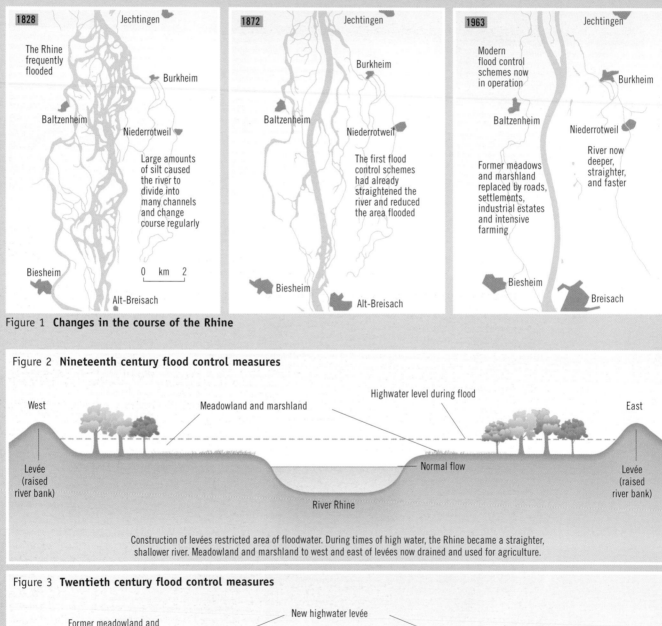

1828
Jechtingen
The Rhine frequently flooded
Burkheim
Baltzenheim
Niederrotweil
Large amounts of silt caused the river to divide into many channels and change course regularly
Biesheim
0 km 2
Alt-Breisach

1872
Jechtingen
Burkheim
Baltzenheim
Niederrotweil
The first flood control schemes had already straightened the river and reduced the area flooded
Biesheim
Alt-Breisach

1963
Jechtingen
Modern flood control schemes now in operation
Burkheim
Baltzenheim
Niederrotweil
River now deeper, straighter, and faster
Former meadows and marshland replaced by roads, settlements, industrial estates and intensive farming
Biesheim
Breisach

Figure 1 **Changes in the course of the Rhine**

Figure 2 **Nineteenth century flood control measures**

West | Meadowland and marshland | Highwater level during flood | East
Levée (raised river bank) | Normal flow | Levée (raised river bank)
River Rhine

Construction of levées restricted area of floodwater. During times of high water, the Rhine became a straighter, shallower river. Meadowland and marshland to west and east of levées now drained and used for agriculture.

Figure 3 **Twentieth century flood control measures**

Former meadowland and marshland | New highwater levée | Old highwater level
New highwater level | Old highwater levée
Normal flow
River Rhine

A deeper channel, reducing area flooded at highwater, allowing more land to be drained. A deeper channel encourages the river to flow faster.

The Mannheim News

Insurance Companies Refuse to Insure Riverside Properties

Some of Germany's leading insurance companies have announced they are unwilling to insure riverside properties in Mannheim and other German towns downstream on the Rhine. The recent number of massive floods are said to be responsible for this change in policy. A spokesperson for one insurance company said that blame for these floods rested with the engineering works upstream. The deeper, straighter Rhine river now transfers water 50% quicker than before its construction. In times of high flow, for example, when the alpine snow melts, the water arrives in Mannheim at the same time as the high flow from the River Neckar. Until a way is found to slow the transfer of water down the Rhine and its tributaries, then properties will have to foot the bill of flooding themselves.

Downstream of Mannheim, riverside homes in the old town of Cologne were also damaged

Figure 4 **Newspaper article**

ACTIVITIES 2

1 Look at Figure 1.
 a Describe the main changes that have taken place in each of the three maps.
 b What effect do you think straightening a river might have?
 c Why might it be a disadvantage to replace the riverbank meadows and marshes with roads, settlements and industrial estates?

2 Examine Figure 2. Explain why the nineteenth century flood control scheme, while successful in reducing floods, would not have been of benefit to shipping.

3 **a** Examine Figure 3. In what ways was the 1930s solution designed to improve upon the nineteenth century version?
 b What problems do think a faster flowing river might create?

4 Read the newspaper article above (Figure 4)
 a What were the main causes of the flooding in Mannheim?
 b Why are insurance companies not willing to insure riverside property?

5 It is suggested that 220 million m³ have to be stemmed above Mainz to help solve the flooding problems downstream. Various proposals have been suggested to help solve this flooding problem on the Rhine. These are listed below:
 ● construct barrages for power plants, which would hold back some 150 million m³ of water
 ● provide overflow areas for floodwater
 ● raise the height of levées
 ● allow some land currently used for settlements and industrial purposes to be returned to meadow and marshland to absorb the floods
 ● construct a network of dams on tributary rivers to delay high water flow reaching the Rhine.
 a For each of the above solutions, discuss the advantages and disadvantages of each scheme, focusing on the economic impact (cost, disruption to settlements and industry, benefits of power generation, etc.), the environmental impact, and the human costs and benefits.
 b From your analysis, decide which scheme or schemes you would implement and explain why.

Sewer of Europe?

The water of the Rhine is used by numerous industrial manufacturing processes, by farmers for irrigation, by power stations for cooling water and by 20 million people for drinking water. All of these discharge waste-water back into the river. In the early 1970s, the annual load of toxic pollutants was 24 million tonnes. Despite this, it was not until the Sandoz accident (Figure 1) that pollution of the Rhine was taken seriously. In 1987 the Rhine Action Programme was introduced (Figure 2).

The main pollutants of the Rhine

Nutrients – phosphates, nitrates found in detergents and in agricultural products were causing algal blooms

Salts – salty water, mainly from potash mines in Alsace

Heavy toxic metals – cadmium, lead and mercury all contaminate the food chain

Toxic products that are not degradable

Warm water discharged back into the Rhine from manufacturing and power station cooling can disturb fish and other forms of freshwater life, causing them to hatch out in winter when there is no food available to sustain life.

Figure 1 The Sandoz incident

On 31 October 1986, a fire broke-out in the Sandoz warehouse in Basel-Schweizerhalle. The warehouse contained over 1000 tonnes of pesticides, solvents and other chemicals. Over 40 million litres of water were needed to put the fire out. With such a large volume of water needed, not surprisingly, some of the chemicals were washed out into the Rhine. Seven days after the outbreak of the fire, the toxic chemicals had flowed as far as Cologne. It took two days for all the poisonous water to pass through Cologne. Dead fish were seen floating everywhere and waterworks operations had to be suspended.

Figure 2 The Rhine Action Programme

This programme aims to:
- return water species such as salmon to the Rhine
- enable Rhine water to be used as drinking water
- reduce the levels of harmful chemicals in the river bed so that the sediment can be dredged to allow easier shipping navigation and then be dumped on land or at sea.

To achieve this, the following measures have been introduced:
- strict laws have been passed, forcing industries to reduce discharges of toxic chemicals into the Rhine by 50% – 70%
- accidental discharges have been cut
- restoration of parts of the river (e.g. side channels off the main river) to encourage the return of water species
- a more advanced, quicker early warning system of any major accidents to enable action to be taken by authorities downstream.

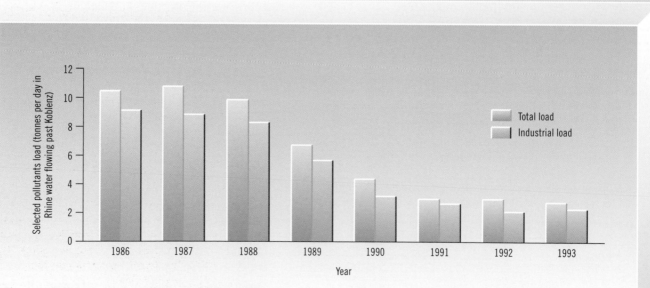

Figure 3 **Pollutant discharge into the Rhine, 1986 – 93**

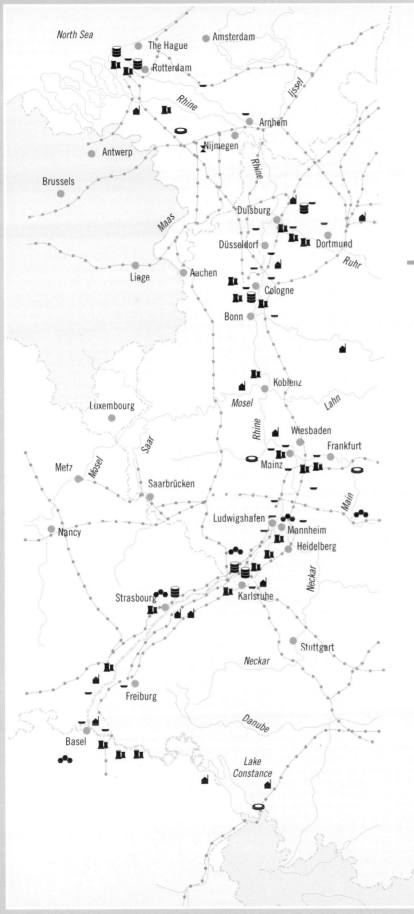

Figure 4 **Sources of pollution along the Rhine**

1 Study the graph and map in Figures 3 and 4.

a Where were the most polluted areas of the Rhine in 1975?

b What industries could be found along these sections?

c Is it generally true to say that areas where the greatest concentration of industry are found were the most polluted in 1975? (See Figure 5, next page.)

d For nearly the whole length of its course through the Netherlands in 1975, the Rhine was extremely polluted with all the pollutants shown in the key, yet the Netherlands does not have such a dense concentration of industry as other places further upstream. How can this be the case?

e Using Figures 2 and 5, describe the success that the Rhine Action Programme has had in reducing pollution in the Rhine?

f Which parts of the Rhine are now the most polluted?

2 Read Figures 1 and 2. If the Sandoz accident were to occur today, in what ways might its effects be different and why?

3 One major initiative is to restore salmon to the Rhine. Given that salmon migrate upstream, apart from pollution from toxic chemicals, what other obstacles might the fish have to overcome?

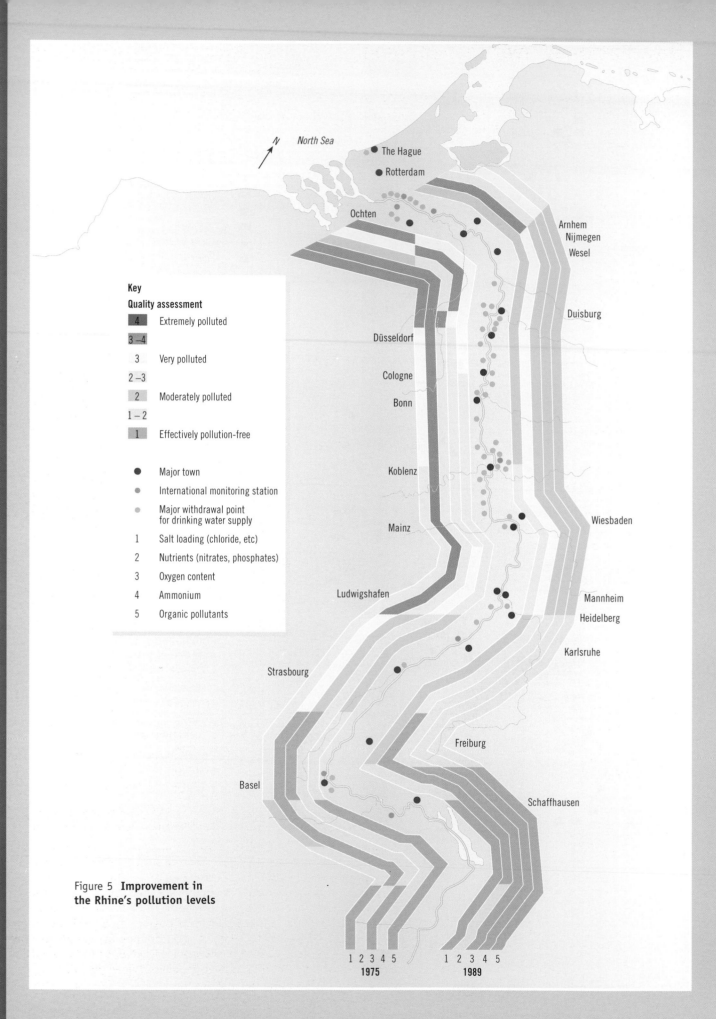

Key

Quality assessment

4   Extremely polluted

3–4

3   Very polluted

2–3

2   Moderately polluted

1–2

1   Effectively pollution-free

●   Major town

●   International monitoring station

●   Major withdrawal point
for drinking water supply

1   Salt loading (chloride, etc)

2   Nutrients (nitrates, phosphates)

3   Oxygen content

4   Ammonium

5   Organic pollutants

North Sea

The Hague

Rotterdam

Ochten

Arnhem
Nijmegen

Wesel

Duisburg

Düsseldorf

Cologne

Bonn

Koblenz

Wiesbaden

Mainz

Mannheim

Heidelberg

Ludwigshafen

Karlsruhe

Strasbourg

Freiburg

Basel

Schaffhausen

1 2 3 4 5
1975

1 2 3 4 5
1989

Figure 5   **Improvement in
the Rhine's pollution levels**

International river management

The Rhine flows through the heart of industrial Europe. It is the Netherlands, however, who most feel the need for urgent international cooperation in the management of the Rhine. In 1993 and 1995, floods from the river caused over $1 billion of damage. Most of the pollutants are already in the Rhine by the time it reaches the Netherlands, meaning that water purification plants are working to their full capacity. At present, the polluted mud at the bottom of the river has to be stored, as it is too contaminated to be dumped at sea. Along the Rhine and in the world's busiest port, Rotterdam, it has to be dredged to keep shipping channels clear. This costs the Dutch government $120 million a year. Various international bodies have been set up to help with the management of the Rhine; these have had some success (as we have seen with reductions in pollution). However, the Rhine is still heavily polluted in places, for example. Many experts are now calling for one overall organisation to be in charge of all aspects of managing the Rhine in all countries through which it flows.

Figure 1 **Industry near Ruhrort, on the banks of the Rhine**

ACTIVITY 4

Imagine you are a minister in the Netherlands government with special responsibility for the Rhine. Your government has decided to press for one international authority to be in charge of all aspects of water management along the Rhine. A special meeting has been called to discuss this proposal and you have been asked to write a speech to be given at the meeting, supporting this proposal. Your speech should include why you feel such a body is required. You should identify the major issues in order of importance that you feel need to be tackled if and when such an authority came into being. You should draw upon all the information given on these pages.

Energy is a vital component of our lives. Domestic heat, light and cooking, industrial processes, farming and transport across the world all require an energy supply. In More Developed Countries, the fossil fuels (coal, oil and natural gas) are the main energy sources (Figure 1).

Almost 80% of the electricity used in the UK is generated by burning fossil fuels. This process, as well as using up non-renewable resources, also makes a major contribution to atmospheric pollution. Most of the remaining 20% of the electricity is produced by nuclear power which also has pollution problems.

In Less Developed Countries (LDCs), a much larger proportion of energy is generated from **biomass,** while a small number of countries are able to exploit the heat generated from volcanic activity in the earth's crust to generate geothermal energy.

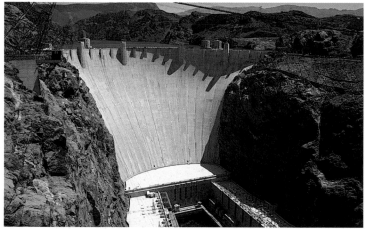

Figure 3 **The Hoover Dam, USA** Steep upland gradients provide a high head of water necessary to drive the turbines.

Figure 1 **Energy terms**

Fossil fuels – a fuel made from the remains of living organisms that has taken millions of years to form. All fossil fuels burn to give off carbon-dioxide.

Non-renewable resources – those which have only a limited, exhaustible supply. Once used, they are effectively 'gone forever'; they cannot be replaced within a human lifetime.

Renewable resources – those resources whose supply cannot be exhausted; they can be replaced within a relatively short period of time.

Alternative sources of energy – those that rely on renewable resources and do not pollute the atmosphere. They are likely to play an increasingly important part in providing for our future energy needs.

Biomass – the burning of organic material such as wood or animal dung.

Figure 2 **Electricity – a convenient source of energy**

There are advantages that electricity has over burning energy sources like coal and oil directly in the home or factory:

■ it is easier to transport

■ it can be used for a range of purposes, from powering a washing machine to smelting metals

■ it provides a continuous supply to the consumer at the flick of a switch and there are no storage problems

■ it does not pollute at the point of use.

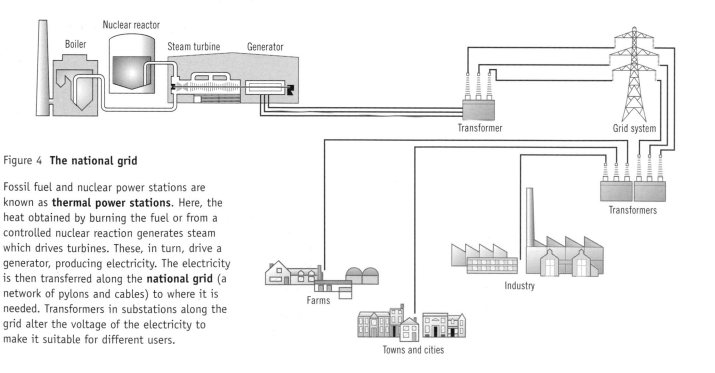

Figure 4 **The national grid**

Fossil fuel and nuclear power stations are known as **thermal power stations**. Here, the heat obtained by burning the fuel or from a controlled nuclear reaction generates steam which drives turbines. These, in turn, drive a generator, producing electricity. The electricity is then transferred along the **national grid** (a network of pylons and cables) to where it is needed. Transformers in substations along the grid alter the voltage of the electricity to make it suitable for different users.

Figure 5 **Location of power stations in the UK**

Coal-fired power stations

■ built on or near coalfields, near large population centres because coal is bulky and costly to transport
■ large amounts of water needed to produce steam to drive the turbines
■ flat sites are required
■ usually located along large rivers, such as the Trent, or by coastal estuaries.

Oil-fired power stations

■ found in sheltered coastal inlets where there is deep water to allow entry for large oil tankers
■ tend to be found close to oil refineries which convert the crude oil brought in by tanker or pipeline into the heavy fuel oil needed by the power station
■ present British and EU fuel policy makes it unlikely that any further oil-fired power stations will be built.

Gas-fired power stations

■ have become more popular in recent years
■ largest are found along the east coast where there is access to gas piped in from the North Sea
■ many are small gas turbine units built in areas remote from other power stations
■ since 1991, when electricity companies switched from coal to gas as their preferred energy source, numerous larger power stations have been built.

Nuclear power stations

■ found along the coast where there are supplies of water to cool the nuclear reactor and areas of flat, stable land on which to build
■ built away from major population centres for safety reasons
■ still require good transport links to allow easy transportation of raw materials and waste products
■ examples include Sizewell B in Suffolk, and Dungeness B in Kent.

Hydro-electric power (HEP) schemes

■ found mainly in the west of the UK in upland areas
■ high rainfall provides a constant supply of water
■ narrow valleys with strong and impermeable rock are ideal for dam construction
■ steep upland gradients provide the necessary high head of water (the height of the water inlet above the turbines).

---

1 Copy out the table shown and complete it by placing the following types of energy into the correct column. (Some may fit into more than one column.)

biomass; coal; geothermal; HEP; natural gas; nuclear; oil; solar; tidal; wave; wind.

Fossil fuel	Non-renewable	Renewable

2 Using Figure 5, explain why the Trent valley is a popular location for coal-fired power stations.

3 Why are each of the following found in coastal locations:
 a oil-fired power stations?
 b nuclear power stations?

4 Make a simple drawing of Figure 3. Use the information given above to add labels to your picture describing what makes an ideal location for an HEP scheme.

ENERGY

The UK has traditionally relied on coal as its main source of energy. However, as Figure 1 shows, coal has become less important with time. In 1950, coal accounted for 94% of total energy consumption while today it provides less than 30%. Coal was first replaced by oil, which was cheap in the 1960s and could be refined to make by-products, as well as be used in power stations. In 1973, Arab oil producers cut exports to Europe, causing oil prices to rise sharply. The British government then decided to invest in North Sea oil and gas as a way of reducing the amount of energy it imported.

Natural gas has become an increasingly important energy source because it is cleaner burning than coal or oil and the UK has its own supply in the North Sea. Gas-fired power stations are also less costly and quicker to build than other types of power stations. The 1990s have seen a dramatic increase in the number of gas-fired power stations in the UK, referred to as the 'dash for gas'.

The British nuclear programme did not begin until the 1950s and it has continued steadily to increase its share of energy production. Fears over safety and the cost of dismantling a nuclear power station once its useful life is over, mean that more stations are unlikely to be built.

The potential for hydro-electric power (HEP) to make up a significant share of energy production in the UK is limited because there are only certain sites that are suitable for dam construction and most of these are already in use.

Figure 1 **Total energy consumption in the UK (%)**					
	1960	**1970**	**1980**	**1990**	**1994**
Coal	76.5	50.7	35.2	30.6	24.2
Oil	22.6	42.7	39.7	34.7	35.5
Natural Gas	0.1	2.7	20.1	25.6	30.1
Nuclear	0.2	3.3	4.5	8.0	9.7
Hydro-electric	0.6	0.6	0.6	0.5	0.5

Figure 2 **The Sea Empress disaster, 15 February 1996**

Accident happened close to the Pembrokeshire National Park, an area of outstanding natural beauty

Wales

Skomer

Oil washed onshore, killing sea birds and affecting seal colonies

Milford Haven

Skokholm

St Ann's Head

On 15 February 1996, the supertanker *Sea Empress* ran aground on its way to Texaco refinery in Milford Haven, spilling its cargo of light crude oil. Over 100 000 tonnes of oil is lost

Pembroke

Threat to livelihood of local crab and lobster fishermen

Force-8 gales and absence of a large salvage tug delay rescue operation

Main oil slick moved south-east by currents

300 oiled seabirds found on Lundy Island off north Devon coast

BRISTOL CHANNEL

Key

⚓ Sea Empress

0   km   10

Conventional energy sources – some positive and negative factors

Coal

Plentiful; over 200 years supply still available from current proven reserves (those already known about) in UK; a 'dirty' fuel, giving off sulphur dioxide (SO_2), nitrogen oxides and large amounts of carbon dioxide (CO_2); linked to acid rain and global warming.

Oil

Cheap and plentiful, but many of world's remaining reserves are found in areas of political instability so supplies could be at risk; world's proven supplies expected to last only another 45 years; gives off CO_2; additional pollution problems from tanker spills (Figure 2).

Natural gas

Cheap and plentiful; current reserves estimated at 50 years' supply but more is likely to be discovered; easy to transport by pipeline; produces no sulphur dioxide and only half as much CO_2 as coal.

Hydro-electric

Renewable source; high construction costs but produces cheap electricity; reservoirs can provide opportunity for recreation but suitable sites are limited; very large schemes flood whole valleys and may force people to leave their homes; variations in rainfall affect the amount of electricity that can be generated.

▼ Figure 3 **Dungeness B nuclear power station**

Figure 4 **The nuclear debate**

In favour of nuclear power	Against nuclear power
Emits no carbon dioxide or sulphur dioxide.	Disposing of radioactive nuclear waste problematic; some waste (a very small quantity) remains highly radioactive for thousands of years and must be buried deep underground.
Nuclear power plants can run continuously for long periods, providing a reliable and uninterrupted supply of electricity.	Although safety is the highest priority in nuclear power stations, always a risk of nuclear leaks or accidents.
Oil and natural gas will run out in the near future but there are still adequate supplies of nuclear power's raw material, uranium.	Nuclear power stations are very costly to build and no-one has yet attempted to decommission (dismantle) one. Reactor core remains radioactive for centuries and must be encased in concrete.
Only small quantities of fuel are needed so there is less environmental impact from mining and transportation.	Produces more expensive electricity than coal or oil but may become cheaper as oil runs out or if a carbon tax is introduced.
It is necessary, for strategic reasons, to maintain a range of energy sources in case supplies of any one of them are suddenly cut (as happened during the 1973 Oil Crisis, when the price of oil rose four-fold).	Threat of terrorist attack.

1 Read the text and study Figure 1. Describe the trend in energy consumption for each energy source. You should mention figures from the table and graph to support what you write.

2 Using the information on these two pages, give reasons for the changes in the contribution of each energy source.

3 Why might nuclear power still be a valuable energy source in the future?

4 What else is oil used for apart from as an energy source?

Type	Definition	Potential	Advantages	Disadvantages
Wind	Wind energy turns rotors which drive the generator	The UK is one of windiest countries in the world with many suitable sites, mainly in western upland areas; could supply 20% of nation's energy	No atmospheric pollution; wind is free and widely available; no fuel to transport or store; large amounts of cooling water not required; low running costs once built; ideal for small, remote communities, e.g. in the Highland	Major visual impact on landscape, often in scenic upland areas; noise from turbines; wind is unreliable so cannot be turned on when demand for power is highest; a large windfarm is expensive to build (photo below)
Solar	Energy from the sun	Limited; the UK is too cloudy; solar energy expected to provide less than 1% of UK's needs by year 2000; much potential in LDCs with more sun	Clean; suited to small-scale schemes such as heating water in individual houses	Quite expensive to develop on a large scale; large area of solar panels needed to generate large amounts of electricity; difficult to store energy when sun is not shining
Tidal	Electricity is generated at river estuaries with large tidal ranges	Significant; west coast of UK has several large estuaries that could be dammed; could provide 15% of the UK's present needs (Figure 2)	No atmospheric pollution; cheap electricity; increase in water sports behind barrage	Would interfere with flow of sediment along estuary, possibly encouraging coastal erosion; would destroy wetland habitats and interfere with movement of fish along estuary; expensive to build
Wave	Waves enter a narrow channel, increase in height and spill over into a reservoir. As water is let out from reservoir, it drives the turbines	Great potential but more research needed; 20% of UK's electricity could be generated this way	No atmospheric pollution; largest storm waves occur in winter when demand for energy is highest	Wave power variable depending on weather; only possible in certain locations; often remote from where demand is
Biogas	The burning of methane gas given off by rotting plant matter	Small but significant potential; increasingly common at waste disposal sites where methane is collected	Helps to dispose of large quantities of waste such as pig or sewage slurry; can be carried out anywhere; burning of methane prevents it from directly entering the atmosphere, where it is a very powerful greenhouse gas (30 times worse than carbon dioxide)	Burning of methane produces carbon dioxide
Geothermal	Heat from the earth is used to heat water that has been injected into the crust and then piped back to the surface	Limited potential in the UK	Successfully developed in Iceland and New Zealand	Attempts to exploit this form of energy in Cornwall proved too expensive
Combined heat and power (CHP)	Heat from conventional power stations is used to warm water for nearby buildings (Figure 1)	Considerable potential on a local scale	Power stations normally waste up to 70% of the heat they generate through their cooling towers; scheme can reduce waste to 20%	Laying of heat pipes is costly
Energy conservation	Reduce the demand for energy altogether by minimising wasteful energy loss (Figure 3)	Several measures can be adopted to conserve energy in the home, including double-glazing and loft insulation	Heat loss reduced in buildings; reduced cost of domestic energy bills	Inital cost of installation is still quite high

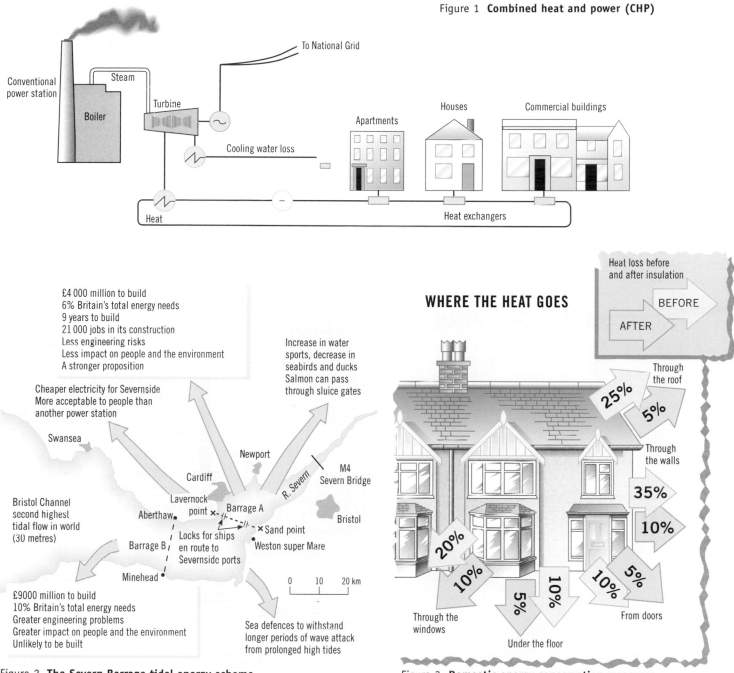

Figure 1 **Combined heat and power (CHP)**

To National Grid

Conventional power station

Steam

Boiler

Turbine

Cooling water loss

Heat

Heat exchangers

Apartments

Houses

Commercial buildings

£4 000 million to build
6% Britain's total energy needs
9 years to build
21 000 jobs in its construction
Less engineering risks
Less impact on people and the environment
A stronger proposition

Cheaper electricity for Severnside
More acceptable to people than another power station

Increase in water sports, decrease in seabirds and ducks
Salmon can pass through sluice gates

Swansea

Newport

Cardiff

M4
Severn Bridge

Lavernock point

Barrage A

R. Severn

Bristol Channel second highest tidal flow in world (30 metres)

Aberthaw

Sand point

Bristol

Barrage B

Locks for ships en route to Severnside ports

Weston super Mare

Minehead

0   10   20 km

£9000 million to build
10% Britain's total energy needs
Greater engineering problems
Greater impact on people and the environment
Unlikely to be built

Sea defences to withstand longer periods of wave attack from prolonged high tides

Figure 2 **The Severn Barrage tidal energy scheme**

WHERE THE HEAT GOES

Heat loss before and after insulation

BEFORE

AFTER

Through the roof
25%
5%

Through the walls
35%
10%

Through the windows
20%
10%

5%

10%

10%

5%

From doors

Under the floor

Figure 3 **Domestic energy conservation measures**

1 Assess the environmental impact of all the energy sources discussed in this unit by completing the table. (One energy source has been started for you.)

Energy source	Environmental problem	Scale of problem (local, national, international)
Coal	carbon dioxide emissions; contribute to global warming;	international
	sulphur dioxide emissions; cause of acid rain	national / international

2 Rank the energy sources in question 1 from best to worst in terms of their environmental impact. Give reasons for your ranking.

3 a Find the area shown in Figure 2 in an atlas.
  b Which counties surround the area shown?
  c What economic advantages might result from the barrage development?

4 What advantages does energy conservation have for (a) the user and (b) the environment?

5 Using the information given in Figure 3 and ideas of your own, design and label your own energy-efficient house.

An important environmental consequence of burning fossil fuel is acid precipitation or acid rain. All rainwater is naturally slightly acidic but **pH values** (the scale on which acidity is measured) of between 4 and 4.5 are now common in industrial parts of the USA, Russia and north-western Europe.

Acid rain is formed when sulphur dioxide (SO_2) and nitrogen oxides (NO_2) are released into the atmosphere as gases. They then fall directly back to earth as **dry deposition,** or are dissolved into rainwater to form dilute sulphuric and nitric acid. These acidic water droplets may be carried over long distances until they eventually fall as rain or snow, far away from where they were formed (Figure 2).

The main sources of sulphur dioxide and nitrogen oxides are the burning of fossil fuels, often high in sulphur, in power stations, motor vehicle exhaust emissions and industrial processes such as oil refining and metal smelting. Areas in Europe with the highest concentrations of sulphur dioxide in rainwater are shown in Figure 3.

The effects of acid rain

Scandinavian countries were the first to express their concern at the threat of acid rain in the early 1970s. They put much of the blame on the coal- and oil-burning power stations of the UK, France and western Germany. The problems became worse when taller chimneys were constructed on UK power stations in an attempt to reduce the problem of its local acid rain. This had the effect of pumping emissions higher into the atmosphere where they could be carried further by the prevailing westerly wind, transferring the problem elsewhere.

Some areas are better able to withstand acid rain than others. Soils rich in calcium (such as limestone) can neutralise the acid while already acid soils on top of granite or sandstone are more easily affected (Figure 3).

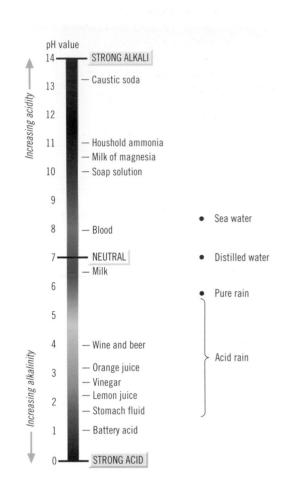

Figure 1 **A scale of pH values**

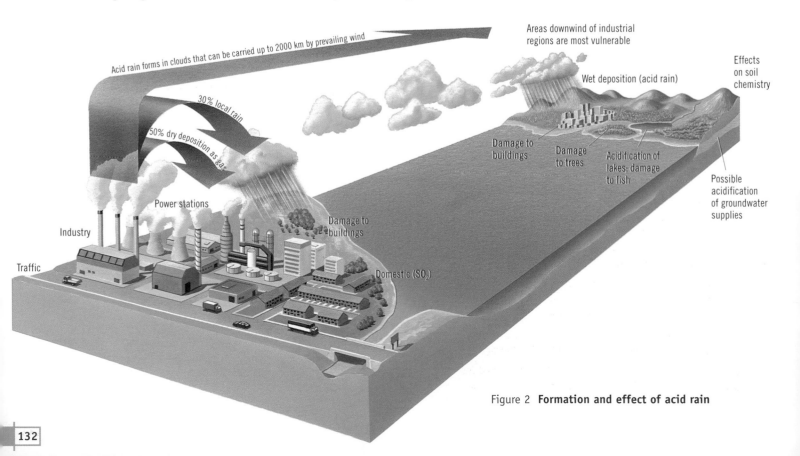

Figure 2 **Formation and effect of acid rain**

Lakes and rivers

Lakes and rivers in Scandinavia became increasingly acidic, causing the death of fish and plant life. By 1984, 75% of lakes and rivers in south Norway had no fish in them. Many lakes and rivers in the UK have also suffered.

Forests and soils

Conifer forests in northern Europe have suffered badly. As the acid percolates through the soil, it leaches (removes) important minerals such as magnesium, causing mineral deficiency and the yellowing of needles and leaves. As the soil becomes more acidic, it releases aluminium which then poisons tree roots. Trees are weakened and are more likely to be affected by insect attack and disease. Over half of western Germany's fir and spruce forests are now in decline, including much of the Black Forest.

Buildings

The more acidic rain that falls over towns and cities has increased the rate at which buildings and statues are being dissolved by chemical weathering. Rocks such as marble and limestone are particularly vulnerable. The Acropolis in Athens is reported to have deteriorated more in the last three decades than in the previous 2000 years.

Health

Acid rain increases the rate at which metal pipes dissolve. This can release harmful lead and copper into the water supply.

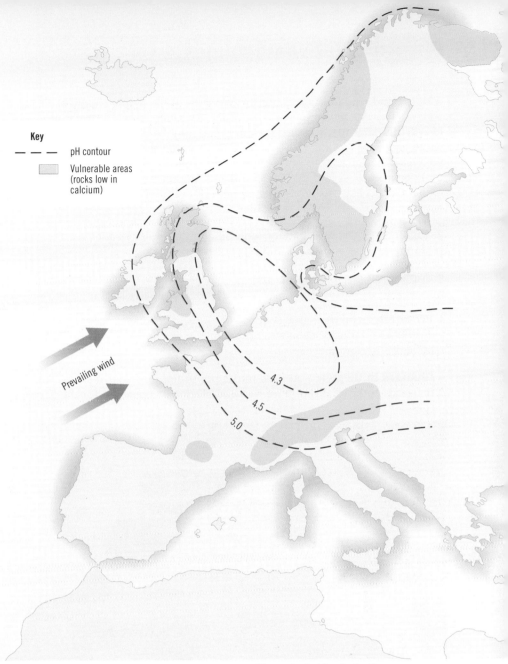

Key

— — — pH contour

▢ Vulnerable areas (rocks low in calcium)

Prevailing wind

4.3
4.5
5.0

Figure 3 **Acid rain in Europe**

Possible solutions to the acid rain problem

■ Reduce the number of coal burning power stations in favour of cleaner burning gas or nuclear power. This has already been done in Germany, France and the UK.

■ Fit desulphurisation equipment to existing coal-burning power stations. This can remove up to 90% of sulphur from emissions but is expensive to install. In 1989, the UK committed itself to spending £1.8 billion on cleaning up its fossil fuel power stations. It is cheaper to import low sulphur coal from overseas.

■ Set strict emission controls for vehicles. Catalytic converters on vehicle exhausts can reduce emissions of nitrogen oxides by 90%. All new petrol cars in Germany and the UK must be fitted with a catalytic converter.

■ Sweden has added lime to its lakes and soil to try to neutralise the acid. It has also restricted the sulphur content of its heating oil.

■ Sensible use of energy in the home and at work would reduce the demand for electricity from power stations.

1 What is acid rain?

2 Study Figure 3.
   a Which parts of Europe have the lowest pH values?
   b What do these areas have in common?

3 How does acid rain affect vegetation?

4 Why are some areas more vulnerable to acid rain than others?

5 What can be done
   a to lower harmful emissions?
   b to reduce the effects of acidification once it has happened?

6 How do you think acid rain might affect humans?

7 Why is international co-operation necessary in dealing with acid rain?

Coal, oil and natural gas account for over 80% of the global energy used, with nuclear energy supplying most of the remaining needs. LDCs still rely heavily on other fuel sources, such as wood, and biomass, such as crop waste and animal dung. These countries are still in the process of building their own power stations and national grid. They do not have their own coal or oil supplies and find it expensive to import them. People living in rural areas do not have access to supplies of coal and oil nor to electricity, whereas biomass is readily available.

As Figure 4 shows, world energy consumption has risen steadily for the past century and is set to rise still further for several reasons:

● **Population growth** – Every new individual creates additional demand for energy.

● **Economic growth** – As a country develops, it becomes more industrialised. Industry generates an enormous demand for energy. Agriculture is more mechanised and these machines also require energy.

● **Changes in lifestyle** – As a country's population becomes more wealthy, it demands and can afford more cars and electrical appliances for the home.

Figure 1 Energy consumption for select countries, 1991

Country	Consumption per head (kg of coal equivalent)
USA	7655
UK	3756
France	3704
Japan	3306
Brazil	813
China	580
Nigeria	150
Nepal	23

Figure 2 **A modern kitchen requires a considerable amount of energy to power the cooker, food mixer and dishwasher. This does not include the energy needed to build these machines in the first place**

▲ Figure 3 **In LDCs, electrical appliances are rare and humans do most of the work. Energy is more likely to come directly from burning wood**

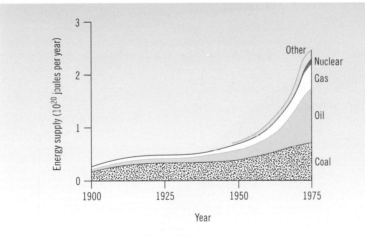

Figure 4 **World energy supplies, 1900 – 75**

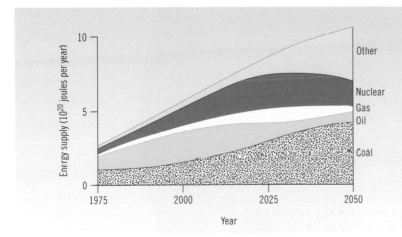

Figure 5 **Projected energy demand, 1975 – 2050**

1 Study Figure 1.
  a Give reasons for the differences in each county's consumption per head.
  b Why is energy consumption given in kg of coal equivalent?

2 Study Figure 4.
  a By how much has total energy supply increased since 1900?
  b Which energy source has shown the greatest increase in its share of energy production?
  c Suggest what types of energy source might be included in the 'other' category.

3 Describe what Figure 5 shows about projected energy demand in the future.
  a What are the possible environmental consequences of these projected changes?
  b What developments might mean that the prediction in Figure 5 is inaccurate?

Population density around the world

Humans are capable of living almost anywhere. They can live in polar regions, in deserts or in rainforests. However, these extreme environments do not encourage a high population density.

Population density is the number of people who live in a given area. It is calculated for a particular country, using the equation:

$$\text{Population density} = \frac{\text{Number of people in a particular country}}{\text{Size of that country (km}^2\text{)}}$$

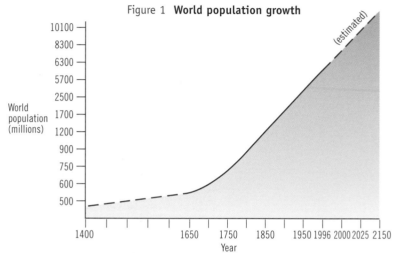

Figure 1 **World population growth**

Figure 2 **Humans can live in extreme environments**

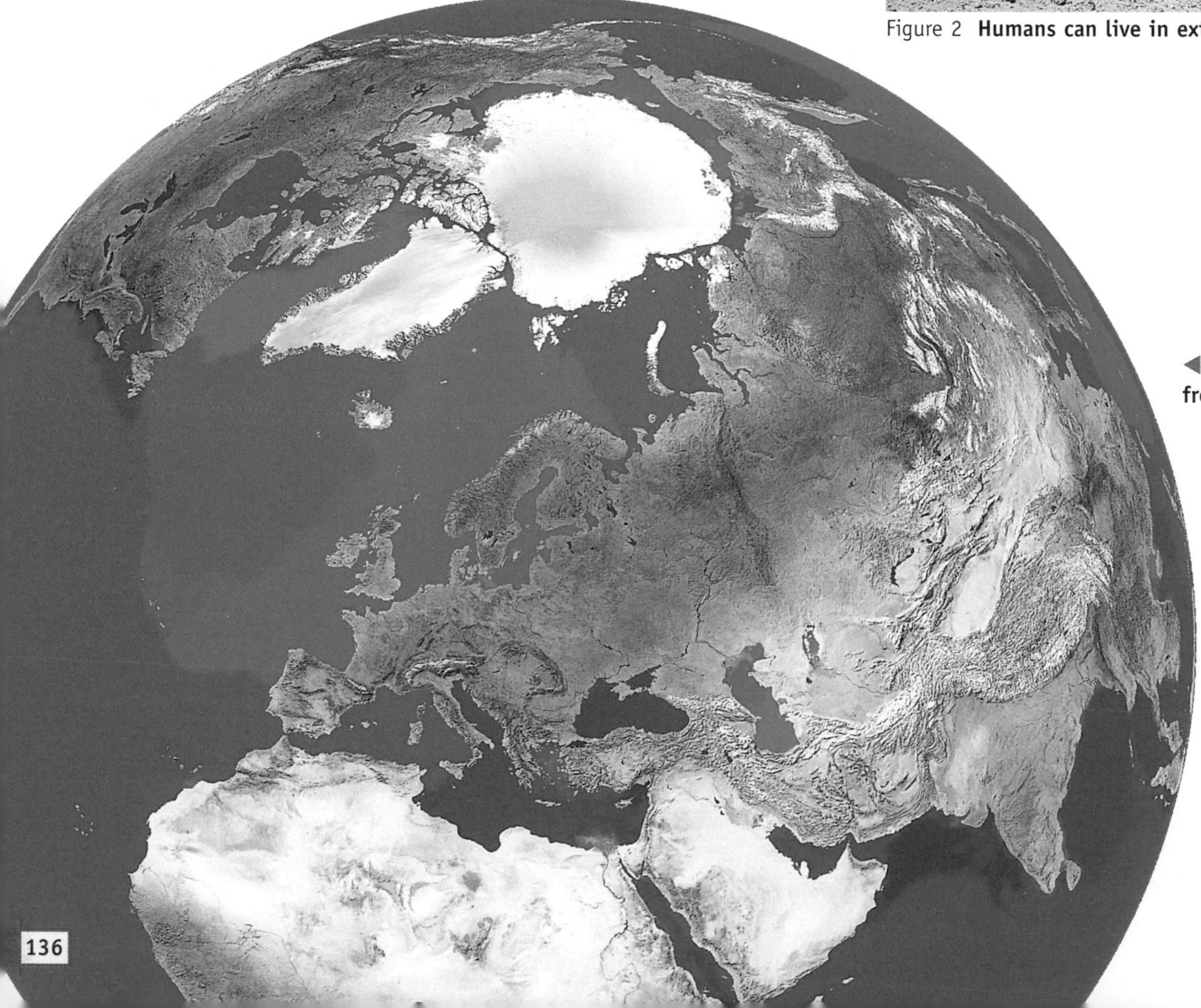

◀ Figure 3 **The world from outer space**

India's population distribution is largely a result of physical factors. The Ganges River provides water for drinking and irrigation. Its flood waters provide rich alluvium for crops spread across a broad, flat plain. In addition, the river has religious significance for Hindus, with many religious festivals and ceremonies taking place along its banks. These factors encourage a high population density.

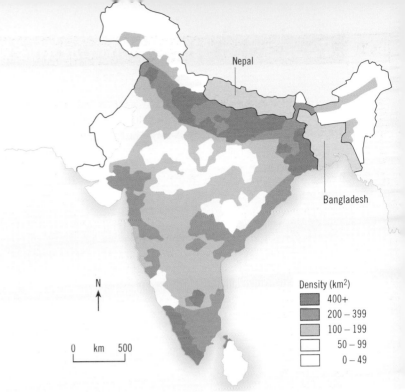

Figure 4 **India – population density and distribution**

Density (km²)
- 400+
- 200 – 399
- 100 – 199
- 50 – 99
- 0 – 49

0   km   500

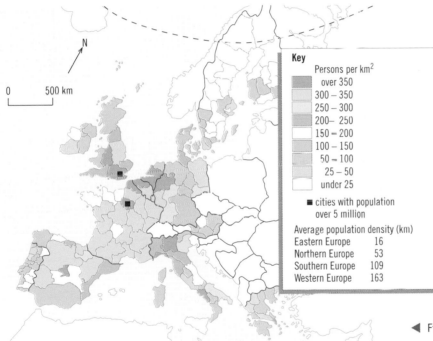

Key

Persons per km²
- over 350
- 300 – 350
- 250 – 300
- 200 – 250
- 150 – 200
- 100 – 150
- 50 – 100
- 25 – 50
- under 25

■ cities with population over 5 million

Average population density (km)
Eastern Europe	16
Northern Europe	53
Southern Europe	109
Western Europe	163

As well as being influenced by relief, soils, water and climate, the distribution of people can be affected by human factors. Economic growth encourages migration to an area of employment. The high population densities around the major European cities are largely a result of economic opportunities. North-west Germany has a very high population density based on the industrial strength of cities such as Dortmund, Essen and Duisburg, founded on the Ruhr coalfield.

◀ Figure 5 **Europe – population density, 1992**

1 Study Figure 3 and an atlas.
   a Name the physical features that can be seen from the satellite image which prevent a high population density e.g. the Himalayas.
   b Name the areas with the highest population densities.
   c Explain why these areas have high population densities. Divide your answer into Physical factors and Human factors.

2 Study Figure 4.
   a Explain why a neighbouring country, Nepal, has a very low population density.

b Explain why another one of India's neighbouring states, Bangladesh, has a very high population density.
c What problems has the high population density caused for Bangladesh?
d Which are India's major cities and what are their influences on it's population distribution?

3 Study Figure 5.
   a Which are the most densely populated countries of Europe?
   b What are the reasons for this concentration?
   c What are the advantages of having a high population density?
   d Which European countries have the lowest population densities?

Population distribution across the UK

The population distribution across the UK is influenced by a number of factors. The highest population densities are found around the major conurbations. A conurbation is an area that has formed from a number of towns or cities that have merged. Physical features such as a river crossing, harbour and proximity to coal deposits would have given the towns an initial advantage but their growth was due to the industries and the jobs which developed.

Within the cities themselves, the population is very unevenly spread (Figure 5). The highest population densities are found in the central areas where terraced housing had been built in the nineteenth century to accommodate the increasing workforce. The lowest population densities are found in the suburbs and outer suburbs, where larger houses and gardens ensure the density is reduced.

Figure 1 **UK – population density, 1991**

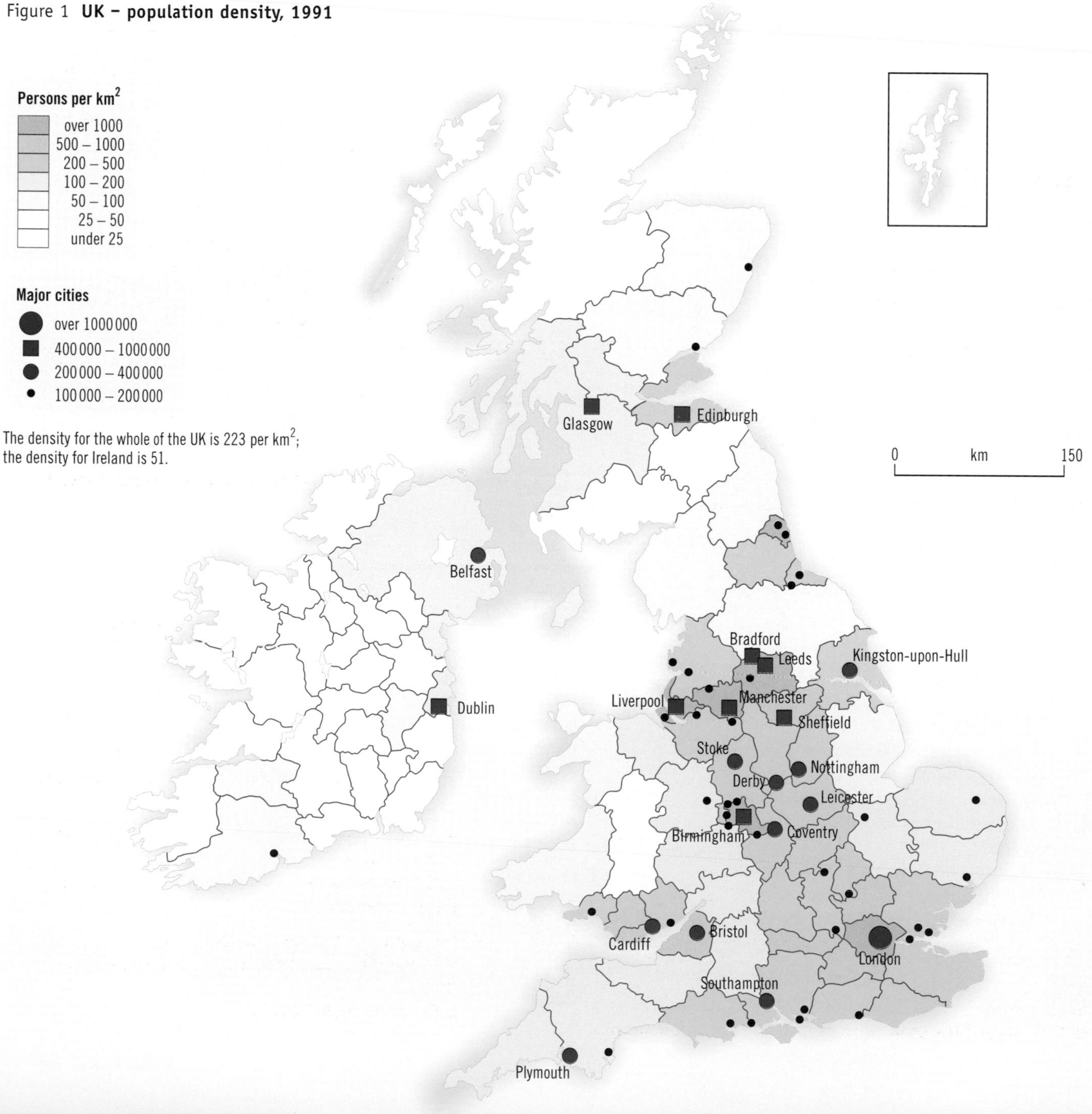

Persons per km²
over 1000
500 – 1000
200 – 500
100 – 200
50 – 100
25 – 50
under 25
Major cities
over 1000000
400000 – 1000000
200000 – 400000
100000 – 200000
The density for the whole of the UK is 223 per km²; the density for Ireland is 51.
0 km 150
Glasgow
Edinburgh
Belfast
Dublin
Bradford
Leeds
Kingston-upon-Hull
Liverpool
Manchester
Sheffield
Stoke
Nottingham
Derby
Leicester
Birmingham
Coventry
Cardiff
Bristol
London
Southampton
Plymouth

Figure 2 **Population densities can vary within a region**

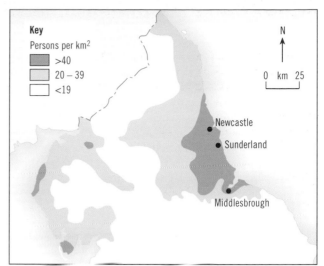

Figure 3 **Population density for northern England, 1990**

Key

Persons per km²

>40
20 – 39
<19

N

0   km   25

Newcastle
Sunderland
Middlesbrough

Figure 4 **Compact housing points to a high population density**

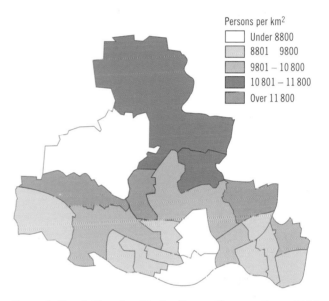

Persons per km²

Under 8800
8801   9800
9801 – 10 800
10 801 – 11 800
Over 11 800

Figure 5 **Population density for Newcastle upon Tyne, 1991**

Figure 6 **Large back gardens show a lower population density**

1 Study Figure 1.
   a Name the least populated counties of the country.
   b Explain why they are sparsely populated.
   c Name seven conurbations with the highest population densities.
   d Suggest reasons for the growth in these conurbations.

2 Write a few paragraphs which describe and explain the distribution of population in the UK.

3 Study Figure 3.
   a Around which cities are the highest population densities found?
   b Which industries encouraged the growth of these populations?

4 For your nearest town or city:
   a Name the areas with the highest population densities.
   b Describe their location.

9.3 An exploding population

The world's population has often been described as a 'demographic time bomb'. The population is expanding so quickly that people fear the resources of the planet may not be able to sustain the increase. In mid-1996, the population was 5771 million. If current growth rates are to continue, this population will double by the year 2042. This growth has not been constant over time and is not constant across the world as a whole.

1950

Africa 8.6%

Asia 52.9%

Developed world 32.1%

Latin America 6.4%

2025

Asia 57%

Developed world 15.8%

Africa 18.4%

Latin America 8.9%

Figure 1 **Past and future population distributions**

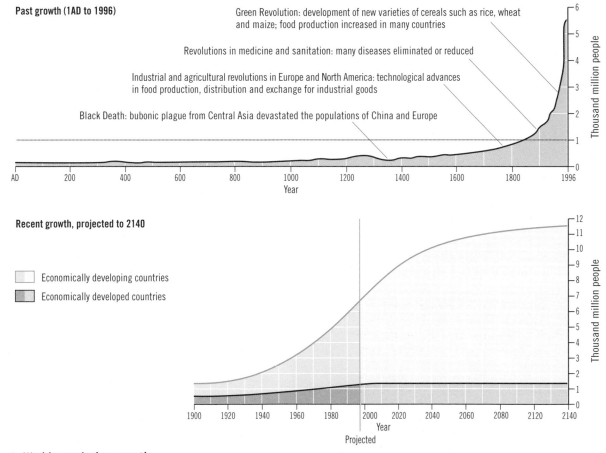

Past growth (1AD to 1996)

Green Revolution: development of new varieties of cereals such as rice, wheat and maize; food production increased in many countries

Revolutions in medicine and sanitation: many diseases eliminated or reduced

Industrial and agricultural revolutions in Europe and North America: technological advances in food production, distribution and exchange for industrial goods

Black Death: bubonic plague from Central Asia devastated the populations of China and Europe

Recent growth, projected to 2140

Economically developing countries

Economically developed countries

Figure 2 **World population growth**

The change in population numbers in a country will depend on the birth rate, the death rate and migration. The **natural increase** in population of a country is calculated using the following equation:

Natural increase = Birth rate − Death rate

There are significant differences between the rates of natural increase of different countries (Figure 3). Population growth rates vary with time, and from place to place.

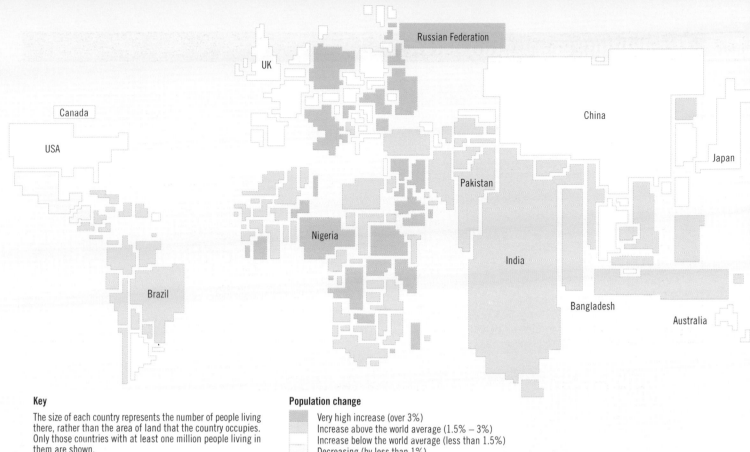

UK
Russian Federation
Canada
USA
China
Japan
Pakistan
Nigeria
India
Brazil
Bangladesh
Australia

Key

The size of each country represents the number of people living there, rather than the area of land that the country occupies. Only those countries with at least one million people living in them are shown.

One small square represents one million people.

Population change

- Very high increase (over 3%)
- Increase above the world average (1.5% – 3%)
- Increase below the world average (less than 1.5%)
- Decreasing (by less than 1%)

Figure 3 **Change in global population**

Birth rate – the number of children born per 1000 people per year

Death rate – the number of deaths per 1000 people per year

Migration – the balance between immigrants and emigrants

Immigrants – people entering a country

Emigrants – people who leave a country to live elsewhere

Carrying capacity – the number of humans, animals and plants an area of land can support

---

Figure 4 **Population statistics for selected countries, 1996**

Country	Birth rate	Death rate	Natural increase
Australia	14	7	7
Brazil	25	8	
China	17	7	
Ethiopia	46		30
Italy	9	10	
India	29	10	
Indonesia		8	16
Japan	10		3
Mexico	27	5	22
Nigeria		12	31
Russia	9	15	
Saudi Arabia	36		32
Sweden		11	1
USA	15		6

---

1 Study Figure 2.

a Describe the growth of the world's population

(i) up to 1650

(ii) from 1650 to 1900

(iii) from 1900 to 1996.

b Using your knowledge of natural increase, birth rate and death rate, explain the changes in the growth rate.

2 Study Figure 1.

a Describe the distribution of the world's population in 1950.

b Describe the projected distribution of the world's population for 2025.

c How will this distribution affect food supply and global markets for manufactured goods?

3 Study Figures 3 and 4.

a Copy the table and fill in the missing figures.

b Calculate the % increase for each country, using this formula: $\dfrac{\text{Natural increase}}{1000} \times 100$

c Group the countries into the following categories: Increase over 3%, Increase 1.5% – 3%, Increase less than 1.5%.

d Which regions of the world have the highest natural increases?

e Which regions of the world have the lowest natural increases?

9.4 | The demographic transition model

The demographic transition model shows what might happen to the birth rate, death rate and natural increase, with time. This model is good for describing population changes in Western Europe but it does not account for changes in the less economically developed countries (LDCs). It does show that LDCs experience different problems to those of Europe a century ago.

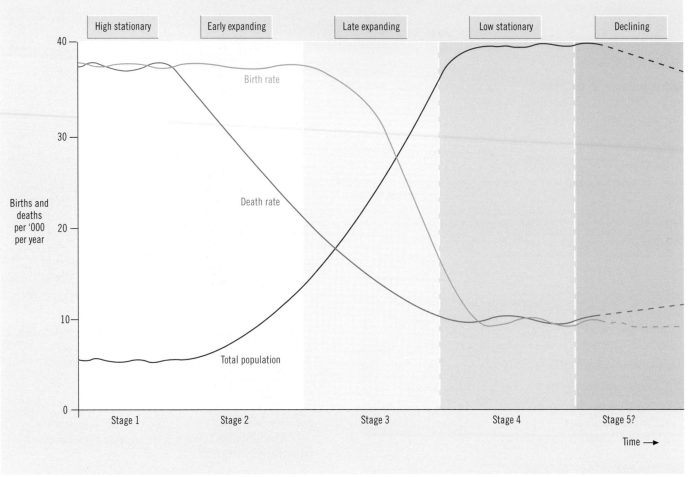

Figure 1 **The demographic transition model**

Stage 1 – High Stationary Stage

Death rate: high due to infectious diseases, such as typhoid and cholera, poor nutrition and even famine and wars

Birth rate: high due to lack of family planing, low status of women and a high infant mortality; children add to the family income through child labour; encourages large families.

Stage 2 – Early Expanding Stage

Death rate: begins to fall due to improved medicines, nutrition, sanitation and water supply

Birth rate: remains high.

Stage 3 – Late Expanding Stage

Death rate: continues to fall due to greater improvements in health, sanitation and nutrition; care for elderly introduced

Birth rate: starts to fall as children are prevented from working and so become a drain on the families, wealth; infant death has been reduced; family planning techniques become more widely available and acceptable; status of women rises and the marriage age increases.

Stage 4 – Low Stationary Stage

Death rate: remains low

Birth rate: levels off; through family planning, the desired size for the family matches the achieved family size.

Stage 5 – Declining Stage

Death rate: could increase as a greater proportion of the population is elderly

Birth rate: continues to be low; financial and job insecurity may reduce it even further.

Figure 2 Demographic change in England and Wales, 1770 – 1990

Year	Birth rate per 1000	Death rate per 1000
1700	36.0	30.5
1710	33.0	31.0
1720	35.5	34.0
1730	36.0	38.0
1740	38.0	36.0
1750	39.0	30.5
1760	36.5	30.0
1770	38.0	30.5
1780	38.0	29.0
1790	40.0	26.0
1800	38.5	22.0
1810	37.0	20.5
1820	36.0	20.5
1830	35.0	21.0
1840	31.0	20.0
1850	32.5	22.5
1860	34.0	22.5
1870	34.5	22.0
1880	33.0	20.0
1890	30.5	18.5
1900	28.0	17.0
1910	25.0	14.5
1920	20.0	12.5
1930	17.0	12.0
1940	14.5	13.0
1950	16.0	11.0
1960	17.5	11.5
1970	16.5	11.0
1980	14.0	12.0
1990	14.0	11.0

1 a Plot the information shown in Figure 2 on a graph. Use the same key as for Figure 1.
b Label the following points on the appropriate line:

Death rate

1780	Improvements in farming techniques start
1850	Banning of public cesspools in London
1860	Infectious diseases have a reduced impact
1872	Public Health Acts
1929	Penicillin discovered
1946	National Health Service introduced

Birth rate

1842	Women and children banned from mining
1870	Increased family planning awareness
1876	Compulsory Education Act
1906	Illegal for children under 11 to work

2 Place each of the countries in Figure 4 (page 141) into the following table:

Stage on demographic transition model				
High stationary	Early expanding	Late expanding	Low stationary	Declining

3 Plot the following information for Sri Lanka on to graph paper.

Year	Birth rate	Death rate
1911 – 20	38	30.5
1921 – 30	39	26.5
1931	37.5	22
1936	34	22
1940	36	20.5
1946	38.5	19
1953	38.5	11
1963	34.5	8.5
1971	30	8
1976	28	8
1983	26	6
1996	20	5

a What stage of the demographic transition model do you think Sri Lanka has reached? Give reasons for your answer.
b Divide the following list of explanations into *Influences on the birth rate* and *Influences on the death rate*:
malaria control; nutrition improved; more women employed; increased family planning; more women educated; average marriage age rose; health system improved; increased urbanisation; values such as monogamy introduced.
c Compare Sri Lanka's birth rate and death rate figures for the twentieth century with those of England and Wales.

Population change in LDCs

Less developed countries experience growth rates quite different to those of European countries. Birth rates are high and death rates, declining.

Birth rates

In some countries, such as Mali, Uganda and Niger, the birth rate is over 50 per 1000 per year. The rates are affected by a number of factors.

Children are a valuable resource, particularly in LDCs. They help with work on the farm in rural communities; in towns, they can work for money. It is believed that if poverty was reduced, this would reduce the need to have as many children.

Children also provide security and support for old age. A large family ensures that there will be children to look after the parents when they are elderly.

Some societies place considerable value on the number of children that a couple have, particularly male children. This encourages an increase in the birth rate.

Even though women tend the crops, prepare the food and have a good idea as to the number of children a family can support, they have relatively little status. As a result, they have relatively little power over the high birth rate.

High infant mortality encourages the population to have even more children in the hope that some will survive. For example, if a family were to have eight children, they have hopes that at least five will survive. A lack of family planning further encourages an increase in birth rate.

Death rates

Medical improvements, such as the discovery of penicillin and immunisation in the developed countries, helped to lower the death rates in LDCs as technology spread. The combined factors of improved health care, water, sanitation and nutrition helped the death rate decline within a few decades.

Since LDCs have a relatively small elderly population, the numbers of deaths among them are not significant enough to affect the overall rate. The average death rate for North Africa, a rate of eight per 1000 per year, is lower than the UK's rate of 11 per 1000 per year.

Figure 1 **Population pyramids and how they relate to the demographic transition model**

The structure of a population can be seen by a **population pyramid**. The pyramid shows the proportion of males and females at 5-year age intervals. From the population pyramids, it can be determined whether the population is growing, stable or likely to decline. As a country moves through each stage in the demographic transition model, the shape of the population pyramid will change.

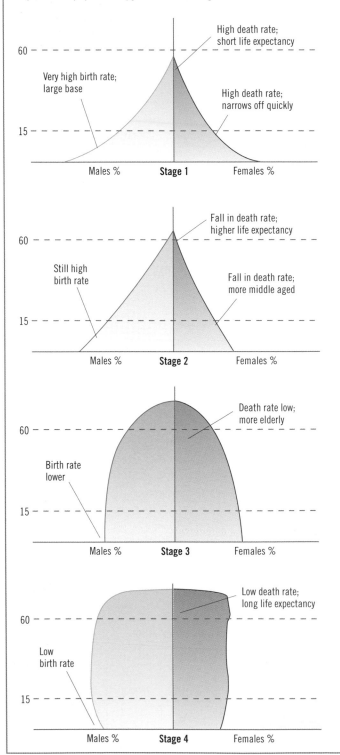

Effects of a rapidly growing population

Depletion of resources

If a population grows too large, the land may not be able to support it. Food supplies will be exhausted and the population will starve. The carrying capacity of the land will have been exceeded by the increasing size of the population. This observation was first suggested by Thomas Malthus in 1798. Some geographers now try to account for the famines in sub-Saharan Africa by using this theory.

In contrast, other geographers suggest that the natural disasters are more to do with civil wars and poor infrastructure than lack of resources. As the population grows, the ability of farmers to improve their yields increases. Farmers use agricultural innovations to improve their crops, such as those which contributed towards the **Green Revolution**. Yields increased, enabling a larger population to be supported.

Both suggestions agree that a rapidly expanding population does put a considerable strain on the environment. This results in desertification, deforestation and an increased dependence on artificial fertilisers.

Changing age structure

A rapidly expanding population will give rise to a high proportion of young people (Figure 1). Over 40% of Africans are under the age of 15 years. This puts a tremendous strain on the economies of those countries as they try to provide education, food and health care for the masses. Later on, housing and unemployment becomes a problem.

Figure 2 UK population, 1990		
Age group	Male %	Female %
0 – 4	6.99	6.33
5 – 9	6.68	6.04
10 – 14	6.23	5.61
15 – 19	7.49	6.78
20 – 24	8.49	7.78
25 – 29	8.36	7.79
30 – 34	7.15	6.73
35 – 39	6.8	6.47
40 – 44	7.32	6.93
45 – 49	5.93	5.62
50 – 54	5.53	5.29
55 – 59	5.23	5.13
60 – 64	5.01	5.15
65 – 69	4.86	5.46
70 – 74	3.14	4.04
75 – 79	2.59	3.91
80 – 84	1.45	2.8
85 +	0.75	2.14
Total	100	100

1 **a** Explain why less economically developed countries have a rapidly expanding population.
b What problems will this cause?

2 **a** Match the four population pyramids (Figure 3) to the examples shown in Figure 1.
b Give reasons for your answers. Write at least one paragraph for each pyramid, justifying your choice.

3 **a** Using the data in Figure 2, draw a population pyramid for the UK for 1990.
b Describe the shape of the pyramid and explain what it shows about the population structure.

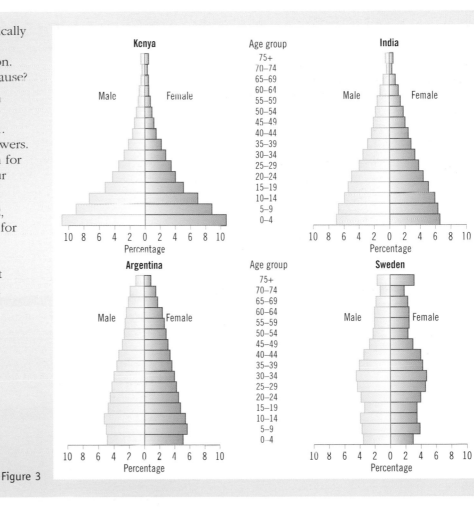

Figure 3

9.6 Controlling population growth

Many countries are trying to reduce the growth in their populations. However, the problems they encounter are complex, and depend on a number of social, political, economic and geographical factors.

Figure 1 **Statistics for Asia, China, India and Mauritius**

Country	Population (millions)	Birth rate (per 1000)	Death rate (per 1000)	Natural increase (per 1000)	Doubling time at present rate (years)	% using modern contraception	Literacy rate %	GNP per capita ($US)
Asia	3501	24	8	16	43	54	63	2150
China	1217.6	17	7	10	66	81	78	530
India	949.6	29	10	19	37	36	48	310
Mauritius	1.1	20	7	13	54	49	80	3180

Mauritius

Being a small island, Mauritius is very different to India and China. In the 1960s, it had the fastest growing population in the world, which quickly outstripped its limited resources. To combat this growth a number of developments were introduced, including organised family planning through a network of clinics around the island, and improving health care and the status of women.

Also, a surge in economic growth resulted in better standards of living for the population in general. New areas were converted into farmland and new techniques of double cropping were introduced; potatoes and groundnuts were grown alongside rows of sugar cane. Multinational companies invested in the island, taking advantage of the financial incentives and tax relief set up by the local government. A large, educated workforce provided cheap, skilled labour, making the size of the population an asset rather than a burden.

The small size of Mauritius, coupled with its economic potential, meant that it could combat the fear of famine.

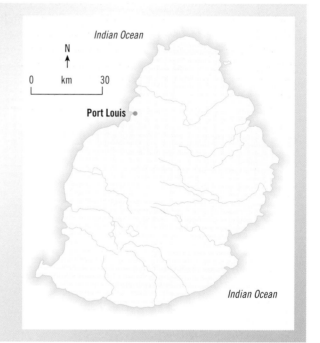

India

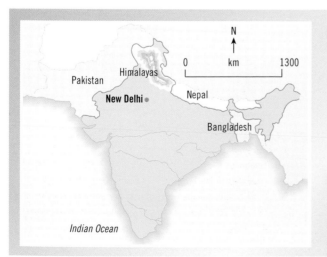

Despite having a family planning programme since the 1930s, India has struggled to reduce its growth rate. India is a large and diverse country. It is also a democracy and as such, could not use some of the strict laws which China had implemented. For example, in the 1970s, India tried a compulsory sterilisation for men with more that three children but public objection was so great that they have had difficulty in carrying out a family planning programme since then.

India is not wealthy. It covers a large area, making communication extremely difficult. The population is made up of a variety of cultures, of different languages and religions. A high percentage of the population is rural and education is not widespread.

China

China has the world's largest population with over 1.2 billion people. One fifth of the world's population lives there. China's leaders were faced with a rapidly growing population and a fear of mass starvation by the end of the century.

A 'one-child' policy was introduced. This policy has been altered since its introduction but generally, couples are encouraged to have only one child through a number of means:

- a 5% – 10% salary bonus for limiting to one child
- a 10% salary reduction for having two children
- no extra space allocation for second or third children
- priority in education and health care for 'only' children.

The government recommended a later age for marriages and couples had to apply for the right to start a family.

These measures have been largely successful. However, such policies could only be implemented by a strong authoritarian government. Chinese culture and tradition is based around a large family, with male offspring being particularly important. If a female baby is born, she is sometimes killed to allow the couple to have another baby, hopefully, a male. In 50 years time, there will be a high proportion of elderly Chinese, with only a few young people of working age to provide for them. The population balance has been thrown.

The 'one-child' policy has led to international criticism and claims of abuse of human rights. However, China had been faced with potential catastrophe and has managed to slow its population growth considerably. Despite this success, China's population is still set to double by the year 2062.

1 Use the information in Figure 1 to compare China, India and Mauritius. Write brief notes on their similarities and differences.

2 India has had problems in implementing a family planning programme. Give reasons for these problems, using the following headings: economic; social; political.

3 What are the main reasons for the success of Mauritius' population controls?

4 a Do you think China's 'one-child' policy is acceptable? Why/why not?
b Do you think that because China managed to slow its growth rate through this policy, that the result has been justified by the method used? Give reasons for your answer.

147

Not all countries have a problem with a growing young population. If the country is at the fourth or fifth stage of the Demographic Transition Model, a large proportion of its population will be at an old age. The elderly are usually not working and are dependent on the rest of the population. In addition, the younger population is also dependent on the rest. A **dependency ratio** can thus be calculated.

$$\text{Dependency ratio} = \frac{\text{number of children} < 15 + \text{number of elderly} > 60}{\text{number of people of a working age}} \times 100$$

The higher the dependency ratio, the higher the proportion of dependent population. Some countries have a high dependency ratio because they have a high proportion of children, such as India and Kenya. For other countries, such as Sweden and the UK, the high ratio is caused by a high proportion of elderly people.

Figure 1 Distribution of retired age groups in the UK

Key
%

	13.6– 15.5
	12.5–13.5
	12.0–12.4
	11.5–11.9
	11.0–11.4
	9.1– 10.9

N

0   km   150

Figure 2 **Retired people are often attracted to coastal areas**

The geography of age

The UK's elderly are not evenly distributed through the country (Figure 1). Certain areas, such as the larger cities, have fewer elderly than average, while others, such as the south coast of England, have more than average.

The uneven concentration of elderly people is due to migration. Once people retire, they tend to move away from their original county of work, often to be near their families and away from cities. In the UK, retired people have tended to move to the south coast. They are attracted by the milder climate and a perception of a high quality of life. As there is a concentration of elderly in this area, additional facilities are provided for them.

Bournemouth

Bournemouth is an ideal location to retire. It has a relatively warm climate, is situated by the sea and because of its high percentage of elderly, has facilities for health care, entertainment and accommodation.

The high number of elderly also puts a strain on the resources. Services such as *meals on wheels*, home help and health visitors need to be provided. Cinemas are being turned into bingo halls, and playgrounds into bowling greens. An increasing number of residential homes are being created. This breeds resentment among some of the local people.

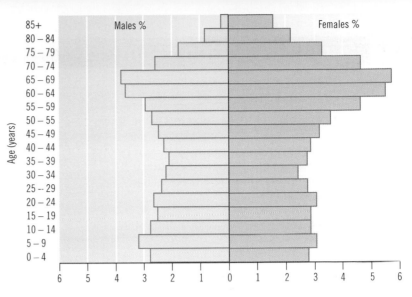

Figure 3 **Population pyramid for Bournemouth**

However, the increase in elderly does have its advantages. With a number of UK holiday makers travelling to the beaches of America and Europe, the local tourist industry had gone into decline. Hotels and guest houses have been converted into homes for the elderly. These and other facilities provide a guaranteed year-round employment, rather than the seasonal jobs generated by the tourist trade.

Figure 4 **Location of Bournemouth on the south coast**

Some countries experience more deaths than births, resulting in a declining population. Eastern Europe has an average natural decrease of four per 1000 per year. This causes a number of problems:

- an increase in the proportion of elderly
- increasing demands from pensions
- increasing demands on health care and provision
- a reduced workforce
- a fall in consumer demand and house demand.

Many European governments recognise these problems and are trying to solve them. In the UK, people are encouraged to take out private pensions to supplement the state pension. Much of the health care is provided by private companies. Employers in formerly male-orientated industries are now recruiting women. Retailers are employing staff of pensionable age.

In some countries, such as Germany, immigrants help to steady the population balance.

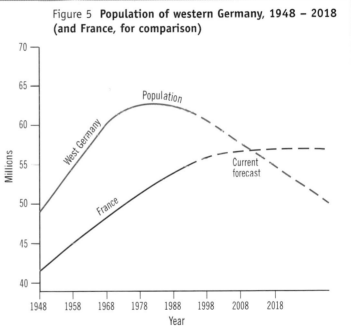

Figure 5 **Population of western Germany, 1948 – 2018 (and France, for comparison)**

1 Study Figure 1.
   a Name five counties with less than 10.9% between pensionable age and 74 years.
   b Describe the distribution of the counties with the highest percentage of elderly.
   c Give reasons for their distribution.

2 Study Figure 3. Calculate the dependency ratio for Bournemouth.

3 **a** What are the implications of providing health care for the town if a large percentage of the population is elderly.
   b Why might local residents resent the number of elderly people.

4 **a** Calculate the dependency ratios for the UK and four other countries, using the population pyramids on page 145 (Figures 2 and 3).
   b What does this tell about the populations of those countries?

5 **a** What are the advantages of employing older people in a large DIY superstore?
   b What are the advantages and disadvantages of increasing the number of women in the armed forces?

Migration, the movement of people or animals, can take place over vast or short distances. It may be a one-way movement with migrants not returning to their origins, or it may be **temporary**. People may choose to migrate (**voluntary migration**) or may become refugees subject to **forced migration**.

Reasons for migrating are varied and complex. E S Lee devised a model to help explain the reasons for migrating (Figure 1). The migrant is influenced by a number of positive and negative factors. In each case the individual's decision will be affected by personal choice. A big city may be an attraction to some, while others might prefer a smaller town. Thus, the individual's perception of the various factors affects the decision.

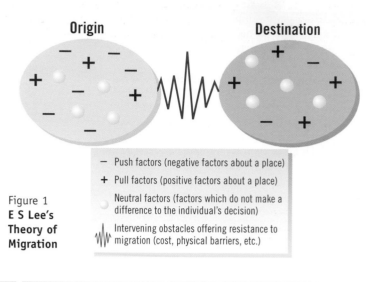

Figure 1
E S Lee's Theory of Migration

−   Push factors (negative factors about a place)

+   Pull factors (positive factors about a place)

○   Neutral factors (factors which do not make a difference to the individual's decision)

⟿   Intervening obstacles offering resistance to migration (cost, physical barriers, etc.)

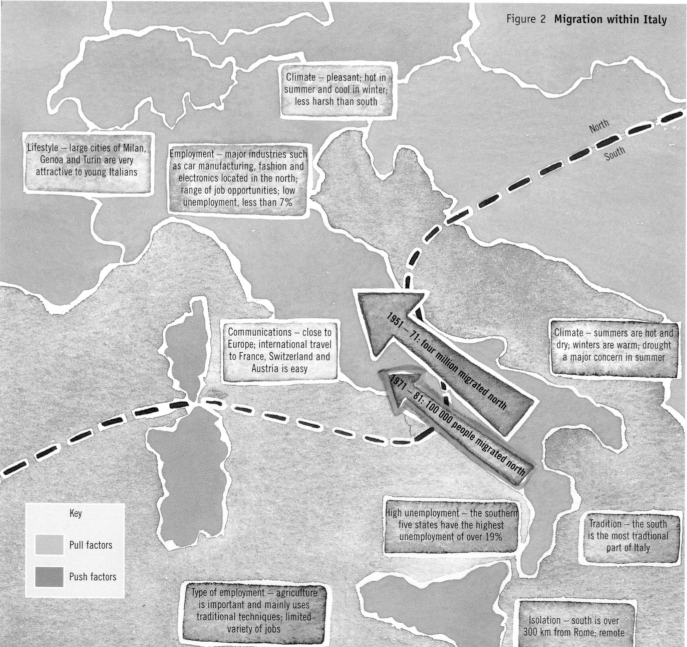

Figure 2 **Migration within Italy**

Climate – pleasant; hot in summer and cool in winter; less harsh than south

Lifestyle – large cities of Milan, Genoa and Turin are very attractive to young Italians

Employment – major industries such as car manufacturing, fashion and electronics located in the north; range of job opportunities; low unemployment, less than 7%

North
South

Communications – close to Europe; international travel to France, Switzerland and Austria is easy

Climate – summers are hot and dry; winters are warm; drought a major concern in summer

1951 – 71: four million migrated north

1971 – 81: 100 000 people migrated north

High unemployment – the southern five states have the highest unemployment of over 19%

Tradition – the south is the most tradtional part of Italy

Type of employment – agriculture is important and mainly uses traditional techniques; limited variety of jobs

Isolation – south is over 300 km from Rome; remote

Key

Pull factors

Push factors

Indonesia

Indonesia has the fourth largest population in the world. Its population is unevenly distributed; over 70% of the people live on 7% of the land. The island of Java has over 105 million people; some areas have a population density of over 1000 people per km².

The government developed a Transmigration Scheme to move people from Java to the more remote islands. They wanted to relieve pressure on the resources in Java, to spread economic development to the other islands and to improve national unity by mixing the populations. They offered a number of incentives to families to migrate, namely, two to five hectares of land, a simple wooden house and tools, seed and food to get established.

The Transmigration Scheme was the largest and most ambitious migration plan. Due to the costs of the scheme, original targets had to be halved and money borrowed from the World Bank. The numbers migrating have decreased in recent years to such an extent that those on the scheme are outnumbered by voluntary migrants.

Key

Cities

- ■ over 5 000 000
- ● over 1 000 000
- ● over 500 000
- ● over 100 000
- over 50 000

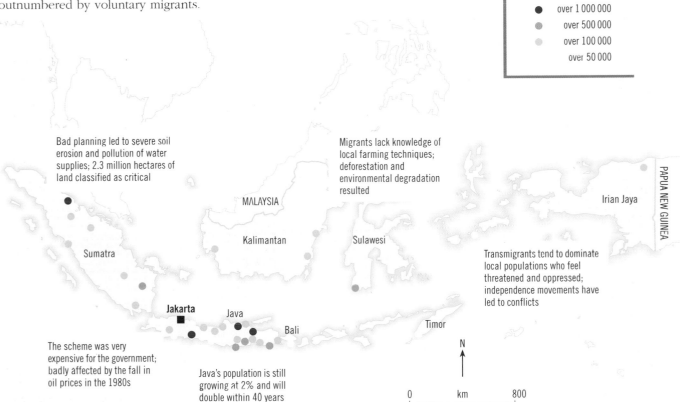

Bad planning led to severe soil erosion and pollution of water supplies; 2.3 million hectares of land classified as critical

Migrants lack knowledge of local farming techniques; deforestation and environmental degradation resulted

MALAYSIA

Kalimantan

Sulawesi

PAPUA NEW GUINEA

Irian Jaya

Sumatra

Transmigrants tend to dominate local populations who feel threatened and oppressed; independence movements have led to conflicts

Jakarta

Java

Bali

Timor

N

The scheme was very expensive for the government; badly affected by the fall in oil prices in the 1980s

Java's population is still growing at 2% and will double within 40 years

0   km   800

Figure 3 **Indonesia – population distribution and effects of transmigration**

1 a Set the following migrations into the correct columns in the table: a businessman commuting to London; a Brazilian migrating to São Paulo; a Mexican migrating to the USA; a refugee from Rwanda migrating to Tanzania; a Florida family fleeing Hurricane Hugo.

	Temporary	Permanent
Voluntary		
Forced		

b Add more of your own examples of different types of migrations.

2 Construct a table to show the push and pull factors which would encourage a young person from Sicily to migrate to the north of Italy.

3 List the consequences of the Indonesian Transmigration Scheme under the following headings: environmental effects; social effects; economic effects.

4 Research and write short notes on Indonesia's religion, industries, sports, tourist destinations and climate.

9.9 Migration between countries

Often there are more intervening obstacles to migrations between countries. Migrants usually have to prove their financial security, skills and health as part of the immigration procedure. However, the push and pull factors are still strong enough to encourage the migration. In some cases, migrations are forced; the migrants are called **refugees**.

Germany

Germany has experienced a wide range of migrations: Jews fled the Nazis in the 1930s and 40s; southern European workers arrived in the 1950s, 60s and 70s; eastern European migrants moved in after the destruction of the Berlin Wall in 1989.

After the war, migrants were attracted to Germany by the number of jobs on offer. For example in 1961, 500 000 jobs were available but only 180 000 local people had applied for them. The demand for workers was largely due to a rapidly growing economy since the mid-1950s, and a declining German labour force due to a rise in school-leaving age and a fall in retirement age. Working conditions and wages were among the best in Europe.

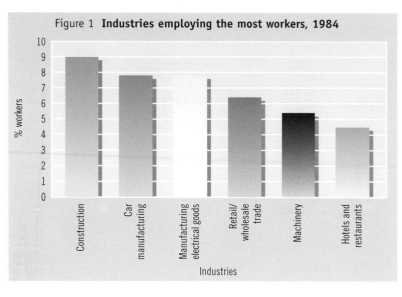

Figure 1 **Industries employing the most workers, 1984**

The pattern has changed more recently, however. A decrease in economic growth meant a rise in unemployment. The unification of Germany in 1989 brought a flood of former East Germans into the West, hoping for employment and better standards of living. The recession of the early 1990s led to a further rise in unemployment.

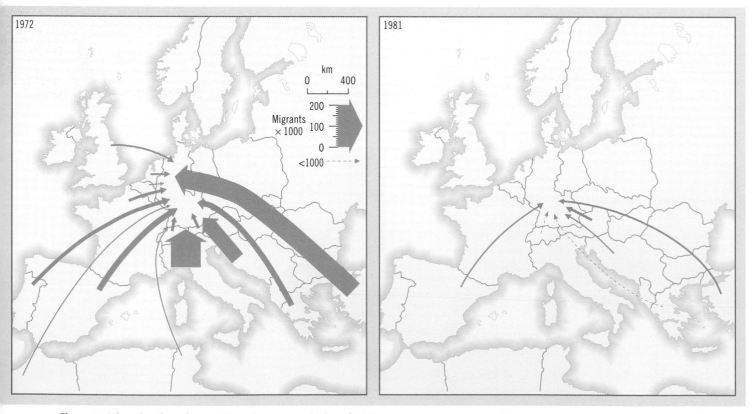

Figure 2 **Migration into former West Germany, 1972 and 1981**

Effects of migration

Economic effect in Germany

Immigrant labour was an essential part of Germany's economic progress; the country tended to stagnate in their absence. Following the 1990 recession, however, there has been increasing unemployment. Infrastructure, such as hostels, had to be built to house the labourers. Money was leaving the country as labourers sent their earnings to their families in the countries of origin. For example, between 1975 and 1980, $US 900 million was sent home by Greek migrants.

Political effect in Germany

Stricter controls were imposed. Liberal asylum laws were tightened in 1993 to restrict the influx of migrants, especially from East European countries. Right wing groups grew in strength and numbers, and increased their violent attacks on migrants.

Social effect in Germany

Gastarbeiter (guest workers) cannot easily claim German nationality and therefore, do not have equal rights. If it were not for the influx of migrants, the German population would have declined since the war.

Effects in the countries of origin

Countries such as Turkey and Greece which provided many of the migrants, will have benefited by the fall in their own unemployment rates. Their economy would have improved from the money sent home by the migrants. However, the departure of so many young males, especially from the rural areas, would have pressurised the agricultural sector. Often it is the most able workers who migrate. Their original societies might tend to stagnate in their absence.

Figure 3 **A Turkish migrant worker in a German factory**

Figure 4 **Turkish workers were killed in the arson attack on their hostel**

Figure 5 **Population structure for western Germany**		
Age groups	Males %	Females %
0 – 4	7.2	7.1
5 – 9	4.0	3.9
10 – 14	3.0	2.0
15 – 19	4.8	3.0
20 – 24	10.0	4.8
25 – 29	12.0	4.2
30 – 34	9.0	3.8
35 – 39	6.0	5.0
40 – 44	4.3	4.2
45 – 49	4.0	3.8
50 – 54	3.4	4.3
55 – 59	2.1	2.6
60 – 64	3.1	4.3
65 – 69	2.7	4.0
70 – 74	2.4	3.5
75 – 79	1.3	2.5
80 – 84	0.8	1.5
85 +	0.5	1.0

1 Study Figure 2.
   a Which five countries provided the largest number of migrants to Germany in 1972?
   b Use the key to calculate the number of migrants from each country.
   c Describe the distribution of these countries.
   d Suggest likely push factors which would encourage the migrants to leave their home countries.

2 Using Figure 2, describe the changes to the pattern of migration in 1981.

3 Using Figure 5:
   a Draw a population pyramid for the western part of Germany.
   b Which three age groups have the highest percentage of male population?
   c Compare the differences between the male and the female populations.
   d Explain these differences.

Measuring development

Figure 1 shows what has been described as the **North-South divide**. North of the line are the richest, most economically developed countries. South of the line are the poorest countries. However, just because a country is rich does not necessarily mean that it is developed.

There are many different ways of measuring a country's level of development. Each **development index** has its own advantages and disadvantages.

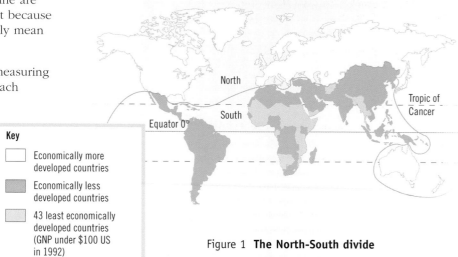

Figure 1 **The North-South divide**

Key

☐ Economically more developed countries

■ Economically less developed countries

▨ 43 least economically developed countries (GNP under $100 US in 1992)

Figure 2 Development statistics for selected countries, 1996

Country	GNP per capita ($US)	Population growth rate %	Infant mortality per 1000 live births	Adult literacy rate %	Urban population %	Daily calorie supply as % of requirements, 1988 – 90	% of population with access to health services, 1985 – 93
Australia	17 980	0.8	5.8	99	85	124	100
Brazil	3370	1.7	58	82	76	114	n/a
China	530	1.1	44	78	29	112	90
Ethiopia	130	3.1	120	24	15	73	46
Ghana	430	3	66	60	36	93	60
India	310	1.9	79	48	26	101	85
Indonesia	880	1.6	66	82	31	121	80
Iran	2 230	2.9	57	54	58	125	80
Italy	19 270	0	8.3	97	97	139	100
Japan	34 630	0.2	4.2	99	78	125	100
Latvia	2 290	– 0.7	19	99	69	n/a	n/a
Mali	250	3.1	106	32	26	96	n/a
Mexico	4 010	2.2	34	88	71	131	78
Nigeria	280	3.1	87	51	16	93	66
Papua New Guinea	1 160	2.3	63	52	15	114	96
Peru	1 890	2.1	60	85	70	87	75
Russia	2 650	– 0.5	18	99	73	n/a	n/a
Sweden	23 630	0.1	4.4	99	83	111	100
UK	18 410	0.2	6.2	99	90	130	100
USA	25 860	0.6	7.5	99	75	138	100
Industrialised countries	18 130	0.6	9	98	76	134	100
Developing countries	918	2.1	69	66	36	107	79
Least developed countries	236	2.7	111	43	22	90	48

Development indices

GNP per head (US$ per capita per year) – the total value of the goods and services produced in that country in a year divided by the country's population

Infant mortality rate (number per 1000 per year) – the number of deaths of infants of under 1 year old per every 1000 live births

Population growth rate (%) – the percentage by which a country's population is growing

Adult literacy rate (%) – the percentage of persons aged 15 and over who can read and write

Urban population (%) – the percentage of population living in urban areas

Daily per capita calorie supply (%) – the daily food supply as a percentage of the required food supply for each country

Access to health care (%) – the percentage of the population with access to health care.

There are problems in interpreting all of these indices. A value for a country as a whole can hide a considerable difference within sectors of the country. Collection of data may be unreliable and some countries may be unwilling to release figures.

Separate indices offer particular problems. For example, when comparing GNP between countries, those with a mainly subsistence economy will feature poorly as the subsistence sector will not contribute to the country's earnings. However, those people may be well fed and employed and so better off than those in an apparently richer country.

For this reason a number of indices, combining a range of indicators, have been created. The latest is the **Human Development Index** developed by the United Nations Development Programme. It combines indices on a country's wealth, health and education. Some countries, such as Sri Lanka and Tanzania, feature more highly in the HDI than they would if just GNP were taken into account. Others, such as Saudi Arabia and Iraq, feature less well. Critics of the HDI say that wealth is still the dominant feature of the index and other factors, such as law and order, civil rights and freedom of speech, should also be considered.

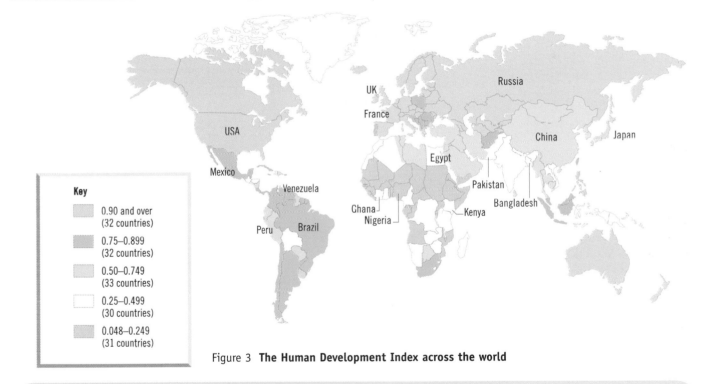

Key

- 0.90 and over (32 countries)
- 0.75–0.899 (32 countries)
- 0.50–0.749 (33 countries)
- 0.25–0.499 (30 countries)
- 0.048–0.249 (31 countries)

Figure 3 **The Human Development Index across the world**

1. Select four development indices. Draw up a table showing how each one is calculated, which units they use, and the advantages and disadvantages of using them as a measure of development.

2. Study Figure 2.
   a Pick out the top five and bottom five countries in each category of index.
   b Is there a pattern between the different indices?

3. Compare the summary information for Industrialised, Developing and the Least Developed Countries in Figure 2. Combine this information with Figure 1 on page 156. Write a speech for presentation to a school assembly with the title *An Unfair World*.

4. Compare Figure 1 with Figure 3
   a Describe in detail the distribution of the 43 least economically developed countries.
   b How similar are the patterns between the two maps?
   c What does this tell us about the value of using GNP as an indicator of development?
   d What does this tell us about how the Human Development Index is calculated?
   e If you were designing an index to show development, what factors would you consider?

10.2 The development gap

Less Economically Developed countries differ to the More Economically Developed Countries on a number of indices. Figure 1 represents the share of the world's resources and wealth. A variation exists across the globe due to numerous interlinked factors.

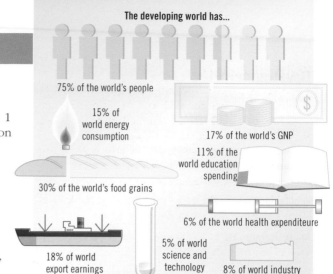

The developing world has...

75% of the world's people

15% of world energy consumption

17% of the world's GNP

11% of the world education spending

30% of the world's food grains

6% of the world health expenditeure

18% of world export earnings

5% of world science and technology

8% of world industry

Figure 1 **An unfair distribution of resources**

Historical factors

The slave trade

Slaves taken from West Africa to provide labour in the Americas had a profound effect on the development of the African regions. The slaves, often the strongest and most capable men and women, and the goods taken in exchange, namely guns, alcohol and textiles, had a detrimental effect on the region's development.

Colonisation

European explorers began colonising countries from the sixteenth century onwards. Before colonisation most of the countries were self-sufficient and in some cases, well developed compared to Europe. The economies of the colonies were altered and national boundaries imposed to ensure the provision of raw materials for European industrialisation. This severely restricted their own development and has left them with major economic and political difficulties. In particular, the trade patterns that developed were problematic (page 158).

The influence of the Europeans included opening up the mineral wealth of the country, creating farms and plantations, roads, railways, schools and hospitals. However, many people claim that colonisation and slavery are the sources of many of the problems facing the LDCs today.

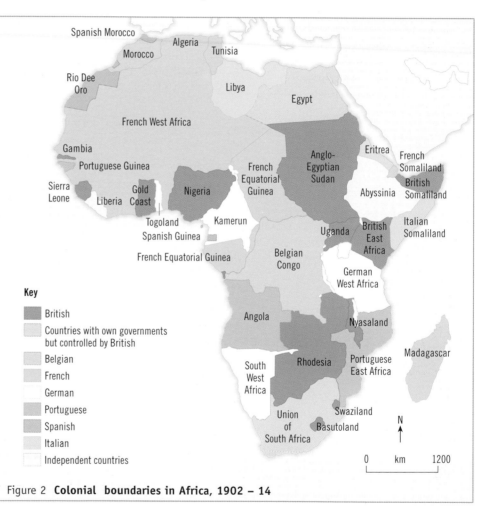

Key

- British
- Countries with own governments but controlled by British
- Belgian
- French
- German
- Portuguese
- Spanish
- Italian
- Independent countries

Figure 2 **Colonial boundaries in Africa, 1902 – 14**

Debt – an economic factor

A number of LDCs have borrowed money from other governments, international bodies and high street banks. The interest repayments on these loans are high. As a result, LDCs find it difficult to repay or even reduce the debt. Failure to keep up with repayments mean that the LDCs now owe more than they borrowed in the first place. Mexico and Nigeria have to pay over 30% of their income from exports in debt repayments; each person in Tanzania owes the West £134. In 1990, four times the amount of British aid given to the LDCs was received by the high street banks as interest repayments. It is almost impossible to progress or improve the standard of living under these circumstances.

Political factors

Some LDCs have inefficiently-run governments. Many are dictatorships with poor civil rights and no freedom of speech. In others, bribery, corruption and tribal loyalty guarantees votes. A vast bureaucracy and promotion of relatives are common problems. Incompetent and corrupt officials occur in many wealthier countries as well but the problems are exaggerated when a country is vulnerable.

Environmental factors

Many LDCs are subject to harsh extremes of climate. Although Europe and America suffer droughts, hurricanes and flooding, they have the resources and technology to cope them. LDCs on the other hand, do not have the money to deal with these environmental problems. In addition, the rapidly expanding populations make the land more vulnerable and more susceptible to the next disaster.

Figure 3 **Ken Saro-Wiwa, executed in Nigeria in 1996**

Figure 4 **The effects of natural disasters can be reduced with technology and money** A flooded street in the Mekong delta, and the Thames Barrier, London

1 Study Figure 2.
  a Create a table showing the 1924 name for ten different countries, its 1996 name and the colonial power.
  b Describe the distribution of the French colonies within Africa.
  c What links do countries like France and the UK still have with their former colonies?

2 Droughts in the UK cause only minor inconveniences yet in LDCs they lead to famine and death. Explain why LDCs are more vulnerable to natural disasters.

QUALITY OF LIFE

Most of the LDCs' economies are based on a few primary industries. These are often the farming of cash crops in plantations, such as coffee, tea or rubber, or the extraction of natural resources, such as timber, oil or copper. The products are then sold to the MDCs to manufacture and in many cases, are then sold back to the original country at increased rates. This trade pattern is based on historical factors and is exaggerated by trade barriers.

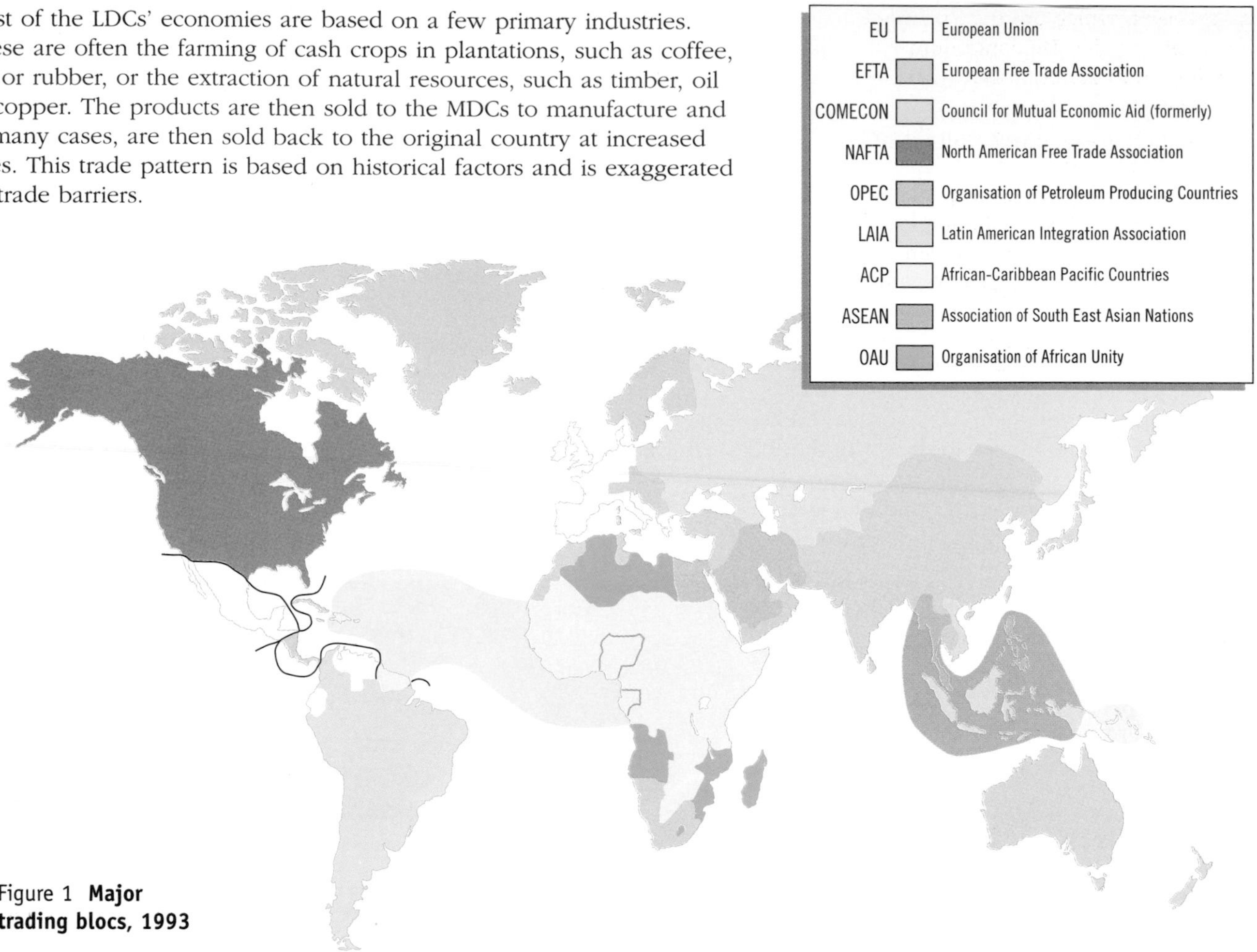

EU	European Union
EFTA	European Free Trade Association
COMECON	Council for Mutual Economic Aid (formerly)
NAFTA	North American Free Trade Association
OPEC	Organisation of Petroleum Producing Countries
LAIA	Latin American Integration Association
ACP	African-Caribbean Pacific Countries
ASEAN	Association of South East Asian Nations
OAU	Organisation of African Unity

Figure 1 **Major trading blocs, 1993**

Most countries of the world now belong to a **trading bloc**, a group of countries which have grouped together and have removed tariffs and trade barriers. This enables free and easy trade between those countries within the bloc while at the same time hindering trade with countries outside the group. The UK is a member of the European Union and so has tariff-free trading within Europe. One of the biggest blocks is the NAFTA (North American Free Trade Association), involving Canada, USA and Mexico. Mexicans hope the removal of tariffs will allow their cheaply produced goods to be sold in the USA. However, American firms are planning to move factories to Mexico to use the cheap labour and so increase their profits, which will be kept in the USA. American firms can now export their goods to the rapidly expanding Mexican market, swamping local suppliers.

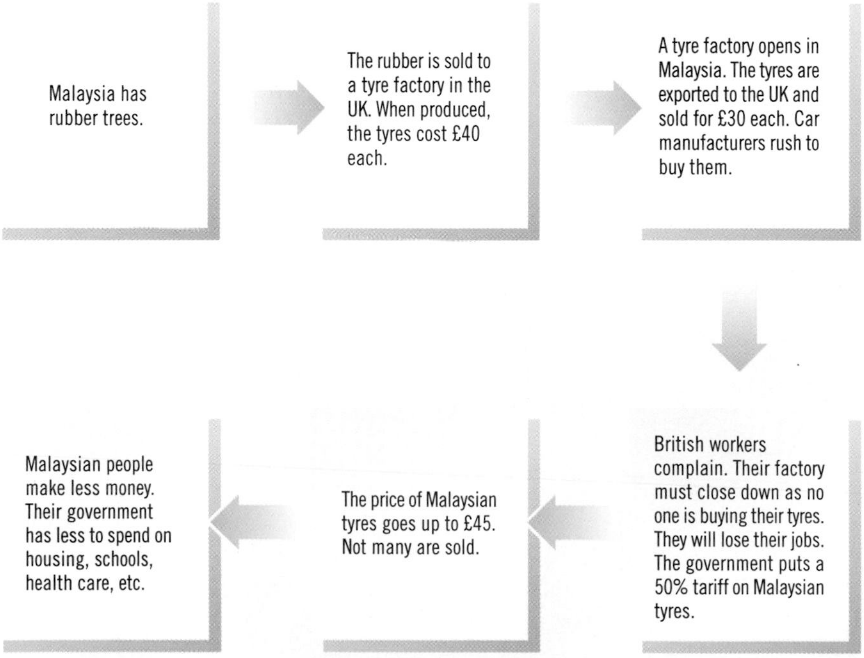

Malaysia has rubber trees.

→ The rubber is sold to a tyre factory in the UK. When produced, the tyres cost £40 each.

→ A tyre factory opens in Malaysia. The tyres are exported to the UK and sold for £30 each. Car manufacturers rush to buy them.

↓ British workers complain. Their factory must close down as no one is buying their tyres. They will lose their jobs. The government puts a 50% tariff on Malaysian tyres.

← The price of Malaysian tyres goes up to £45. Not many are sold.

← Malaysian people make less money. Their government has less to spend on housing, schools, health care, etc.

Figure 2 **How tariffs work**

Coffee is a common cash crop in LDCs. The UK imports 90% of its coffee in the form of beans, which are then processed into instant powder. By controlling the processing and transport, the UK makes more money from coffee than the producing countries. To prevent those countries processing the coffee themselves, the import tax on processed coffee is six times that on the imported beans. In addition, because so many LDCs grew coffee in the hope of gaining foreign capital to reduce their debts, there is considerable overproduction across the world. Prices are controlled by the markets in the West causing prices to fall. For example, in 1970 Ethiopia could buy one truck with the money it earned from 63 bags of coffee. A decade later it would need to sell over 127 bags to buy a similar truck. Today, approximately 500 bags would be required. To make the trade 'fairer', some companies ensure that a larger share goes to the people who grew the coffee.

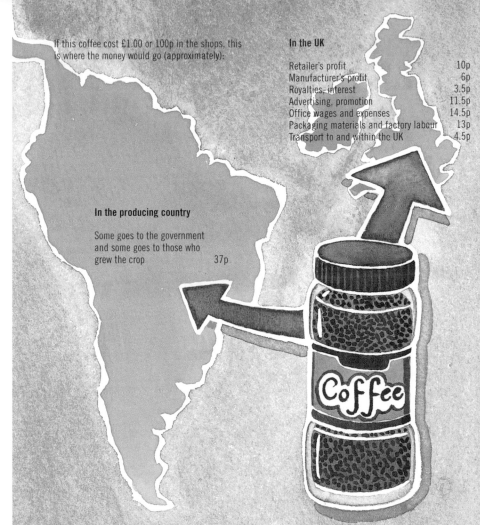

If this coffee cost £1.00 or 100p in the shops, this is where the money would go (approximately):

In the UK

Retailer's profit	10p
Manufacturer's profit	6p
Royalties, interest	3.5p
Advertising, promotion	11.5p
Office wages and expenses	14.5p
Packaging materials and factory labour	13p
Transport to and within the UK	4.5p

In the producing country

Some goes to the government and some goes to those who grew the crop   37p

▶ Figure 3 **Where the money goes**

◀ Figure 4 **Fairly traded goods on sale in a developed country**

1 **a** Select two trading blocs and name the countries within them.
  b In what ways does a trading bloc help the strongest countries?

2 Why might some people in the UK be against the removal of import tariffs?

3 Study Figure 3.
  a Draw a pie chart showing the share of the coffee profits retained in the UK and that which goes to the producing country.
  b Explain why more coffee is not manufactured into coffee powder in the LDCs.
  c Design a poster encouraging people to buy fairly traded goods.

4 Explain how trade patterns exaggerate the difference between the rich and the poor countries.

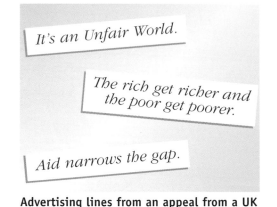

It's an Unfair World.

The rich get richer and the poor get poorer.

Aid narrows the gap.

Advertising lines from an appeal from a UK aid agency

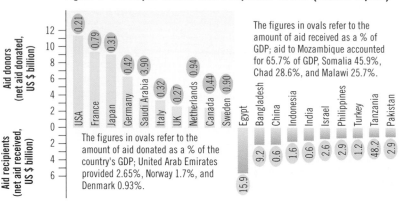

Figure 1 **Principal donors and recipients of aid (Brandt report)**

The figures in ovals refer to the amount of aid received as a % of GDP; aid to Mozambique accounted for 65.7% of GDP, Somalia 45.9%, Chad 28.6%, and Malawi 25.7%.

The figures in ovals refer to the amount of aid donated as a % of the country's GDP; United Arab Emirates provided 2.65%, Norway 1.7%, and Denmark 0.93%.

Note: In 1980 the Brandt report recommended that all developed countries should be providing 1% of their GDP for international aid by the year 2000.

Types of aid

Bilateral aid – this is given directly by one government to another. It usually takes the form of **tied aid.**

Tied aid – the donor government states what money should be spent on health care, education or infrastructure, for example.

Multilateral aid – governments donate money to world organisations such as the World Bank or The European Commission, which then distribute the aid themselves.

Voluntary organisations – these are funded by the public and organise their own aid programmes, for example, Oxfam, Comic Relief and VSO. They make up about 5% of all aid given.

Examples of aid

Sustainable logging in Papua New Guinea

The EU have set up a scheme to reduce the rate of logging. Mobile sawmills have been given to a number of villages. These 'walkabout' sawmills enable the villagers to process the timber in the forest, resulting in less deforestation as the rate of removal is slower than by machine. By processing the timber themselves, the villagers make more money than if they just sold the untreated logs.

The Victoria Dam, Sri Lanka

Approximately £100 million of UK aid provided equipment, advisors and technicians to build a large hydro-electric dam in Sri Lanka. Much of the equipment was manufactured in the UK.

Earthquake relief, Armenia

Blankets and temporary shelters were sent out to the earthquake area. In addition, tracker devices and firemen trained in their use were flown out by the UK government.

Figure 2 **A Russian helicopter helps with rescue work after an earthquake**

Reasons for lending aid

Governments lend aid for a number of reasons:

Economic

LDCs, with their large populations, will form an important market for manufactured goods in the future. It is in the best interests of more developed countries to help the LDCs develop.

Many of the larger projects, such as building dams, require further purchases from the donor country in the future. Often UK engineers and scientists will be employed on the scheme.

On a smaller scale, for example, donating some four-wheel-drive vehicles to projects will ensure continued demand for spares in the future

Political

By giving aid to a country, the bonds between the two countries are strengthened. Egypt, for example, is an important ally for America in the Middle East. The bond is strengthened as the USA lends more aid.

If the gap between the North and South gets too large it is likely to lead to global instability, hence the importance of maintaining the aid relationship.

Moral

Many people believe the rich have a duty and obligation to try to give to the poor

▶ Figure 3 **Boomerang aid**

1 Study Figure 1.
   a In actual terms, which were the biggest donors of aid?
   b Redraw the graph, this time representing the amount of aid donated as a percentage of the country's GDP. Include those countries mentioned in the text.
   c Which are the biggest donors of aid in relative terms?
   d How many of the countries shown have obtained the figures suggested by the Brandt Report?
   e Write a paragraph commenting on these figures.

2 **a** What different types of aid have been identified in the text?
   b Classify the examples given in *Examples of aid* under each type of aid.
   c Construct a table for each type of aid, outlining the advantages and disadvantages for the donor country.
   d Construct a table for each type of aid, outlining the advantages and disadvantages for the recipient country.

3 Study Figure 3.
   a Explain what is meant by 'boomerang aid'.
   b In what ways can aid generate wealth for the donor country?

Case study | Papua New Guinea

Papua New Guinea is a LDC, a former colony of the UK and Germany, and then an Australian Protectorate until its independence in 1975. The country consists of a beautiful Pacific coastline, thick rainforest and high mountain ranges. Over 850 different languages are spoken due to the landscape which prevents free access between valleys. The coastal regions were involved in trade since the beginning. The inaccessible highlands, however, did not have contact with the outside world until the 1930s when gold diggers developed routes into the mountains.

Logging

Logging in the coastal regions is growing fast. Corruption and bribery mean that restrictions and replanting are often ignored. The hardwood logs are exported, often to be made into chipboard for construction work in the 'tiger economies' of the Far East. Some local landowners set up their own companies and have started to manufacture the wood into planks themselves. The logging companies have built roads and provided money for education and health services to many remote parts of the country.

Food

Still predominantly a subsistence population, the growing towns mean that more people are buying food. The most common foods are rice and tinned fish. Subsidised rice is imported from Australia. Rice could be grown in Papua New Guinea, but local producers cannot compete with the imported product. If the government were to remove the rice subsidy, the price would escalate and the government would lose its votes.

Tinned fish is imported from Japan, much of which had been caught off the Papua New Guinea coast. Without a fish processing plant, Papua New Guinea is forced to import from Japan.

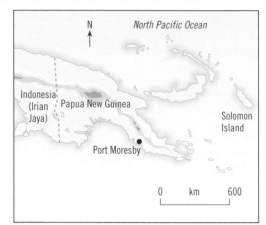

Figure 1 **Papua New Guinea**

Mineral reserves

The highlands provide an immense mineral wealth. Gold, copper and, recently, oil are extracted. Multinational companies such as RTZ (Rio Tinto) operate the huge mines, employing local tribesmen and women, and engineers from Australia. The income is divided among the local landowners, the government and the multinationals, who have the largest proportion. Disputes over the share going to locals have led to armed resistance and the closure of one mine. A mine operator is being sued in the world's largest claim for pollution to a river.

The mining companies donate water supply equipment, school buildings and health care. However, the local society which was formerly subsistence is now struggling to cope with the influx of money, alcohol and guns.

◀ Figure 2 **Porgera Mine, Chimbu Province**

Figure 3 **New classrooms being built with the help of foreign aid**

Aid

About 20% of the government's budget is paid for by Australian aid. Countries such as Canada, Japan and organisations like the UN and EU have donated aid in terms of money, technical assistance and infrastructure.

Sustainable logging

The EU have started to fund a project to reduce the rate of logging. They are providing 'walkabout sawmills' which allow the villagers to cut and process the wood themselves. The mills are mobile and so cause less destruction to the forests than dragging the wood to one large mill. The pace of deforestation from these small mills is less than if the wood was being removed by a logging company. It is hoped that the forest will have longer to recover and regrow. Not only will the logging be sustainable but the large profits to be had from processing the wood will remain with the villagers rather than go to the foreign logging companies.

Farming in schools

Voluntary Service Overseas, a UK charity, has sent a number of farmers to work in schools. They are given money to establish farms in each school. The school farms grow local produce which can be used to feed the students or can be sold in local markets. It is also hoped that the students will learn new farming methods and how to farm profitably.

1 **a** Write a paragraph describing the location of Papua New Guinea.

b Using Figure 2 *Development statistics for selected countries, 1996* on page 154, compare Papua New Guinea with the UK and Mali. To what extent is Papua New Guinea not a typical developing country?

2 Outline the advantages that the logging and mining companies bring to the local people and the country.

3 Write a letter to your local newspaper explaining the problems that multinational companies bring to a country such as Papua New Guinea.

4 **a** Do you consider aid projects such as those shown in unit 10.4 will help the country cope with its problems?

b In what other ways could the more developed countries help Papua New Guinea face the future?

The word 'civilisation' is derived from the same word as 'city'. In the past the city showed the highest form of art, architecture and 'civilisation' that society could attain. Today large cities still reflect the values of the societies in which they are located.

Urbanisation is the increase in the proportion of people who live in cities. Globally, there is a great increase in the rate of urbanisation. In the UK urbanisation occurred in the nineteenth century during the Industrial Revolution (Figure 1). It appears that the growth of urban population in developed countries is slowing down, and that most urbanisation is taking place in the less developed countries. In addition to the global rise of urbanisation (Figure 5), there is a great increase in the number of large cities (Figure 2).

Measuring growth in a city is difficult. The general pattern, however, is that there is a relationship between level of development and urbanisation (Figures 4 and 6).

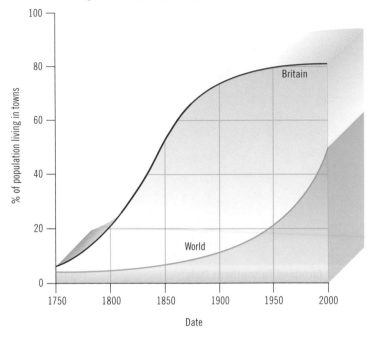

Figure 1 **Rates of urbanisation since 1750**

Figure 2 **The rise of the supercities**
Cities with more than ten million inhabitants

Year	City
1950	New York
	London
1975	New York
	Tokyo / Yokohama
	Los Angeles
	London
	Mexico City
	Shanghai
	São Paulo
1995	São Paulo
	Beijing
	Shanghai
	Paris
	Bombay
	Calcutta
	Tokyo
	Seoul
	Mexico
	Los Angeles
	New York
	Buenos Aires

Figure 3 **New York, long-time supercity**

Figure 4 **Problems of measuring urban population**

■ Different countries have different measurements of urban levels. In Norway, a settlement with over 200 people is classified as urban. This would be the size of a village in the UK.

■ In a country where literacy rates are low, keeping track of the birth and death rates may be very difficult. The record of migration to the cities may be equally difficult to track.

■ Even in wealthy countries, a census is usually only taken once every ten years. Figures for dates in between the census years are estimates.

■ As a city grows, settlements on the edge of the city may become absorbed. If new boundaries are drawn to include these settlements, there may be a false impression of sudden growth.

■ Different authorities may use different boundaries of settlements. Estimates of the size of the very large cities, in particular, vary greatly.

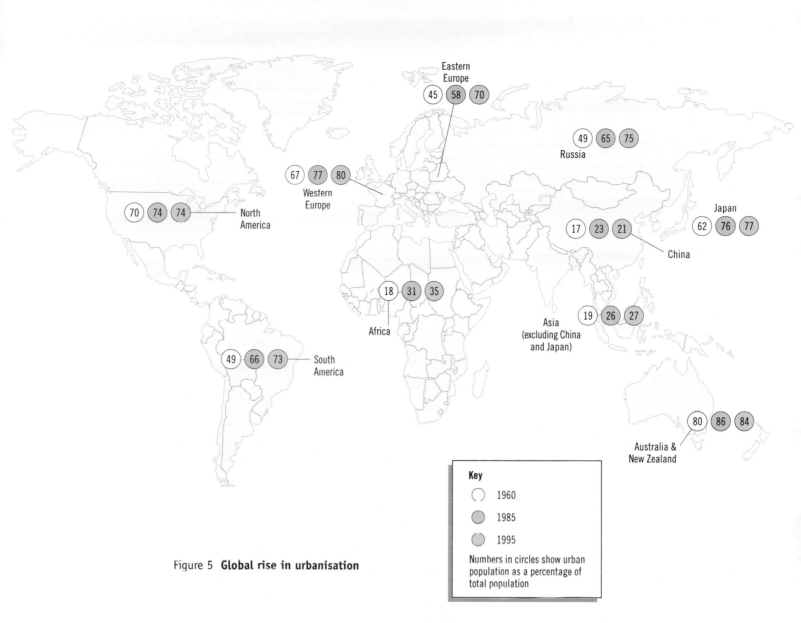

Figure 5 **Global rise in urbanisation**

Key
○ 1960
◑ 1985
◕ 1995

Numbers in circles show urban population as a percentage of total population

1 Use the statistics and an atlas to plot the location of cities with more than five million inhabitants on a blank map of the world.

2 Why do you think London does not appear in the list of largest cities in 1995 (Figure 2)?

3 Where are most of the 'supercities' located?

4 What problems do countries with 'supercities' have?

5 Plot a scattergraph with the information shown in Figure 6. What is the relationship between the two sets of data?

Figure 6	**Relationship between urbanisation and development**	
Country	% urban population	UN Human development index *
Australia	86	0.97
Bangladesh	18	0.185
Brazil	77	0.739
Chile	86	0.863
Denmark	76	0.953
Iran	55	0.547
Japan	77	0.981
Malawi	15	0.166
Peru	70	0.6
Turkey	48	0.671
USA	74	0.976
UK	93	0.962

* An index calculated by the UN includes income, life expectancy, adult literacy and years in education.

Examining the period when each settlement first developed can help explain why settlements are located in particular places. Often the reasons for the original settlement location are no longer important (Figure 1). Some villages with accessible sites or other advantages grew into towns (Figure 2) but many failed to expand and even today, remain small settlements. As the economy shifted from agricultural to industrial, towns grew in locations best suited to the new technology.

The spacing of settlements is determined by the physical landscape and history of an area, and the sphere of influence of the settlement itself. The satellite photograph in Figure 3 shows how difficult it is to identify settlement patterns.

Spacing of settlements

All settlements provide a service to the surrounding area. A farm, for example, offers storage of tools and grain for the fields, whereas a capital city will offer government and media services to the whole country. The higher the order of the service or function, the larger the area that the settlement will serve. This area is the **sphere of influence**.

All services have a **range**, the maximum distance over which people are willing to travel to use a service. The higher the order of service, the larger the range.

All services have a **threshold**, that is, the number of people required to make the operation of a service or shop viable. A newsagents will have a smaller threshold than a large department store, for example.

Where physical features are not important, it is the interaction of the range, threshold and sphere of influence of services in different settlements in an area which will determine their spacing.

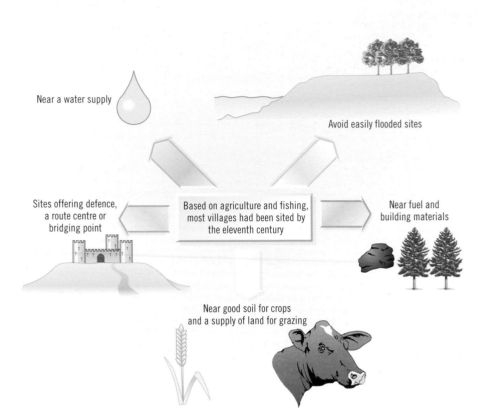

Figure 1 **Hamlets and villages in the UK**

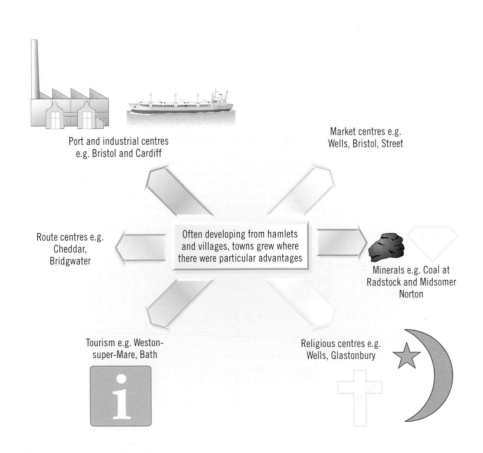

Figure 2 **Towns in the UK**

Figure 3 **Bristol and surrounding area** On this satellite photograph, water is black, urban areas are dark blue, and agricultural land is red.

1 **a** Using tracing paper and an atlas map of the area to guide you, trace the outline of the land and settlements shown on the satellite photograph. Label as many of the towns and cities as you can. Is it possible to see if the settlement pattern is related to the physical landscape?

b Explain why Wells, Glastonbury and Cheddar remained small settlements while Bristol and Cardiff grew.

c Why have Bristol and Bath both survived and grown although they are so close?

2 How would you identify the sphere of influence of a village or a small town?

11.3 The growth of urban areas

One of the greatest periods of urbanisation was in nineteenth century Britain during the Industrial Revolution. Until this period the largest settlements had been market towns, ports or administrative and religious centres that served the surrounding rural population. With the new techniques of manufacturing, settlements on the coalfields or near raw materials, at port sites, or at nodal points became the best places to expand. Increased efficiency meant fewer people were required on the land. Migration to the new job opportunities in urban factories took place. City growth was also caused by rapid population growth which was over 10% for most of the century.

Commerce thrived. The cities expanded without structure or plan. Low-cost terraced housing, often in the back-to-back style, was supplied by local builders for rent. These cheap houses were near the city centre, adjacent to factories, canals and railways. Such housing has now largely been cleared from British cities, but a typical grid street pattern remains in some areas. The rapid growth and the problems in supplying adequate services, such as street lighting, water and sewage disposal, led to a series of parliamentary Acts to control these utilities.

The better quality housing built during the nineteenth century has survived. Today as the city has expanded, many of these buildings have been occupied for commercial uses such as offices and shops. Parks, gardens and institutions, such as libraries, hospitals and schools dating from the Victorian period, remain a part of the urban landscape.

Figure 1 **Development in Birmingham, 1570 – 1996**

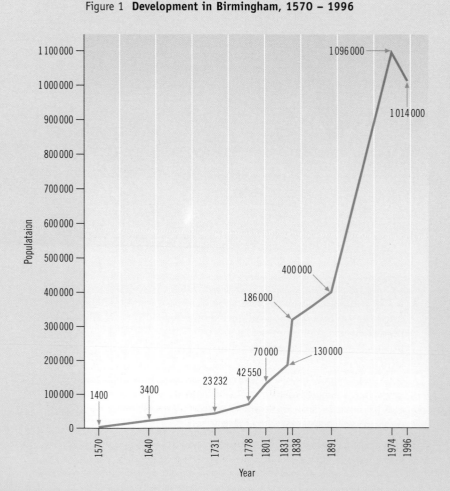

The growth of Birmingham

The poor soils of the area encouraged the development of trade and skills such as metal working rather than reliance on agricultural wealth. Although not on a coalfield, the south Staffordshire coalfield was nearby.

Canals and railways linked the area to London (1838), Liverpool (1837) and Gloucester (1840). Although not a port, and with no textile tradition, the city grew, based on a variety of small metal working industries and food processing. By 1873 there were 745 different trades and skills listed in the city.

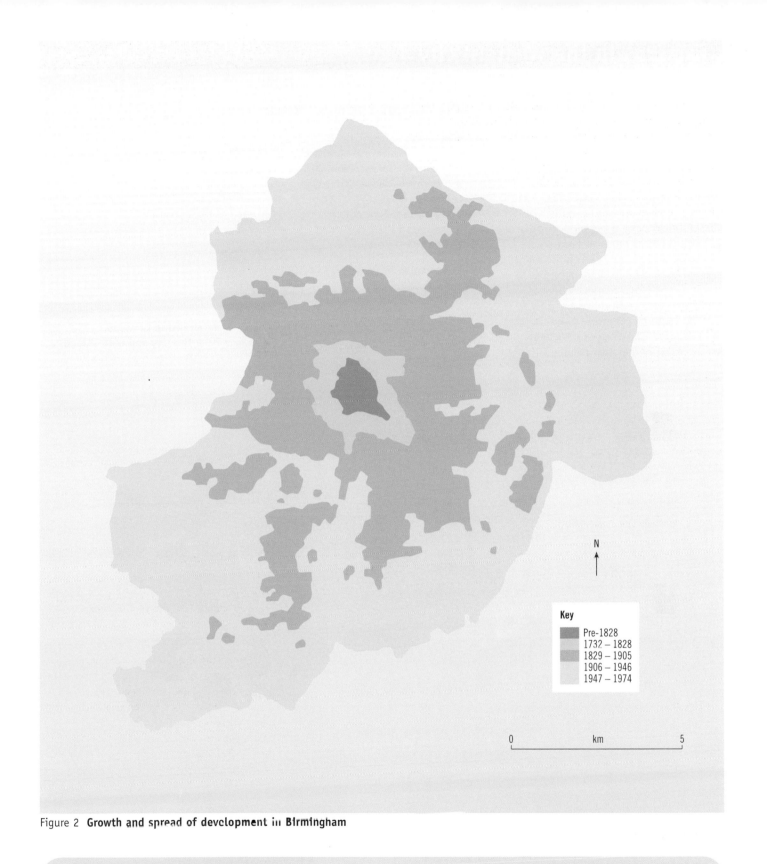

Figure 2 **Growth and spread of development in Birmingham**

Key
- Pre-1828
- 1732 – 1828
- 1829 – 1905
- 1906 – 1946
- 1947 – 1974

N

0   km   5

1 Use a geology map of Britain to identify areas of coal deposits. Which large urban areas are located on these deposits?

2 a Most nineteenth century developments of workers' housing have now been cleared. Why?
b What sorts of buildings and urban areas remain from the Victorian era in a city known to you?

3 a Study Figures 1 and 2. Why may there have been such a rapid population growth in 1838?
b Although peak population growth was before the twentieth century, why has this century contributed the most physical growth?

4 What has happened to the population of Birmingham since 1974? Suggest reasons for this.

The photographs on page 174 show the main areas of a typical Western city. Although different land uses tend to be located in different areas of the city, all cities have a Central Business District, some industry, and housing which occupies most of the space. These land uses are described on the right. Geographers have used models to account for the layout of land use. Figures 2 and 3 show the two earliest and simplest models suggested by Burgess and Hoyt, respectively. Individual cities will differ from these general patterns (Figures 4 and 5). The models were drawn up before high levels of car ownership changed the city.

The Central Business District (CBD)

■ At a focus of routes, the CBD is usually the oldest part of the city. It has historic buildings and parks as well as new buildings.
■ Competition for accessible sites makes land expensive. Tall buildings maximise space.
■ Only commercial and business concerns can afford the high rents. There is little residential land use.
■ Few industries are located in the CBD.
■ The street pattern may date from the period when the city first expanded, causing congestion.

Land values in the city

Land values decrease with distance away from the central, accessible and prestigious sites.

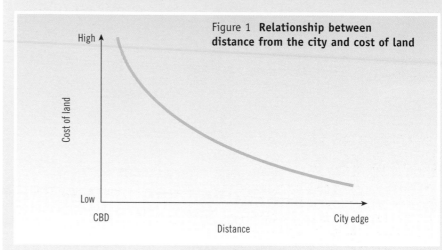

Figure 1 **Relationship between distance from the city and cost of land**

Key

1	The central business district (CBD)
2	Wholesale light manufacturing
3	Low class residential
4	Medium class residential
5	High class residential

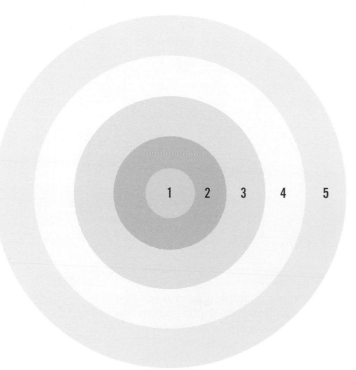

Figure 2 **The concentric ring model, Burgess 1924**

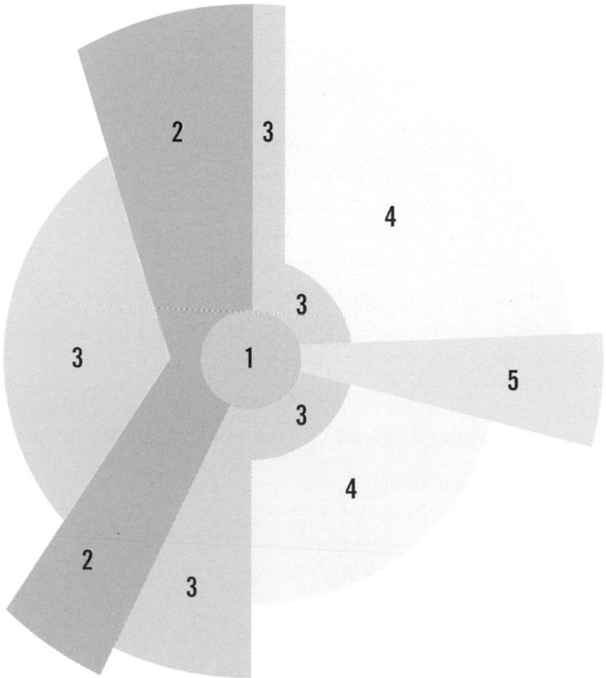

Figure 3 **The sector model, Hoyt 1939**

Industry in the city

Heavy industry

Heavy industry is usually located in the inner city near the docks, canal or railway links. Much of the industry has declined, although brewing, food processing, and industries which typically serve the CBD, such as printing, are still located here.

Light industry

Industrial estates from the early 1900s are located on what would have been the city edge, next to roads and railways. Suburban development has surrounded these industrial areas.

High technology industry

These new industries are located most often on city-edge sites, adjacent to motorways and airports.

Housing in the city

Low cost housing

The cheapest housing is on relatively expensive land surrounding the CBD. People with low incomes live here to avoid the cost of commuting to the CBD. The high cost of housing is offset by high densities and older properties in particular are subdivided. Housing is typically rented or has been purchased from the council. On the city's edge, low cost housing is often found where councils have located estates as a result of clearance from the inner city.

Medium cost housing

Suburban development typically provides more living space beyond the inner city. There is a higher proportion of owner occupation than nearer the CBD. Villages which have become engulfed by the city may create local pockets of higher and lower cost housing, as may be the case in the other residential zones.

High cost housing

The largest owner-occupied houses are found on the edge of the city where commuting to the CBD is expensive. A recent trend is for high cost housing to be built in exclusive locations near the CBD.

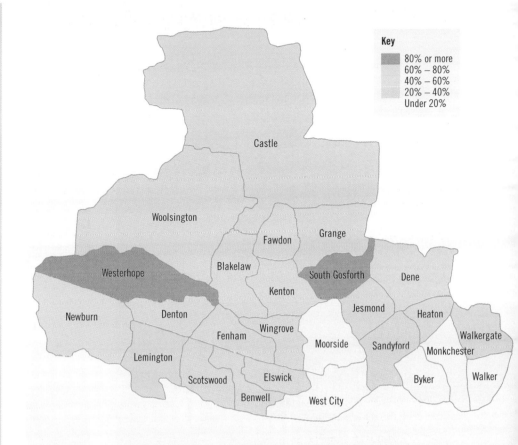

Figure 4 **Newcastle upon Tyne – households in owner occupation, 1991**

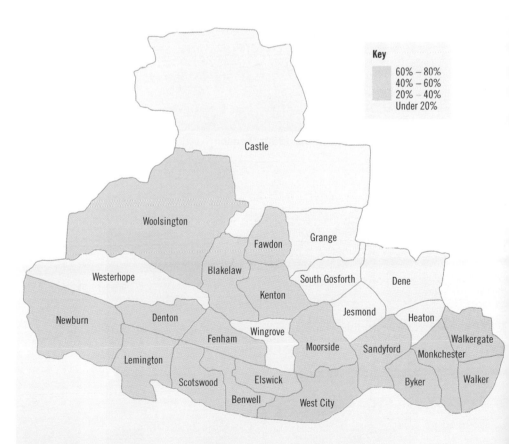

Figure 5 **Newcastle upon Tyne – households in Local Authority rented accommodation, 1991**

Figure 6 **The Central Business District, Perth, Australia**

Figure 7 **Toxteth, inner city Liverpool**

Figure 8 **Housing built in the 1930s, London**

Figure 9 **Modern executive housing, edge of Bristol**

Figure 10 **Edge-of-city council development, Wester Hailes, Edinburgh**

Figure 11 **Outer business district, Brislington, Bristol**

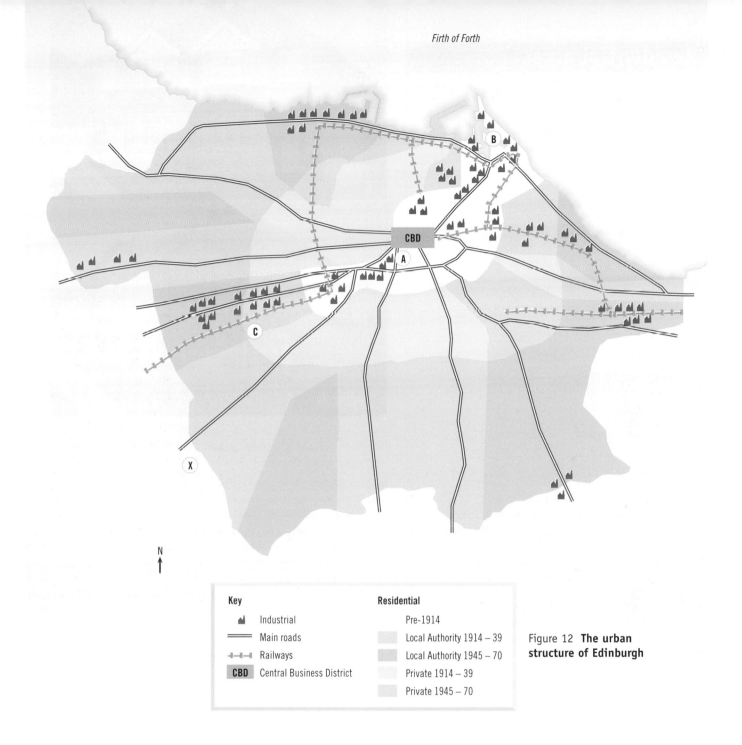

Firth of Forth

CBD

Key

⛭ Industrial

══ Main roads

╈╈╈ Railways

CBD Central Business District

Residential

Pre-1914

▨ Local Authority 1914 – 39

▨ Local Authority 1945 – 70

▨ Private 1914 – 39

▨ Private 1945 – 70

Figure 12 **The urban structure of Edinburgh**

N ↑

---

1 Using the urban land use models in Figures 2 and 3 (page 172), place the photographs in the appropriate zones shown in the models.

2 Does the housing pattern in Newcastle upon Tyne (Figures 4 and 5) correspond to either the concentric ring or sector model? Give reasons for your answer.

3 Study Figure 12 which shows the main areas of industry, and private and Local Authority housing for select periods in Edinburgh. Using tracing paper, draw:
a an overlay shading the housing according to two groups: private and local authority.
b an overlay shading the areas according to age: pre-1914, 1914 – 1939 and 1945 – 1970.

c Comment on the patterns you have produced. In what ways does Edinburgh correspond to the models in Figures 2 and 3?

4 Match these industries to the locations A, B, and C:
a long-established brewery
b animal foodstuff processing using imported grain
c light engineering established in the 1930s.

5 Why have modern research and development industries been located to the west of the city, rather than the east?

6 Modern private housing has been developed at Bonaly and Balerno, marked at X on the map. Why has this location been selected for private housing?

11.5 Residential areas

Different areas of the city have different residential characteristics (Figure 4). Residential choices are determined mainly by the ability to pay for housing. The age of the population, family circumstances, stages in the life cycle, aspirations, and religious and ethnic influences may also be important. The 'urban gatekeepers' such as city councils who allocate council houses, landlords and estate agents, may also control flows of information about houses. However, the extent of such controls is difficult to measure. Figure 1 shows how these various factors can strongly influence residential characteristics.

£79,000

£98,000

LYNWOOD DRIVE

The price of a similar property may vary across a city. Cost is the determining influence as to who can live in a particular area. Factors which help determine demand include:

■ the perception of the area. Leafy spacious suburbs, often in areas of high relief, are considered more desirable, while proximity to an area perceived as unsafe lowers prices.

■ proximity to services, such as good schools, transport links, and neighbourhood shops will enhance house prices.

■ proximity to industry, railway lines, derelict land, or busy traffic-congested roads can have a negative effect on house prices.

Figure 1 **The cycle of residential choice**

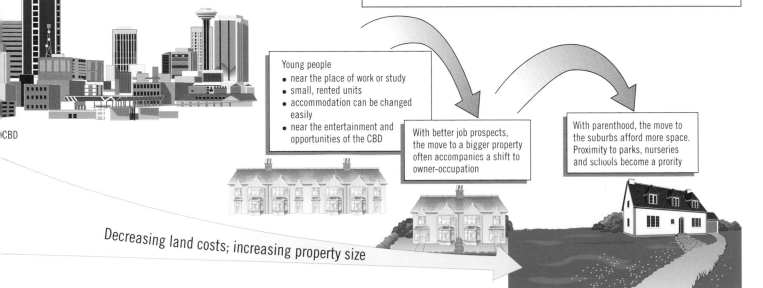

CBD

Young people
- near the place of work or study
- small, rented units
- accommodation can be changed easily
- near the entertainment and opportunities of the CBD

With better job prospects, the move to a bigger property often accompanies a shift to owner-occupation

With parenthood, the move to the suburbs afford more space. Proximity to parks, nurseries and schools become a prority

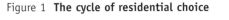

Decreasing land costs; increasing property size

Movement tends to take place along transport routes.

This analysis of the stage in the cycle of housing preference overlooks the following:

■ Migration to the suburbs may be reduced due to job insecurity and unemployment.

■ An increasing number of young professionals are moving out of the city altogether.

■ An increase in the number of households with only one adult and the tendency for family breakdown limits movement to the suburbs.

The trend to migrate out along transport routes has been noted in relation to 'age and stage' and also as migrant groups become more established. Thus children of first generation immigrants have moved out to larger houses and better opportunities in the suburbs, but kept to areas linked to familiar transport routes.

Figure 2 **Housing near the Shankill Road**

In addition to the usual factors that cause differences in residential areas, Belfast's housing areas are segregated according to religion. As new housing estates were built on the city edge, the religious divide extended outwards from inner Belfast, along lines of public transport. Thus the Roman Catholics from the Falls Road area settled in the Anderstown estate, and Protestants moved from the Shankill to the Ardoyne.

Only 1% of children in the province attend integrated schools. The continued demand for separate schooling and the desire to prevent children from crossing boundaries and 'peace lines' has encouraged people in Belfast to move to their respective majority areas. The 1991 census revealed that of Belfast's 51 district council wards, the population of 35 000 is at least 90% of one religion or the other.

Figure 3 **The peace line in Belfast**

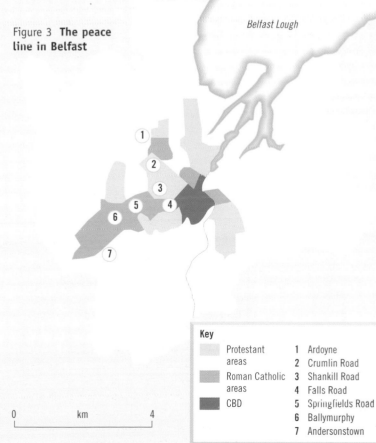

Key

	Protestant areas	1	Ardoyne
		2	Crumlin Road
	Roman Catholic areas	3	Shankill Road
		4	Falls Road
	CBD	5	Springfields Road
		6	Ballymurphy
		7	Andersonstown

0   km   4

Figure 4 **Location of Kelvindale and Easterhouse, Glasgow**

The table shows information for two contrasting areas in the city of Glasgow. Kelvindale is a Victorian suburb, with the city's main university, art gallery and public buildings dating from this period. Easterhouse is an area of housing built in the 1960s to accommodate people from the cramped inner city.

Factor	Kelvindale	Easterhouse
Housing		
owner occupied	79%	15%
rented from local authority	3%	58%
vacant dwellings	4%	20%
Land		
% of land in ward in industrial use	0.4%	6.2%
% vacant land in ward	3.8%	10.5%
Households		
with car	74%	20.5%
with a professional or managerial member	44.5%	6.8%
with children	22%	45%
with lone parent	2.3%	16.5%
Percentage of workforce unemployed	6.3%	34.2%

Study Figure 4.

1 Produce two pie charts (one each for Kelvindale and Easterhouse) to show the information for housing in Figure 4.

2 What types of housing are not shown, which could account for the incomplete statistics?

3 Describe the differences between the two wards. Show the other information in graphic form.

11.6 Ethnic patterns in cities

Migrants to a country tend to settle in cities, and often in the inner areas (Figure 2). In the UK, migration from the New Commonwealth territories of the West Indies, Pakistan, India and West Africa, encouraged by job opportunities and a higher standard of living, occurred before restrictions were set in 1963 and 1964. Since then the flow of migrants' relatives and those with special skills has continued on a smaller scale.

Many ethnic groups are located in the large conurbations (Figure 1). The Indian groups have become more integrated into British society; between 1971 and 1984 the move to administrative jobs increased by 50%. The 1991 census indicates that 15% of Indian males had a post-school qualification or degree, compared with only 9% of white males. These groups are prepared to move further apart and locate in different parts of the city.

Figure 2 Reasons for settling in the inner cities

Migrants settle in the inner cities for a number of reasons:

■ cheap rented accommodation – often migrants were single males, their dependents arriving much later

■ older, large properties were easily subdivided and let by private landlords

■ the availability of jobs in the CBD and public transport

■ the proximity of services catering for a newly arrived population e.g. launderettes, cafes, and, once the groups had become settled, specialist services catering for different language and cultural groups e.g. mosques, food stores

■ negative discrimination may have discouraged migrants from settling elsewhere.

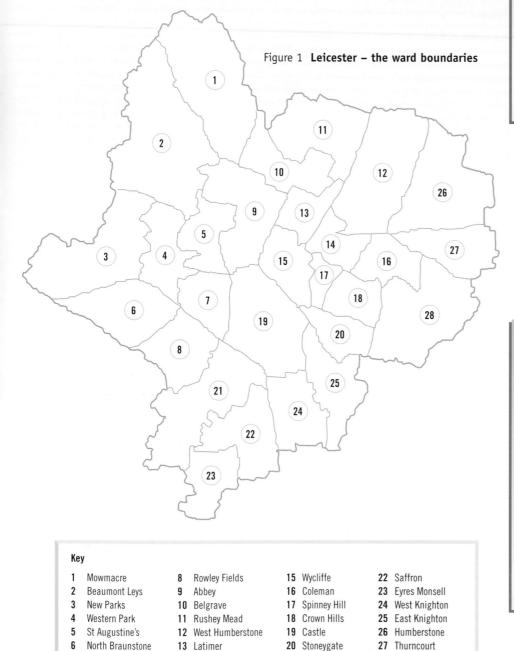

Figure 1 **Leicester – the ward boundaries**

Location Quotient

The Location Quotient is a means of recording variation in the distribution of a population. It shows how the pattern differs from what would be expected if all its members were evenly distributed throughout the area. Thus in Leicester, where 22% of the population is Indian, one would expect each ward to have an Indian population of 22% if the distribution were even.

$$\text{Location Quotient LQ} = \frac{\text{Observed}}{\text{Expected}} \quad \frac{22}{22} = 1$$

New Parks ward, for example has 1% Indians. The Location Quotient is 1/22 = 0.045. Thus a LQ of less than 1 suggests under-representation of the population, while a value over 1 suggests over-representation.

Key

1	Mowmacre	8	Rowley Fields	15	Wycliffe	22	Saffron
2	Beaumont Leys	9	Abbey	16	Coleman	23	Eyres Monsell
3	New Parks	10	Belgrave	17	Spinney Hill	24	West Knighton
4	Western Park	11	Rushey Mead	18	Crown Hills	25	East Knighton
5	St Augustine's	12	West Humberstone	19	Castle	26	Humberstone
6	North Braunstone	13	Latimer	20	Stoneygate	27	Thurncourt
7	Westcotes	14	Charnwood	21	Aylestone	28	Evington

Figure 3 Indian population of wards in Leicester

Ward	% population Indian
Abbey	47.1
Aylestone	2.7
Beaumont Leys	9.9
Belgrave	47.5
Castle	6.3
Charnwood	47.2
Coleman	24.3
Crown Hills	65.6
East Knighton	6.8
Evington	18.1
Eyres Monsell	0.4
Humberstone	5.5
Latimer	66.7
Mowmacre	0.9
New Parks	1.2
North Braunstone	0.7
Rowley Fields	12.6
Rushey Mead	60.5
Saffron	1.7
Saint Augustine's	6.9
Spinney Hill	60.9
Stoneygate	39.5
Thurncourt	5.9
Westcotes	18.9
Weston Park	7.6
West Humber Stone	13.9
West Knighton	14.4
Wycliffe	29.8
% Indian population in Leicester	22.3%
% Indian population in Leicestershire	8.4%

Attitudes to ethnic communities

Riots in Liverpool, London, Nottingham and Bristol's inner cities have had a racist dimension. The issue of ethnic and racial identities is confused. In 1996 a Hindu temple was opened in Neasden, North London (see photo). Responses to the building, which was constructed in a record two and a half years, provide an insight into attitudes to ethnic groups in cities.

"It's good to see so much private investment in the neighbourhood."

"Nonsense! A temple on a London skyline!"

"I'd hoped, in time, my family would have become less obviously different. The mosque encourages us to look and be different."

"If separate worship and schooling continue, our society is going to become split."

"We're losing our national heritage."

"Our culture with emphasis on family is much superior to the culture we see around us."

"Part of the wealth of a society is in its variety of traditions. People should be able to learn from each other."

1 Using Figure 3, complete the LQ index for the Indian population of each ward in Leicester.

2 **a** On a copy of the map (Figure 1; also on page 251), produce a choropleth map, dividing the LQ indices into suitable categories e.g. LQ 0 – 1.2 = low concentration, LQ 1.3 – 5.0 = medium concentration. Use a light colour for the lowest concentration and darker colours for higher concentrations.

b Identify the wards where the highest and lowest concentrations of Indians are located. Do these correspond to any pattern identified in the urban land use models (page 172)?
c What other ward information would you need to draw conclusions about the relative status and wealth of the Indian population?

3 Why do you think dispersal from the concentrations of ethnic groups takes place in clearly defined directions?

4 What factors will encourage ethnic groups to integrate more and become less concentrated in certain areas?

The **inner city** is defined as the area adjacent to the CBD, with many social, economic and physical problems. In the USA, **ghettos**, which are defined as areas having a high percentage of ethnic minorities, are located in the inner city. British inner cities date from the nineteenth century, when industry and housing for the workers expanded rapidly. By the late 1950s and early 1960s traditional industries had declined and housing was in a poor state. Planners redeveloped the inner cities by clearing the existing housing and replacing it with flats and new houses, in a process called **comprehensive redevelopment**.

Thirty years later, the inner cities were once again problem areas. The new housing designs were unpopular and some had structural problems. New industries were not attracted to these inner areas. Teesside, for example, suffers inner city decline and has tried renewal (Figure 1).

Nineteenth century expansion

- high density terraced housing built on the original edge-of-the-city

- new furniture, iron and steel, and railway-related factories built near docks.

Patterns of industrial change from the 1920s

- railways and shipbuilding declines

- furniture manufacturing moves to greenfield sites

- steel manufacturing moves to edge-of-city

- chemical works on city edge in 1950s employ most of the workers.

Regeneration

- Urban programme

- Teesside Development Corporation established 1992

- City Challenge

1960s

- new council housing supplied based on American style 'Radburn' layout with shared gardens and curving roads

- derelict and contaminated land left as firms move out

- land is difficult to sell; firms prefer new sites near city edge

- migration of people to newer houses on city edge, nearer jobs

- increasing proportion of households with social problems left behind

- housing vacated

- vandalism and crime increase

- deterioration of shops and services

- pollution – litter, dumping and graffiti

- investment not attracted to area.

Figure 1 **Decline in the Stockton on Tees inner city**

Reversing the trend

The UK government has implemented solutions to the problems of the inner city. Enterprise Zones were among the first initiatives. They have brought changes to the affected areas, but many question the effectiveness of the policy. Urban Development Corporations were established later, first in London Docklands, and subsequently, in other cities. They attract private funds.

Figures 2 to 3 show the changes which have occurred in Teesside Development Corporation. Other schemes, including the City Challenge scheme, the Task Force and Derelict Land Grants, suggest that the government is attempting to compensate for policies which, until the mid-1980s, favoured the city edges.

The Teesside Development Corporation

Teesside Development Corporation was created in 1987 to regenerate 48 km² of derelict urban land. It is the largest regeneration site in Europe. Initial clearing of the land cost more than £75 million. Schemes have included the building of a barrage which holds the Tees at high tide level and has created 17 km of navigable water. An international standard canoe course adds to the leisure facilities. In addition to the facilities marked on the map, a new offshore base serves the North Sea Oil and Gas industries. The base is made up of 22 companies, including OTEC (Ocean Technology Centre), which together employ 1400 people. A new nature reserve costing £11 million to establish makes use of land formerly used by ICI. Over 26 km of new roads, walkways, canals and bridges, including the barrage, make the area more accessible.

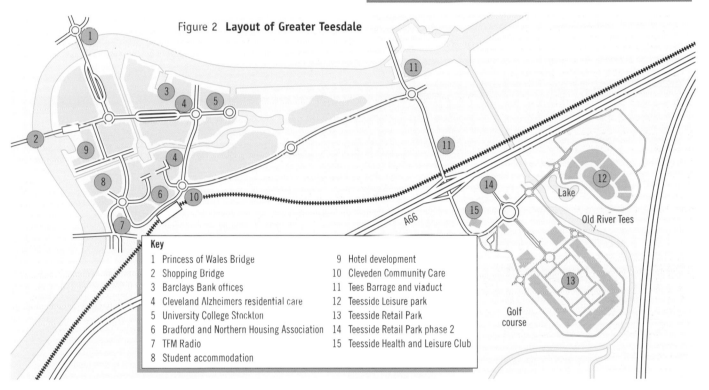

Figure 2 **Layout of Greater Teesdale**

Key

1 Princess of Wales Bridge
2 Shopping Bridge
3 Barclays Bank offices
4 Cleveland Alzheimers residential care
5 University College Stockton
6 Bradford and Northern Housing Association
7 TFM Radio
8 Student accommodation
9 Hotel development
10 Cleveden Community Care
11 Tees Barrage and viaduct
12 Teesside Leisure park
13 Teesside Retail Park
14 Teesside Retail Park phase 2
15 Teesside Health and Leisure Club

Figure 3 **The Tees Barrage** The permanent high water level makes for a more attractive riverside.

The **Task Force** is aimed at tackling unemployment and low skill levels in the inner cities through training and educational investment. In Teesdale, areas such as Parkfield (25% unemeployment) and Hardwick (20% unemployment) have been targetted.

City Challenge

A competition was set by the government between selected inner cities to raise money from private sources to regenerate an inner city area. As a result, Stockton was given City Challenge status in 1992. Within two years, 368 jobs were created in 66 new new businesses and 1004 houses were improved.

Enterprise zones

Enterprise zones were designated to attract industry to old, declining industrial areas. A series of financial rewards encouraged firms to locate in these areas. The main incentives were that firms would be exempt from paying rates for ten years, grants of up to 100% would be available for machinery and capital, and planning permission would be considered with sympathy and speed.

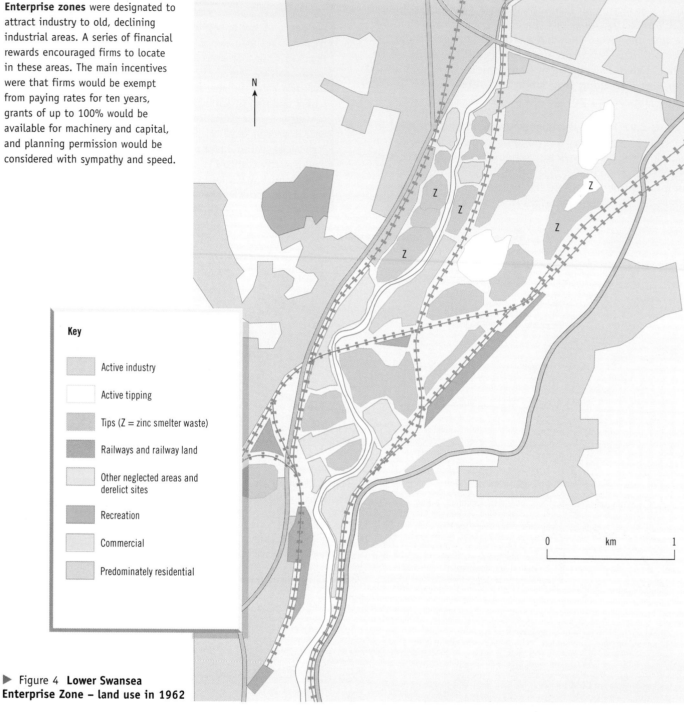

Key

- Active industry
- Active tipping
- Tips (Z = zinc smelter waste)
- Railways and railway land
- Other neglected areas and derelict sites
- Recreation
- Commercial
- Predominately residential

0   km   1

▶ Figure 4 **Lower Swansea Enterprise Zone – land use in 1962**

1 a Locate Swansea on a map of the UK. The city grew on coal and metal manufacture. From Figure 4, what evidence is there of these industries?

b 'Footloose' industries are not tied by particular locational factors. What advantages could Swansea offer to modern 'footloose' industries?

2 Roughly 60% of the Swansea inner area was derelict land in 1962. Why had it not been reused?

3 Compare Figures 4 and 5. Describe the changes which have been made in the area between 1962 and 1986.

4 a Study Figure 7. Why do you think so many of the relocating firms were from Swansea?

b What criticisms do you think have been made of creating a zone in a city, within which there are attractive benefits for industry?

c What important information does Figure 7 not reveal?

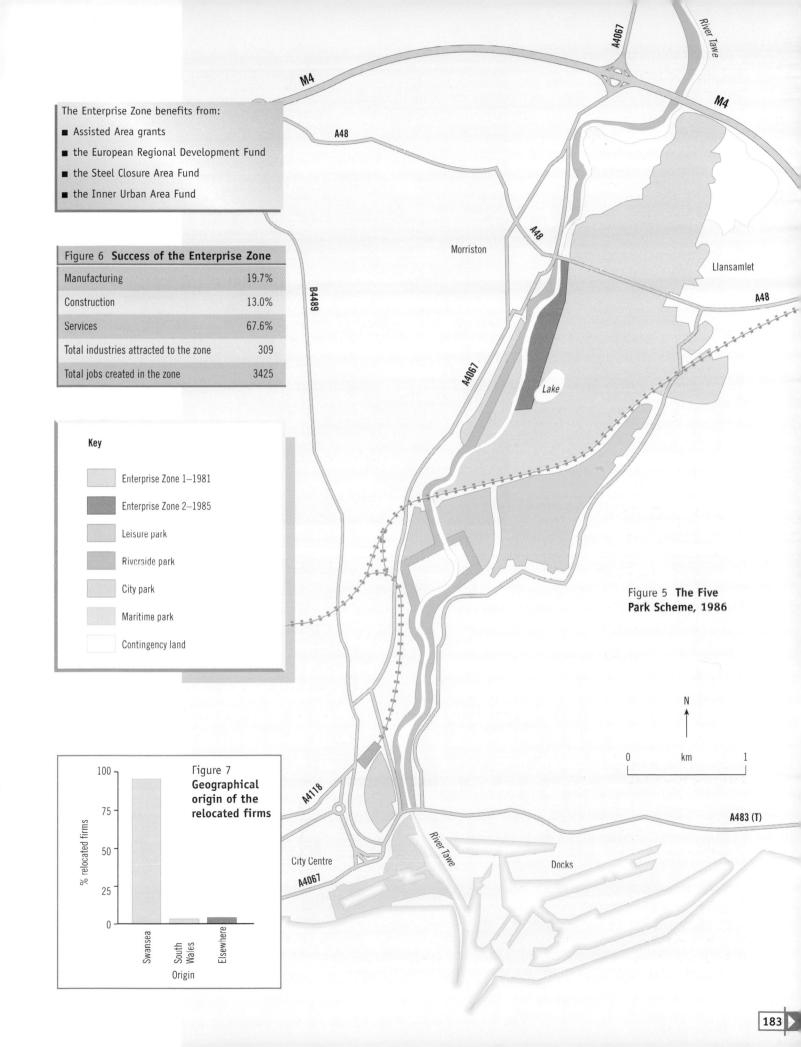

The Enterprise Zone benefits from:

■ Assisted Area grants
■ the European Regional Development Fund
■ the Steel Closure Area Fund
■ the Inner Urban Area Fund

Figure 6 **Success of the Enterprise Zone**	
Manufacturing	19.7%
Construction	13.0%
Services	67.6%
Total industries attracted to the zone	309
Total jobs created in the zone	3425

Key

Enterprise Zone 1–1981

Enterprise Zone 2–1985

Leisure park

Riverside park

City park

Maritime park

Contingency land

Figure 5 **The Five Park Scheme, 1986**

Morriston

Llansamlet

Lake

N

0   km   1

Figure 7 **Geographical origin of the relocated firms**

% relocated firms

100
75
50
25
0

Swansea   South Wales   Elsewhere

Origin

City Centre

Docks

River Tawe

Derelict Land Grants

Derelict land in cities was created by:

- the out-migration of industry to the city edges

- delays in planning permission

- areas of housing being cleared and rebuilt elsewhere

- the difficulty of co-ordinating the many owners of derelict land in the inner cities. The most notable owners were industries, port operators, gas and electricity boards, railways, Local Authorities and Health Boards.

Derelict Land Grants operate in two ways:

- money for reclamation of land
e.g. at Listerhills in Bradford railway land and mills have been converted into warehousing and a distribution centre

- promotion of Garden Festivals
e.g. This festival made a profit in Stoke on Trent, 1986, and left a legacy of 160 ha of wood and park land in the urban area.

▶ Figure 8 **The labyrinth left from the 1986 Garden Festival, Stoke on Trent**

Gentrification

Not all areas surrounding the CBD are caught in a negative spiral. Some pockets of high-class housing have retained their identity, such as the seventh arrondissement in Paris, or Chelsea and Kensington in London. In many British cities the affluent middle classes have seen the potential of period housing in the inner urban areas. They value:

- the proximity of the CBD

- the mix of people compared with the suburbs

- the mix of land use in such neighbourhoods

- the relatively cheap cost of older properties

- the possibility of restoring and improving properties to their own taste.

Local shops and services have improved with this injection of energy. The influx of middle class people and subsequent change to properties has been called **gentrification**. House prices increase as gentrification increases. Camden, Islington, and Notting Hill are all areas in London where this process has arrested decline.

Figure 9 **Gentrification has brought new life into declining inner urban areas**
Often the only visible signs that it has taken place are new doors and window frames.

New towns – an alternative to urban problems?

Governments have attempted to build completely new settlements as a solution to urban problems. In the UK, the New Towns Act of 1946 was a response to a number of problems. New towns are separated from the existing urban areas by green belts. The location of the new, and later expanded towns is shown in Figure 10. The towns have their distinctive features but have also been subject to major criticisms.

Reasons for building the new towns

■ London had sprawled during the 1930s

■ Between 1919 and 1939, London had increased by 750 000 through natural increase but by 1.25 million through migration

■ The Barlow report published in 1940 advised the decentralisation of industry out of the capital city

■ Many homes had been destroyed during the War and many slums from the 1930s remained

■ The building programme was part of a new start at the end of the Second World War.

Features of British new towns

■ The towns were administered by a corporation and financed by the Treasury

■ The towns were designed to be self-sufficient in employment services and social life

■ The best of urban life was to be combined with the 'rural' advantages of neighbourhoods

■ The housing was low density, grouped in neighbourhoods and based on road transport

■ The first new towns used greenfield sites; later developments were expanded settlements.

Criticisms of the new towns

■ New towns drew investment away from the conurbations and after 20 years, only 1% of the British population was contained in the towns

■ The first phase of settlements around London were built before commuting became the norm; these towns soon became 'commuter settlements'

■ Low density housing depended too heavily on road transport

■ A lack of cheap housing and the failure of the new towns to attract high income executives means there is a lower social mix than was originally planned

■ Planning did not take into account the peoples' views.

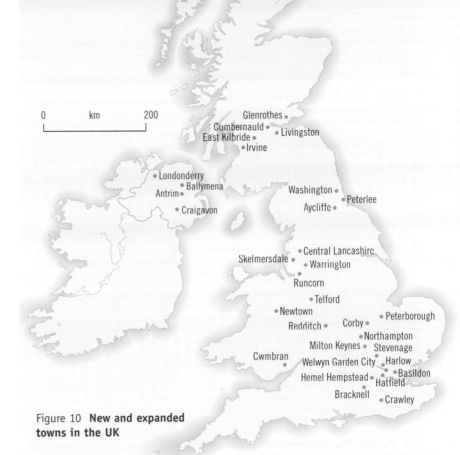

Figure 10 **New and expanded towns in the UK**

Case study | Craigavon – a town with no heart

Designated a New Town in 1964, Craigavon was established to rehouse people from Belfast and to attract jobs to a declining rural area. A linear development links Portadown (population 30 000) with Lurgan (population 32 000) and involved extensive reclamation of marshland south of Lough Neagh. A new shopping centre, offices and a central park were placed between the two settlements. Financial inducements attracted the Goodyear company, which later withdrew, but existing industries in food processing, pharmaceuticals and textiles expanded. The neighbourhood plan has encouraged religious segregation. Brownlow, for example, is predominantly Protestant.

Original plans for services were too ambitious for the population size. Today the original centres of Lurgan in the east and Portadown in the west still exert a powerful hold. Only 15 000 people live outside these two settlements. The villages surrounding the towns have expanded with high class residential developments. There is therefore little high class residential development in Craigavon. Use of the new town favours those with private transport, since bus journeys through the different neighbourhoods are long and the scale of low density building discourages walking.

1 What are the advantages and disadvantages of setting up a new town on a greenfield site by (a) expanding an existing settlement and (b) by linking two settlements?

2 Do you think Craigavon was a success? Give reasons for your answer.

In the early 1970s Glasgow was one of the most depressed cities in the UK. Its reliance on traditional heavy industry, such as shipbuilding, iron and steel, and textiles, meant that when these industries declined, unemployment and urban decline set in. In the East End, an inner area, large-scale demolition of old slum housing reduced the population from 151 000 in 1951 to 80 000 in 1971. The high-rise housing built to replace the slums and damage caused by the Second World War fell into disrepair. The environment was blighted with derelict land, pollution, poor quality housing, and declining services. This inner urban decay hardly invited investors. New industries were attracted to the new towns such as Cumbernauld, East Kilbride, and Livingstone. Local pride became discouraged in this negative spiral; crime and vandalism increased.

In the 1990s, however, Glasgow is recognised as a leader in showing how a city can achieve economic and physical renewal. In 1990, it was voted European City of Culture, signalling its transformation.

By assessing existing advantages and building on them, the city has achieved much (Figure 1). Many of the projects such as the GEAR project have achieved international recognition.

Locational advantages

- It is well linked with the rest of the UK by the M8 motorway, a port and an airport

- With access to fine coastal and highland scenery, 200 golf courses within two hours' driving, and an attractive rural environment on the outskirts, the city could be attractive to 'footloose' industries

- The decline of heavy industry meant that sites of a variety of scales were available for development.

Labour advantages

- It is the third largest urban centre in the UK, with a population of over 700 000

- It has a labour force with traditional skills in mechanical and electrical engineering, printing, clothing, textiles and food processing

- Two universities in the city, producing 5000 graduates each year, 12 colleges of further education, and 70 private training concerns, ensure a high calibre workforce.

Resource advantages

- Energy costs are amongst the lowest in Europe

- It has plentiful supplies of soft water, free of calcium and magnesium salts.

Building on the advantages

Glasgow attracted funds from central government, the EU and a variety of private and public initiatives. These were used in the following ways:

Transport and communications

By 1995, a £110 million investment in Glasgow airport has increased its capacity to six million passengers. A fully integrated bus, rail and underground network has been developed; only London has a larger commuter network in the UK. An investment of up to £1 million each week in the 1990s in one of the most inexpensive and efficient telecommunication systems in the world has been made.

Environmental improvements

A number of initiatives, including the cleaning of buildings, temporary landscaping of vacant sites, traffics control measures, and the improvement of parks and play areas in the centre has been undertaken.

Retail developments

Glasgow has avoided out-of-town retail developments. It is actively developing the existing 20 district shopping zones and promoting pedestrianisation of the city centre.

Housing improvements

Between 1990 and 1994, 10 000 new private houses were built at a cost of £300 million. There has also been extensive improvements, replacements of unsuccessful high-rise housing with smaller units and refurbishments of tenement 'yards', mostly through the GEAR project.

Investing in people

In the GEAR project and elsewhere, the need to consult has been recognised. Improvements in the built environment have been matched with investment in training and skills.

Successful marketing

Glasgow's council adopted an energetic approach to marketing. The *Glasgow's miles better* campaign reflected its new positive image.

Two adult training centres

Piping of Camlachie Burn

Heavy investment in an integrated transport system with social and environmental benefits

Shoppabus services from Duke Street and Shettleston

New health centre (at Bridgeton)

Old peoples homes; housing for disabled; sheltered housing

Dennistoun

Calton

Camlachie

Shettleston

Sandyhills

River Clyde

Bridgeton

Parkhead

Tollcross

Argyle line through Bridgeton and Dalmarnock opened

Dalmarnock

2500 houses and flats refurbished in 5 years

Fullarton

Carmyle

Rutherglen

71 new factories and houses workshops

900 private homes in 5 years

Landscaping

Cambuslang

Anti-pollution measures

Glasgow Eastern Area Renewal

Glasgow

Figure 1 **The GEAR project**

One of the many initiatives to improve Glasgow was the Glasgow Eastern Area Renewal strategy. Set up in 1976, this became a model for city improvements and was the first project to bring together many different agencies. Central government, Strathclyde Regional Council, Glasgow District Council, The Scottish Special Housing Association, the Greater Glasgow Health Board, the Housing Corporation, the Manpower Services Commission, and the Scottish Development Agency were all involved. The local people were consulted at all stages of the development. The project targeted an area of 1600 hectares of land, with a population of 45 000 in 17 000 homes. The main aims were:

- to help residents secure employment
- to retain and create jobs
- to improve the quality of life
- to improve the environment
- to create better housing
- to involve the community.

Figure 2 **Good for Glasgow**

Glasgow has retained its manufacturing base, with over 1000 firms in engineering, food processing, clothing and printing. The manufacturing industry employs over 70 000 people. Coats Viyella, the Wier Group, the Howden Group, Collins publishing house, and Tennent Caledonian are all located in the city.

Glasgow's proximity to Silicon Glen and access to centres of learning has led to a thriving Research and Development sector, including marine consultation (Yard), Artificial Intelligence (Turing Institute) and the British Telecom Software Development Centre.

Glasgow has been able to attract financial and stockbroking firms because it has one of the few trading floors of the UK Stock Exchange, outside London.

The civil service has located extensions to the Passport Office, Ministry of Defence, and the Office for Population Censuses and Surveys in the city.

Glasgow has successfully developed its cultural heritage. It is home to 200 arts and cultural organisations, more than 20 art galleries and 11 working theatres, with a large 'Mayfest' and jazz and poetry festivals. It also hosts a thriving fashion industry.

Since 1982, there has been a 300% increase in visitors to the city.

1 Design a leaflet to be produced by the City Council that promotes Glasgow as a city in which to live and work.

11.9 The rural-urban fringe

The **rural-urban fringe** is defined as the area where different land uses associated with city and countryside meet. Growth of the city 'invades' rural areas. In the UK, Green Belt controls have been used to try and limit such change.

The fringe areas are characterised by a typical mix of land use which usually fall into the categories shown in Figure 2. Change of land use at the fringe takes many forms, as Figure 1 indicates, and can result in much debate.

Figure 1 Bristol's urban fringe

Bristol has all the characteristic land uses of the rural-urban fringe. Developments on the city edge during the 1980s have included:

■ a large retail park at **Cribb's Causeway** – many high street names have stores here, adjacent to the M4-M5 interchange. The John Lewis store is vacating its city centre site for premises here.

■ **Aztec West Business Park** – this business park guarantees every employee a parking place and provides high quality buildings in an attractively landscaped environment. A central precinct provides bars, restaurants, and recreational facilities. The high level of security, and thoughtful design has attracted prestige firms such as Canon and Digital, and 5000 people are employed here in 86 firms. Other less well serviced businesses have been attracted to the area, causing traffic congestion at peak hours.

■ **Bradley Stoke** – one of the largest private housing developments in Europe. Over 6000 homes had been built by 1996. Many houses were built at the peak of the property boom in the 1980s. House prices have since fallen and many residents now own homes which are worth far less than their original value. The amenities which should have grown for an affluent, settled community have not yet materialised.

Figure 2 Land use on the fringe

Urban services

Cities need water storage facilities, sewage works, electricity sub-stations, power stations and waste disposal sites, and the tendency is to locate these in empty areas on the city edge.

Industrial land use

Modern industrial estates, with their requirements of large sites, access to a motorway network and proximity to an urban workforce, have been developed on the city edge.

Transport

Airports, bus depots, large garages, repair yards and roads bypassing the city, are located on the margins.

Retailing and out-of-town developments

The attraction of large, new sites, with the possibility of purpose-designed buildings, ample car parking space, easy access for deliveries, and the relatively cheap cost of city-edge land has encouraged the growth of retail parks and warehousing.

Recreation

Golf courses, stables, playing fields and country parks all serve the city population.

Housing

'Exclusive' new developments by private companies in sites near attractive countryside, are marketed in terms of their easy access to motorways and to city centre services.

City councils have rehoused people from the inner city on relatively cheap land, on sites that are more easily developed and pose fewer design problems than rebuilding on cramped plots in the city.

Farms and villages

Many villages have become absorbed into the suburbs. Intensive farming, such as horticulture, is located near the urban markets. Farming is protected from the commercial pressure to change land use by Green Belt legislation, which forbids building on designated 'green' land.

Derelict land

Fields are cut up by all the above land uses. Awkward shaped plots or areas inaccessible to farm machinery are left uncultivated.

Figure 3 **Phoenix, Arizona** Planning controls are less strict in American urban fringe areas. There is less pressure on land than in Europe and fuel has always been cheaper. The result is a sprawl of low density buildings and land uses which use a lot of space.

Each land use is connected to a group of people, each with different needs and interests. When the land use changes, so does the mix of people. Their spending and leisure habits, and their transport patterns may change the area. This is seen clearly at the city margin. The advertisement which appeared in a Midlands newspaper is typical of change on the fringe (Figure 4) and the people listed would all have interest in such change.

Home owner, who bought a detached home with a paddock 'in the country' 20 years ago.

A company chairman relocating her firm from London, seeking properties to encourage managerial staff to move

The owner of a local post office and convenience store

FOR SALE

30 Quality homes in an exclusive environment

Landscaped with mature trees, with views of open countryside, the homes are only minutes from the M5 and M42. With the cultural and social opportunities of Birmingham ten minutes, and an international airport twenty minutes drive away, and green fields on your doorstep, you can have the best of both worlds.

Figure 4 **An estate agent's offer**

The Secretary of the local golf club

Chairman of Belvoir Resident's Association representing inhabitants of a nearby council housing estate, where 40% of households use public transport

The farmer who owns the land

A local council member who has recently moved from the inner city to the area

1 Draw a table with columns headed with each category of land use shown in Figure 2. Using an OS 1:25 000 map or a land use map of a city margin, identify features belonging to each land use group.

2 Write short letters to a local newspaper for each of the people listed in Figure 4 giving their reaction to proposed new housing developments.

11.10 Accessible rural areas

One of the most significant trends identified in the UK's 1991 census was the migration of people from urban areas. For example, Merseyside saw a net loss of 5.3% of its population, and the Tyne and Wear urban area a loss of 2.6% between 1980 and 1990. By contrast, the small regional towns and some rural areas, such as Cornwall and Dorset, saw a net increase in population, due to immigration, during the same period. This shift of population out of urban areas has been traced in most developed societies, and is called **counterurbanisation**. The consequences of counterurbanisation are both positive and negative (Figures 1 and 2).

Reasons for counterurbanisation

■ a growing dissatisfaction with urban services, such as schools, hospitals and public transport. The cost of housing in urban areas with good services has risen. The growing gap between 'service rich' and 'service poor' areas of London, in particular during the 1980s, has forced many middle income families to look beyond the city for housing

■ city congestion, pollution and the stress associated with urban living

■ changing work patterns. People no longer need to group together in cities to communicate, and 'teleworking' allows people to work from home

■ the perceived quality of life in rural or small town environments.

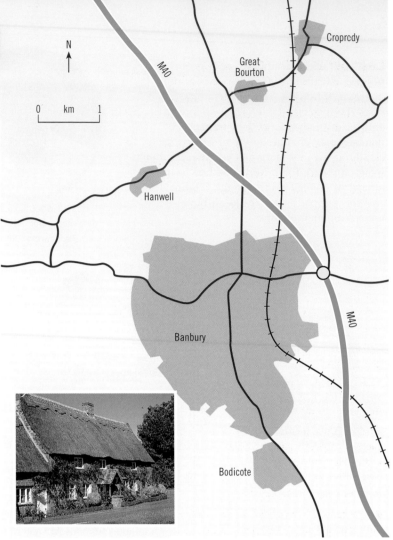

Figure 1 **The villages of North Oxfordshire have become attractive places to live for people who work in Birmingham and London. The M40 has made commuting easier.**

Figure 2 **The pros and cons of counterurbanisation**

The shift of people to the rural areas which are accessible to the large cities has brought losses and gains.

The rising costs of fuel, and of properties in desirable villages may, however, slow counterurbanisation in the UK. The combined effect of long distance commuting, out-of-town retail and industrial developments, and home building on the fringe of urban areas may lead to the 'death of cities'. This trend has been recognised and many cities are now taking the redevelopment of their centres seriously.

Gains	Losses
Incoming residents may inject energy into declining village activities. Schools, clubs and churches may be saved from closure.	Newcomers may not appreciate rural life, and may not respect farmers' property and appreciate the smells and noises of farming.
New residents may campaign for better services.	The declining use of public transport to local towns may cause these services to be withdrawn. Most incomers have at least one car per household.
Buildings may be restored and improved.	Housing may become more expensive, and local people may not be able to compete with relatively wealthy urban residents.
Local labour may be employed.	Farmland may become neglected if the new residents buy farms.
	Social life in commuter villages may die as the residents continue to work and socialise in the city.
	Urban areas may lose vitality and income.

Less accessible rural areas

Rural areas beyond the commuting distance from urban centres have distinct characteristics and problems. These are typical of all remote areas in Western Europe. Figure 3 shows England's Rural Development Areas, which have special status to try and help solve their problems and where a variety of solutions to the problems are used.

Reasons for decline of rural services

■ economies of scale – it costs less to provide services to large numbers. New housing and services have tended to be located where there is already a nucleus of services

■ the Post Office, breweries, oil companies and doctors' practices have all tried to reduce their expensive rural outlets. With the rise in car ownership, people have been able to travel further for these services

■ 75% of rural households have at least one car. Bus passenger numbers have been reduced and higher fares result. Villages without shops, post offices and schools have usually suffered from resulting cuts to the service

■ rural schools have closed due to a falling birth rate and pressure on public expenditure

■ village shops have been unable to compete with urban stores which are accessible by car.

Features of remote rural areas

■ unemployment

■ low range of job opportunities

■ population decline or a sparse population

■ net out-migration of those of working age

■ an age-structure biased towards the elderly

■ poor access to services and facilities.

Solutions to the problem of supplying services

■ mobile services – delivery services of milk, post and library and banking services by van

■ mail order services – 'catalogue shopping' was pioneered in rural North America

■ car pooling, minibus services and subsidies to car owners to share lifts.

Such schemes require careful organisation, however, and 80% of the rural households in the UK without a car also lack a telephone.

0   km   200

Figure 3 **Rural Development Areas of England**

Figure 4 **Many village shops and post offices have closed for good**

12.1 Urban growth in the less developed world

Towns and cities in less economically developed countries (LDCs) are growing rapidly. In addition, an increasing proportion of people in LDCs are living in cities, a trend called **urbanisation**. A high proportion of people live in cities in LDCs (Figure 1). It seems that LDCs are undergoing a period of urban growth and urbanisation similar to that in Europe during the nineteenth century. There are, however, important differences (Figure 2).

The growth of cities in less developed countries is accounted for by a high rate of natural increase of population. This is the surplus of births over deaths. More significantly, a high rate of migration from the rural areas causes **urban growth**. It is estimated that 3000 migrants arrive in urban areas every hour in the less developed societies. This reflects the poor conditions in the rural areas, but also the perception of opportunities in the cities. Often the hopes for a better life are based on false or biased information. The reality in the cities is quite different.

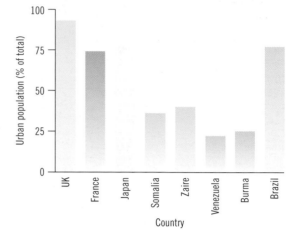

Figure 1 **Urban population in selected countries (%)**

Figure 2 **Differences in urbanisation between developed and less developed countries**

	Factor	Developed countries	LDCs
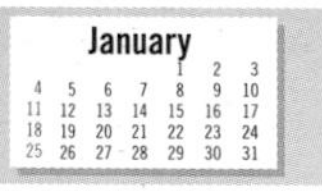 January	Time	nineteenth century	post 1950
	Industry	linked to the process of industrialisation	not necessarily linked to industrial change
	Technology	labour intensive	not necessarily labour intensive
	Employment	rural migrants employed in the new industries	migrants find jobs in the 'informal' sector e.g. selling fruit on the street, or service sector e.g. as servants
	Population growth	death rates fell slowly, then birth rates	death rates fell rapidly, birth rates still remain high in many countries giving rapid population growth
	Trade	many European countries had access to colonies to allow trade and the means to feed the rapidly expanding population	debt and unfavourable trading relationships; imported food is expensive

Figure 3 **Urban population in selected countries (% of total), 1950 – 2000**

Country	1950	1970	1990	2000
Botswana	0	8	24	33
Brazil	36	56	77	83
Canada	61	76	76	79
UK	84	89	93	94
Nigeria	10	20	35	43
India	17	20	28	34

1 **a** Using Figure 3, draw a line graph to show the growth in urban population for selected countries.
b Describe the pattern shown.
c Suggest reasons for this pattern.

Push factors in the rural areas

■ Change such as a new reservoir, a new cash crop or change in land ownership may force farmers off their land

■ Hazards such as over-grazing, drought, crop failure, fire, pests and floods make the farmers' lives difficult

■ Workers may not own land and may feel powerless

■ There are often too many mouths to feed.

Figure 4 **A village in Anhui Province, eastern China**

Pull factors in the urban area

■ Those with education or the will to change may want a better life

■ Jobs in factories pay more than farming

■ Food supplies can be easily bought, rather than grown or exchanged

■ Housing may be better serviced with electricity and water supplies

■ The idea that smart people live in the city may be a powerful factor

■ Services such as street lighting, schools, clinics, and transport may be better.

Figure 5 **Xianen, a city in south-eastern China**

The pattern of rural-urban migration continues in LDCs because the cities exert a powerful 'pull'. Flows of information back to the rural areas are often inaccurate. Few migrants will admit to failure in the cities and only the successful migrants can afford to pay fares to return to their place of origin. The description of an area in Rio de Janeiro (Figure 1) suggests that many would like to return to the land but cannot. Often there is a short supply of housing to rent. Many migrants cannot afford rents and end up making 'squatter housing' from materials they have found or bought cheaply. These areas of informal housing have different names but all have features in common. In contrast to the squatter areas, the areas where the rich live have the best services in the city. In LDCs, the gap between the rich and poor is greater than in most developed societies.

▶ There was a time when this place was covered with orange groves, as far as the eye could see. Today, Baixasa Fluminense, about twelve times the size of Paris and located a few kilometres north of the centre of Rio de Janeiro, is one of Brazil's poorest and most dangerous areas. Three stinking streams, thousands of narrow unpaved lanes regularly rutted by rain, a high voltage power line stretching across it, two expressways and a railway line – that is the setting. Two and a half million people are struggling to survive in this Brazilian-scale cesspit stretching between the municipalities of Nova Iguazu, Duque de Caxias, San João de Meriti and Nilopolis.

The stench from the gutters leaves you no doubt as to the origin of their murky contents. Cars are rare, the horse-drawn cart is everywhere. No neat shops, just small corner stores selling liquor, tobacco and groceries. The water supply is irregular, electrical connections are a wild jumble and schools are very rare. Everywhere there are heaps of rubbish which are sometimes burned, but seldom collected. In summer the place is plagued by mosquitoes and hit by devastating floods.

Jobs are hard to find other than those available in the chemical and petrochemical industries which are present in the region. The luckier ones commute to jobs in Rio, in heavily overcrowded trains or rickety buses. The vast majority of inhabitants – often migrants from the Nordeste, attracted by the city lights – lead hand-to-mouth lives, doing odd jobs, smalltime trade and raising chickens or pigs.

Of the 200 doctors supposedly working in Baixada Fulminense's only general hospital, only 30 are actually there. The rest have moved away. Four-hour waiting times are common and many patients do not even bother to come. Disease and undernourishment are thus free to take their toll. The six so-called neighbourhood medical centres lack the most basic drugs, and two years after opening, one of the centres has had to close.

Violence and insecurity are everywhere: 2575 murders, and more than 25 000 burglaries, rapes and muggings were committed in 1990. Vigilante groups have sprung up as people have tried to protect themselves. But these groups sometimes turn into criminal organisations. The director of Baixada Fluminense's police force says 35 groups of 'exterminators' have been identified.

Then there are the ravages caused by corruption. It is a lawless area where payments are levied for going or coming into certain neighbourhoods.

The director of Radio Mauna Soimoes said 'We get calls every day from Nordestinos asking for help to go back to their province, for they don't have the money to pay the bus fare'. For most people the word 'future' does not figure in their vocabularies. ■

Figure 1 **Report from Rio** – from a newspaper article

Names of shanty or squatter areas	
Favelas	Latin America
Bustees	India
Bidonvilles	French-speaking Africa
Gecekondu	Turkey
Shanties	English-speaking Africa

Features of squatter settlements

- often illegal
- built rapidly from a variety of materials (gecekondu means 'built in the night')
- usually built by residents themselves
- poorly served with drains, paved roads, electricity
- unplanned and haphazard development
- usually at the edge of cities, along rail or road routes, or on vacant land nearer the city centre
- often on unsuitable sites (near factories, on steep slopes, near waste sites)
- populated with large families.

1 Read Figure 1. Imagine you are part of an aid agency trying to solve the problems of a shanty area, such as that in Baixasa Fluminense. Write a development plan to try to solve the problems. Some solutions you might like to consider are listed below.
- improving public health
- incentives and grants to small industries
- cheap loans to residents to improve their homes
- education and social centres

Give reasons for your choice of action.

2 Why is there so little migration back to the rural areas from the cities?

Figure 2 **A bustee near the centre of Calcutta**

Figure 3 **A favela perched on a hillside above Rio de Janeiro**

Shanty areas are a major feature of cities in the less developed countries. Another feature common to all cities is the CBD. With their use of concrete and international architecture, these areas are similar across the globe (Figure 1). Cities in less developed countries also have industrial areas, although they do not employ enough people. Many people are forced to work in the casual or **informal sector**. The wealthy live in distinct areas. Cities in different continents tend to reflect their different histories. For example, some of the sub-Saharan African cities retain their original walled settlements and the areas once occupied by Europeans.

Figure 1 **The CBD in Calcutta, India, has similar characteristics to cities of the developed world, although the presence of street sellers and temporary markets points to a different economy**

The industrial areas, often not segregated from other land uses, represent all types of manufacturing. Most industries are located near railways and ports, as in the western cities. The lack of planning controls, however, often means a lack of zoning and the poorest housing is often near industrial areas. Many people cannot find jobs in the formal industrial sector and so accept low paid casual work. Here, children in Manila in the Philippines, sort rubbish for materials which they can sell.

Children sort rubbish for sale in Manila

Pollution in Mexico City

Housing for the wealthy

■ located near or with rapid access to the CBD for jobs, entertainment and other services

■ contain the best services in the city, or may have private services e.g. private roads, policing or electricity

■ tends to be grouped in one zone since the cost of services is high

■ occupies a disproportionate amount of space for the size of the wealthy population

■ occupied by small families with expectations of high levels of education

■ takes the form of exclusive apartments set in spacious grounds and often grouped around leisure facilities

■ employs a large number of servants, maids and gardeners.

▶ Figure 2 **More expensive apartments in Kinshasa**

▼ Figure 3 **Marrakesh** Within the old city of Marrakesh, some buildings still have their original uses. Modern buildings are simply built alongside.

Models of the city in the developing world

Each city reflects a distinct history in its land use, but general patterns can also be observed. The cities of sub-Saharan Africa, like those of India, tend to have grown in a pattern of different areas, but those in Latin America have grown in a ring pattern. The presence of squatter settlements is typical of most cities in developing countries. Figure 4 shows a pattern of land use typical of most South American cities. Figures 5, 6 and 7 show why places rarely conform to the theoretical model.

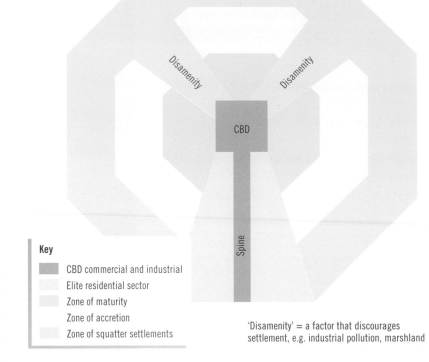

Disamenity
Disamenity
CBD
Spine
Key
CBD commercial and industrial
Elite residential sector
Zone of maturity
Zone of accretion
Zone of squatter settlements
'Disamenity' = a factor that discourages settlement, e.g. industrial pollution, marshland

▲ Figure 4 **The structure of Latin American cities**

Population in millions
0
1
2
3
4
5
6
7
8
1820
1900
1920
1940
1960
1996
Year

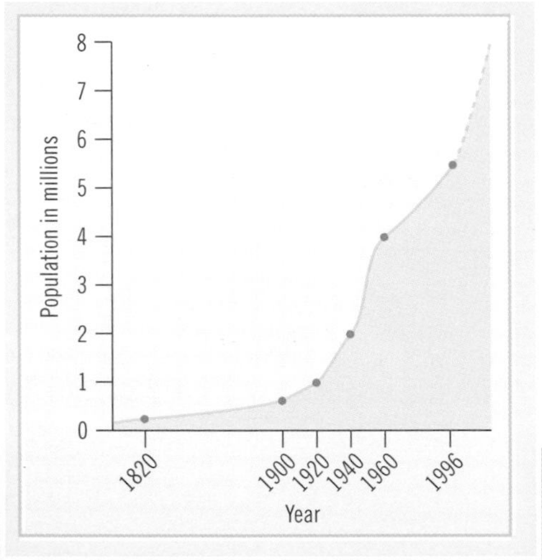

◄ Figure 5 **The growth of Rio de Janeiro**

▼ Figure 6 **Rio de Janeiro looking towards the harbour**

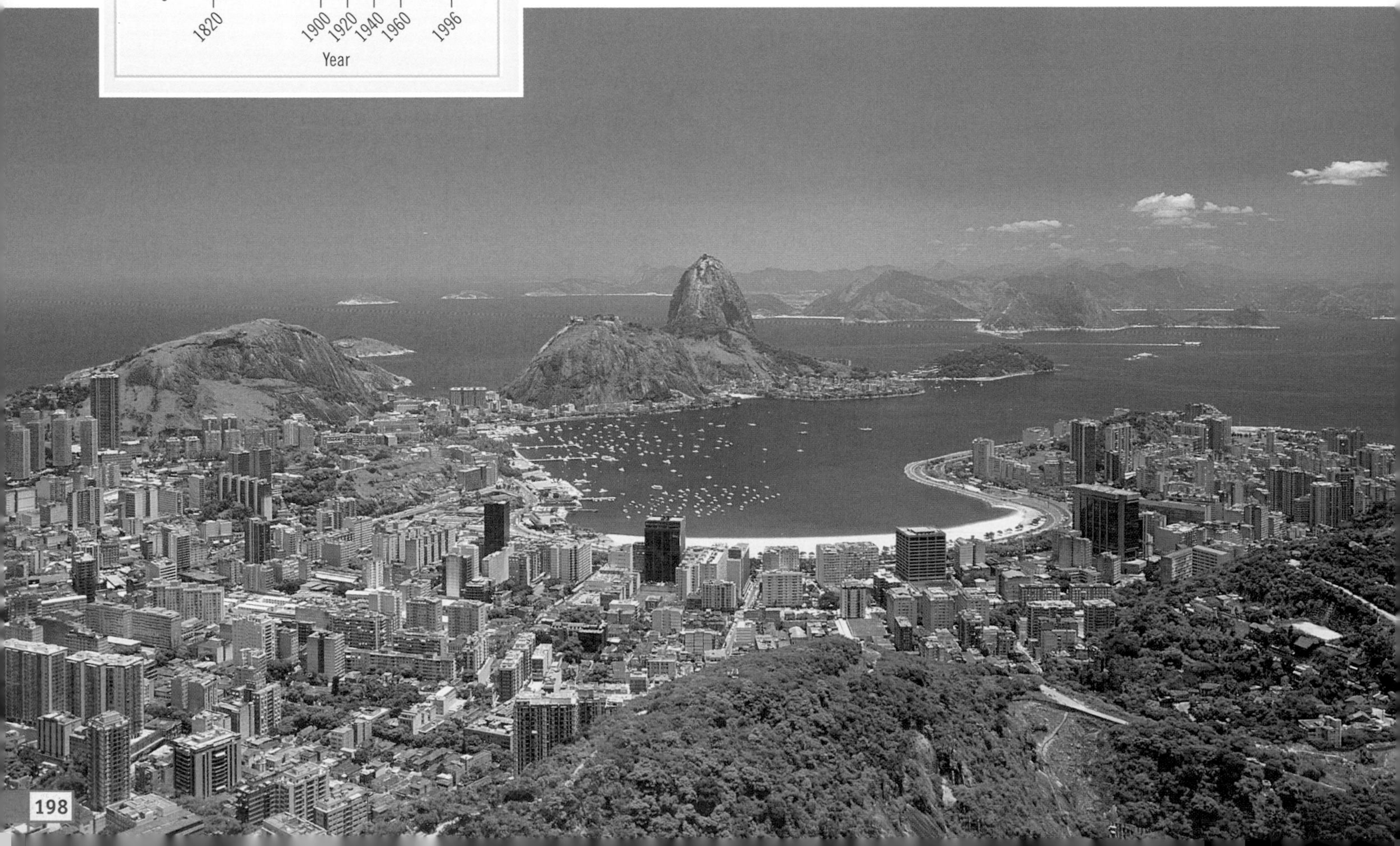

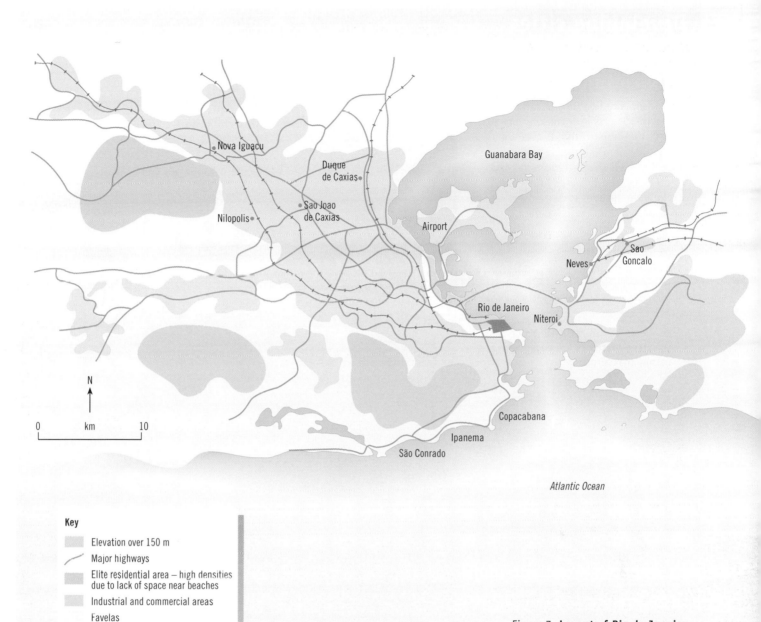

Key

Elevation over 150 m

Major highways

Elite residential area – high densities due to lack of space near beaches

Industrial and commercial areas

Favelas

Figure 7 **Layout of Rio de Janeiro**

1 Study the graph in Figure 5 showing the growth of Rio de Janeiro. Why do you think there is some doubt over the size of this and most other cities in less developed countries?

2 Why do the elite residential areas often occupy large areas of land quite out of proportion to the size of the population?

3 What sorts of features will cause 'disamenities' which richer residents will want to avoid?

4 What is the difference between the location of the low grade housing in the western city and the city in less developed countries?

5 Study Figures 6 and 7 of Rio de Janeiro. Suggest why the city does not conform to the model shown in Figure 4.

Developing cities

Case study | Niteroi – a growing city

Niteroi, connected to Rio de Janeiro by a bridge in 1974, is a dormitory city. It houses commuters to Rio as well as migrants. It is a wealthy city and many people live well. Nevertheless, favelas have crept up the hillsides and even in this relatively affluent area, environmental damage is evident.

Year	Population
1970	292 000
1990	480 000

▶ Figure 1 **Niteroi** Like Rio de Janeiro, the steep hillslopes are edged with a narrow coastal plain

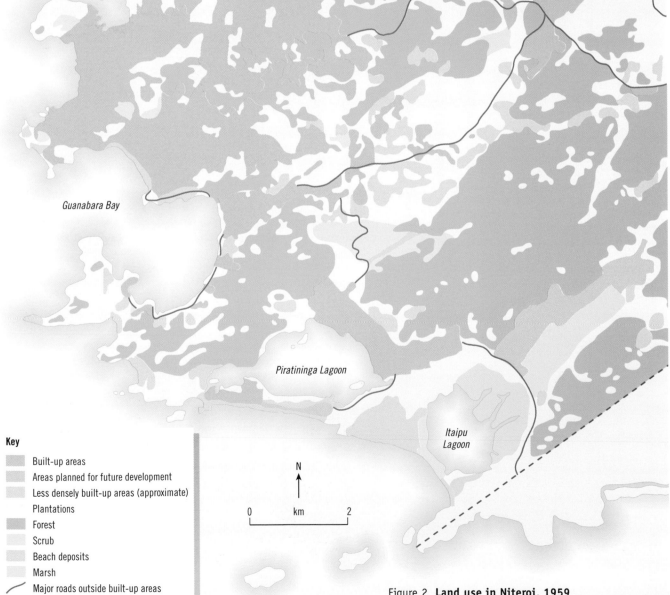

Key
- Built-up areas
- Areas planned for future development
- Less densely built-up areas (approximate)
- Plantations
- Forest
- Scrub
- Beach deposits
- Marsh
- Major roads outside built-up areas

Guanabara Bay

Piratininga Lagoon

Itaipu Lagoon

N

0   km   2

Figure 2 **Land use in Niteroi, 1959**

Key

Built-up areas

Areas planned for future development

Less densely built-up areas (approximate)

• Quarry

Plantations

Forest

Scrub

Beach deposits

Marsh

Major roads outside built-up areas

Figure 3 **Land use in Niteroi, 1987**

1 The development at Camboinhas was built between 1959 and 1987. This exclusive estate has a police post at the entrance. What additional attractions may make Camboinhas a sought-after area?

2 What changes to the two lagoons have taken place between 1959 and 1987? Why?

3 Why do you think the expensive housing does not extend as far as the coast at the Itaipu Lagoon?

4 Some of the forest areas, nearly all occupying the steeper slopes, have become occupied by favelas. Why have the favelas developed on these areas and on the marshy areas at the coast?

5 Why have some forest areas become scrub?

6 Suggest some differences the tunnels through the steep ridge separating Icarai from São Francisco may have made to the southern suburbs.

7 Look at Figures 2 and 3. Compare the two developments at Itaipu and Cachoeiras. What are the differences?

12.5 Solving the problem

Solutions to the squatter problem fall into two broad categories. A traditional solution is to rebuild and provide new housing. New towns have been constructed in Singapore and Cairo, and new capitals have been created in Brazil (Brasilia) and in Nigeria (Abuja). Creating capital cities is an expensive solution, however, and many less developed societies are burdened by overpopulation and cannot keep pace with their housing needs.

Less formal solutions, often involving aid agencies, try to maximise the resources of the local people, most notably their enthusiasm and labour. 'Site and service schemes' supply basic building materials, construct water pipelines, electricity and street lighting, but the home building is left to local people. Often a granting of legal status to the squatter settlements encourages local and government investment.

When Abuja was officially designated the capital of Nigeria, the aims were:

- to provide a new capital, to relieve pressure on Lagos which was growing rapidly and rather European in outlook
- to unite the Christian south with the Muslim north of the country
- to provide housing and services in the country's interior
- to signify power and wealth.

Funded by oil revenues, the scheme first involved clearing the area of villages. Compensation was offered in some states. Over 7000 people were moved and settled elsewhere. Delays, allegations of corruption and ambitious plans that have proved difficult to fulfil, have dogged the new capital. Few jobs have been supplied, apart from those in the construction industry. The flow of migrants to the south continues.

◀ Figure 1 **Abuja was an expensive gesture and remains unfinished**

▼ Figure 2 **Layout of Abuja**

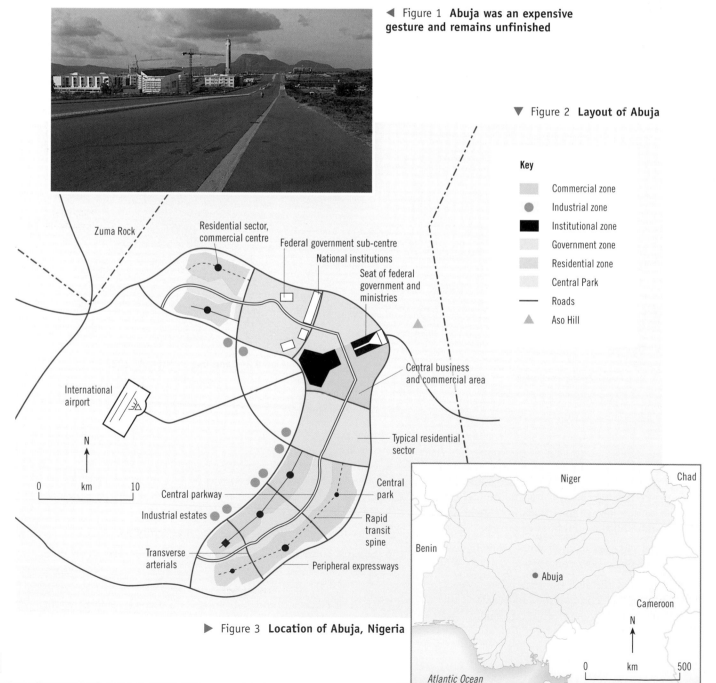

Key

- Commercial zone
- Industrial zone
- Institutional zone
- Government zone
- Residential zone
- Central Park
- Roads
- Aso Hill

▶ Figure 3 **Location of Abuja, Nigeria**

Achieving legal status and slum improvement in Brazil

Once a slum, or squatter settlement in Brazil is granted legal status the inhabitants are secure. Landowners cannot legally claim the land back from the squatters. Some speculators wait for squatter settlements to develop, become improved and then evict the inhabitants. They then sell off the housing.

The inhabitants have a right to representation on *Commissions of Urbanisation and Legalisation*. These are urban development commissions which can draw on government funds.

For example, Entre a Pulso is a fifty year old slum in Recife. The oldest houses are quite established, and made of concrete, the newest made from waste materials and wood. The area is sandwiched between smart beach-side apartments by the coast and a new shopping centre further inland. The Arruar project, partly financed by a British charity, is seeking to upgrade the slums by drawing teams of professionals together with the local people.

Lawyers help inhabitants obtain legal title to the land, architects help draw up plans for community centres, clinics and houses, and engineers help develop urban improvement plans.

Figure 4 **In the shanty towns poor health is a problem for many people and infant mortality is high** Vaccination schemes for children are an important part of many aid programmes.

▼ Figure 5 **Self-help housing**

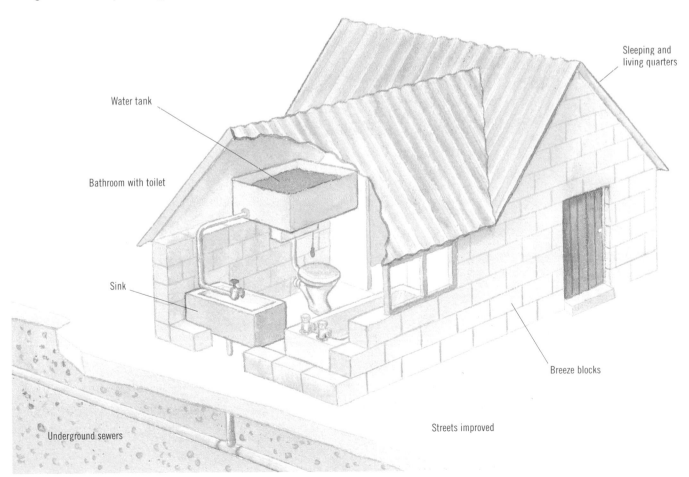

Water tank

Bathroom with toilet

Sink

Underground sewers

Sleeping and living quarters

Breeze blocks

Streets improved

Build Your Own Home Game

The aim of this game is to enable you to enter into the hazards and opportunities involved in developing a home in a shanty area. You will work in groups. Each group will need **two dice**, each of a different colour. One will be used for expenditure points, the other for income points. You will need some **card** cut to represent the building materials listed below, and **pencil and paper** to record your points.

To obtain points roll the dice. The number you will gain or spend will correspond to the numbers on the dice. If, for example, your red expenditure die shows a five, and your blue income die a six, you have one point to spend. Locate the dice pattern on the chart opposite and follow any additional instructions. There is no limit to the points you may accumulate, but you cannot buy materials if you have minus points.

For each home you will need:

- 4 walls – 2 points each
- 1 roof – 6 points
- 1 bag of cement – 3 points
- 1 water pipe – 3 points
- legal status for the group's area obtained by any member rolling a double six.

Within your group you could trade materials or share a wall with a neighbour. The first group to legally house all its members wins.

As you work through the activity, consider the following points to discuss at the end:

1 Are all factors either positive or negative, or is it more complex than this?

2 What combination of factors enabled one group to win?

3 What difference could (a) aid agencies and (b) city authorities make in the shanty towns?

4 Why are hazards hardest on the poorest?

5 Do 'opportunities' tend to favour the wealthiest?

Your brother dies. His small inheritance is spent on the fare back home for his funeral.

Electricity black-out. You lose an afternoon's work.

You lose a load of shoes you have been repairing for extra cash.

The neighbour to whom you loaned some money disappears.

The baby is ill and requires expensive medicine.

If you do not have legal status, the local authority bulldozers remove your group from the land. Start again.

You find a dumped pram and sell its wheels.

A son gets a place at school. Take another turn.

A daughter lands a job as a maid and needs travelling expenses.

Someone steals your cement which you lose in addition to these two points.

You hear there may be jobs at a new factory. Your expensive journey to the factory is a waste of money.

Your money is stolen at the carnival. Lose all your positive points.

Someone gives you a lift to the city centre where you pick up a day's work.

An aid agency sets up a building scheme and you borrow a power drill for a day.

Your cousin arrives from the country. More earnings or another mouth to feed?

A landslide destroys one of your wall panels. Lose this in addition to the two points.

Drought means you have to walk further to water delivered by tanker. You lose a lot of time.

A fire destroys the community centre where the children go two mornings a week.

You find a 20-point bank note. Add this to your score.

An aid agency buys your group a cement mixer. Two points for everyone.

Someone rigs up an illegal electricity supply from the mains. Free power for a week.

A new hamburger chain opens a branch near your home. Your son finds work for two weeks but your other children want hamburgers which are expensive.

A student on his gap year with an aid agency makes a mistake with the cement.

A gang rob you for money for drugs.

A photographer works in your area and gives each of your six children two points.

You borrow a sewing machine from the community centre and save money on clothing.

Your son buys a bicycle and can visit a market which is cheaper than your nearest food store.

You cycle out to a forested area and pick firewood which you later sell.

Your daughter starts school and needs writing materials.

Your son is ill. No earnings this week. Lose a point.

A local road accident with a lorry gives your group three 'free' water pipes. Add these to your five points.

An aid agency sets up carpentry lessons in the community centre.

You find some abandoned roofing materials. Add half a roof in addition to these three points.

The bottles and cans you have been collecting from the streets are sold for recycling.

A new rapid transit system speeds your journey to the city centre. You go there once a week for odd jobs.

The local authority grant your group the right to live on the land for a very low rent.

Traffic on the roads in the UK has increased dramatically in recent years. In 1996, there were 23 million cars on Britain's roads (compared with 15 million in 1980), each travelling an average of 6000 miles per year (compared with 4000 miles in 1980). That amounts to a total of 138 billion car miles travelled in Britain in 1996 alone (or 378 million car miles every day!). It is not surprising that many of Britain's roads, particularly those in urban areas, suffer chronic traffic congestion! Yet, within all this travelling, patterns of **traffic flow** can be identified. **Peaks** (high points) and **troughs** (low points) of traffic flow can be seen on roads at particular times of the day (e.g. peaks during the 'rush hour' before and after work), and on particular days of the year (e.g. peaks on Bank Holidays).

People could be travelling for any number of reasons, perhaps going to work or school, to a leisure activity or a special event. When the road network cannot cope with the demands of traffic, **congestion** occurs. Serious congestion where traffic is at a standstill for prolonged periods of time is known as **gridlock**.

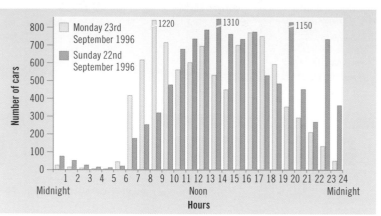

Figure 1 **Frequency of cars per hour in Warwick, 1996**

Local data

Warwick – market town; population 47 000

Leamington Spa – busy shopping town; population 100 000

Stratford-upon-Avon – popular tourist town; population 25 000

Figure 2 **Warwick Castle from the River Avon**

1 Study Figure 1 which shows the frequency of cars per hour on Myton Road in Warwick measured from a sample point over a 24-hour period on two consecutive days in 1996. Peaks and troughs can be identified.
a Use the information on these pages to account for the patterns found in each of the graphs in Figure 1. Explain the differences between the two graphs, including differences in flow rates and the times of the peaks and troughs.
b What further information would be helpful to you in understanding traffic flows along Myton Road?

2 **a** What roads in your local area suffer from traffic congestion? Are there particular times of the day or year that the congestion is worse?
b Can you give reasons as to why the congestion occurs?
c What could be done to solve the problem?

3 Design a traffic flow survey that could be carried out along a road in your local area. Consider the equipment needed, length of survey, frequency of measurements and what specific data you want to record.

4 Study Figure 3. Draw a similar plan of the road in your survey and add the features around it that might affect its traffic flow.

5 **a** What variations in traffic flow would you expect to see in your survey data?
b How could these variations be explained?

6 Expand your survey so that information can be gathered on the modes of transport used, distances being travelled, average speeds and the purpose of people's journeys. Plan how these could be accurately measured.

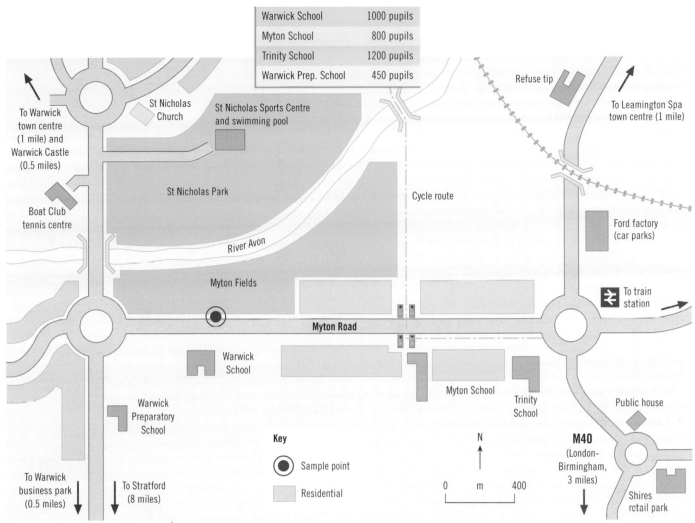

Warwick School	1000 pupils
Myton School	800 pupils
Trinity School	1200 pupils
Warwick Prep. School	450 pupils

Figure 3 **Myton Road, Warwick**

Key

● Sample point

Residential

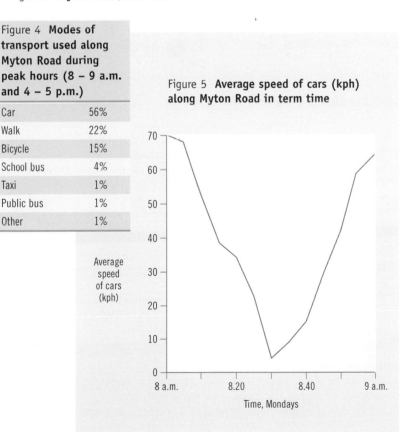

Figure 4 **Modes of transport used along Myton Road during peak hours (8 – 9 a.m. and 4 – 5 p.m.)**	
Car	56%
Walk	22%
Bicycle	15%
School bus	4%
Taxi	1%
Public bus	1%
Other	1%

Figure 5 **Average speed of cars (kph) along Myton Road in term time**

Traffic congestion on Myton Road

From 8.20 a.m. to 8.40 a.m. and from 3.30 p.m. to 4.10 p.m. Monday to Friday, Myton Road traffic comes to a virtual standstill. Average speed of vehicles drops dramatically (Figure 5) as queues can extend to up to half a mile in length. The distribution of modes of transport used along Myton Road at these times is shown in Figure 4.

7 What factors do you think might contribute to the times of gridlock?

8 How might town planners be responsible for this congestion?

9 What steps could be taken by town planners to get rid of the congestion?

10 Study Figure 4. How could this distribution help explain the congestion along Myton Road?

11 a Find out how pupils travel to your school.

   b Compare the data in Figure 4 with that of your school. How might the differences you see be explained?

A **transport network** is where several places are joined together by a series of routes to form a pattern. A network consists of two elements:

● **Links** – these are the routes between places (e.g. the M40 joining the West Midlands to the South East)

● **Nodes** – these are the places where two or more links meet (e.g. Bristol where the M5 and the M4 meet).

Networks vary both within a country and between countries. They can vary in their **accessibility** (the ease by which a place can be reached from other places) and in their **density** (the number of routes and how closely packed together they are).

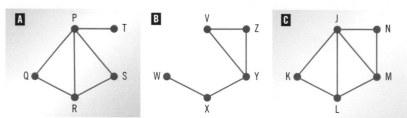

Figure 1 **Three transport networks**

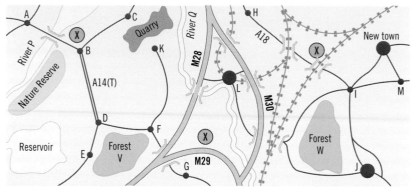

Figure 2 **A modern transport network**

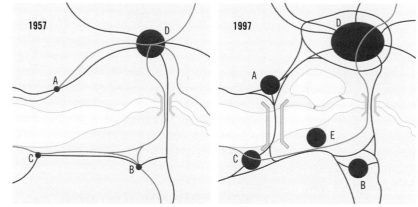

Figure 3 **The district of Manson, 1957 and 1997**

Modifying transport networks

In order to increase the effectiveness of a transport network, modifications may be made to increase its accessibility, density and overall efficiency. For example:

■ Increasing access along a congested link to improve traffic flow, such as adding more lanes to a busy road

■ Diverting access away from a congested node to redistribute traffic flow, such as adding a by-pass to direct traffic around a busy urban settlement

■ Adding a link to improve accessibility between nodes, such as building a bridge over a river estuary to link two large towns

■ Adding a new node and links to it to reduce congestion in existing nodes, and increase accessibility and density of the whole network, such as building a new town and access roads to it

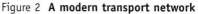

---

1 Study diagrams A, B and C in Figure 1. Which network appears to be (i) the most efficient? (ii) the least efficient? Explain your answers.

2 Study Figure 2.
a Suggest ways in which the transport network may have been modified. Can you see any examples of modified transport patterns in Figure 2 ?
b Are there any obstacles that might determine the shape and pattern of the transport network?
c Three sites (circled cross) are being considered for three projects: a rail freight terminal, a Business Park and a power station. Which project should be located at which site? Explain your choice.

3 Study Figure 3.
a Describe the changes that have taken place in the transport network of nodes and links over the last 40 years.
b Explain why you think these changes have taken place.

Hinterland expansion

A **hinterland** is the area served or influenced by a town or city. Hinterlands of towns and cities in developed countries expanded as the distances travelled by commuters increased. A **commuter** is a person who lives in a smaller town or village in the hinterland of a larger town or city, who travels to the larger settlement for work. The increase in car ownership (Figure 4) and improvements in the road and rail network (Figures 5 and 6) mean that more commuters can choose to live further from their place of work, thus altering the size and shape of the hinterland in which they live.

Why people commute

There are several reasons why people choose to commute:

● Many wish to work in a large city yet live in a more pleasant environment such as a quiet rural village some distance away, enjoying the best of both environments.

● Young people may commute because housing is cheaper in outlying towns and villages than it is in a large city.

● Elderly commuters may have bought property in rural areas in preparation for their retirement.

However, there is a considerable amount of **cost** and **time** involved in commuting, so not everyone can afford to do it.

Improvements in the road and rail network

The National Motorway Network

In 1953 the first few kilometres of motorway were opened. The government realised that the road system needed modernisation and that the UK needed fast, straight roads that avoided urban areas and linked the major centres of population and industry. Motorway construction has continued at a rapid pace as the network has struggled to keep up with ever increasing demand. In 1996, with over 5000 km of motorway, the network was nowhere near completion (Figure 5).

Advantages of an integrated motorway network include shorter journey times, relieving of congestion around urban areas and greater accessibility to the rest of the country. Disadvantages include loss of countryside, the huge cost of building and maintaining them and 'bottlenecks' where motorways join smaller roads.

Electrification of the railway network

In the 1980s improved technology brought about the electrification of the railway network in the South-East of England, the commuting hinterland of London (Figure 6). Such **space-time convergence** (shorter travel times which effectively 'bring places closer together') has allowed increased commuting. For example, on the Bedford to London St Pancras line, a journey formerly of over an hour is now 45 minutes. This has produced a 50% increase in the number of commuters using the line. Demand for housing has increased along these newly electrified lines, especially around certain towns such as St Albans, with the consequent inflation in house prices.

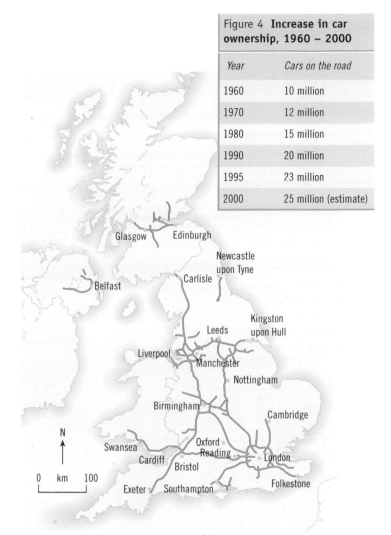

Figure 4 **Increase in car ownership, 1960 – 2000**	
Year	Cars on the road
1960	10 million
1970	12 million
1980	15 million
1990	20 million
1995	23 million
2000	25 million (estimate)

Figure 5 **Existing motorway network and upgrading schemes**

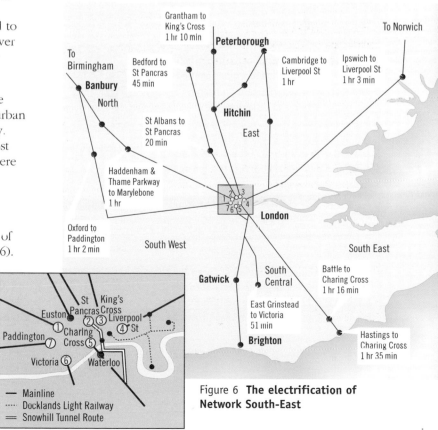

Figure 6 **The electrification of Network South-East**

13.3 Problems of urban transport

Most cities of the world are facing a transport crisis. Rapidly increasing populations with an increase in car ownership have made traffic congestion and gridlock a way of life. Existing transport systems are unable to cope. It is generally agreed that current policies are inadequate but there is widespread disagreement over how the crisis should be tackled.

▶ Figure 1 **Congestion outside the Gare de Nord, Paris**

Case study | London

London, like so many cities of western Europe, is strangling itself to death. Every day, more and more cars and lorries flood into the city centre. Average car speed in the city centre is now less than 10 mph, no faster than a horse and carriage one hundred years ago! Before long the entire city could be at a standstill.

Many of the transport problems of London and other major cities are described below.

Environmental pollution

Motor vehicles are the single largest source of **air pollution. Smog** can be created when the nitrogen oxides and hydrocarbons emitted by cars react with sunlight to form **ozone.** Carbon monoxide, ozone and other emissions aggravate bronchial and lung disorders and can be deadly to old people, the very young and sufferers of asthma. Exhaust gases also contain carbon dioxide, which is a greenhouse gas.

Pollutants emitted from vehicles (e.g. soot from diesel engines) can make buildings and monuments look unsightly. It is costly to return the stone to its original state.

Revving of engines, sounding of horns and the thundering roar of heavy lorries and coaches all increase the city's **noise pollution** to levels which are damaging to health and peace of mind.

Traffic queues, smog, multi-storey car parks and motorway fly-overs can all be described as forms of **visual pollution**, blots on the urban landscape that spoil how the city looks.

Harmful to people

In London last year, over 6000 people were killed or seriously injured in **traffic accidents**. The annual global figure was 300 000. Of those, more than half were pedestrians and pedal cyclists struck by vehicles.

Traffic congestion delays **vital servies** (police, fire, ambulance) from getting to emergencies. For example, it took seven minutes for the nearest fire engine to travel 1300 metres to the King's Cross underground fire in 1987.

Greater levels of **stress** are experienced by drivers as they wait in long queues and are delayed for work and meetings.

Loss of land

Coping with the car has become a top priority for many urban planners, with the car taking control of the whole character of cities. Over 25% of all land in London is taken up with roads and parking spaces (over 60% in Los Angeles).

Harmful to economy

The movement of goods is slower within urban areas. Time and manpower is wasted in traffic jams. The CBI (Confederation of British Industry) estimates that each year London loses more than £20 billion as a result of traffic congestion.

Why urban traffic has increased

Increases in car ownership and **commuting** have brought about a greater volume of vehicles wanting to travel on urban roads. The Department of Transport predicts traffic volume in UK cities will increase a further 50% over the next 30 years.

Reduced public transport funding by governments over consecutive decades in favour of road-building and private transport has resulted in a **decline in the service** offered, leading to a decrease in the number of people wanting to travel by public transport. In London the use of buses and trains has remained relatively high, but like most other European cities, the car has replaced the bus and train as the principal means of travelling to and within urban areas. People also prefer the comfort and convenience of their own cars to public transport.

Improvements in urban road networks and the inflexibility of the railways has attracted **freight** companies to the roads (Figure 2). Over 90% of Britain's urban freight now travels by road. Movement of goods is quicker and easier during the early and late hours of the day when the roads are less congested.

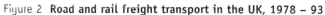

Figure 2 **Road and rail freight transport in the UK, 1978 – 93**

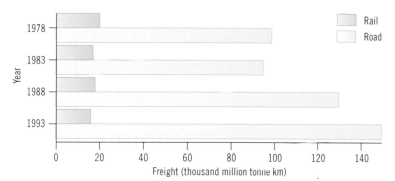

Figure 3 **The benefits of private transport**

Figure 4 **The benefits of public transport**

Figure 5 **Public vs private transport**

1 Study Figure 5. These are comments from people who use different modes of transport.
   a What mode of transport is each comment referring to?
   b Who might be making each comment?
   c Divide the comments into those about private transport and those about public transport.

2 Construct a table giving arguments for and against public and private transport. The comments in Figure 5 may help you.

3 **a** Construct a questionnaire to discover people's attitudes to different modes of transport. You could ask young people and old people about their views and compare the results.
   b Do the views expressed help you to understand why urban traffic congestion is such a huge problem?

4 **a** Figures 3 and 4 show contrasting views. What is the message of each illustration?
   b Design your own advertisement poster to highlight the advantages of public transport over those of private transport.

13.4 | Urban transport solutions

As traffic congestion in the world's cities has worsened and environmental concern has grown, many different schemes have been implemented to ease the situation. These range from small-scale projects to large-scale investments of millions of pounds. They have met with varying degrees of success.

Solutions to the urban traffic problem can be divided into two main approaches:

● to allow private transport to continue expanding by building new roads, motorways and car parks to cope with increased traffic volumes

● to limit private transport by restricting their use and encouraging alternative methods of travel, particularly public transport.

Case study | Singapore

Singapore is an independent state located at the tip of the Malaysian Peninsula (Figure 1). The main island is only 618 sq. km in area yet is home to a population of three million. This makes it one of the highest population densities for any country in the world (4854 people per sq. km). Singapore, like other world cities, has chronic traffic congestion. Despite various disincentives to car ownership, the number of vehicles has increased greatly over the last four decades. This has been caused by a mix of growing affluence, inadequate public transport services and a lack of road space. By 1995, the total number of vehicles registered in Singapore was 620 000, a 50% increase on the figure for 1981. If present growth rates continue, increased congestion will have disasterous effects on the economy, environment and public health.

In the past, efforts to solve the traffic problem were small-scale and included widening roads, changing two-way streets into one-way streets and creating more car parks. However, the steady increase in vehicle traffic made such efforts ineffective. The next attempt was to increase duties on imported foreign cars, to increase car tax and the vehicle registration fee but these methods proved inappropriate for regulating car travel at congested times and in congested areas. Since 1975 a number of large-scale schemes have been implemented with overall success:

Higher parking fees

In 1975, parking fees in the Central Business Disrtict (CBD) were set at $0.50 for the first hour, $1.00 for the second hour and $2.00 for every hour after that, disuading traffic from remaining in the centre for a prolonged period of time.

Area Licensing Scheme (ALS)

The ALS came into effect in 1975. The CBD was cordoned off as a restricted zone between the morning peak hours of 7.30 and 10.15 (Figure 2). A special daily or monthly licence had to be bought and displayed on the windscreen of any car entering the restricted zone during those hours. The only vehicles allowed in without a licence were commercial vehicles, buses and car pools (cars or taxis carrying at least four people). The aims of the ALS were to alleviate peak hour congestion in the CBD and to encourage more people to travel in each vehicle. By 1991 the ALS had been extended to include evening peak hours as well and in 1993 the ALS was fully automated.

Figure 1 **Location of Singapore, in south-east Asia**

Figure 2 **Singapore's Area Licensing Scheme**

The Weekend Car Scheme (WCS)

In 1991 this scheme was introduced to allow more people to own private cars without adding to traffic congestion. WCS licensed cars could be used between 7 p.m. and 7 a.m. Monday to Friday, after 3 p.m. on Saturday and all day Sunday. Each WCS car owner is given a licence for unlimited travel on five days of the year, but any days beyond that cost $20 each.

The park-and-ride scheme

Fifteen fringe car parks with a capacity of 10 000 cars were built around the edge of the ALS restricted zone (Figure 3). Motorists entering the city could use the car parks and continue their journey into the CBD by the public transport shuttlebus.

Figure 3 **An efficient bus service reduces congestion**

Improved public bus service

Besides the existing Singapore Bus Service (SBS), the Supplementary Public Transport System (SPTS) was introduced in 1974 to encourage greater use of public transport and meet the needs of commuters. The SPTS used the existing pool of privately owned school buses during peak hours to provide extra services on specified routes. An air-conditioned service was later introduced. Reserved bus lanes along major roads were introduced to give priority of movement to public buses during peak hours. This system affected 16 km along 23 roads in the CBD.

Expressways

Seven new expressways, 141 km long, were added to the existing road network to speed up traffic flow all over the island. These expressways allow through-city traffic to avoid the city centre altogether (Figure 5).

Vehicle quota system

Set up in 1990, this scheme limited the number of vehicle licences available. Anyone buying a new car has to bid for an allotted licence, only gaining the licence if he or she were the highest bidder. Every three months the licence has to return to the bidding process again.

Figure 4 **New expressways divert traffic around Singapore's CBD**

Mass Rapid Transit (MRT)

The MRT, opened in 1987, is similar to the underground networks in London (Underground), Paris (Metro) and New York (Subway). It has an east-west line and a north-south line with interchanges at two central stations. It is now widely used as an alternative to car travel to and from work (Figure 6).

Figure 5 **The Mass Rapid Transport system, Singapore**

The changing division of labour

Industry has changed a great deal over the last 50 years. Mines have closed, machinery has replaced farm labourers, and manufacturing industry has been revolutionised by the introduction of robots and high-technology equipment. Today more and more people work in service industries, such as shops, hospitals, finance and research. Industry can be classified into four sectors (Figure 1).

In the UK, there have been significant trends in each of the industrial sectors shown in Figure 1. Figure 2 shows these trends. The occupations where employment has in increased has been in the tertiary and quaternary sectors, while manufacturing industry has declined. These trends have been called **deindustrialisation**.

Figure 1 The industrial sectors

Industrial sector	Definition	Example
Primary	The extraction of raw materials from the ground and sea	
Secondary	Processing of raw materials and manufactured goods	
Tertiary	Provision of a service	
Quaternary	Provision of information and administrative services	

Deindustrialisation

Deindustrialisation is the term given to the decline in manufacturing industries and the growth of tertiary and quaternary industries. Deindustrialisation in the UK has resulted from:

■ machinery replacing people in most manufacturing industries

■ competition from countries abroad producing manufactured products at much cheaper prices

■ prices for UK goods being too high, due to low labour productivity (output per person) and a lack of investment in new machinery

■ highly qualified people preferring jobs in the tertiary and quaternary sectors

■ high interest rates in the late 1980s and early 1990s making UK products expensive to buy abroad.

The effects of deindustrialisation have been felt the most in the traditional manufacturing regions of the UK. Areas such as the West Midlands, the North East and North West have all experienced huge job losses in manufacturing. While new developments have taken place, notably in retailing and other services, there are never enough jobs to replace those lost. In many cases, the new jobs are not suited to the former manufacturing workers.

Despite these concerns, some people are pointing to a new phase of growth in manufacturing, a process that has been called **reindustrialisation**.

There are definite trends in employment in the four industrial sectors for the UK; on a world scale there are also definite patterns emerging. Figure 4 shows some of these.

The globalisation of industry

Today many firms have different aspects of their manufacturing operations around the world. This is so that they can make use of cheaper labour and other favourable factors offered by developing countries in places such as South East Asia or South America. Not all countries have benefited from this shift in operations, but it is clear that one result of this change is mainly to service industries in the developed countries.

Figure 2 The changing structure of industry in the UK, 1981 and 1995

	% people employed		
	1981		
Region	Primary	Secondary	Tertiary
North	7	34	59
Yorkshire and Humberside	7	35	58
East Midlands	8	39	53
East Anglia	7	31	62
South East	3	27	70
South West	5	29	66
West Midlands	4	42	54
North West	3	37	60
Wales	8	29	63
Scotland	5	31	64
Northern Ireland	5	29	66
United Kingdom	**5**	**32**	**63**
	1995		
North	3	28	69
Yorkshire and Humberside	3	28	69
East Midlands	3	33	64
East Anglia	5	24	71
South East	2	18	80
South West	3	21	76
West Midlands	2	32	66
North West	2	27	69
Wales	4	27	69
Scotland	4	24	72
Northern Ireland	4	22	76
United Kingdom	**3**	**24**	**73**

Figure 3 **Standard regions of the UK**

Reindustrialisation

Reindustrialisation is the name given to the growth of some sectors of manufacturing and service industries. Reindustrialisation in the UK has the following characteristics:

■ the growth of high-technology firms – these are firms that produce very advanced products with a great deal of scientific research and development e.g. pharmaceuticals and micro-electronics

■ such new firms that set up manufacturing often only have a small, highly skilled labour force

■ the new firms are located in the less industrialised areas of the UK, such as East Anglia.

Figure 4 **The global structure of industry**

Country	Percentage of workforce in		
	Primary	Manufacturing	Services
Brazil	25	25	50
Bangladesh	59	13	28
Germany	4	30	66
Mali	85	2	13
Nepal	92	1	7
North Korea	17	27	56
Romania	31	44	25
Taiwan	21	30	49
UK	2	20	78
USA	3	18	79

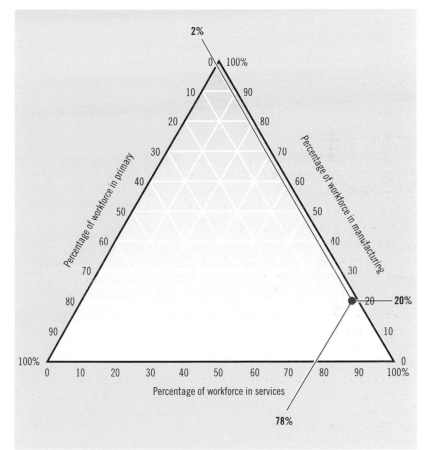

Figure 5 **The changing division of labour**

1 Copy and complete Figure 1 by adding at least one example of an industry found in each industrial sector.

2 **a** Using the information in Figure 2, calculate the percentage change (the difference between the 1981 and 1995 figure) of people employed in each region of the UK for primary, secondary and tertiary industries.
b Using the outline map in Figure 3 (see also page 252), draw three choropleth maps to show the percentage change of people employed in primary, secondary and tertiary industries, for each of the regions of the UK.
c Describe what trends your maps show.
d How might deindustrialisation and reindustrialisation help explain the patterns on your three maps?

3 **a** Figure 5 shows a triangular graph (see also page 253). Using the information in Figure 4, plot the position of the countries on the triangular graph. The UK has already been completed for you.
b Which countries are found with mainly primary industries?
c Which countries are found with predominantly secondary industries?
d Which countries are found with predominantly tertiary industries?
e Can you suggest any reasons for this worldwide pattern?

The location of industry

Figure 1 shows that manufacturing industry can be thought of as a system. For a factory to manufacture or produce a product, it requires a certain number of inputs before the product can be made and transported to market. Figure 2 shows the main factors that are taken into consideration when a suitable location needs to be found for a new factory

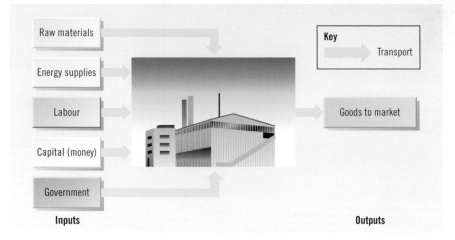

Key
Transport

Raw materials

Energy supplies

Labour

Capital (money)

Government

Goods to market

Inputs   **Outputs**

▶ Figure 1 **Industry as a system**

Figure 2 **Factors that affect industrial location**

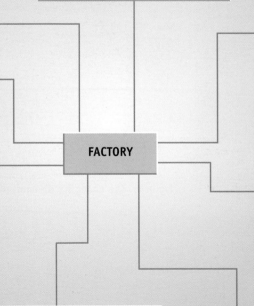

Government

Due to special incentives, such as grants and subsidies, industries are attracted to areas that they may otherwise have not located in some parts of the UK.

Raw materials

During the industrial revolution, close access to raw materials such as coal and iron ore was essential for most industries, as they were heavy, bulky and expensive to transport. Today, fewer manufacturing industries use raw materials directly to make their products. Instead, many firms now assemble component parts to make their final products, which are cheaper and lighter to transport.

Energy supplies

While many early manufacturing industries were established close to sources of energy, such as coalfields, modern industries can almost be guaranteed to have an energy supply anywhere in the country due to the National Grid of electricity.

Access to market

The market can be anything from another factory wanting to use components parts for a larger product, to shops and retailers in the UK or worldwide. Easy access to the transport network (road, rail, air, sea) is important in getting products to the market.

Labour

Labour is important to manufacturing industries in many ways. Industries with large scale production lines, such as the car industry, require lots of labour to assemble products. Smaller high-technology firms do not require large amounts of labour, but do require very skilled workers to design, manufacture and research into ways of improving their products.

FACTORY

Accessibility

While the cost of transport is no longer a major factor, getting from the factory to the market is. Most industries, therefore, require quick and easy access to the road and motorway network – another factor that encourages location on the edge of towns and cities.

Site

Most modern industries look for a flat site on which to build a single-storey factory with room for expansion. Such sites tend to be found at the edge of towns and cities where land is cheaper and not congested, unlike the inner city.

Capital

All industries require some money in advance of selling their products to set up and start manufacturing.

Figure 3 **Toyota's assembly plant at Burnaston**

Key

| 1 160 000 workers live within 45 minutes | 290 000 workers live within 30 minutes | 163 000 workers live within 15 minutes |

Figure 4 **Commuting distance for workers at Toyota**

What Burnaston had to offer Toyota

Communications – close to the motorway network, with a proposed M1-M6 link, and two international airports at nearby Leicester and Birmingham

Labour – a large potential workforce in surrounding towns and cities, with a tradition of high-quality work in a variety of engineering-type industries

Linkages – Birmingham, Nottingham, Coventry, Leicester, Nottingham, Derby and Burton-on-Trent, all have a wide range of industries that could supply component parts for car manufacture and provide a host of other necessary services

Site – a 580-acre flat site with room for expansion

Environment – the Peak District National Park is close by; there are also numerous sporting activities, such as golf courses, and entertainment facilities, like theatres, cinemas and restaurants, located near to the Burnaston site

Houses and schools – a wide variety of housing is available in pleasant surroundings with a large choice of schooling.

---

1 Explain why raw materials, energy supplies and transport costs are less important factors of location when deciding where to build a factory today.

2 Look at the information in Figures 3 to 4.
a Redraw the systems diagram in Figure 1 so that it represents the Toyota factory at Burnaston. Add information that is specific to the Toyota factory.
b Using the photograph and map, describe the advantages of the site at Burnaston for locating a factory.
c What were the essential factors that attracted Toyota to the site at Burnaston?

d Construct a table to show the likely impact of the Toyota decision to move to Burnaston. Use the following headings: Economic, Social, Cultural, Environmental.
e Overall, do you feel the region will benefit from having Toyota located there? Explain why.

3 How easily could you attract industry to locate in an area? Imagine that your school buildings and grounds were being offered for future industrial development. In small groups, produce a marketing poster that shows the advantages of the site, and nearby facilities and services that would attract an industry to locate there. You may also give a small presentation to the rest of the class.

Location of heavy industry

Case study | Teesside – centre of heavy industry

For convenience, many geographers divide manufacturing industry into two classes. **Heavy industries** are usually large-scale in operation, deal in bulky products and are heavily dependent on their raw materials. They tend to be located close to the source of their raw materials. Iron and steel making is one example.

Light industries are usually small-scale in operation, deal in lighter, compact products and are not tied to a raw material location. They tend to emphasise accessibility as their most important factor. The electronics industry is one example of light industry.

Teesside, in the North East of England, is one of the largest areas of heavy industry in the UK.

Figure 1 **The location of industry at Teesside**

Key

Steel

Oil refining

Chemical and petrochemicals

Nuclear Power Station

Built-up area

Hartlepool

Oil pipeline from North Sea

Redcar

ICI Wilton

River Tees

ICI Billingham

Stockton-on-Tees

Middlesbrough

N

0   km   5

Teesside's early development

Since 1850 when railways had become established, the iron and steel industry was founded. With 800 iron furnaces opening in 20 years, the working population grew from 7000 in 1850 to 30 000 in 1881. The nearby Cleveland Hills was the source for the iron ore, while neighbouring Durham coalfield provided coking coal.

During the First World War, Billingham was chosen to make nitric acid for wartime explosives. Good road and rail communications, the navigable river Tees, local supplies of coal and salt water (which could be brought to the surface in the form of brine, an essential raw material of the chemical industry), were all important factors. After World War 1, fertilisers were made. Sulphur, one of the main raw materials required, was obtained from anhydrite, which was mined under the Billingham site.

Figure 2 **Steelworks on Teesside**

Teesside today

Teesside remains an important centre for heavy industry, although the number of people employed in the region's industries has declined and a number of factors responsible for the area's early development are no longer relevant.

The iron and steel industry is based around the steelworks at Redcar. Iron ore is now imported from countries such as Brazil, Canada and Sweden. Coking coal too, is cheaper to import from countries such as Australia and Poland. What keeps the steelworks at Redcar is the deepwater ore terminal where coking coal and iron ore are unloaded from bulk carriers of up to 150 000 tonnes.

The chemical industry now imports most of its raw materials, again relying on the deepwater port on the Tees. Coal and anhydrite are no longer used in the manufacture of chemicals.

There is a large petrochemical plant at Wilton. Oil, the raw material, is provided from the oil refineries on the Tees estuary, which in turn receive their supply from the North Sea fields via pipeline. The plant at Wilton is linked by pipeline to Billingham and Merseyside. Polyester, nylon, perspex and PVC, are examples of the products produced at Wilton.

Some industries, such as those on Teesside, have remained at a location, even though the original factors responsible for their location are no longer relevant. This is called **industrial inertia**.

All the industries at Teesside have experienced change in recent years, with vast amounts of money being invested in new advanced technological equipment. This often means, however, that the number of workers required is less and there have been many redundancies in the region over the last 15 years.

1 Using the text, list the factors that encouraged Teesside to develop as a centre for heavy industry up to the First World War.

2 Using Figure 1, describe and explain the distribution of heavy industry in Teesside.

3 **a** What is industrial inertia?
b Why are the industries on Teesside an example of industrial inertia?
c What changes have taken place more recently on Teesside? How will this affect the local population?

High-technology industry

A high-technology (high-tech) industry is one which makes products that are very sophisticated, involving a great deal of scientific research and development. The industry always looks to improve its products and employs highly skilled labour. Some examples of high-tech industries are shown in Figure 1.

High-tech industries grew very rapidly in the 1980s and early 1990s. They are often referred to as **footloose industries** as they have relatively free choice of where to locate. With a wider choice of location, many high-tech industries are found on the edge of towns and cities on purpose-built industrial estates, business and science parks (Figure 2).

Despite having a freedom of choice, high-tech industries are still found in distinct locations. This is partly due to the desire to be close to centres of research, such as universities but is mainly due to the structure of many high-tech firms (Figure 3).

The tendency to split up operations has led to concentrations of research and development establishments in the South-East and branch plant factories that require larger labour inputs in areas where labour is cheaper. Once an area has become attractive to a firm, it tends to attract more companies of a similar nature, leading to concentrations or **agglomerations** of industries.

Figure 1 **Examples of high-tech industries**
Electronic equipment
■ computers
■ telecommunicators
■ industrial control systems
■ testing and measuring equipment
■ office equipment
■ aerospace and military equipment
■ incorporation in consumer products, e.g. automobiles, washing machines, ovens, etc.
Consumer electronics
■ colour and monochrome television receivers
■ radio receivers
■ video cassette recorders
■ audio-tape recorders
■ record players
■ hi-fi equipment (tuners, amplifiers)
■ pocket calculators
■ electronic games.

Footloose industries – factors that favour a free choice of location

■ light industries that often do not use raw materials but component parts

■ power requirements, usually only electricity – available from the national grid

■ end product is small and often cheaper and easier to move

■ employs a small labour force

■ non-polluting industries which can locate near to residential areas

■ accessibility; needs to be near a road network

Industrial Estates, Business Parks, Science Parks

Footloose industries tend to be attracted to purpose-built estates on the edge of towns and cities. These offer a number of advantages over inner city locations:

● space for single-storey factories and future expansion
● cheaper land values on edge-of-city
● accessibility to main roads and motorways
● pleasant environment (often located on a greenfield site)
● labour supply from nearby residential areas and commuter villages.

1 **a** Define what is meant by high-tech industry.
  b Name three examples of high-tech industry.
  c Name three examples of the products of high-tech industry found in your home.

2 **a** What is meant by the term 'footloose industry'?
  b Explain why footloose industries tend to locate on the edge of towns and cities.
  c Examine Figure 4. Give reasons for the location of electronics and instruments firms in south-east England.
  d Why do the firms shown on Figure 4 tend to cluster or 'agglomerate'?

3 Explain the differences between industrial estates, business parks and science parks.

There are three types of estate:

● **Science parks** are industrial estates with direct links to universities. Often found in university towns, they are out-of-town greenfield sites which mainly concentrate on research and development for high-tech firms.

● **Business parks** are similar to science parks in that they are pleasant out-of-town working environments for offices or high-tech research and development companies, but are not directly linked to a university. Some business parks have retail outlets such as hypermarkets. Like science parks, they are heavily landscaped with grass and trees to create a pleasant working environment.

● **Industrial estates**, although often found on the edge of towns and cities, are also common further towards city centres. While attracting some research and development, many of the factories perform more of a manufacturing function. Often buildings will have been constructed before a company considered locating there. While a pleasant environment is still important, such estates tend to be less landscaped than science or business parks.

Figure 2 **Location of science parks in the UK**

N

0   km   200

Key
1 Aston Science Park
2 Brunel Science Park
3 Cambridge Science Park
4 Cefn Llan Science and Technology Park
5 Chilworth Research Centre
6 Co-operative Education Centre
7 University of Durham Industrial Research Laboratories
8 University of East Anglia Industrial Liaison Unit
9 University College Galway Industrial Liaison Office
10 Heriot Watt Research Park, Edinburgh
11 Keele University Science Park
12 Listerhills High Technology Development
13 Liverpool University R & D Advisory Unit
14 Loughborough Technology Centre
15 Manchester Uiversity / Manchester Science Park
16 Merseyside Innovation Centre
17 St John's Innovation Park, Cambridge
18 Surrey University / Surrey Research Park
19 University of Warwick Science Park
20 Scottish Development Agency and Universities of Glasgow, Strathclyde, and West of Scotland Science Park
21 Applied Statistics Research Unit, University of Kent, Canterbury
22 Stirling University Innovation Park
23 St Andrews Technology Centre
24 Dundee Technology Park
25 Aberdeen Science and Research Park

Figure 3 **Structure of a major high-tech firm**

Part of company	Process	Location factors
Research and development	New ideas, prototypes, testing new products; often takes place in purpose-built research establishments	Close to highly skilled labour force; near a research centre, such as a university; must have pleasant environment in which to work
Product manufacture	Assembling of various component parts or raw materials, usually in branch plant factories	A labour force that is cheap to employ but skilled in precision assembly of small parts; often female labour employed; areas where government grants or incentives are offered are popular
Administration and sales	Marketing the product and dealing with administration of the company	A city location, or close to city, usually in the South-East; managerial workforce required

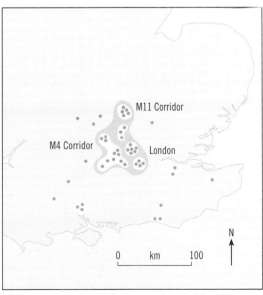

Figure 4 **Locations of electronics and instruments firms in south-east England**

Case study | Aztec West Business Park

Aztec West business park was developed in the 1980s and 1990s on an area of flat land adjacent to the M5 motorway, on the outskirts of Bristol. A large number of houses have been built nearby. The site has good services and amenities (such as local shops and a public house (pub) in the 'office village'). Like most business parks, it is landscaped to provide what the owners call 'quality of life in a business environment'.

Aztec West is located at the western end of 'Silicon Strip' or the 'M4 Corridor'. These are the terms given to the large number of high-tech companies that have located at sites along the M4 motorway between London and Bristol. The quick travelling time to London and Heathrow airport, and the existence of a number of other research centres are the principal reasons for such growth.

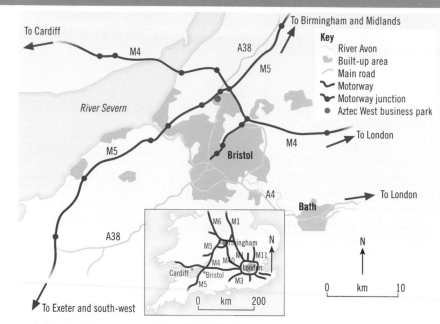

Figure 5 **Location and plan (bottom) of Aztec West business park**

Name of firm	Activity
Mercury Communications	Telecommunications
Benson Electronics	Computer systems
Digital Equipment Ltd	Computer systems
Panasonic UK Ltd	Distribution centre
Radio Rentals	Distribution centre
Sutcliffe Vending Services Ltd	Catering services
Stat Plus	Legal and commercial stationery
Inmos	Computer systems and design
Pirelli General Ltd	Distribution depot

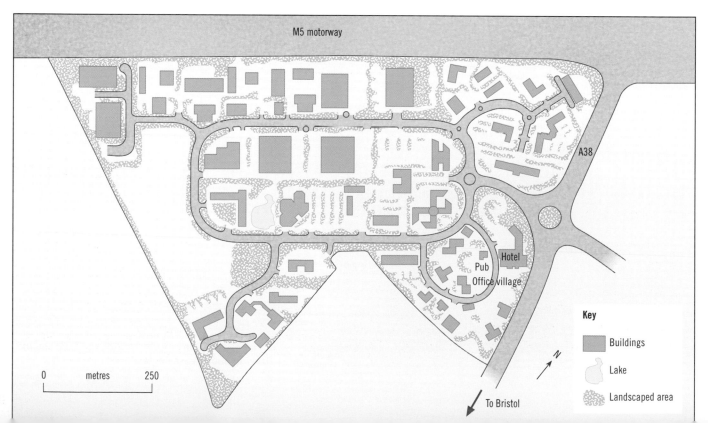

Scotland's Central Valley has been called Silicon Glen because of the number of electronics factories that have located there. In 1996, more than 45 000 people were employed in over 300 electronics factories in the region.

This area of central Scotland has traditionally been an industrial area. Coalfields first attracted industry and the area became famous for its iron and steel, shipbuilding and heavy engineering industries. Today, however, employment in these industries is declining, while employment in the electronics industry is increasing.

Silicon Glen has been successful in attracting overseas companies. Household names such as Seiko, NEC, IBM and Texas Instruments can all be found in the Glen. The problem is that most of these companies only set up branch plant factories that assemble raw materials and/or component parts, most of which are imported from outside the region, so local firms do not benefit from 'spin-off trade'.

Country of origin	% of firms
USA	44
UK	42
EU	3
Rest of world	11

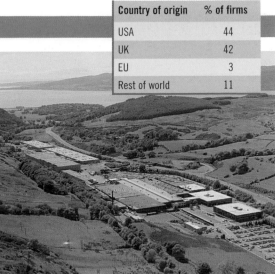

Figure 6 An IBM branch plant at the mouth of the Clyde

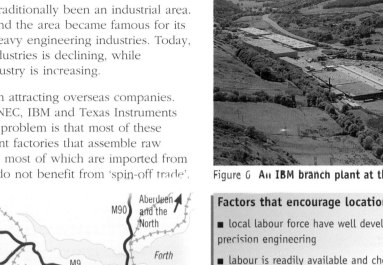

Figure 7 **Communication links in Silicon Glen**

Factors that encourage location in Silicon Glen

- local labour force have well developed skills in precision engineering

- labour is readily available and cheap due to decline of traditional heavy industry

- government grants and incentive packages are available (although less so today than 15 years ago)

- excellent transport links with airports and road and rail

- Scotland's pleasant rural environment is very accessible.

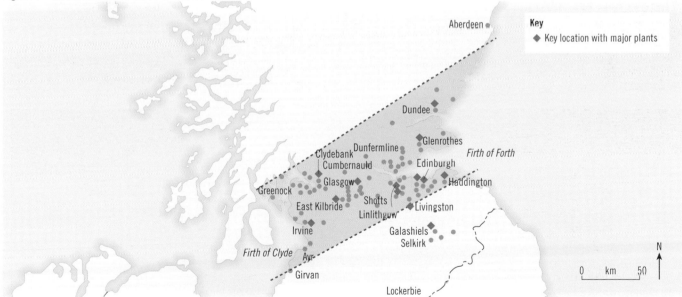

Figure 8 **Location of the Scottish electronics industries at Silicon Glen**

1 a Examine Figure 5. What features of the layout of Aztec West business park are designed to attract high-tech firms to it?
b What other features about Aztec West's location make it attractive to high-tech firms?

2 a Using the data in Figure 6, construct a pie chart to show the country of origin of electronics companies in Scotland.

b Why might so many overseas companies not be good for Silicon Glen?
c Imagine you were the Marketing Advisor for Silicon Glen. A major American electronics company has expressed an interest in locating there. Write a letter to the company director explaining why you feel Silicon Glen would be an ideal location for their company.

The fall and rise of South Wales

The Industrial Revolution of the nineteenth century was dominated by heavy industry located close to raw materials. Industrial areas grew up on Britain's coalfields and attracted workers from rural areas. South Wales was one such area. Coal mining and iron and steel manufacturing were the main industries.

The effect of the industrial revolution was dramatic. Towns and cities grew rapidly and the region prospered. A huge export trade developed through the coastal ports of Cardiff, Newport and Swansea to all parts of the British Empire.

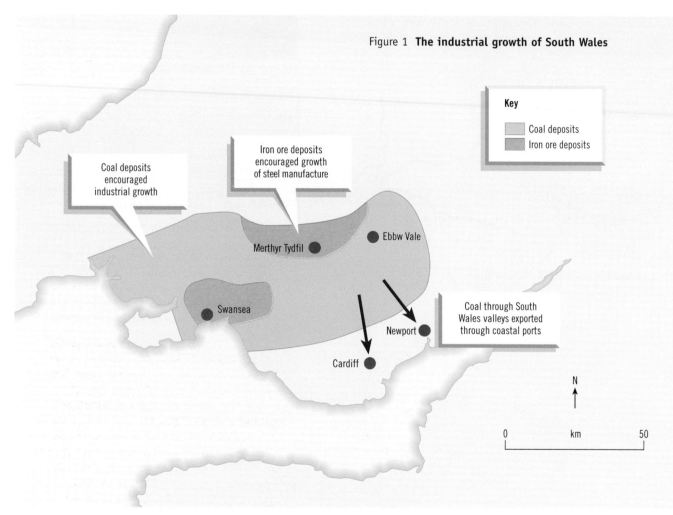

Figure 1 **The industrial growth of South Wales**

Economic development did, however, come with a price. Pollution was a real problem, as was poor housing and low wages. By the end of the Second World War other problems also emerged. The main market for South Wales' products was the British Empire. Countries of the Empire were seeking independence and beginning to use their own raw materials or import from neighbouring countries. Back in Britain, industries that used raw materials from South Wales were now finding it cheaper to import those materials from countries abroad. The region needed other industries to sustain its economy. Since all its industries had been based on a narrow range of industrial products, South Wales had entered a **cycle of decline** (Figure 2).

In 1961, a government report described South Wales as 'an industrial desert'. From that time onwards South Wales, along with other depressed traditional industrial regions, has been an **Assisted Area** (Figure 4).

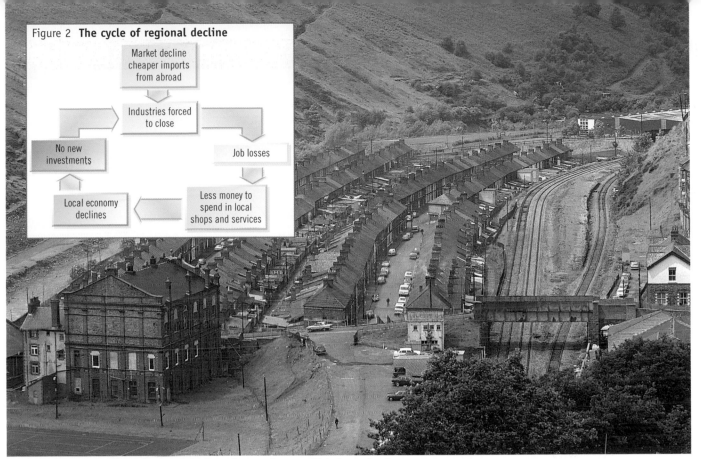

Figure 2 **The cycle of regional decline**

Market decline cheaper imports from abroad → Industries forced to close → Job losses → Less money to spend in local shops and services → Local economy declines → No new investments →

Figure 3 **A mining village in South Wales when coal was still being mined**

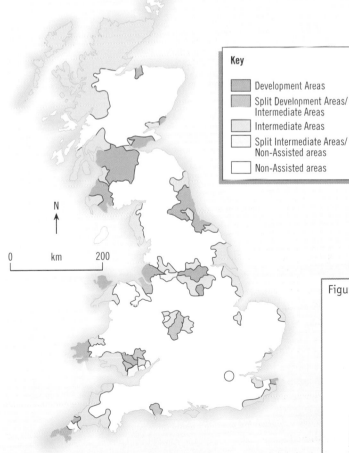

Key
- Development Areas
- Split Development Areas/ Intermediate Areas
- Intermediate Areas
- Split Intermediate Areas/ Non-Assisted areas
- Non-Assisted areas

N

0   km   200

Figure 4 **Assisted Areas of the UK, July 1993**

Assisted Areas are parts of the country that qualify for a series of **grants** (money given as a gift) or **loans** (money that is borrowed but has to be paid back), to help their industries improve, develop and, hopefully, attract new investment.

Industry is important to a region as it provides jobs and money. By attracting industry through these financial incentives, the government hope that regions which have suffered a cycle of decline, will experience a **cycle of growth** or **multiplier effect** (Figure 5). Once a region starts to be successful in terms of attracting industry, it will produce wealth and in turn, attract other industries to locate, providing employment. By making the costs of setting up an industry cheaper, firms may be encouraged to move to a declining region.

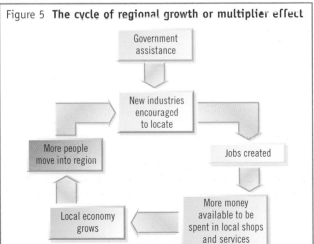

Figure 5 **The cycle of regional growth or multiplier effect**

Government assistance → New industries encouraged to locate → Jobs created → More money available to be spent in local shops and services → Local economy grows → More people move into region →

225

One of the main reasons why the economy of South Wales has grown in recent years has been the number of high-tech firms, especially foreign-owned companies, which have taken advantage of the incentives on offer and located in the region (Figure 8).

Cardiff Bay

Like the city of Swansea, Cardiff has recently made a huge effort to attract industry. By redeveloping the site of Cardiff docks (once a thriving port which exported coal, iron and steel from the South Wales Valleys), the hope is to eventually create 30 000 jobs in high-tech industry and offices. The development will also build 6000 homes, provide services and amenities such as restaurants, sports facilities, shops and hotels, and a freshwater lake.

The development began in 1987 and is already near completion. It will help attract new industry and provide jobs in an area which suffered a loss of trade and jobs as the coal and steel industries of South Wales declined.

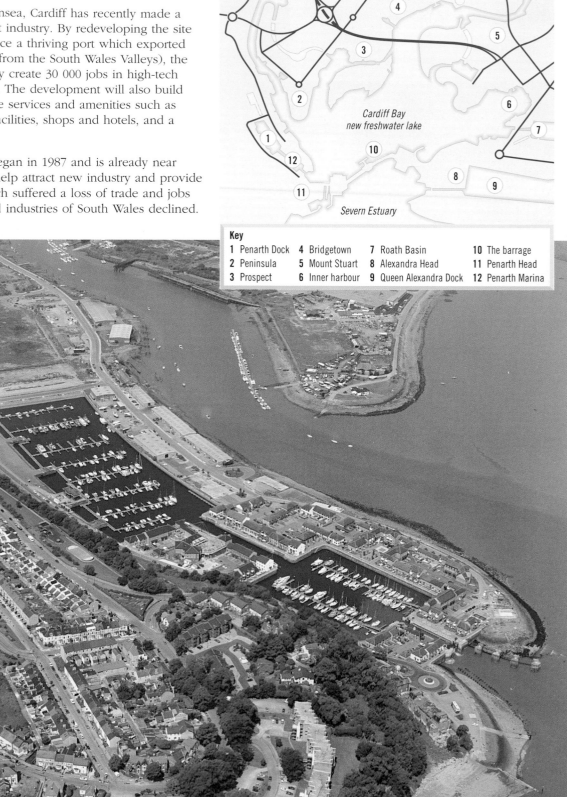

Cardiff Bay
new freshwater lake

Severn Estuary

Key

1	Penarth Dock	4	Bridgetown	7	Roath Basin	10	The barrage
2	Peninsula	5	Mount Stuart	8	Alexandra Head	11	Penarth Head
3	Prospect	6	Inner harbour	9	Queen Alexandra Dock	12	Penarth Marina

Figure 6 **Part of Cardiff Bay today**

Figure 7 **The Sony factory, South Wales**

The call of the high-tech valleys

Wales is changing with the disappearance of traditional heavy industry and the arrival of the new sunrise industries of the future.

Instead of pit-head winding gear and smoke-belching chimney stacks, the valleys of South Wales are becoming home to bright new factory units on high-tech industrial estates. Unlike the one pit still working in South Wales, the new industries are clean and danger free.

So what is attracting industry to the region? Certainly, the close proximity to the Brecon Beacons National Park and the dramatic coastal scenery of places like the Gower Peninsula are encouraging factors. Perhaps most importantly, however, there has been a huge

investment programme in roads, with dual carriageways running down through the valleys linking into the M4 motorway. London is only a one and three-quarter hour train journey from Cardiff and with a range of government incentives available, it is not surprising that the region has attracted so many firms. To add to this, Wales has some of the cheapest labour to employ. Recent surveys have shown that international companies now find it cheaper to pay the workforce in Wales rather than in some developing countries.

It is not surprising, therefore, that South Wales now boasts the highest concentration of Japanese companies in Britain, as well as over 100 UK firms who have chosen to relocate to the region.

Figure 8 **Newspaper article**

1 What were the main advantages of South Wales that originally attracted industry to locate there?

2 Why did the early industries begin to decline?

3 **a** How does having Assisted Area status help attract new industries?
b Look at the map of the UK's Assisted areas (Figure 4). Why do you think some of those regions are to be found in the inner city areas of the UK's cities?

4 Imagine you are a member of the Welsh Development Agency. A Japanese electronics firm is considering locating in South Wales. Write a letter to convince the directors of the firm that South Wales is the place for them to locate. Use Figure 8 to help you.

14.6 The new Industrial Revolution

Although the large industrial nations such as USA and Japan continue to dominate manufacturing, there have been some significant changes in world manufacturing industry in recent years. A number of developing countries have started to catch up with the large industrial nations. Countries like Singapore, Taiwan and Brazil have all rapidly developed a large manufacturing industry and as a result, are seeing their economies grow and their countries become richer. Such countries are called **Newly Industrialising Countries (NICs)**.

With the growth of the east Asian NICs, combined with the industrial superpowers of Japan and USA, many people now believe that manufacturing will shift its traditional home of Western Europe to what has been called the Pacific Rim (Figure 1).

The growth of NICs has brought rising prosperity to many countries. However, with economic growth also comes problems. The following pages show how two NICs, Malaysia and Thailand, have experienced rapid industrial expansion.

Factors that have encouraged eastern Asia's industrial growth

Labour – wages are much lower in NICs, so large multinational companies can employ people more cheaply than in their own country and make goods at a cheaper cost. Asian workers are also well known for their willingness to work hard.

Government – NICs have tried very hard to attract new industries by offering financial incentives.

Communications – global communications are now more advanced than ever. Computers and satellites all help firms that have set up manufacturing factories in an NIC but have their headquarters in the developed world. It is also much quicker to transport goods around the world with the constant improvements in shipping and aircraft.

Market – the market for most manufactured goods is worldwide. Thus the actual location becomes less important.

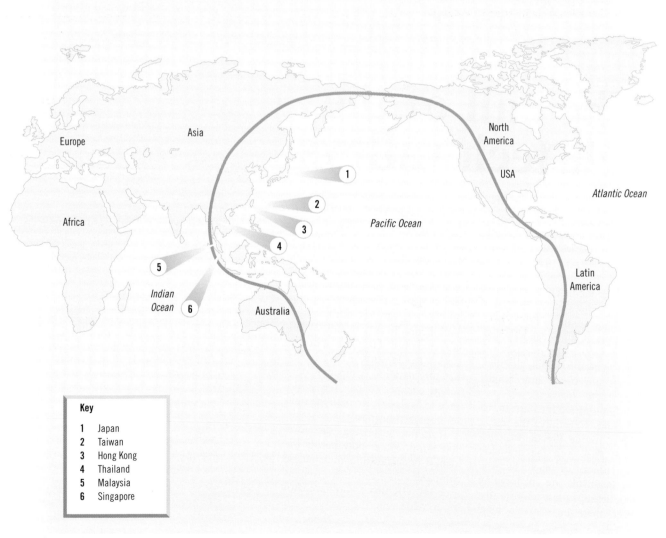

Key

1   Japan
2   Taiwan
3   Hong Kong
4   Thailand
5   Malaysia
6   Singapore

Figure 1 **The Pacific Rim**

Malaysia – an NIC within the Pacific Rim

Malaysia is a country that is not only expanding its manufacturing industry rapidly, but is fast becoming one of the richest countries in the developing world. Most of Malaysia's growth has been based on electronic industries. Over half of its exports are of electronic goods. The government has tried to attract mutinational companies to Malaysia, with some notable success.

Within Malaysia, this new industrial revolution has been most evident on the island of Penang. The map shows why Penang has proved to be such a popular location for industry.

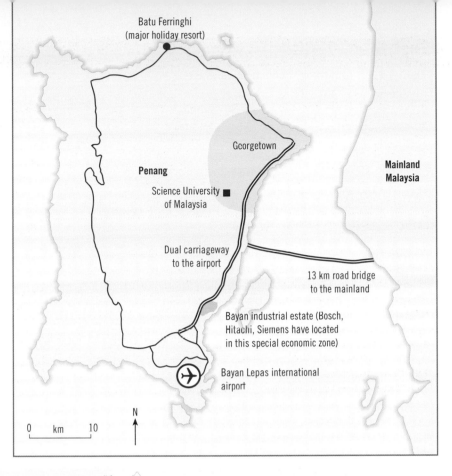

▶ Figure 2 **Location of industries in Malaysia**

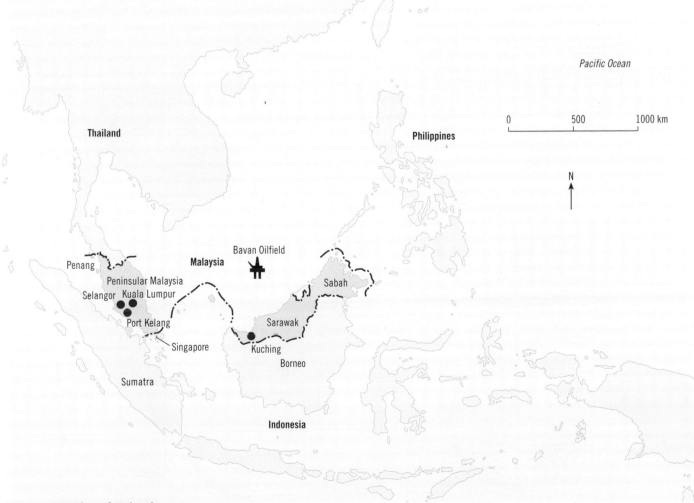

Figure 3 **Location of Malaysia**

Thailand – a country of industrial contrasts

Thailand is one of the world's fastest growing economies. Thailand has undergone a huge transition from an agricultural-based economy to one dominated by manufactured goods (especially electronics). Personal wealth has increased while the ownership of goods such as televisions has grown rapidly.

Despite these improvements in living standards, the benefits of economic growth have not been shared by everyone. Bangkok, the capital city, has emerged as the prosperous industrial growth region. Average incomes in Bangkok are ten times higher than in the north-east of the country. As a result, people have flocked from the countryside to Bangkok and the city is struggling to cope. The roads are congested and the main port cannot handle the volume of traffic. Pollution in the city is so serious that people walk around with handkerchiefs over their mouths. The rapid development of the city has meant that many buildings have been constructed rapidly and without proper services – only 2% of Bangkok's residents have access to sewage facilities. The canals are choked with litter and raw sewage. Industries have also released so many pollutants into the sea that the Gulf of Thailand, south of Bangkok, has virtually no marine life in it.

The government have tried to do something about the growth of Bangkok at the expense of the rest of the country.

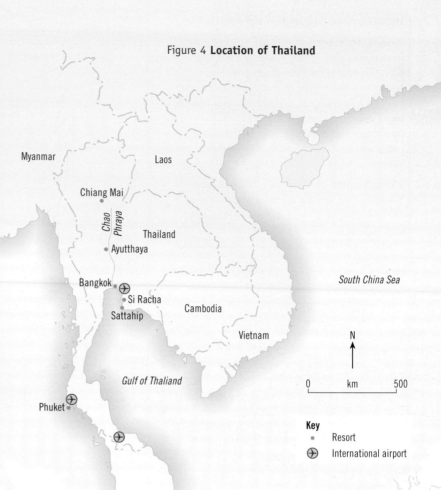

Figure 4 **Location of Thailand**

▼ Figure 5 **The structure of Thailand's economy**

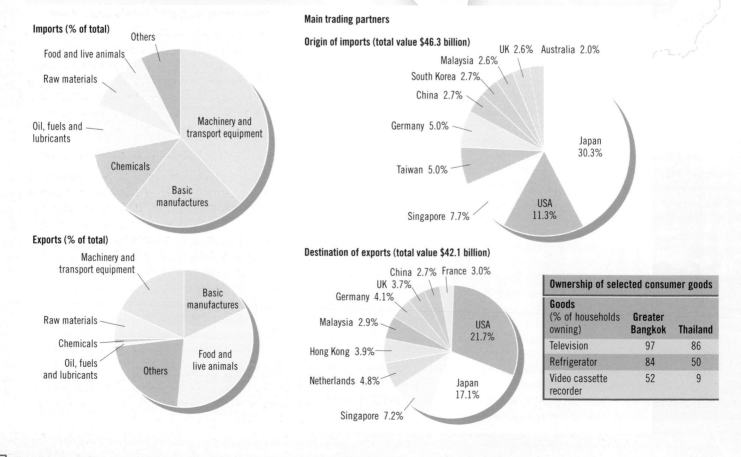

Imports (% of total)

Others
Food and live animals
Raw materials
Oil, fuels and lubricants
Chemicals
Machinery and transport equipment
Basic manufactures

Exports (% of total)

Machinery and transport equipment
Raw materials
Chemicals
Oil, fuels and lubricants
Others
Basic manufactures
Food and live animals

Main trading partners

Origin of imports (total value $46.3 billion)

UK 2.6%   Australia 2.0%
Malaysia 2.6%
South Korea 2.7%
China 2.7%
Germany 5.0%
Taiwan 5.0%
Singapore 7.7%
Japan 30.3%
USA 11.3%

Destination of exports (total value $42.1 billion)

China 2.7%   France 3.0%
UK 3.7%
Germany 4.1%
Malaysia 2.9%
Hong Kong 3.9%
Netherlands 4.8%
Singapore 7.2%
USA 21.7%
Japan 17.1%

Ownership of selected consumer goods		
Goods (% of households owning)	**Greater Bangkok**	**Thailand**
Television	97	86
Refrigerator	84	50
Video cassette recorder	52	9

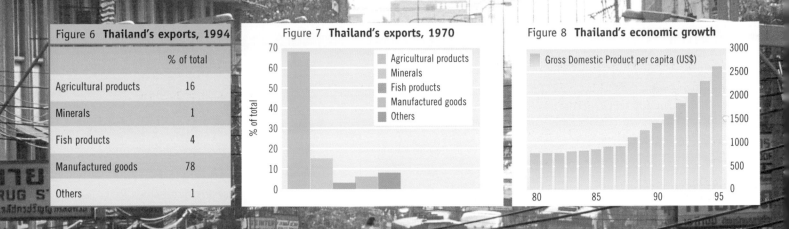

Figure 6 **Thailand's exports, 1994**	
	% of total
Agricultural products	16
Minerals	1
Fish products	4
Manufactured goods	78
Others	1

Figure 7 **Thailand's exports, 1970**

Agricultural products
Minerals
Fish products
Manufactured goods
Others

Figure 8 **Thailand's economic growth**

Gross Domestic Product per capita (US$)

The Eastern Seaboard Development Zone

This is an attempt by the government to decentralise industry to two zones about 100 km south of Bangkok. Designed to try and attract industry away from Bangkok, this new industrial area will make use of the natural gas reserves of the Gulf of Thailand and will be based around a huge petrochemical works which, it is hoped, will attract new related industries.

The Southern Seaboard Development Zone

This is designed to transform the peninsula south of the country into an industrial area. Two new ports are to be built and large areas of land around the ports have been set aside for industrial development. A free trade zone and the development of tourism is also planned for the areas closest to Malaysia.

1 What is the Pacific Rim and why is it growing so rapidly?

2 Using page 229, list the advantages to a company wishing to locate in Malaysia.

3 **a** Using the information in Figure 6, produce a bar graph to show exports in 1994.
b Compare your graph to the one for exports in 1970 (Figure 7). What are the major changes? Why?

c What benefits has manufacturing growth brought to Thailand?
d Using page 230, describe the problems that rapid economic growth has brought to Bangkok.
e Thinking back to the multiplier effect, how is Thailand's government hoping that the Eastern and Southern Seaboard Development Zones will even out Thailand's industrial growth?

15.1 The world's fastest growing industry

Tourism is estimated to become the world's biggest industry by the year 2000. In 1990 it earned $(US) 316 035 million world wide. The industry has grown considerably, around 70% in the last decade.

The importance of tourism is widely recognised – qualifications can even be gained in Leisure and Tourism in the UK.

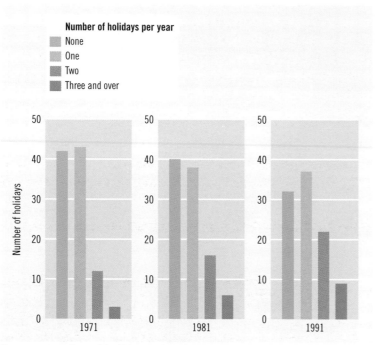

Number of holidays per year
- None
- One
- Two
- Three and over

Figure 1 **Number of holidays taken in a year, 1971 – 91**

" Tourism in Britain is a success story. Our history and heritage, culture and countryside provide an unrivalled tourism experience. The industry provides jobs for 1.5 million people and contributes £33 billion to the economy – 5% of our GDP. Over 20 million visitors from overseas came here last year. But we all know what happens if we sit back and rely on past success to continue. Other tourist destinations will simply shoulder us aside. Already the warning signs are there when we look at our foreign competitors. "

Rt Hon. Stephen Dorrell MP

Secretary of State for National Heritage

Figure 2 **An extract from a speech made in 1996**

Why tourism has increased

More leisure time
An increasingly elderly population and a younger retirement age has meant a significant increase in the number of people retired from work.

A shorter working week has meant that people have more leisure time at weekends and at the end of the day. There has also been an increase in the length of the entitled paid leave for employees.

Affluence
The average income in the UK has increased considerably since the early 1900s. Spending on consumer goods such as televisions, computers and cars has increased, as has spending on holidays.

Greater mobility
Car ownership has increased due to a rise in affluence and a fall in car prices. This has enabled people to travel on holiday more frequently and more independently.

Advances in aircraft design have meant a decline in the relative cost of air travel, making air travel affordable to more people.

Figure 3 **Car ownership per family, 1961 – 91**

- 2 cars
- 1 car
- No car

1961

1991

Holiday destinations

There has been an increase in the number of international holidays taken as people have more time and money to spend, and as communications, particularly air travel, has increased. International holiday destinations are further abroad since the number and quality of long-haul flights have improved.

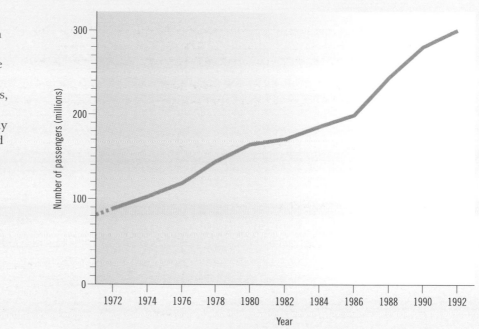

Figure 4 Number of air passengers carried on scheduled international flights, 1972 – 92

Types of holidays

A wider range of holidays are on offer. Package holidays (where the travel company fixes flights, accommodation and meals) have grown in popularity. The variety of personal interests have led to more specialist holidays and adventure holidays. Flexibility at work and improved communications have encouraged a further growth in short break holidays. More recently, there has been an increase in 'all inclusive holidays'.

Figure 5 **Number of people taking holidays of 4 or more nights**

Year	Number or people (million)		
	UK	Abroad	Total
1965	30	5	35
1970	35	6	41
1975	40	8	48
1980	37	12	49
1985	33	16	49
1992	32	22	54

1 Study Figure 2
   a According to Rt Hon. Stephen Dorrell MP, what attracts tourists to Britain?
   b In what way is 'Tourism in Britain' a success story?
   c Draw a graph using the data shown in Figure 5.
   d What are 'the warning signs' Mr Dorrell mentions?

2 Study Figure 1
   a What percentage of the population
   (i) had no holiday in 1971?
   (ii) had no holiday in 1991?
   (iii) had one holiday in 1981?
   (iv) had two holidays in 1971?
   (v) had two holidays in 1991?
   b Describe the pattern shown from this graph.

3 Explain why the tourist industry has grown over the past 50 years?

People are attracted to different environments for different types of holidays. For example, coastal environments such as Eastbourne and Cannes in the south of France, are popular among families with young children. Mountain environments, such as Snowdonia, the Alps and the Rockies, have also become increasingly popular over the past few years as they support a range of active sports, such as mountain biking, climbing, walking and skiing.

Some people like to visit famous towns, museums, art galleries and monuments in places like Bath, Venice, New York, and the West End of London.

Recently, whole new environments have been created just to attract tourists to areas previously unvisited, for example, Disneyland, Paris and CentreParcs, Somerset.

Figure 2 **Mountain biking in California**

Figure 1 **Top 20 attractions charging admission, 1994 (in thousands)**		
1	Alton Towers, Staffordshire	3011
2	Madame Tussaud's, London	2632
3	Tower of London	2407
4	St Paul's Cathedral, London	1900
5	Natural History Museum, London	1625
6	Chessington World of Adventures	1614
7	Blackpool Tower	1305
8	Science Museum, London	1269
9	Thorpe Park, Surrey	1235
10	Drayton Manor Park, Staffordshire	1104
11	Windsor Castle	1091
12	London Zoo	1047
13	Edinburgh Castle	992
14	Kew Gardens	989
15	Royal Academy, London	952
16	Roman Baths and Pump Room, Bath	871
17	Chester Zoo	774
18	Warwick Castle	756
19	American Adventure, Ilkeston	723
20	Stonehenge, Wiltshire	697

Case study The Lake District – a landscape loved to death

The Lake District is an area that has inspired artists and poets such as Wordsworth and Coleridge. The landscape is a glaciated environment of high mountains, deep valleys and beautiful lakes. It also has a number of very attractive traditional settlements. The area has a population of only 41 000 yet has over four million tourist trips each year. Many jobs are created as a result of the tourist industry and some facilities (roads and telephones) are improved. In 1994 tourists spent £425 million. However, these advantages are off-set by several problems.

Traffic congestion

Over 80% of the visitors arrive by road, most of them between April and September. The traffic quickly becomes congested in the narrow, steep roads, especially behind slow-moving caravans and tractors.

Pollution

Road traffic creates pollution from their exhausts as well as noise pollution. Tourists inevitably drop litter. Large campsites can also spoil the view, creating 'visual pollution'.

Soil erosion

Sites and walks are very popular. When thousands of walkers trample along the same paths the vegetation is destroyed and the soil exposed. Wind and rain can then erode the soil, creating gullies.

Conflicts between tourists and locals

There are potential conflicts between walkers and farmers, for example, gates are left open by careless walkers and sheep are worried by dogs. Local residents may resent the crowding in their towns and shops. Many tourists end up buying second homes in the area, which they occupy for only a few weeks in the year. The houses then become too expensive for the local people to buy.

Conflicts between different types of tourists

Many different activities (sailing, water skiing, jet skiing, wind surfing) have to compete for limited space on the lakes. At some lakes, different activities are restricted to limited areas. Many of these sports may disturb the tranquillity of other tourists.

These problems are magnified in some of the busiest centres. Certain towns such as Windermere, Ambleside and Bowness attract many visitors who swarm around the attractions like bees. The busiest centres are often referred to as **honeypot** sites.

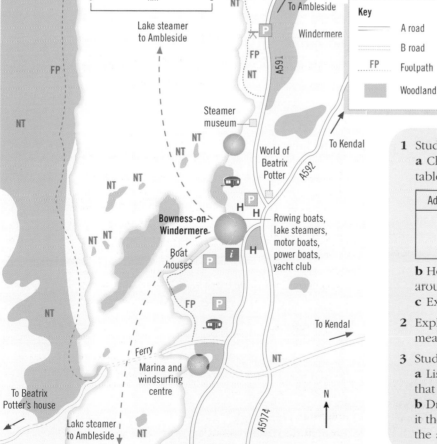

Figure 3 **Holiday activities at Bowness, the Lake District**

1 Study Figure 1
   a Classify the 20 attractions in the following table:

Adventure	Museum	Historical	Other

   b How many of the attractions are based in or around London?
   c Explain why so many are located there.

2 Explain, giving specific examples, what is meant by 'a landscape loved to death'.

3 Study the map of Bowness (Figure 3).
   a List five different activities and attractions that would attract visitors to Bowness.
   b Draw a sketch map of the area marking on it the main communication network. Identify the areas that will suffer from bad congestion.

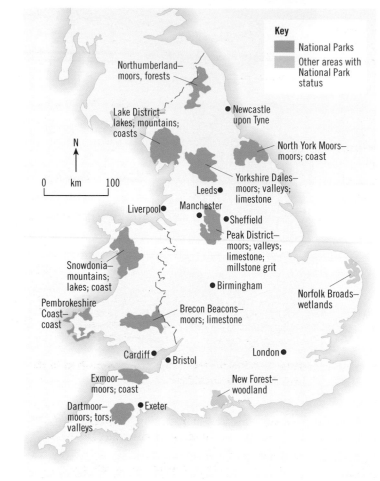

Figure 1 **Location of National Parks in England and Wales**

An Act of Parliament in 1949 founded ten National Parks in England and Wales. The Norfolk Broads and New Forest were later added. Altogether, they make up 10% of England and Wales and constitute a wide range of environments, ranging from high mountains (Snowdonia, Lake District), moorland (North York Moors, Dartmoor) and coasts (Pembrokeshire), to woodland (New Forest) and wetlands (Norfolk Broads).

The aims of the National Parks are to conserve the physical and human environments of the Park, to enable the use of the Park for a range of leisure activities, to support local jobs and industries, and to protect the quality of life of the local residents.

Figure 2 shows the percentage of land ownership in the National Parks; most of it is owned privately. The different owners will have different demands from the land, many of which conflict with the aims of the Parks.

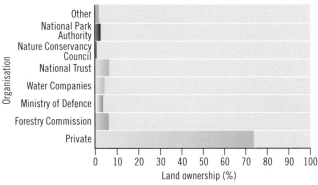

Figure 2 **Land ownership in National Parks, 1990**

Conflicts in Dartmoor National Park

Ministry of Defence

About 14% of Dartmoor is owned by the Ministry of Defence. The firing ranges are frequently used and so access for walkers, riders and other tourists is restricted.

Water Authorities

There was considerable argument about the building of reservoirs in Dartmoor. There are currently eight reservoirs but in 1970 plans for a ninth were refused following resistance from local farmers, walkers and environmentalists.

China clay

Dartmoor's underlying rock is granite which can be quarried for building stone. In some conditions granite weathers to form china clay. There is a large china clay quarry at Lee Moor on the edge of Dartmoor.

Figure 3 **Lee Moor quarry, Dartmoor**

The Lake District National Park Authority

As the Lake District is so popular, it needs to be very carefully managed by the National Park Authority. The Authority only has limited power and has to encourage landowners and county councils into making the right decisions for the Park. The Lake District National Park Authority has a number of carefully considered plans to cope with the problems of over use.

Zoning of leisure activity (Figure 4)

Certain areas of the Park are designated as busy, heavily used areas while other areas are to be lightly used. For example, planning applications for caravan sites are discouraged. They try to limit the development of caravan parks to two corridors along the two main access routes. In this way certain areas to the west and north are less likely to be busy.

Hierarchy of lake use

Certain lakes are identified as free access lakes. Lake Windermere has been heavily used for recreation since the last century. As it has the main 'honeypot' sites along the eastern shore, it attracts many visitors who can participate in almost all water activities. Other lakes are designated natural lakes such as Wastewater and Haweswater, allowing only lakeside owners to use them. These lakes are in the quiet zones of leisure activity.

Both these plans involve trying to restrict heavy use to a limited area – a damage limitation exercise. The problems of pollution and congestion are confined to one area while other areas remain quieter.

The Lake District Traffic Management Initiative

This scheme is a joint project between the National Park Authority, the Cumbria County Council, the Countryside Commission and the English and Cumbria Tourist Board. It aims to:

- reduce periodic traffic parking congestion
- offer alternative modes of transport to the car
- reduce the impact of increasing levels of traffic on the countryside
- tailor traffic to the availability of the existing road
- ensure that the National Park remains accessible for quiet enjoyment, irrespective of income or disability
- enable the local community to proceed with its usual business.

Road hierarchy

The roads have been classified as to the use they should have. Main trunk roads such as the A561 will have little restriction. In some cases smaller lanes will be down-graded to form 'lakeland lanes' which carry *no vehicles except for access'*.

Public transport services

Rail, bus and lake steamer transport routes are to be co-ordinated. A comprehensive Travel Card is planned to be introduced. Public transport will be made more appealing by increasing guided commentaries on buses, improving visibility at bus stops, and renovating lake jetties.

Information

Public transport timetables should be printed in the free newspaper produced by the main bus company, *Stagecoach*. Road signs are to be improved, with a common style and explanation for the restrictions.

Catering for users' needs

The Initiative has worked imaginatively to promote the use of public transport to fell walkers. Leaflets recommending 'linear' walks with return links by bus or boat are being produced. Posters with telephone numbers of taxi companies have been displayed as taxis provide a guaranteed service for walkers fearful of missing the last bus home.

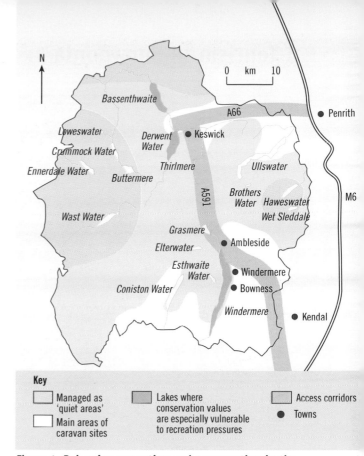

Figure 4 Balancing recreation and conservation in the Lake District National Park

1 Study Figure 1. On an outline map of the UK:
   a Copy and label the distribution of the National Parks.
   b Mark on the following conurbations: London, West Midlands (Birmingham), South Yorks (Sheffield), West Yorks (Leeds), Manchester, Liverpool, Tyne and Wear.
   c Mark on the following motorways (you may use a road atlas map): M1, M3, M4, M5, M6, M11, M62, A1(M)
   d Explain why the Peak District is the most visited National Park.

2 **a** Draw a divided bar graph to represent the following information on Land Ownership of the Lake District Park. Use the following information:

Private	58.9%
Forestry Commission	5.9%
Ministry of Defence	0.2%
Water companies	6.9%
National Trust	24.2%
National Park Authority	3.9%

   b How does the pattern of ownership in the Lake District differ from the average for the National Parks shown in Figure 2?
   c How does the pattern of landownership in the Lake District make it easier for the National Park Authority.

Tourism in Snowdonia

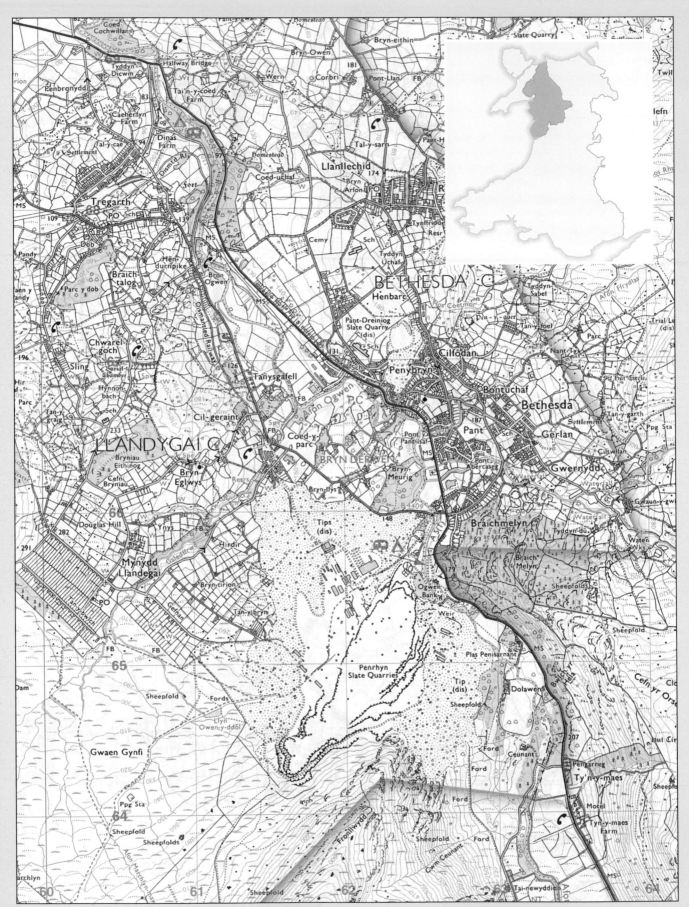

Figure 1 **Snowdonia – an extract from an OS 1:25 000 map**

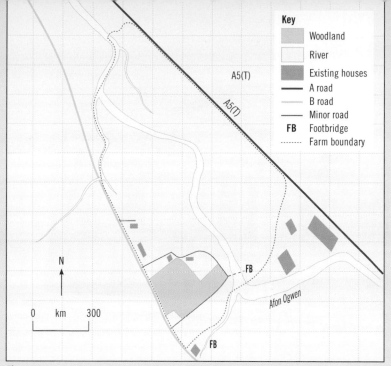

Figure 2

Proposal

Permission has been sought by Mr and Mrs I. Morris of Tanysgafell to develop a large campsite on their land. The campsite is to consist of the following:

Accommodation

- 40 permanent caravans
- 60 sites for visiting caravans
- campsites for 50 tents.

Facilities

- showers and toilets (either two large blocks or four separate units)
- shop
- restaurant
- games room (table tennis, pool and darts)
- adventure playground.

Infrastructure

- access tracks about the site
- one new bridge across the Afon Ogwen for campers' use only
- enlargement of two entrances to the B4409; no access to the A5 (T).

Landscaping

Visual disturbance is to be reduced to a minimum by planting trees, building grass banks and carefully planning the location of the various facilities in the campsite.

Figure 3 **Application to a planning committee**

1 Figure 3 shows an application for planning permission to turn some farmland into a campsite. Imagine you are the farmer concerned. Write a speech to be made to the planning office at the public hearing. You should consider why you want to build the campsite, what benefits it will have to the local community both in the short term and long term, likely objections and ways to reduce some of the concerns.

2 At the public hearing there were some strong arguments against the proposal. Name three reasons why local people might object to the development of a campsite.

3 Despite these objections the campsite was given planning permission. You have been asked by Mr and Mrs Morris to plan the campsite. On a copy of Figure 2 (from OS map grid squares 6166 and 6167), locate the facilities shown on the proposal (Figure 3). Allocate the following space for each landuse:

Land use	square allocation
Permanent caravans	4
Visiting caravan sites	4
Tents	3
Showers	1
Shop	1
Restaurant	1
Games room	1
Adventure playground	2
Total	**17**

Among other considerations, you should be aware of visual pollution within the campsite and to local residents, noise pollution, and the likelihood of flooding. Woodland can be removed but must be replaced elsewhere on the land. There is no limit to the area of grass mounds and trees planted.

4 Write a report of 250 words explaining your plan, what considerations you had to take, how you decided on the location of each landuse and what extra developments you have suggested.

Bethesda – five miles south-east of Bangor

This busy quarrying town at one time housed more than 2000 workers from the Penrhyn slate quarries, but these now operate on a very much reduced scale. The quarries existed in the time of Elizabeth I, but were not systematically worked until the period when Richard Pennent of Liverpool married the Penrhyn heiress and himself became Baron Penrhyn in 1783. To cater for workers' souls, several grandiose chapels were built. notably Jerusalem, Siloam and Bethesda in the High Street, after which the town is named. The town is hemmed in on the west by enormous spoil heaps. The quarries, which produce a variety of coloured slate in blue, green and red, are open to groups of visitors.

The greatest industrial impact upon the area in the nineteenth century was the demand for cheap house-roofing materials. This demand was met by the development of massive slate quarries – an activity which was to change the landscapes in which it took place. The slate industry, which in its time spawned railways, ports, mines, vast non-conformist chapels and even great country houses, has all but gone. Despite this collapse, there are many fascinating remains to be seen.

The Snowdonia National Park offers superb opportunities for the hill walker. Snowdon, the UK's highest mountain, dominates the area like an angry giant. It even has a railway if you would like a more leisurely trip to the top. For those interested in more sedate walking, there are many options. Streams tumble down off the mountains creating beautiful waterfalls. Woods cling tightly to the steep valley sides broken by a network of clearly mapped trails.

There is much evidence of the tribes that lived in the region in the ancient past. Hut circles, cairns and old settlement sites abound. The more recent past is represented by the old slate quarries which provide dramatic scars on the landscape.

There are old woodlands in the Lake District and in Wales, too, but here they consist of oaks clinging tenaciously to the hillsides in areas where the land was simply not worth the effort of clearing. Among these woods are Woodwarbler and Redstart, Pied Flycatcher and Tree Pipits. There are prospering populations of Buzzard and, in south-central Wales, a growing number of Red Kite.

The forests of coniferous trees such as the Norway and Sitka Spruce provide a less popular habitat for the birds but even the widely condemned tracts of planted conifers, as they mature, are much appreciated by the now widespread Crossbill.

Two important words of caution for the walker – almost all the land in the National Park is privately owned and so should be treated with consideration and respect. Every year this environment claims the lives of unsuspecting walkers. Do ensure you have the right level of experience and proper equipment before heading for the hills.

ACTIVITIES 2

1 Refer to the Ordnance Survey map (Figure 1 on page 238). On a blank piece of A4 paper, draw a sketch map of the area bounded by northings 64 and 69 and eastings 60 and 64. Mark on it the following: A45 (T); B4409; the main rivers; quarries and slate tips; land over 350 metres; woodland.

Use an appropriate scale and key.

2 Choose one of the following
● a cycle route starting at Mr and Mrs Morris's campsite. This should be a circular route using only minor roads where possible. It should take in sites of possible interest.

● a nature trail based within walking distance of the campsite. It should be no more than 6 km.

● a long distance hill walk of over 10 km. The campsite will provide a minibus to drop walkers off and collect them at the end of their walk. It can only use existing paths and rights of way. Note the drop off and pick up points.

a Mark the route on your sketch map.

b Write a brief guide for the route. Give directions and points to look out for along the way.

3 On a sheet of A4 paper, produce an advertising leaflet for the campsite giving information on the campsite itself, the local area, it's attractions and history, and the range of activities on offer.

4 In the future, how would you see the campsite changing? What other attractions could be developed?

'Spain is the number one destination for British holiday makers. In 1995, Spain accounted for almost half of all summer bookings and this trend seems set to continue in 1996. The most popular Balearic island is likely to be Majorca, while Ibiza and Menorca will compete with the Spanish Costas for business.'

The Association of British Travel Agents – report on the best holiday destinations for 1996

Figure 1 shows how much Spain dominates the UK package holiday industry. The Balearic Islands have taken advantage of the tourist trade but tourists also present associated problems and challenges.

Figure 1 **Top package holiday destinations, 1994**

Majorca is the largest of the Balearic Islands. It has a wide range of stunning scenery from golden sandy beaches to dramatic limestone gorges. Small fishing villages tucked into narrow bays contrast with the windmills and olive groves of the interior. Majorca and the other islands took advantage of the increase of mass tourism in the 1950s offering cheap holidays in the sun. Large high-rise hotels and apartments were quickly built to accommodate the millions of tourists.

Advantages

With the tourists the number of jobs increased. People were needed to build the accommodation, work in the tourist industry and sell farm produce to the hotels. The worst quality farmland by the coast is now the prime site for hotel complexes and can be sold at high prices. As a result, Majorca is one of the richest areas of Spain. The standard of living is high and the infrastructure is excellent.

Disadvantages

Despite its high income, much of the money from tourism leaves the island as many of the hotels and facilities are owned by mainland Spanish and multinational companies. This has caused considerable resentment and unrest among the local people.

Most of the jobs in the industry are seasonal, therefore, in the winter months there is high unemployment (in March 1995 there was 15.2% unemployment in the Majorcan workforce).

Many of the large tourist developments have little regard for preserving the local environment and beauty, causing considerable environmental degradation.

Tourism places a drain on water supplies. The vast majority of rainfall falls in the winter months yet the highest demands for both the tourists and irrigation are in the summer. A severe lowering of the water table has led to salt water seeping into supplies.

Many of the resorts have a reputation for catering for the young. Rowdiness and bad behaviour of some tourists have proved especially troublesome, adding to the social problems.

Figure 2 **The Balearic Islands**

Figure 3 **Fishing village**

Figure 4 **Modern tourist development**

The future

The Local Authorities are attempting to redefine the Majorcan tourist industry. They are moving away from the mass market of cheap package holidays and trying to attract a more 'discerning and wealthy' tourist through a number of ways:

● emphasising the historical and cultural traditions of the island and highlighting the environmental attractions.

● protecting the environmental beauty. There has been recent local legislation, with strong local support, to preserve and enhance the local environments. As shown in Figure 5, over 30% of the island is now protected.

● redesigning some of the worst areas. Figure 6 details a dramatic redevelopment. Other plans include grassing over existing derelict land, adding benches and tables along the sea fronts and tidying up the beaches.

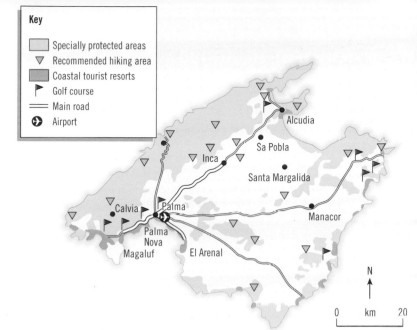

Figure 5 **Resorts, protected areas and 'green' tourism in Majorca**

Majorca blows up habitat of the great British yob

The mayor of Magaluf has 'resorted' to extreme measures to improve the image of her town – 60 kg of dynamite was enough to bring the walls of the Hotel Atlantic crashing down. As the hotel fell to the ground in a cloud of dust, local dignitaries cheered and clapped. More than 20 other hotels are going to be demolished in an attempt to improve the image of the town and try to discourage the British holiday makers from using and abusing the resort.

The authorities had attempted to solve the problems caused by the young holiday makers before. Excessive alcohol consumption and violent behaviour by young British holidaymakers led the authorities to decide that a radical change of approach was needed. They would try to take the resort upmarket, increasing the quality of the hotels and hence the price. Consequently, it is hoped that the type of tourists who have caused the problems in the past will not be able to afford the

increased costs and so will stay away. As well as the demolition programme, the authorities are spending £25 million in an attempt to upgrade the resort, hoping to recreate a pleasant, peaceful ambience.

Figure 6

1 **a** Use the following information to draw a climate graph for Majorca.

Month	Jan	Feb	Mar	Apr	May	Jun	July	Aug	Sept	Oct	Nov	Dec
Temperature (°C)	10	11	13	15	17	20	25	24	20	16	15	11
Rainfall (mm)	50	55	45	30	25	10	5	5	15	50	55	50

b Compare the climate of Majorca with that of Britain.

2 **a** What are the main attractions of a family holiday in Majorca as opposed to one in Britain?
b What are the main disadvantages?

3 Study Figure 6
a What problems did the young tourists cause?
b What measures had been taken by the local authorities in an attempt to solve the problem?

c How do you think the authorities will try to make the resort more 'upmarket'?
d Why are some local residents unhappy about the plan?

4 Imagine you were the Minister of Tourism for Majorca. Write a letter to the British Travel Operators emphasising the changes you are trying to make and the attraction of your island to a wealthier range of more 'discerning' tourist.

A mixed blessing?

Tourism is seen by some LDCs as a mixed blessing. For some, it is a chance to earn some much needed foreign capital as well as an opportunity to show off its landscapes and proud traditions; for others, it is thought to cause more problems than it solves. With many of the tourist facilities being owned and run by foreigners and tourist numbers fluctuating according to fashion and the exchange rates, the country becomes even more vulnerable and dependent on the rich world.

Tourism is Kenya's largest foreign exchange earner. The country is keen to encourage tourists who bring in valuable income which can then be spent on infrastructure, health care and education for its rapidly expanding population. Kenya's environment has a wide range of attractions for the tourist: beautiful beaches and reefs, a tropical savanna climate, Mount Kenya and the game reserves. It also has a rich and diverse tribal culture and heritage.

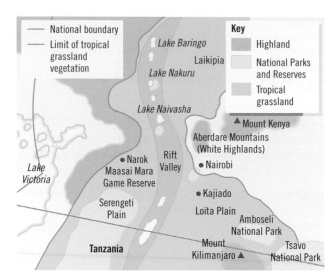

Figure 1 **Location of game reserves in Kenya**

Day 1

We landed on a dirt runway and were driven to the campsite past lots of wild animals. It was frightening watching six large elephants walk in front of the jeep.

Allison is our safari co-ordinator. She is Kenyan but speaks with an American accent as she has been educated in San Francisco.

Day 2

Up at 5 o' clock for the first 'game drive'. Joseph was our driver and was very friendly. He was not from this part of Kenya but had been working here for several years. He spotted a group of lions feeding on a dead antelope. After some time driving around, Joseph received a call on his 'walkie-talkie' saying that some leopards had been spotted in a different part of the park. We then drove off at speed to find them. They were well camouflaged but easy to see as there were six jeeps surrounding them.

While we were out our tent had been cleaned and the hot water boiler had been stoked.

Day 3

Went to visit a traditional Maasai village. The village is just outside the game park as only planned tourist developments are allowed in the game reserves. We had to pay £10 a person to go. The villagers lined up to sing us a song that used to be sung to welcome their hunters back from a long journey. They were very friendly and didn't mind having their photo taken. They showed us into one of their homes which they share with their goats. I had a look around the back of their hut and was surprised to find a pile of old coke and beer bottles. Before we left they showed us some of the crafts they had made. I bought a spear and necklace.

Day 4

Another early start. Allison had encouraged us to go on a balloon ride. We had a short drive to the start point and climbed into the big basket. Soon we were drifting over huge herds of antelope and wildebeest. We saw some hippos in a river. The balloonist, Greg, was from Australia. At the end of the trip he served us with a champagne breakfast. French Champagne in the middle of the African savannah – bizarre!.

Our tent

Smile please!

Buying souvenirs

Figure 2 **Extract from a tourist's diary**

Disadvantages of tourism

Environment

Extensive use of the parks by jeeps and tourist minibuses has created a network of tracks. Heavy rains and strong winds add to the erosion of these tracks leaving scars on the landscape. On the coast, tourist boats and coral collectors have destroyed many of the reefs.

Animals

Motor vehicles and even balloons can disturb the animals and alter their behaviour. Their hunting, mating and living patterns may be changed by the presence of tourists.

People

The Maasai were nomadic pastoralists. Much of the area they formally migrated around is now in the game reserves, denying them access. Often the wild animals which are now protected destroy tribal crops. In addition, many of the local skills and traditions are being forgotten and the young are keen to get jobs in the tourist trade. Ironically, one way to ensure the continuation of their customs is by performing for the tourists.

Economy

The rise in political unrest and poverty-led violence affected international tourism. Earnings fell by 15% in 1992 and again in 1993. In addition, as newer destinations are opened up, such as South Africa and Zimbabwe, competition for the foreign tourist will increase.

Figure 3 **Soil erosion caused by motor vehicles**

Father joins hunt for safari murderer

British tourist murdered in game reserve

Tragedy in paradise – tourist found murdered

1 Study Figure 2, an extract from a tourist's diary. The author mentions a number of different people and jobs. Rank the jobs in order of the highest paid first to the lowest paid last. Which of these jobs are likely to go to local people and which will probably go to people from elsewhere? Explain your answers.

2 Produce a table showing the advantages and disadvantages of tourism to a LDC such as Kenya. You should include the effects on the people, environment and economy.

3 Write a letter to the chairman of The Big Travel Company explaining the problems their business causes LDCs and suggest ways to reduce some of the problems.

Ecotourism

An expanding industry

Recently, we have become more aware of the vulnerability of the world's environments and the problems created by tourists. There has been a growth in 'green' tourism or **ecotourism**. Ecotourism can take place anywhere and involves tourists taking an active part in ensuring that their visits do not have negative effects on the environment.

> *"... we become ecotourists not simply by visiting a rain forest, but by behaving 'responsibly' towards it and its indigenous peoples. It is low impact, low density tourism, experienced predominantly in small groups. Education as well as pleasure and excitement are part of the experience. An important characteristic of ecotourism is that it can and should be controlled by, and hence benefit, local communities. They are the owners and guardians of the attractive resources. Without their involvement, ecosystem conservation is unlikely."*
>
> Robert Prosser, 1995

The Amazon Lodge, Brazil

Having arrived in Manaus, the tourists have a gruelling journey by boat and bus to the Lodge. The Lodge is made of local materials and sleeps only 25 guests. It is basic and does not provide hot water nor air conditioning. It has solar power and any waste is taken away in containers. Meals are prepared by one of the 14 local people employed using local fruit, vegetables and meats. The tourists can visit local families in groups of no more than ten. Alternatively, they can go in smaller groups on a three- to five-day canoe trail into the rainforest, learning about the flora and fauna. A different part of the forest is used for each visit so no long lasting damage is caused.

As well as ensuring the environment and indigenous people are treated with respect, the holiday is sustainable in ensuring the tourists have an enjoyable, educational and unique experience. By doing this it is hoped the tourists will keep coming back.

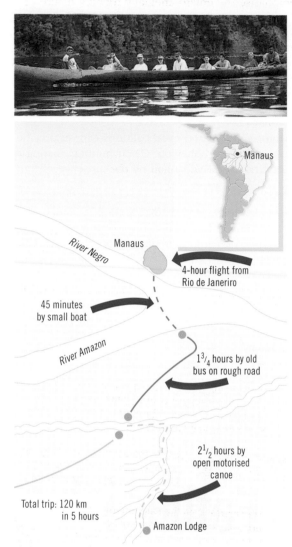

Figure 1 **Location and route to Amazon Lodge**

(Map labels:) Manaus · River Negro · Manaus · 4-hour flight from Rio de Janeiro · 45 minutes by small boat · River Amazon · 1¾ hours by old bus on rough road · 2½ hours by open motorised canoe · Total trip: 120 km in 5 hours · Amazon Lodge

Walindi

Walindi is world renowned. Its guest book reads like a guide to Who is Who in the world of Sport Diving and Underwater photography. Voted as 'the best diving resort, anywhere in the world' by reader surveys, the staff and hospitality at Walindi will ensure your stay is memorable.

Dives with names like Emma, South Bay, Inglis Shoals, North Emma, Cape Campbell, Marie-Helene's, Susanne's and Resthof Island are world famous; they are only a few of the more than 200 reefs and dive sites sprinkled throughout Kimbe Bay. All are pristine and undamaged by a policy of Look but don't touch!

Walindi is not a large dive resort and that's the way we like to keep it. Catering to a maximum of 22 divers means that you get the undivided attention you deserve, yet the freedom to feel that every dive has been made for you alone.

Walindi Dive Resort, Papua New Guinea

Coral reefs are one of the most fragile ecosystems and the increasing popularity of scuba diving means that they are very vulnerable to damage. The operators are keen to emphasis the conservation of the reefs and the quality of the holiday for the tourist.

They protect the reefs by creating one mooring site which the boat can tie up to every visit. Consequently, there is no need for anchors which destroy the reef. Divers are strictly monitored to ensure they do not touch or damage the reef. The guides are highly qualified and can educate the divers about the coral and fish they see. The resort has a library for further study.

Accommodation consists of wooden huts covered with palm leaves. Hot water is produced by solar panels on the roof and electricity is provided from a diesel generator for only part of the day. The hotel employs local people and buys fish and vegetables from the local markets.

Most modern tourist developments in the UK emphasise the environmentally friendly nature of their business. Park wardens and volunteers have a full-time role to educate and inform. The negative issues concerning tourism are more widely known and advice is readily available. However, because of its success, ecotourism is facing a difficult future. Some less than committed operators are taking advantage of the 'eco' label and not ensuring environmentally friendly practices. In addition, with more people taking these types of holidays it will become increasingly hard to maintain the small numbers and low impact of the trips.

▶ Figure 2 **Signs like these help to promote conservation**

A lakes-friendly guide

When to go Some of the quietest months are May and June, when the weather is often at its best, and September and October.

Getting there Do not travel by car; go by train. There are railway stations at Staveley and Windermere for the southern lakes, Penrith for the north.

Transport within the Lake District Where possible, use public transport or bicycle rather than private car. Bus and boat services give surprisingly free movement.

Where to stay Do not use hotels. If possible use your stay to subsidise those working in traditional trades in the National Park. The National Trust publishes a list of 38 working farms which take guests and Tourist Information Centres have accommodation lists which include farms.

What to bring Do not bring all your food with you. If you spend money in local provisions shops you will make it less likely that they close through lack of trade perhaps to be replaced by a shop catering purely for tourists.

What to buy and not to buy Buy products made locally. If you buy a locally produced garment using Herdwick wool you help the Lakes. If you buy a garment made from the wool of a sheep not reared here you do not help. Watch for companies with names that suggest they sell local produce but in fact import their wares.

1 Study the extract on ecotourism.
  a Define in your own words the meaning of the term 'ecotourism'.
  b Why is it important for the tourist to be in small groups?
  c Why is it so important that local communities are involved?

2 With reference to *The Amazon Lodge*
  a Make a list of ways the Lodge is environmentally friendly.
  b Produce a table comparing the holidays experienced by a visitor to the Amazon Lodge and the visitor to the Maasai Mara game reserve in Kenya (page 244). Compare the vegetation and wildlife likely to be seen, the type of accommodation and the service provided. Which holiday would you have wanted to go on and why?

3 Study the *lakes-friendly guide*.
  a How can tourists themselves reduce the negative effects of their visits to National Parks in the UK.
  b How would you encourage tourists to become more environmentally friendly to an area you have studied.

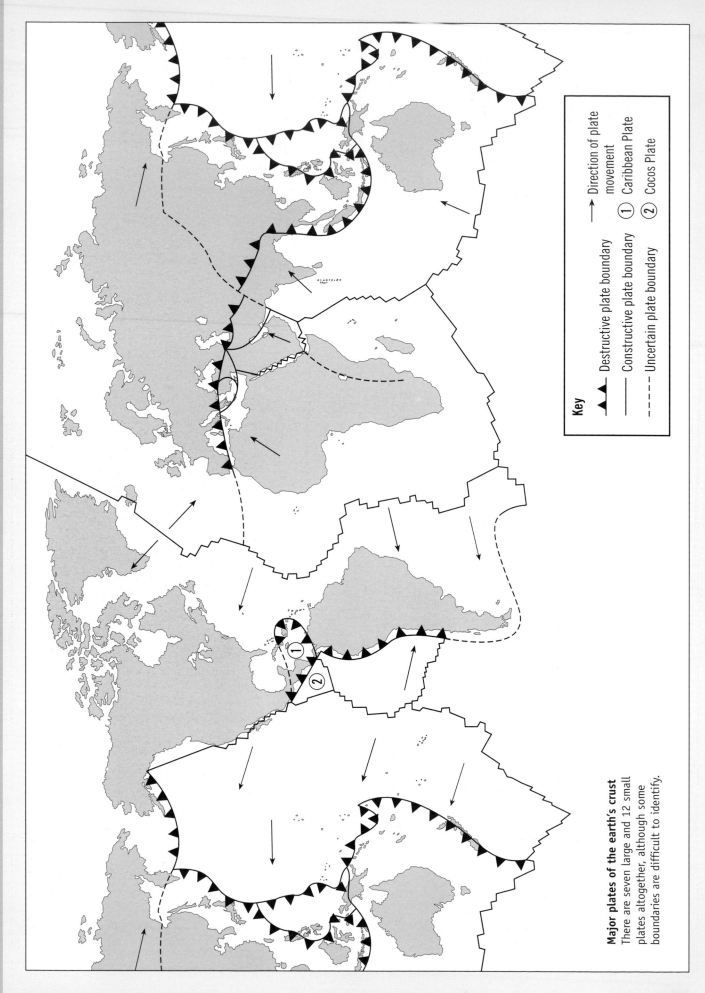

Key

▲▲▲	Destructive plate boundary
——	Constructive plate boundary
-----	Uncertain plate boundary
→	Direction of plate movement
①	Caribbean Plate
②	Cocos Plate

Major plates of the earth's crust
There are seven large and 12 small plates altogether, although some boundaries are difficult to identify.

C G

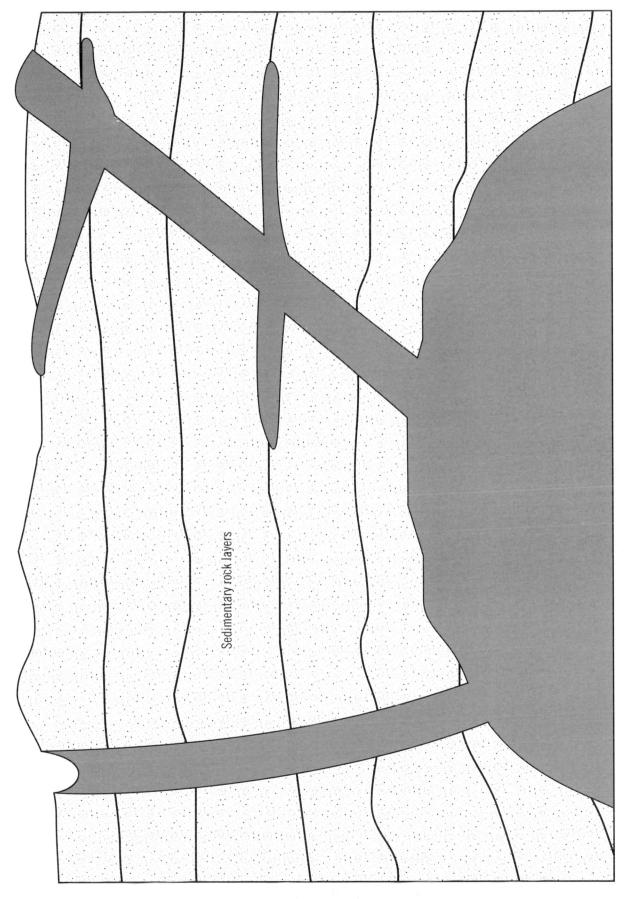

Sedimentary rock layers

Igneous intrusions

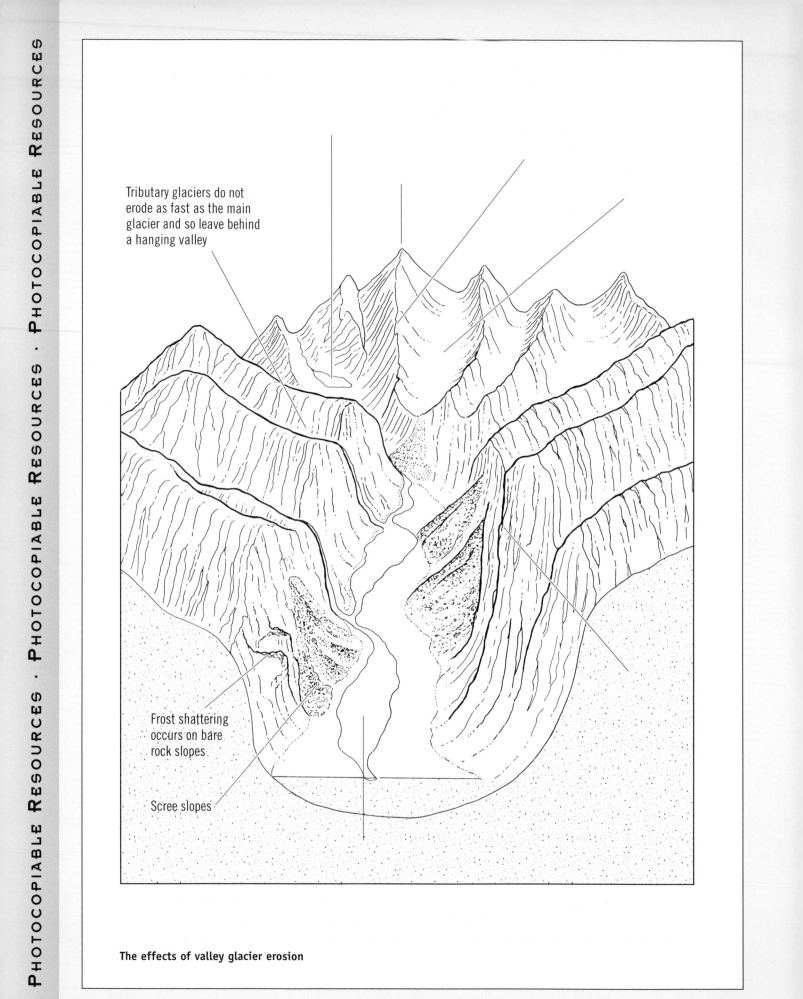

Tributary glaciers do not erode as fast as the main glacier and so leave behind a hanging valley

Frost shattering occurs on bare rock slopes

Scree slopes

The effects of valley glacier erosion

C G

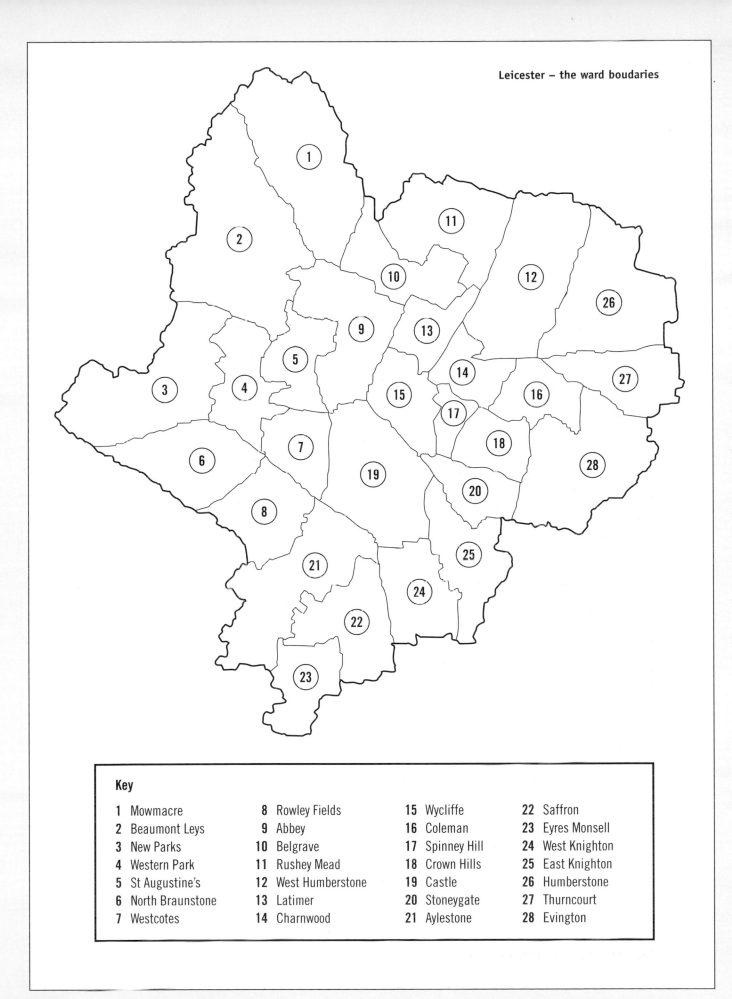

Leicester – the ward boudaries

Key

1 Mowmacre	**8** Rowley Fields	**15** Wycliffe	**22** Saffron
2 Beaumont Leys	**9** Abbey	**16** Coleman	**23** Eyres Monsell
3 New Parks	**10** Belgrave	**17** Spinney Hill	**24** West Knighton
4 Western Park	**11** Rushey Mead	**18** Crown Hills	**25** East Knighton
5 St Augustine's	**12** West Humberstone	**19** Castle	**26** Humberstone
6 North Braunstone	**13** Latimer	**20** Stoneygate	**27** Thurncourt
7 Westcotes	**14** Charnwood	**21** Aylestone	**28** Evington

Standard regions of the UK

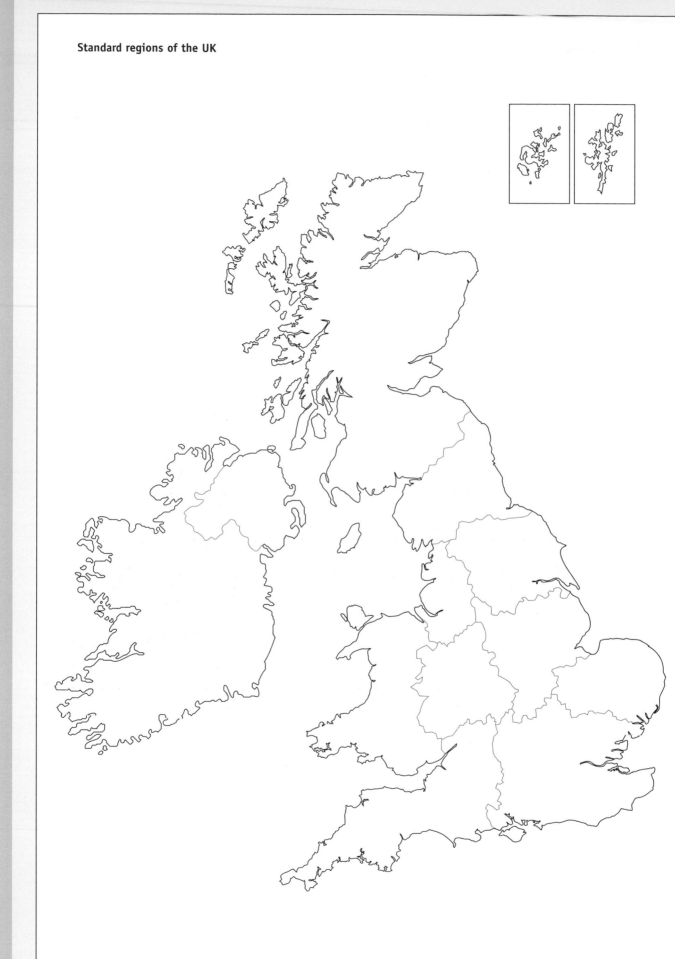

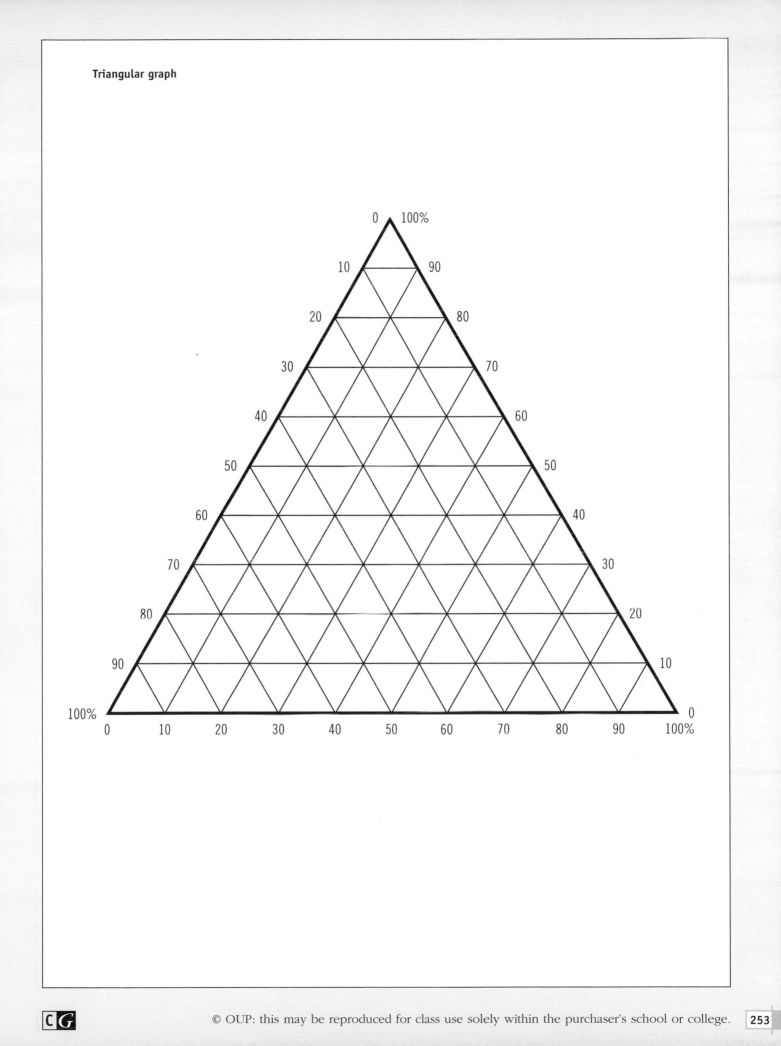

Index